Architecture of the Night

Dietrich Neumann

Architecture of
The Illuminated Building the Night

With essays by

Kermit Swiler Champa, Dietrich Neumann,
Werner Oechslin, and Mary Woods

Prestel Munich · Berlin · London · New York

Introduction

Dietrich Neumann

When the American architect Raymond Hood coined the term "Architecture of the Night" in 1930, the concept behind it had been enthusiastically debated for a number of years by lighting designers, critics and architects. They all were convinced that the nocturnal appearance of architecture had to be a carefully planned, important part of its design concept. Electric light was considered a potential new "building material" that could bring about conceptual changes as profound as those caused by the arrival of steel and plate glass in the nineteenth century and justify visions of a future luminous architecture. Indeed, thousands of buildings were illuminated in American cities in the 1920s and '30s, often in changing colors and with special lighting effects, significantly altering the appearance of skylines at night. In many cases provisions for the lighting had been made in the early design stages, and particular choices of color, form and materials changed a building's appearance by day as well.

Similar debates and applications took place at the same time in Europe. In Germany, for instance, the term *Lichtarchitektur* (light architecture) became popular around 1926/27 both for buildings with carefully integrated outside illumination devices as well as for ephemeral spatial formation from searchlight displays. Architects like Erich Mendelsohn, Bruno Taut or Ludwig Mies van der Rohe carefully considered their designs' nocturnal appearance and artists such as Fernand Léger and László Moholy-Nagy described visions of projected light frescoes and a luminous urbanism.

The history of architectural illumination provides encounters with a long forgotten aspect of twentieth century architecture, with fascinating projects and intensive debates. On both sides of the Atlantic, the expected effects of architectural illumination were considered a motor for stylistic change: in the United States, setback skyscrapers were promoted by architects such as Wallace Harrison or Harvey Wiley Corbett as ideal for an application of floodlights, and utmost simplicity in surface treatment and ornamentation was recommended to avoid distorting shadows. Instead of conventional advertising, many firms were persuaded by lighting designers to simply use abstract color illumination of their buildings—an approach whose success was less measurable but added greatly to the spectacular appearance of many skylines. In Europe, members of the architectural avant-garde accommodated advertising in the horizontal elements of modern urban buildings, supported at night by indirect lighting or luminous, translucent glass elements. At the same time visions of an unsubstantial architecture of light and color emerged, considered the ultimate fulfillment of modernity. Comparing the diurnal and nocturnal appearance of a building to an image and its photographic negative, some theorists of the Modern Movement expected a less rational, illusionist approach by night to complement the "new sobriety" with its emphasis on structure, function and materials.

Both in Europe and the United States, nocturnal architectural design was seen by its proponents as a potential all-encompassing art form for the future, combining architecture, mural painting, stage design, and film projection. Beyond the often quoted "painting with light" and "theaters in the air," artists predicted a "luminous urbanism," choreographing a city's lights into a visual nocturnal symphony, or "space light architecture" projected by light beams into the air above a city. Many lighting designers had begun their careers at the theatre. Electricity companies made precise suggestions regarding materials, colors, and surface treatment and presented imaginary nocturnal skylines in large illuminated models.

The first wave of enthusiasm, rich debate and a multitude of projects ended with the blackouts of World War II and subsequent changes in stylistic taste. A fresh approach to integrating nocturnal illumination into modern architecture followed in the 1950s and '60s until the energy crisis of 1973 terminated all such projects. Since the 1980s there has been an increasing revival and a renewed interest in artificial light as a planning parameter and an artistic tool.

Just as this current interest flourishes without much knowledge of its long prehistory, the art of architectural illumination has suffered more than other historical phenomena from an astonishingly thorough, collective amnesia. Several times throughout the twentieth century it was introduced as a new phenomenon without mentioning the earlier achievements. There are many potential reasons for this. Important contemporary debates happened in electric trade journals rather than in those for architects, who had been hesitant to take outside illumination seriously. The art's ephemeral and temporary nature, its lack of physical traces and adequate visual documentation also might have contributed to the selective hindsight of historians and their "bias of survival" (to use Daniel Boorstin's perceptive phrase).

No other artistic medium of the twentieth century has crossed the boundaries between art and commerce, technological display and utopian vision, easy entertainment and demagogic politics as effortlessly as this. "Architecture of the night" or "light architecture" could mean installations as different as the enormous spatial illusions of Albert Speer's "Lichtdome" at National Socialist party rallies and the replicas of Parisian buildings outside the city, brightly illuminated at night to deceive aerial attackers during World War I. Throughout the twentieth century the discussions center, however, on buildings whose nocturnal appearance stood in relation to that of the day. Driven by technological and stylist changes, outline lighting with incandescent bulbs was joined around 1915 by floodlight illumination, and by the application of luminous translucent glass in the 1920s and '30s. Laser and LED technologies as well as computer applications have broadened the field of applications in recent years.

The richness of the debates, their daring utopian visions and the unfulfilled potential of this aspect of modern architecture, deserve the attention of our time. The following pages offer a first attempt at presenting projects and debates considered essential by their contemporaries. They cover aspects of the prehistory, the 1920s and '30s in Europe and the U.S. and the development since World War II. Kermit S. Champa's essay examines the enormous potential of colored light as an abstract art in the late nineteenth and early twentieth century, while Mary Woods contextualizes paintings and photographs of nocturnal Manhattan in the 1920s by artists such as Georgia O'Keeffe and Alfred Stieglitz. Werner Oechslin's essay combines an analysis of debates about light architecture in the 1920s with ideas of the Enlightenment. The second half of this book documents prime examples of architectural illumination in the twentieth century (some are unique and exceptional, others are typical for a particular type or approach). Several of the large industrial and world fairs, which often provided testing grounds for new architectural lighting, are also included. While their architecture was usually short-lived, it was designed with a particular emphasis on its nocturnal appearance and initiated discussions about lighting as a fine art. The large number of building examples from the 1920s and '30s in the United States and Europe reflects the coverage and focus of the debates in contemporary publications, while, similarly, the absence of projects in the 1970s documents the lasting influence of the energy crisis in 1973. We have limited our selection to cases where the lighting concept was contemporary to that of the architectural design, often the result of a collaboration between architect, client, and illuminating engineer, and frequently influencing the design of the building itself, its form and materials, selections of color and ornamentation. This excludes illuminations of historic architecture that enjoyed great popularity throughout the century and occasionally rendered equally striking effects. Our selection also confines itself to buildings whose exterior lighting became a visible part of the urban environment.

The bibliography at the end of this volume contains a brief selection of both historical and contemporary sources that provided important information for our research. The most essential contributions came from the work of social and technological historians, in particular Wolfgang Schivelbusch, David Nye, and John A. Jakle. Special editions of the architecture magazines *Daidalos* (1988) and *Lotus* (1993) have addressed architecture's relationship with artificial light. Art and architectural historians Robert Bruegmann, Timothy Rub, and Christian Zapatka were among the first to address aspects of our particular topic in their essays in the 1980s. Apart from their coverage in architectural and trade magazines, contemporary lighting applications have been chronicled continuously over the last fifteen years in individual publications by architects, lighting professionals and journalists, such as Wanda Jankowsky, Heinrich Kramer, and Ingeborg Flagge. A historical glossary at the end and brief biographies of major lighting designers conclude this volume.

Despite increasing numbers of successful projects and the beginnings of a new historical and theoretical debate, architects still rarely plan for the nocturnal appearance of their buildings. Our selection of projects, ideas and protagonists is meant as a first attempt at providing points of orientation in uncharted territory and will, we hope, invite responses, challenges, and reconsiderations in the future.

Architectural Illumination before the Twentieth Century

Dietrich Neumann

The spectacular illumination of architecture in the twentieth century has a long prehistory. Since the Renaissance, public and private festivals in Europe often included architectural illumination and fireworks at night. Among the often cited and well illustrated examples are the spectacular illumination of the canals in the Versailles gardens of 1674 or of the buildings of Ghent honoring Emperor Charles VI in 1717. The history of such festivals, their structures, rituals and illumination have been subjected to considerable scholarly research.[1]

While the introduction of electricity in the late nineteenth century changed the duration, intensity and character of such illuminations, and, for the first time, had a substantial influence on architectural forms and theory, there are also important continuities. In fact, the theoretical concepts behind architectural lighting efforts and their reception in the twentieth century are deeply indebted to their predecessors. Be it their occasions, political implications, the vocabulary in contemporary descriptions, or the comparisons with the abstract art of music and the combination of "marte et arte"—martial and fine arts—many tropes were scarcely affected by the profound technological change. As Werner Oechslin has pointed out, temporary structures in Renaissance and Baroque festivals, often with significant roles at night, already served as occasional test cases for a future architecture.[2] Many descriptions of illuminations in the eighteenth and nineteenth centuries reveal a longing for permanence or at least a longer duration of the spectacle, and perceptive observers often express concern for the illumination's influence on architecture. Both notions are essential for the development of an "architecture of the night" in the twentieth century.

Johann Wolfgang Goethe's vivid description of "La Girandola" in Rome on June 30, 1787 may serve as an example of many accounts of the time: "To see the colonnade, the church and, above all, the dome, first outlined in fire and, after an hour, becoming one glowing mass, is a unique and glorious experience. When one thinks that, at this moment, the whole enormous building is a mere scaffolding for the lights, one realizes that nothing like it could be seen anywhere else in the world.... The fireworks were beautiful because of the setting, but they did not compare with the illuminations of the church... it seemed entirely like a scene from a fairy tale. To see the beautiful form of the church and its dome as a fiery elevation is a view both grand and charming."[3]

The fireworks above the Castello St. Angelo and the architectural illumination of St. Peter's that Goethe witnessed on his Italian journey were held regularly between the fifteenth (since 1481) and nineteenth centuries,[4] and were typical of the numerous festivals of this time (Goethe had witnessed "at least half a dozen" on his trip). Artists like Wright of Derby and popular printmakers welcomed the subject. (Figs. 1, 2). In preparation for the festival's regular return, the dome of St. Peter's had been equipped with permanent candleholders in 1547. Goethe was more impressed with the lasting illumination of St. Peter's than with the fireworks, and observed how the illumination changed the appearance of architecture, turning it into "a mere scaffolding" while letting the dome appear "as a fiery elevation" suggesting a two-dimensional, linear drawing.

More drastic changes of architecture through illumination could be enacted when temporary structures were involved. The 1814 festivities in London's Green Park after the victory over Napoleon, for example, included a wooden "castle of discord" which an evening crowd saw vanish behind fire and smoke at night and reemerge as the "temple of unity." The design by the architect John Nash was transformed with the help of a mechanism that rotated the upper part of the entire structure, developed by the inventor and artillery officer Sir William Congreve.

At this time the new technology of gas lighting had just begun to appear in London's streets.[5] As part of another celebratory spectacle in the summer of 1814 in London, a wooden pagoda, supported by a Chinese bridge in St. James' Park (Fig. 3) was bedecked in more than 10,000 new decorative gas lights. While the application and potential appearance was similar to an outline lighting with oil lamps, gas promised a great advantage for festive illumination, such as indeterminate duration as well as easier application and control as all lights could be ignited simultaneously. While the involvement of a pagoda in the victory celebration over Napoleon was perhaps a little far-fetched, it had been chosen in order to demonstrate that gas lights could adorn a steep and tall structure in places difficult to reach for any conventional lamplighter. When Lord

Nelson's battle on the Nile was reenacted with rowboats on the canal beneath the bridge one night in August, 1814, the pagoda illumination was turned on. The wooden building, however, caught fire almost immediately and burned down. The visitors mistook this for a well-calculated effect and applauded passionately.[6] The dangers that accompanied gas lighting and the need for central supply systems were among the reasons for its slow acceptance. In the 1840s, finally, it had been generally embraced as a new technological reality, even if reports about gas explosions and serious accidents continued throughout the century.[7]

In 1851, the German architect Gottfried Semper witnessed spectacular gas illuminations in Paris and London and discussed their aesthetic shortcomings and potential: "What a glorious discovery is the gaslight! How its brilliance enhances our festivities, not to mention its enormous importance to everyday life! Yet in imitating candles or oil lamps in our salons, we hide the apertures of the gas pipes; in illumination, on the other hand, we pierce the pipes with innumerable small openings, and all sorts of stars, firewheels, pyramids, escutcheons, inscriptions, and so on seem to float before the walls of our houses, as if supported by invisible hands.

This floating stillness of the liveliest of all elements is effective to be sure (the sun, moon, and stars provide the most dazzling examples of it), but who can deny that this innovation has detracted from the popular custom of *illuminating* houses as a sign the occupants participate in the public joy? Formerly, oil lamps were placed on the cornice ledges and window sills, thereby lending a radiant prominence to the familiar masses and individual parts of the houses. Now our eyes are blinded by the blaze of those apparitions of fire and the facades behind are rendered invisible.

Whoever has witnessed the illuminations in London and remembers similar festivities in the old style in Rome will admit that the art of lighting has suffered a rude setback by these *improvements*."[8]

Semper noticed, as Goethe had before him, how the illumination changes, even obscures the appearance of the architecture. We sense his uneasiness towards the commodification of the new element, as he pinpoints the typical aesthetic conflicts at the threshold between two technologies.

Contrary to electric light's monopoly in the twentieth century, the nineteenth century is characterized by a fruitful coexistence of different lighting technologies, which were sometimes used in conscious contrast, engaged in dialogue or encountered aesthetic conflicts akin to the ones described by Semper. Gas and oil lamps were joined at mid-century by the blindingly bright electric arc lights, used mainly outdoors for experimental illumination of squares and streets (Fig. 4). Electric illumination only became widely aceptable after its initial brightness had been tamed to a level comparable to that of gas lighting in the 1880s and 1890s.

1 Joseph Wright of Derby
Fireworks on Castel Sant'Angelo
1774–75, oil on canvas, 42.5 × 71.1 cm
Birmingham Museums & Art Gallery

2 St. Peter's Basilica, Rome, historical view, *c.* 1800–25. Etching, perforated. Anon.

3 London, St. James' Park, Wooden Pagoda equipped with 10,000 gaslights, Print, English, 1814.

4 Deleuil, Joseph. Arc Lighting Experiment using Foucault Type lamp in the Place de la Concorde. Print, French 1844.

Electric Illumination at Large Exhibitions

Hand in hand with the progress of illumination technology, artificial light increasingly lost its role as a tool of social stratification and helped to democratize the night. While the illuminated night had been the realm of the privileged, who could afford to stay up late and to have their own lantern, the appearance of amusement parks, such as Vauxhall and Ranelagh in the late seventeenth century, had begun to perforate the sharply drawn lines of privilege.[9] Amusement parks became increasingly nocturnal affairs (see Kermit Champa's essay in this volume), absorbing elements of Renaissance and Baroque festival culture and helping to prepare for the large international and "World's" fairs in the nineteenth and twentieth centuries.

International exhibitions in the 1880s (e.g. Milan, Munich, Paris and Louisville) showcased the newest technical developments in electric lighting and often presented first attempts at its architectural integration. A street in Milan, for instance, would, during the national exhibition of 1881, be converted into an illusionary interior space with arches made of "colored light,"[10] and the cathedral's facade was floodlit by arc lamps, while more than 200,000 gas lights illumined its architectural details.[11] The International Electricity Exhibition in Paris during the same year celebrated the breakthrough of incandescent light and Edison's design was considered the most efficient among several similar competitiors.[12] A year later Munich hosted an International Electricity Exhibition, and the beam of an arc lamp from the Glass Palace in the Old Botanical Garden illuminated the towers of the Frauenkirche over a distance of more than 2,000 feet (Fig. 5).[13] At the Southern Exposition in Louisville Kentucky, in 1883, the responsible electrical engineer, Luther Stieringer from Edison's laboratory in Menlo Park, developed the first comprehensive lighting scheme together with the architects, outlining the architectural features of the main building and the exhibition grounds with strings of incandescent light bulbs. The awe-inspiring moment at dusk, when all lights were switched on simultaneously, was turned into a choreographed ritual, eagerly awaited by the visitors,[14] a regular feature of many subsequent exhibitions. After his success in Louisville, Stieringer was responsible for the lighting of the exhibitions in Chicago 1893, Omaha 1898 and Buffalo 1901 (see pp. 90–91).[15]

At the Paris World's Fair (May 6–November 6, 1889),[16] external electric illumination had advanced both practically and artistically and was effectively contrasted with other lighting technologies. Strings of incandescent bulbs adorned the cornices of most major palaces, including the central dome of the Main Building, while others were floodlit with arc lamps. Colored bulbs were placed throughout the grounds and along the river banks and bridges. Large fountains, between the Eiffel Tower and the Galerie des Machines, were illuminated from below by colored arc lights installed under glass. A complex mechanism allowed color changes with moveable filters. "[The jets] projected themselves in veritable showers of fire, rebounding in a rain of sparkling gems," wrote one observer[17] (see p. 21, Fig. 5).

The most memorable lighting installation, however, was that of the Eiffel Tower, presenting all available lighting types and technologies.[18] Gas lamps were placed on the great arches at the bottom and on the platforms above. Various parts of the tower were lit by incandescent bulbs. On July 14, a hundred Bengal lights blazed forth from the different levels. The topmost platform outside Gustave Eiffel's office was surrounded by a track with two moveable searchlights that would be trained on different buildings in the exposition grounds or the surrounding cityscape. At the very top of the tower a rotating lighthouse lamp was installed. Surrounded by sheets of colored glass the moving light beam sequentially changed through the colors of the French flag, from red to white to blue (see pp. 20, 27, Figs. 4, 12).

A Turkish newspaper journalist sent the following report: "The night view of the exhibition grounds is beyond one's capacity to describe. One stops in awe before a splendor seen nowhere in the world until now. There is no spot that is not flooded with light to dazzle the eye. As one sees these lights, which with marvelous mirror effects pour a gold dust on the exhibition buildings, one wants to believe that the world illuminating sun is dispersing its power…but the honor of illuminating the nights of the Paris exhibition belongs to the light of "electricity." If electric power did not exist, the exhibition grounds could not be illuminated as they are now….It is estimated that the electricity illuminating the exhibition grounds could bring light to a city of 100,000 people."[19]

5 Electro-technical Exhibition Munich 1882.
Frauenkirche, illuminated by an arc lamp from the roof
of the crystal palace. Print, 1882.

The exhibition memorialized the political revolution of 1789 with the presentation of an equally influential revolution in the realm of technology. The metaphorical potential of light and illumination at a celebration of the French Revolution and the Enlightenment did not escape the organizers and the overwhelming demonstration of technical progress might have overshadowed the recognition of how few of the ideals of the revolution had been realized in late nineteenth-century France.

Instead of the stark contrasts in scale and style at the Parisian Fair—from the tallest and widest buildings ever to an array of hypothetical indigenous dwellings that Charles Garnier had assembled as a "history of habitation"—the Chicago World's Fair (May 1 to October 30, 1893) displayed a remarkable coherence, and, for the first time, served as a testing ground not only for technological advances, but for an urbanistic concept as well.[20] And indeed, the Columbian Exposition's long-lasting influence on American urban planning and the popularity of its Beaux Arts Classicism was remarkable. While celebrating the 400th anniversary of Columbus' arrival in America, the fair revealed the United States' continuous dependence on European cultural ideas. It combined historicist architectural forms with the utopian vision of an urban environment generated by far-reaching comprehensive planning. All elements typical for city life at the time, such as traffic, commerce, advertising and heterogeneous architecture, had been banished to the separate amusement section, the "Midway Plaisance," and the homogeneous temporary structures of the "White City" surrounding large reflecting pools in Jackson Park on Lake Michigan suggested a sedate timelessness through their uniform height, style and color. This urbanistic vision reached its culmination at night, when its centrally planned lighting scheme added a layer of abstraction, of unreality, and of heightened coherence. The nocturnal sights with their "artistic effects in illumination" were considered one of the main attractions.[21]

Apart from the lighting for streets and walkways by arc lamps on twenty-foot-high decorative standards throughout the fair, Luther Stieringer employed around 130,000 incandescent bulbs for his largest scheme of outline lighting to date. "Under the cornices of the great buildings, and around the water's edge ran the spark that in an instant circled the Court with beads of fire. The gleaming lights outlined the porticoes and roofs in constellations, studded the lofty domes with fiery, falling drops, pinned the darkened sky to the fairy white city, and fastened the city's base to the black lagoon with nails of gold"[22] (Fig. 6). In contrast to its appearance as a "White City" of plaster and marble dust during the day, color became an important part of the fair at night. Searchlights (the three largest had been imported from Germany) were equipped with filters and installed at various points around the Court of Honor and moved to bathe different facades in temporary washes of purple, yellow, green, blue, and scarlet.[23] In the lagoon in front of the Administration Building (Fig. 9), a set of three fountains was lit from beneath by lights of changing colors shooting upwards along with the varying jets of water. In the Electricity Building, luminous at night as its interior lights blazed forth through its windows, the Edison Tower of Light stood, an 82-foot-tall crystal-capped column covered with multi-colored bulbs that flashed on and off rhythmically to accompanying music. This, perhaps, was the first structure designed entirely for its nocturnal appearance with electric light and was a predecessor to buildings such as the monumental gate at the Paris fair in 1900 (Fig. 7, see also p. 89).

While the Beaux-Arts planning strategies and unified aesthetic vision of the World's Fair had a respectable impact on urban planning in the United States in the first three decades of the twentieth century, the coherent lighting scheme that had been the culmination of these visions did not survive the transition from the temporary environment on Chicago's lakefront to the large urban projects in cities such as Washington, D.C., Cleveland or Detroit.

The opposite is true for the realm of the fairs: here, the lighting schemes continued to evolve, while the urban layout and aesthetics remained close to that of the Chicago fair. The Trans-Mississippi Exposition in Omaha, Nebraska from June 1, 1898 to October 31, 1898, for example, followed Chicago in style and layout. Luther Stieringer's lighting concept marked another important step in the evolution of comprehensive lighting schemes. For the first time it was based solely on outline lighting and, instead of the white surfaces in Chicago, the color scheme

7 World's Fair Chicago 1893. Electricity Building,
Edison's Tower of Light. Contemporary Illustration

8 Statue of Liberty with its original lighting, New York City,
Photo taken during Hudson Fulton Celebration, 1909.

here tended more toward ivory and yellow tones with occasional color decorations. As was by now the general custom, a prominent position was given to the Electricity Building, according pride of place to the most important innovating force of the time. As the critic Octave Thanet wrote: "In the building, one may see the power of electricity; outside, in the open air, every night, is its poetry. Then, ten thousand incandescent lights make Court and Plaza and Park and Midway streets like softened day; and the lagoon mirrors palaces penciled in fire ... while the fountains rain a jeweled shower, opals or rubies or sapphires or emeralds or diamonds—a scene that no one who has seen it can ever forget.... This is what science can do for art."[24]

While the subsequent fairs in Paris, Buffalo, St. Louis, San Francisco, Chicago and New York (see selected projects) continued to draw large crowds especially for their night lighting, amusement parks adopted the new technologies in the 1890s (Coney Island, see p. 96–97), and "Electric Parks" or "White Cities" sprang up around the country. To varying degrees, the structures at the fairs adapted their architecture to the illumination scheme. Materials, colors, surfaces were selected according to their appearance under artificial light and the placement of the outline lighting was carefully planned with the architects. The encounters with this illuminated architecture helped to pave the way for the recognition of lighting as an art form, confirmed by Julius Meier-Graefe's observation at the Paris 1900 fair, that its nocturnal illumination provided glimpses of a future architecture of "concentration and greatness."[25]

Spectacular Urban Illumination

While none of the comprehensive lighting schemes as such could be transferred from the temporary, homogeneous environment of a fair to a complex and heterogeneous cityscape, both temporary and permanent electric lighting began to change the urban context in the late nineteenth century. In the United States, the night had long been discovered as an ideal realm for spectacular political rallies. For Abraham Lincoln's presidential candidacy in 1860, a torchlight parade and fireworks were organized, and the centenary of the American Declaration of Independence was celebrated in New York City in 1876 with thousands of oil lamps and gas lighting. By 1896, American election campaigns were routinely staged with rich nocturnal festivities and electric lighting installations, even the projection of election results. Three years later, the end of the Spanish-American War was celebrated with a nocturnal Peace Jubilee in Chicago, which featured a baldachin of light over a street and a "Curtain of Jewels" of illuminated glass prisms—both predecessors to successful installations at fairs in the first third of the twentieth century.[26] The return of Admiral Dewey and the fleet to New York City in 1899 caused a two-day illumination of New York City, including an electric outline lighting of the Brooklyn Bridge, adorned with an electric sign, thirty-six feet tall, spelling "Welcome Dewey." Domes, spires and skyscrapers in Manhattan and Brooklyn featured lines of incandescent bulbs while searchlight projectors on the bridge towers were in constant motion. Other searchlights stood still on either side of the East River to form what "looked like the ribs of a vaulted arch" high above the water.[29]

The old Madison Square Garden in New York was lit with electric arc lamps in 1879 for the first time.[27] The subsequent building by McKim Mead and White in 1890 would use electric light already to secure the building's position in the skyline. While the architects had, at first, un-successfully, suggested a steam cauldron lit by an arc lamp at the top, they eventually installed 200 incandescent lights inside the crescent moon of prismatic glass on the head of Diana, the famous weathervane at the top of the tower, which was also illuminated by concealed lamps and - reflectors.[28] The dome of the World Building on lower Broadway carried incandescent outline lighting from 1890 onwards (Fig. 10).

When the Statue of Liberty in New York's Harbor, a French present to the United States in recognition of the American Revolution, had finally been inaugurated on November 1, 1886 with a firework and lighting spectacle, there was general agreement that electric lighting was the only option for its permanent illumination.[29] Eight lamps of 6000 candlepower each were installed in the torch and six lamps around the base, an application whose lack of success taught important first lessons in architectural floodlighting: the base was much brighter than the statue,

where "deep shadows [were] cast on the bosom and throat" and the arm was "invisible from the elbow up"[30] (Fig. 8). In 1917, the statue was fully floodlit for the first time in a scheme that has been updated several times since.[31] The floodlight illumination of the capitol in Washington was inaugurated in the same year.[32]

The technological transfer among industrialized nations was astonishingly swift, much faster than any cultural exchange. The Paris Opera, for example, had been temporarily illuminated with arc lights in 1877, to inaugurate the Avenue de l'Opera, and its architect Charles Garnier, greatly interested in new illumination technologies, had succeeded in establishing permanent electric illumination of the Opera's facade as early as 1881.[33] Germany experienced its transition from traditional to modern lighting methods at festive occasions almost simultaneously. In Berlin, where one of the earliest European branches of the American Edison companies had been established, electric illumination became part of political celebrations in the mid-1880s. While in 1885, the 15th anniversary of the victory in the Franco-Prussian War and subsequent foundation of the German Reich had been celebrated with torchlight parades and magnesium fires, two years later, the city's German and French cathedrals were illuminated in honor of Emperor William's ninetieth birthday with twelve arc lamps of twenty-five Ampere each. The modern minded Emperor William II himself initiated a particularly elaborate light festival for the twenty-fifth anniversary of the Reich's foundation and personally supervised the application of various lighting technologies for a subtle differentiation among buildings in the center of Berlin. Indeed, he was one of the first to discover lighting as a tool for visually editing and interpreting the city. The Royal Palace was conceived as the "brilliant center" with 20,000 gas lights on its facade, arc lamps and incandescent lights illuminating the dome, and incandescent lighting reserved for the palace's two most important facades.[34] Other buildings, such as his grandfather's residence Unter den Linden, for instance, received considerably less light and gas lights only, as if to indicate that he belonged to a bygone era. The three-hour-long spectacular light festival on September 2, 1895 was the most elaborately staged event of its kind in Germany to date.

In all industrialized countries, permanent commercial lighting and electric advertising soon began to compete with the lighting of public events in the urban realm, thus challenging its exceptional nature. Both the artistic vocabulary and the critical tools for electric architectural illumination were in place before the twentieth century began.

9 World's Fair Chicago 1893. Machinery Building, Administration Building. Painting by Charles Courtney Curran. Chicago Historical Society G1943.0019.

10 World Building by night, New York City, c. 1909. Contemporary postcard.

1. The most important publications about the topic are: Alan St. Hill Brock. *A History of Fireworks* (London: Harrap, 1949); Eberhard Fähler. *Feuerwerke des Barock: Studien zum öffentlichen Fest und seiner literarischen Deutung vom 16. bis 18. Jahrhundert* (Stuttgart: Metzler, 1974); Arthur Lotz. *Das Feuerwerk: Seine Geschichte und Bibliographie* (Zürich: Olms, 1978); Wolfgang Schivelbusch. *Disenchanted Night. The Industrialization of Light in the Nineteenth Century* (Berkeley: University of California Press, 1988); Werner Oechslin und Anja Buschow. *Festarchitektur: Der Architekt als Inszenierungskünstler* (Stuttgart: G. Hatje, 1984); Georg Kohler, ed. *Die schöne Kunst der Verschwendung: Fest und Feuerwerk in der europäischen Geschichte* (Zurich: Artemis, 1988); Roger Chartier, "From Court Festivity to City Spectators," In: Forms and Meanings: Texts, Performances, and Audiences from Codex to Computer (Philadelphia: Univ. of Pennsylvania Press, 1995); Kevin Salatino. *Incendiary Art: The Representation of Fireworks in Early Modern Europe* (Los Angeles: Getty Research Institute: 1997).

2. Ibid., Oechslin. 80, 81.

3. Johann Wolfgang von Goethe. *Italian Journey (1786–1788),* trns. W. H. Auden and Elizabeth Mayer (San Francisco: North Point Press, 1982): 344.

4. Occasions were, for example, Easter, the election of a new pope, or here the festival of St. Peter and Paul, on which traditionally the tribute of the Sicilian kings was paid to the pope. This practice and the fireworks on this occasion were discontinued in 1788. Goethe had witnessed the last firework display of this particular kind.

5. Schivelbusch. 31.

6. Jósef Horváth. *The Floodlighting of Budapest* (Budapest: Hungexpo, 1989): 17.

7. Schivelbusch. 32, 34.

8. Gottfried Semper. "Science, Industry, and Art" (1852) in: Harry Francis Mallgrave, Wolfgang Herrmann (eds.). *Gottfried Semper The Four Elements of Architecture and other Writings* (Cambridge University Press: 1989): 135–136.

9. Schivelbusch. 138–140.

10. Piero Castiglioni, Chiara Baldacci and Giuseppe Biondo. *Lux: Italia 1930–1990* (Milan: Berenice, 1991): 12.

11. "Milan and Her Great Fair," *New York Times* (12 July 1881): 2, col. 1.

12. William Henry Preece. "Electric Lighting at the Paris Exhibition," *Journal of the Society of Arts* 30 (16 December 1881): 98–107.

13. Ferrari. "Von der Münchener Internationalen Elektrotechnischen Ausstellung 1882," *Das Licht* 2, no. 4 (1932): 174–176;"Electricians in Munich," *The New York Times* (15 October 1882): 3, col. 5; "The Munich Experiments," *The New York Times* (22 October 1882): 3, col. 7.

14. David Nye. *American Technological Sublime* (Cambridge: MIT Press, 1996); Bridwell, Margaret and Theodore M. Brown. *Old Louisville* (Louisville: University of Louisville, 1961)

15. "Death of Luther Stieringer," *Electrical World* 42, no. 4 (25 July 1903): 132; Stieringer, Luther. "Electrical Installation and Decorative Work in Connection with Exposition Buildings," *American Architect and Building News* 74, no. 1352 (23 November 1901): 61–62.

16. I would like to thank Karen Bouchard for researching information on fairs in this chapter. Richard Joseph Harriss. *The Tallest Tower: Eiffel and the Belle Epoque,* (Washington, D.C.: Regnery Gateway, 1975); John Allwood. *The Great Exhibitions* (London: Studio Vista, 1977); Erik Mattie. *World's Fairs* (New York: Princeton Architectural Press, 1998); Alfred Picard. *Exposition Universelle Internationale de 1889 à Paris: Rapport Général* (Paris: Imprimerie Nationale, 1892); "Electricity on the Eiffel Tower," *Engineering* 47 (21 June 1889): 701–704; "Loitering Through the Paris Exposition," *Atlantic Monthly* 65 (March 1890): 360–374; Murat Halstead. "Electricity at the Fair," *The Cosmopolitan* 15 (September 1893): 577–582.

17. "The Luminous Fountain of the Paris Exposition," *Manufacturer and Builder* 21, no. 11 (November 1889): 232.

18. Schivelbusch. 128–134.

19. The Ottoman Newspaper *Sabah,* 1889, quoted in: Zeynep Celik. *Displaying the Orient* (Berkeley: University of California Press, 1992): 47.

20. "The World's Fair at Night." *World's Columbian Exposition Illustrated* 3, no. 7 (September 1893): 163; "To Light the Fair," *World's Columbian Exposition Illustrated* 2, no. 1 (March 1892): 15; "Under the Electric Glare: The First Grand Illumination of the Exposition Grounds," *The New York Times* (9 May 1893): 2, col. 3; John Allwood. *The Great Exhibitions* (London: Studio Vista, 1977); Hubert Howe Bancroft *The Book of the Fair* (Chicago: Bancroft Co., 1893); Carolyn Marvin. "Dazzling the Multitude: Imagining the Electric Light as a Communications Medium," in *Imagining Tomorrow,* ed. Joseph Corn (Cambridge: MIT Press, 1986); Erik Mattie. *World's Fairs* (New York: Princeton Architectural Press, 1998); John A. Jakle. *City Lights. Illuminating the American Night* (Baltimore, London: Johns Hopkins, 2001): 149–154.

21. "In a Frame of Light: White City Gleams under the Glare of Electricity," *Chicago Tribune* (9 May 1893): 1. Cf. also the voices of Theodore Dreiser, Frederick Law Olmsted and Clare Louise Burnham, as quoted in: Jakle. 153–54.

22. Rossiter Johnson, ed. *A History of the World's Columbian Exposition* vol. 1 (New York: Appleton, 1897): 510.

23. "The Great German Search Lights at the World's Columbian Exposition," *Scientific American* 69 (2 September 1893): 145, 152.

24. Octave Thanet. "The Trans-Mississippi Exposition," *The Cosmopolitan* 25 (October 1898): 599–614.

25. Julius Meyer-Graefe. *Die Weltausstellung in Paris 1900* (Paris, Leipzig: F. Krüger, 1900): 40

26. Jakle. 124–128.

27. "The Centennial Fourth. Decorations and Illuminations," *New York Times* (June 30, 1876): 8. "Testing Electric Illumination. Madison-Square Garden to be Lighted Tonight by Electricity," *New York Times* (16 June 1879): 8.

28. "The Tower of Madison Square Garden in New York" *The American Architect and Building News,* vol. 34, no. 830 (21 November 1891): 110.

29. "Lighting the Statue of Liberty," *Electrical World* (26 April 1884): 136.

30. "Liberty's Torch Lighted," *The New York Times* (2 November 1886): 1, col. 3; "Liberty's Face Darkened," *The New York Times* (5 November 1886): 8, col. 2; "Liberty's Torch," *The New York Times* (17 November 1886): 2, col. 4; "Liberty to be Lighted," *The New York Times* (18 November 1886): 5, col. 3; "Liberty Resumes her Task," *The New York Times* (23 November 1886): 5, col. 3.

31. The lighting was updated in 1932, 1944 in anticipation of V-Day (See: "Miss Liberty's New Robes of Light to Glow on V-Day," *New York Times* (28 December 1944): 11.) and again in 1986. Each lighting was celebrated with elaborate ceremonies.

32. "A radiant monument to freedom and democracy," *Literary Digest,* 54, 1991 (30 June 1917): 9.

33. Christopher Curtis Mead. *Charles Garnier's Paris Opéra: Architectural Empathy and the Renaissance of French Classicism* (New York: Architectural History Foundation, 1991): Schivelbusch. *Disenchanted Night....*: 47, 50. See also: "Electric Light in Paris," *New York Times* (29 December 1879): 1. Charles Garnier. *Le Nouvel Opéra de Paris* (Paris: Ducher et. Cie., 1881): vol. 2, 131.

34. See: Douglas Klahr. "The Kaiser Builds in Berlin: Expressing National and Dynastic Identity in the Early Building Projects of Wilhelm II," (Diss., Brown University, 2002): 244–249.

11 1898: Transmississippi Exhibition, Omaha, Nebraska. "Bird's eye view of the Central Court by night." From the Collections of the Omaha Public Library.

A Little Night Music: The Play of Color and Light

Kermit Swiler Champa

"The only rival to sound as a vehicle for pure emotion is colour, but up to the present time no art has been invented which stands in the same relationship to color as music to sound .... We have no colour pictures depending solely upon colour as we have symphonies depending solely on sound .... And here I will express my conviction that a colour-art exactly analogous to the sound art of music is possible and is among the arts which have to be traversed in the future, as Sculpture, Architecture, Painting and Music have been in the past .... Why should we not go down to the palace of the people and assist in a real colour-prelude or symphony, as we now go down to hear a real work by Mozart or Mendelssohn?" (Rev. H.R. Haweis, 1872).[1]

"But though each art has thus its own specific order of impressions, and an untranslatable charm ... each art may be observed to pass into the condition of some other art ... not indeed to supply the place of each other but reciprocally to lend each other new forces ... music being that typical or ideally consummate art is the object of the great Anders-Streben of all art, of all that is artistic or partakes of artistic qualities. All art constantly aspires to the condition of music." (Walter Pater, The School of Giorgione, 1877).[2]

"I can't thank you too much for the name "Nocturne" as a title for my moonlights. You have no idea what an irritation it proves to critics and consequent pleasure to me—besides it is really charming and does so practically say all I want to say and no more than I wish."
(James Whistler to F.R. Leyland, undated letter, early 1870s).[3]

Mr. Bowen (defense attorney for John Ruskin): "Now, take the Nocturne in Black and Gold: The Falling Rocket, is that in your opinion a work of art?" Mr. Burne-Jones (witness for defense): "No, I cannot say that it is. It is only one of a thousand failures that artists have made in their efforts to paint night."
(Whistler v. Ruskin trial, November 25/26, 1878).[4]

"But just as now all kinds of musical instruments are used in rendering the works of great composers, so we may expect that all known methods of exciting emotion will be combined in the grand emotional compositions of the future .... In what has proceeded we have spoken only of projecting the motion of a single ball on a wall; but there is no reason why the motion of several balls should not be gazed at simultaneously, nor why the people of a large city should not have an exhibition of the colour and the motion art upon a canopy of clouds on a dark night." (Professors John Perry and W.E. Ayrton, November 23, 1878).[5]

For many millennia the artificial light of the fire and eventually the torch or the candle and the oil lamp provided the low-power illumination necessary for minimum personal and social functioning after dark, but only with the nineteenth century's engineering of the new higher-powered lighting technologies was it possible to conceive of the day, particularly in the cities, as being more or less equally visible in two aspects—the first natural, the second artificial. The twenty-four-hour city of the present day is the historical result. Human activity may vary between day and night based on customs, but it need not and likely will not as visible electric and electronic reality increasingly blurs with actual reality as dictated by the sun's cycle.

Over the second half of the nineteenth century in the industrialized countries of the west and soon including Japan, a generation of urban dwellers which had grown up with the considerable security of domestic and municipal gaslight began to experience the newer and potentially far more flexible and powerful successor (Fig. 2) The arc lamp fed by an electric current was not immediately convenient for multiple uses, but it was capable of achieving never-before-seen levels of brightness which would be variously beamed by lenses and eventually turned into color by means of filters or angled prisms.

Through the 1860s and '70s, the arc lamp was in most respects more spectacular than functional and as such joined fireworks displays and balloons as features of public entertainment before being harnessed into the more overtly useful searchlight and eventually the cinema projector. In rare instances such as Paris' Folies-Bergère large frosted glass domes were set up to receive and disperse arc light in large interiors but for the most part electric light had to wait for the development of the incandescent bulb to become truly domesticated.

What this meant was that for a considerable period of time—nearly twenty-five years—electric light was something to be experienced more or less in pure form rather than something to take for granted as the replacement for and improvement over gas as the practical means for public and domestic lighting. Not until after the turn of the century were the old gas conduits routinely threaded with electric wiring. While waiting to be domesticated, arc-driven electric light could be conceived, and was in fact conceived, as a potential medium of emotional expression—an aesthetic medium.

Whistler versus Ruskin—an Aesthetic Discourse
The quotes offered above all come from England in the 1870s. Two of them, those of Haweis and of Perry and Ayrton (writing together), suggest an awareness of the music-like potential of projected light. The Whistler and Pater quotes establish the particular aestheticist context out of which the awareness develops. Whistler's also underscores a sensuous fascination with the urban night—fascination which made the artist a regular visitor to London's most popular night-time amusement site, Cremorne Gardens, celebrated in several paintings of the 1870s, most notably *Nocturne in Black and Gold: The Falling Rocket*, painted in 1875 (Fig. 1).

It is interesting to pause for a moment and consider what this picture and others of Whistler's *Nocturnes* suggest with regard to the urban night. They are in a sense surprisingly nostalgic (almost before the fact) in their cultivated dimness, as though that dimness (or "moon-light") were something very precious aesthetically. In the *Nocturnes* the interruptions of prevailing darkness seem always either incidental, small of scale, or momentary. The fading fireworks of the Detroit picture are a characteristic instance of light having appeared but being in the process of fading. The light, regardless of source, feels cradled by nature's night even in the city. This is as it had been for centuries and Whistler in London, as in Valparaiso and later in Venice, seems to want it to continue that way even, one must add, in the imminent face of types and intensities of lighting destined to change the situation forever. Like Pater, Whistler approaches the visual

1 James Abbott McNeill Whistler, *"Nocturne in Black and Gold: The Falling Rocket,"* c. 1875. Gift of Dexter M. Ferry, Jr. Photograph © Detroit Institute of Arts.

2 Berlin: Krollgarten at Night, historic view, c. 1900.
Contemporary lithograph. Private collection.

present from the oppositional perspective of a more knowable and understandable visibility of times past, as that visibility is imbedded in innumerable historical images.

Whistler's arguable "refusal" to confront the light of the urban night, and increasingly bright light of any sort in his paintings distinguishes his work from that of his impressionist contemporaries (and friends) in France in every basic way. For their wholesale celebration of colored light which easily embraces modern visuality, Whistler substitutes a rejection of that celebration which can in some sense be seen as equally modern through the arbitrary comprehensiveness of its manner of opposition. Whistler's darkness and his almost defensively fixed tonalities are oppositional statements intended to stand for art's enduring ability to celebrate whatever it chooses and in whatever way it wants, assuming of course, that the celebration is emotion generating in some persistent way. And certainly it is the otherness—the increasing unfamiliarity of Whister's dark yet translucent tonalities given the ever increasing lightedness of the modern city—that constitutes the continuing allure of Whistler's work. The allure is present because as the years pass it is present only in that work and not in any other routine of vision.

Rev. Haweis had shown himself to be responsive to Whistler's paintings, having commented upon them favorably in the mid-1870s.[6] He was considered by Whistler to have been an important potential witness on his behalf in the Whistler versus Ruskin trial, where the artist brought suit against the pre-eminent "expert" critic of the period in matters of the visual arts (and morals), John Ruskin. The "expert" had been so offended (or perhaps so impressed and threatened) by *Nocturne in Black and Gold: The Falling Rocket* when it was first exhibited in 1877 that he accused the artist in print of throwing a can of paint in the public's face and then putting a scandalously high price tag on the occasion (the painting). Whistler then sued for damages. The Burne-Jones quote offered above stems from the testimony offered at the trial, which unfortunately for Whistler did not ultimately include any from Rev. Haweis or from Pater either. Whistler won the trial in principle but without significant damages being awarded and therefore left responsible for paying all his legal fees. Ruskin, on the other hand, considering himself humiliated and his reputation permanently put in question, resigned his professorship at Oxford and increasingly withdrew from writing. This incidentally left the aesthetic field at Oxford open for Pater and the aesthetic and "morals" field increasingly open in London to Rev. Haweis.

The publicity generated by the trial on November 25 and 26, 1878 made of Whistler and his *Nocturnes* something of a household topic in 1878, in London especially. Two days before, on November 23, Professors Ayrton and Perry delivered a lecture to the Physical Society, in which they made their case for a color art eventually to be driven by powerful intensely-focused light and ultimately to be projected into the night sky. It seems highly likely that the timing of the Ayrton and Perry lecture was not totally accidental but rather intended to make use of the current high profile of "night painting" that was being generated by the trial. The fact that neither Whistler and his *Nocturnes* nor Rev. Haweis' 1872 encouragement of some form of color art were mentioned in the lecture might have stemmed from the desire to stay clear of the Whistler versus Ruskin dispute and to want to appear distinctly scientific rather than polemical in the manner of Rev. Haweis. Both scientists could have taken heart after the fact from Burne-Jones' testimony at the trial that suggested painting's seemingly inevitable failure of imaging night. Since night could not be painted, some other art form would have to be devised in order to render night "aesthetic." Colored light was an obvious candidate for such an art form and the means to generate it were close at hand with arc light. But without Whistler's having posed and pursued with such tenacity the issue of the night as potentially aesthetic (rather than simply romantic) space it seems doubtful that Ayrton and Perry's suggestions would have been taken any more seriously than Rev. Haweis' before them.

Ayrton and Perry—Kinetic Art with Sound and Movement

What then were the two scientists' suggestions? The magazine *Nature* reported in detail in the December 5 issue about the lecture. "The authors began by pointing out the well-known fact that emotion is excited by moving bodies, and they believed that on this basis, a new emotional art would be created which would receive a high development in the distant future. All methods of exciting emotion could be cultivated; but of these, music, by reason of the facility with which its effects could be produced, had alone been highly perfected by the bulk of mankind. Sculpture and painting are not purely emotional arts, like music inasmuch as they involve thought. It would take a long time and much culture for the eye to behold moving figures with similar emotional results to those of the ear on hearing sweet sounds; but time and culture only might be necessary." Both authors were able to use their period of professional residence in Japan at the Imperial Engineering College in Tokyo as a credential in the process of introducing the notion that "Eastern nations," or at least one of them, had devised ways of exciting emotion which had as yet no parallel in the West. "In Japan the authors had seen whole operas of 'melodious motion' performed in the theatres, the emotions being expressed by movements of the body, affecting to the audience, which were quite strange to them. The accompanying orchestral music was, withal displeasing to the authors, while on the other hand, Western music is mostly displeasing to the Japanese. The emotions produced by rapidly-moving masses, such as a train bowling up to a bridge, or by changing colours as in sunsets, have been felt by all, and those excited when the moving bodies are very large do not seem to be producible by anything else in nature. [...] Profs. Perry and Ayrton had designed an instrument, which is now in Japan, for effecting these required changes in a combination of harmonic changes given to a moving body and which they claimed to be the first musical instrument in the visual art in question." The matrix of the instrument was a black circle projected on a surface. The instrument then set the circle variously in "periodic" motions. The authors planned "to construct an improved form of the apparatus and to arrange for the blending of colour with the moving body to heighten the emotional influence; for example, they propose having changing mosaics of different hues, thrown upon the screen for a background to the black spot."[7]

When the Ayrton and Perry lecture was finally published in the *Proceedings of the Physical Society of London* in 1880,[8] the essay included the diagrams for the motions of its projected elements (Fig. 3). The authors admitted that, "We have not yet specially turned our attention to the mechanical details of the colour portion of our machine." Instead they concluded with the paragraph quoted at the beginning of this essay relative to the possibility of working with the

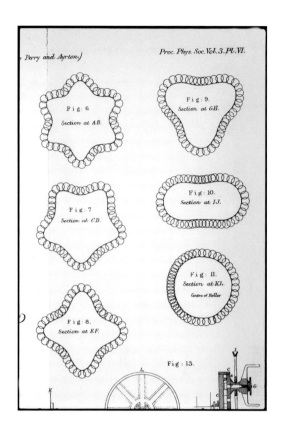

3 Periodic Motions of projected images. Diagram by Professors Ayrton and Perry, 1880.

motions of several "balls" at once in "an exhibition of colour and motion art upon a canopy of clouds on a dark night."

It appears that Ayrton's and Perry's development of a new version of their instrument never transpired. Probably financial and assorted logistical problems were too formidable when seen against the quite speculative and nebulous potential results. But the ideology behind the instrument had a quite durable afterlife and appears still in broad popular circulation in the newspapers as late as the mid-1890s when they are cited in relation to the first demonstration of formally executed "colour-music" in London in 1895.[9]

We will turn briefly to this later in the present text. For this moment however, it is important to see the Ayrton and Perry lecture, its report and its eventual publication as seeming to close off a phase in the consideration of something like an electric light-based medium charged with working in the dark to produce an emotional / aesthetic experience comparable to that understood as issuing from music. As we have seen, this phase was largely introduced by Rev. Haweis, intersected with the celebrity of Whistler's *Nocturnes* and theorized semi-practically by Ayrton and Perry.

What is significant about this phase is that it occurs with new electric lighting technology only beginning to emerge in commercially useful forms. Crude if wildly promising, the technology would have to wait well into the 1880s to emerge as a distinctively flexible medium, and as we have suggested already, it was this period of waiting that gave time for a new light-based medium to be marinated discursively in more or less purely aesthetic terms. But by the 1880s, electric lighting and its various applications was rapidly becoming too important to be managed (even theoretically) by artists and aesthetes. Commerce, and particularly commercial display, now emerged in every heavily industrialized country as the nurturer and developer of electric lighting.

World Fairs of the late Nineteenth Century—Between Aesthetics and Commerce

The key markers of the commercial takeover were the great industrial exhibitions of the decade. The exhibitions were not just spectacularly well lighted so as to function day and night but also had lighting made over into an increasingly prominent aspect of exhibitions and their entertainments. Light was made to do much that was intended to produce public excitement as well as simply to illuminate. In any number of industrial exhibitions, Manchester in 1884 for example, stunning new possibilities for making light spectacular were found. Powerful focused light, diffused light, white light and colored light were joined in an increasingly predictable routine by magical light generators, such as the great fountains of the period that spewed forth seemingly colored and simultaneously illuminated water with many intricacies of force and even direction employed.

Compared to the exhibitions of the 1870s, even large ones like the Centennial Exhibition in Philadelphia in 1876, the newer ones were not engaged in simply using light but also in making light perhaps the most durable feature of the exhibition experience and so conditioning visitors' receptivity to the industrial progress which that feature underlined so powerfully. It is in the exhibitions of the 1880s that complexly manipulated light becomes programmed to constitute what was very nearly a second architectural presence to complement the grand display halls—a veritable "architecture of the night"—where the lighting literally devised its own grand public space and filled it with its own monumental forms, sometimes cooperating with built architecture, sometimes not.

The intentions of the great Expositions' lighting schemes were to overwhelm the public, while entertaining them in great numbers and, in passing, processing all of them into believers in and eventually enthusiastic consumers of the fruits of evolving technology of all sorts. The lighting had, in other words, a highly practical purpose—that of advertising. In this it was marvelously effective as it raised the visual and visceral excitement of the urban / industrial spectacle to what appeared virtually unlimited heights.

At the end of the decade, in 1889, the great Universal Exposition in Paris collected and dispatched in the most complex and elaborate ways essentially all of the illumination technology

4 Eiffel Tower, searchlights outside Gustave Eiffel's office. 1889 Exposition. Contemporary print. Private collection.

that had been developed to date, from ample nighttime ambient lighting of a vast range of buildings and outdoor spaces to the great spotlight on the Eiffel Tower. There, periodic eruptions of
Bengal Lights (reenacted on New Year's Eve 2000) joined in front of the Tower in a park area
with a large array of colored fountains, which were lever controlled by an operator in the Tower
and made to work in coordination with outdoor concerts. Needless to say, the Exposition required
its own electricity-generating station to manage its insatiable hunger for current[10] (Figs. 4, 5, 12).

During the day the buildings of the Paris Expo were themselves already alive with poly-
chrome. Many of the building surfaces were faced with colored ceramic tiles and others colored more
plainly but with an abundance of variety of local hues. Never had an Exposition been so literally
garbed in color. Even the Eiffel Tower was painted a brilliant yellow-orange on the outside. At night
the polychromy shifted gradually from the buildings to the light spectacle, creating a seamless
and continuous visual experience of unprecedented richness and surprising movement. The small
ripples of light penetrating the night at Cremorne Gardens in the mid-1870s were only miniscule
signs of the "spectacle's" conquest of the night, involving the introduction of a continuous light
and color presence in Paris only fourteen years later.

One might rightly observe that the urban industrial night was never to be the same after the
Paris Expo. So much had been introduced and experienced by so many from all over the world that
the flow of the light spectacle from the Expo into the city was rightly imagined to be only a matter
of time in coming. The Expo's effects would be further refined and made even more comprehensively
exciting at later Expositions in Paris, in 1900, (see pp. 92–93) and in a succession of cities in the
United States beginning in Chicago in 1893 and ending for all significant intents and purposes in
New York in 1939 (see pp. 180–181). But none of the later Expositions would substantially alter
the nature of the light and color spectacle first seen in Paris; they would only intensify it by moving
the light and color further and further up into the sky with multiple moving spotlights, often with
colored beams and driven by greater and greater quantities of electricity.

The light and color "language" of the fairs also passed into innumerable urban amusement
parks (the so-called "Luna Parks") throughout the first half of the twentieth century. In this form the
language became a routinely repeated exercise of popular culture for millions of spectators every
summer. And not until the years of World War II, when powerful spotlights became associated

5 Paris World's Fair 1889: Lighted Fountain.
From *L'Illustration*, 29 June 1889.

6 Prof. Alexander Wallace Rimington, *c.* 1911 / 18.

more with anti-aircraft defenses than with entertainment, did their sculpting of the sky weaken as broadly appealing popular spectacle.

Returning to the 1890s, the commercial uses of electric light as understood in the wake of the great Expositions of the previous decade were as varied as the technology permitted. On the one hand, domestic use began to become a true possibility in many cities but the new high-powered spotlights continued to be considered for public potential, particularly for advertising. Indexical of the latter were experiments involving the projections of images (visible for distances of up to twenty miles) on clouds. Huge word and / or number "advertisements" or simply public announcements were the subject of research and engineering already by 1892 in England by Captain Ronald Scott in the London area and by Sidney Hodges in Ealing. Their demonstrations attracted significant attention in New York, where the feasibility of the advertising potential of the idea was seriously reported and debated. Apart from the occasional applications, such as advertising cloud projection in 1920s Germany, however, it appears that little momentum in support of their particular use of high-intensity lighting emerged.[11]

Broadly speaking, the *c.* 1900 status of electric illumination was centered in the manufacture of an endless stream of products capable of being powered by steadily improving municipal power sources. This would be characteristic of the entire century that followed, where it would be up to the later incarnations of the great Expositions to keep the pure excitement of electric lighting in its many new forms alive and publicly interesting. The actual availability of comprehensive urban lighting of the night became an increasingly foregone conclusion. Many new skyscrapers were even designed with exterior night lighting built into their original specifications. By 1930, in major cities both the usefully and the dramatically lighted city had become commonplace, especially in the United States.

The Sound of Color—Rimington's Colour-Music Project

With electric lighting having been largely taken over by commerce in the 1880s and '90s, the "artistic" consideration of it as a proper medium took, as we have noted, a rather distant back seat. Yet the issue never truly died and in the United States (as well as in England) it was sustained by a few quite prominent voices. Preeminent among them were those of the architect, John Wellborn Root, and Harvard philosopher, George Santayana. Both, but likely for different reasons, became interested in what was in fact a rather ancient project to theorize and to enact some form of color analogy to music. The established modern core for this project existed in the writings of Sir Isaac Newton where the presumed similarity between the musical octave and the color spectrum was seen as suggestive of some manner of essential concordance.[12]

Regardless of the fact that no simple measurable concordance could be described scientifically by nineteenth-century physicists, such as Helmholtz,[13] the suggestiveness of Newton's conjectures spawned a substantial discourse in early Victorian England, as several amateurs in aesthetic matters set out variously to offer rationales of more or less scientific sorts. An evolving notion of color-music had come into at least soft focus by the 1880s.

Root, who likely had some knowledge of the English discourse, sensed its coming to life in the stained glass work of Louis Comfort Tiffany which was much beloved by many architects of Root's generation in the United States. By 1883, Root could confidently project the idea of a color art closely analogous to music in its functioning and effects: (describing an "optical instrument" on which artists will perform "arrangements of color") "…the color art will take on itself forms scarcely dreamed of and will occupy a place in the lives of artists and art amateurs similar in all respects to that now held by music."[14] Thirteen years later (1896), but for different reasons, which will be discussed hereafter, Santayana would write: "…a more general development of this sensibility (to the concord and discord of color) would make possible a new abstract art, an art that deals with color as music does sound…."[15]

Santayana, publishing in 1896, had more than Tiffany's work to consider in making his statement. A year before, in June of 1895, the English watercolorist and inventor, A. Wallace Rimington, had given the first public concert featuring his highly sophisticated color organ in

London (Figs. 6, 7). The concert featured the organ in combination with piano, with voice, and with full symphony orchestra. Widely reported by the press in England and elsewhere (especially in the United States), the concert and the repeats in both London and other English cities were major cultural news.[16] All the performances were an instant sensation, if a controversial and short-lived one, as Rimington ceased giving concerts after a single tour and withdrew both himself and his color organ from public scrutiny, choosing instead to describe and defend both in book form. His *Colour-Music* was completed and published in 1911,[17] and with it began in sustained fashion what the present author has termed, in a recently completed book, "The Anglo-American Color-Music Project," which involved besides Rimington, the Englishman Adrian Bernard Klein, and the Americans Thomas Wilfred (born in Denmark) and Mary Hallock Greenwalt.[18] The last three worked through the 1930s and beyond. Interestingly, the two Englishmen began as artists and the two Americans as musicians.

These activities in the 1920s were of great interest to architects and illumination engineers, developing schemes for the color floodlighting of buildings in the 1920s and 1930s. The prominent architect Raymond Hood, for example, ended his seminal essay on an "Architecture of the Night" in 1930 with the following observation: "Anyone who has seen the color organ that has been played in some of our concert halls can realize that the illumination of today is only the start of an art that may develop as our modern music developed from the simple beating of a tom-tom."[19]

The color-music project was in retrospect a brilliant, if unsuccessful attempt to seize colored light back from the "spectacle" and reconnect it with what was understood as "high art." Here, the direct bonding with music was critical, since modern symphonic music was by 1890 the established high cultural paradigm—the most culturally elevated and prestigious of the arts because of its perceived open-ended abstractness and expressiveness.

It was Rimington's sense of this that made his work so foundational. What he did, and what he would be wildly criticized for doing, was to conceive and develop a "mobile color art" that systematically bonded color to music. His color organ began from Newton's speculations regarding concord between the spectrum and the octave. Using multiple arc projectors and color filters Rimington devised mechanisms (most of them new patents) to place the arc and the filters under the control of an organ-like keyboard, which through a combination of mechanical and electrical relays translated musical notations into sequences of pure or mixed colors (Fig. 8). These were projected full screen with both the colors and the tempos of change dictated by extant musical scores. A fixed note-to-color assignment was made but in two variations. In the first, the spectrum and the octave were combined absolutely. Each had only eight "notes," repeatable in ascending degrees of lightness. In the second, the spectrum was spread over four musical octaves (Fig. 8).

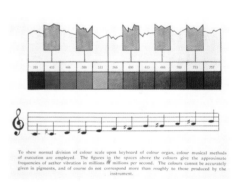

To shew normal division of colour scale upon keyboard of colour organ, colour musical methods of execution are employed. The figures in the spaces above the colours give the approximate frequencies of aether vibration in millions of millions per second. The colours cannot be accurately given in pigments, and of course do not correspond more than roughly to those produced by the instrument.

In essence and probably without knowing it, Rimington was working along lines first marked out in the mid-eighteenth century by a Jesuit physicist, Bertrand Castel, who had used a harpsichord mechanism to elevate colored ribbons in sequence.[20] But what was excitingly new about Rimington's color organ was its use of powerful projected light and, in concert, the combination of color performance with musical performance of the same musical scores. One has to identify as best one can with the cult of symphonic music that so dominated late nineteenth-century aesthetics to understand how exciting the ideological prospects of Rimington's demonstrations actually were. Here for the first time music and color were definitively bonded. And this bonding had been in many respects the aesthetic dream of the century. In addition, the bond was effected through the use of the most modern lighting technology—a use which gesturally at least made an artist's palette out of electric light and set that palette in concordance with the means, methods and established masterpieces of music.

As suggested already, Rimington's concerts and their conceptual presuppositions were highly controversial, especially among musicians, but the very fact of their happening in the culturally super-high profile way they did was sufficient to install their project with sufficient clarity and durability to encourage either acceptance or re-conceptualization by others, especially after the appearance of Rimington's book in 1911.

7 Rimington's Color Organ, *c.* 1911.

8 Keyboard for Rimington's Color Organ, 1911.

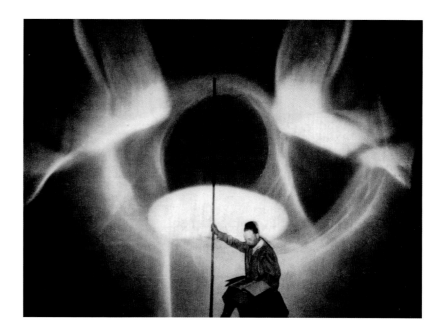

With regard to his concerts of 1895, it is useful to consider exactly how they were staged and for whom, since it was in Rimington's strategy of presentation that one sees perhaps most clearly his effort to distinguish his color-music from the aesthetically unprocessed light play of the commerce of illumination. He hired a prestigious concert hall, publicized the concert via "society" publications and newspapers and offered a Royal preview (by invitation only) prior to the Gala first concert. His color-music was presented as something not of the people, but for the socially and culturally "right" people. His audience was a virtual Who's Who of London society —the elite of the elite, including foreign ambassadors, ranking judges and politicians, dukes, duchesses, etc. With his select audience he named what he intended as the public for his new mobile color art. It was a public of a presumed highest and most diversified culture. It was not, significantly, a public of mere artists and musicians.

Besides installing his color organ and his musicians in a musically prestigious hall, Rimington decorated it, appropriately for the period, with potted palms and oriental carpets at least for the Gala. And of course he went to the considerable expense of hiring an orchestra (large enough to perform Wagner) and a group of soloists of some contemporary renown. For London concerts after the Gala the décor seems to have been simplified somewhat, and for concerts outside London there was no orchestra employed, only vocalists, piano and conventional organ.

Thomas Wilfred later described this historic performance: "On the stage a large white curtain of heavy silk has been carefully draped in deep folds, and down in the center aisle towers a huge cabinet with an attached organ keyboard—the colour organ, with its elaborate mechanism and its fourteen arc-lights within....Wagner's *Rienzi Ouverture* is played by a small orchestra and accompanied by the colour organ. The draped screen pulsates with changing colour; there is no form, only a restless flicker, hue after hue, one for each musical note sounded."[21]

Before each London concert Rimington delivered a lecture, soon published as a brochure and serving as a verbal press release to the newspapers and magazines reviewing the concerts. A few reprinted it verbatim or nearly so. Rev. Haweis, who was out of the country at the time of the concerts, is referenced in the lecture as someone enthusiastic about the Rimington color organ, and in the reviews several journalists noted that Ayrton and Perry were vindicated by Rimington's invention and the concerts.

9 Thomas Wilfred preparing a composition for his Color Organ, *c.* 1925.

With this referencing the aesthetic discourse of the late 1870s was implicitly revived through connection with the Rimington demonstrations of 1895. But the revival was not (with the exception of his mentioning of Rev. Haweis) directed by Rimington himself. In his lecture he proceeded to define himself, his ideology and his machine as pioneering originals in totally uncharted aesthetic territory. Quoting from the lecture,

"Perhaps as this instrument I am about to show you, and the art which it has rendered possible, are so entirely new, you will allow me to say a few words in explanation. [...] Very briefly, my aim had been to deal with colour in a new way, and to place (it) in production under as easy and complete control as the production of sound in music. Until now colour, to a large extent in nature and altogether in art, has been presented to us without mobility and almost completely associated with form....We had not had pictures in which there is neither form nor subject but only pure colour. Even the most advanced impressionism has not carried us this far."[22]

Significantly, Rimington references Impressionist painting, which was, in the period in England along with Whistler's art, seen as the most radical form of visual production—a nearly formless visual production. Rimington positions his art of mobile color even beyond theirs in its abstractness and of course in its absolute bonding with prestigiously established musical abstractness. Historically it is rather surprising that Rimington believed his audience to be seriously interested in his courting of visual abstractness through pure moving color. But the surprise says more about us looking back on the situation from the vantage point of over a century. The degree to which what I have elsewhere called "the cult of music" was in force in the period is difficult, if not impossible to imagine.[23]

Music's abstractness was *the* high cultural standard and whatever aspired to it was broadly believed to be of major aesthetic portent. What Pater had projected in 1877 was securely in place in 1895 in England, and Rimington certainly knew it and relied on it.

As suggested above, it was from musicians and the musical press that Rimington received the most negative criticisms of his concerts and his project in general. The notion of perfect analogy drawn between color and sound was considered largely false and insulting to the independent emotional stature of music. In the reviews of the concert by musicians and a few reporters of a more scientific bent, the post-Helmholtz rejection of measurable similarities

10 Buckingham Fountain, Chicago, employing color projection with musical accompaniment, *c.* 1920. Contemporary postcard.

11 Scriabin performing his composition *Prometheus* with synchronous color projection at Carnegie Hall, New York in April 1915.

between color and sound were often cited in greater or lesser detail. But no matter. Rimington persisted in his belief through his concerts and through his book, and his public seems to have remained generally sympathetic.

Later participants in the color-music project, those already named, varied widely in their commitment to the color-sound analogy. Klein tended to trust it up to a point, while Greenwalt and Wilfred (the two musicians; Fig. 9) rejected it outright, seeing color and its artistic mobility as wholly independent from that of music and their work proceeded without "accompaniment" or, as Greenwalt would eventually theorize, ideally was always accompanying something (or any-thing) to achieve maximum effectiveness. For them, color-music was color-music, no more and no less and they (as well as Klein) developed careers that for practical reasons routinely straddled work in the commercial spectacle and in theater with pure mobile color practice—something Rimington was never really comfortable considering. A personally wealthy individual, he could afford not to.

With his concerts and his book Rimington ultimately constituted himself and his work as a talisman for an art form based in colored light that was unconditioned by anything except its affinity with music, and he addressed himself consistently to a public which he sincerely believed to be "above" the spectacle. He worked with highly controlled colored light (electrically driven of course) in the domestic interior "concert" space of his large studio and in musically dedicated halls. His darkness, as *his* "night," was framed and housed artificially. It was con-ceived as separate from the urban / industrial outside night that was lighted first practically and then spectacularly. His night music invaded privacy and in fact insisted upon it, the governing belief being that any true art, to be such, required an intense intimacy of address—something which the "spectacle" denied in favor of an appeal to an undifferentiated mass public. For Rimington, the making of an art that generated aesthetic emotion of a "significant" sort could never be truly public, because its audience required aesthetic preparation and concentration. Living and working when he did, he was fortunate in being able to have the confidence that serious appreciation of music, a qualified cultural given, could suffice to install such preparation. He may have been right, in his confidence, at least for an historically brief while.

I would like to thank Maureen Meister and Anne Nellis for research help, Judith Tolnick for editorial assistance and Sharon Clark for word processing. KSC.

1. Rev. Hugh Reginald Haweis. *Music and Morals* (New York: Harper and Brothers, 1872): 32–33.
2. Walter Pater. *Three Major Texts*. Ed. by William E. Buckler (New York: New York University Press, 1986): 155–156.
3. Elizabeth Robins Pennell and Joseph. *The Life of James McNeill Whistler* (Philadelphia and London: J. B. Lippincott, 1908): 116.
4. Ibid., 174–175
5. John Perry and W. E. Ayrton. "On the Music of Colour and Visible Motion," *Proceedings of the Physical Society*, III (1880): 18–19.
6. Reverend Hugh Reginald Haweis (1838–1901) was the rector of St. James Church, Marylebone, London. He was a scholar, author, musician and influential as the editor of "Cassell's Magazine." His lectures and sermons were enthusiastically received in England and North America. For Haweis' comments about Whistler cf.: Pennell, 173 (see note no. 3)
7. "The Music of Colour and Motion," *Nature* (London) 10 (Dec. 5 1878): 101–102.
8. Cf. note no. 5.
9. See Kermit Swiler Champa. *The Slang of Aestheticism —The Anglo-American Color-Music Project*, Chapter 2 (Forthcoming) for journalistic response.
10. See *1889 La Tour Eiffel et L'Exposition Universelle* (Paris: Musée d'Orsay, 1889)
11. "Cloud Illumination for Advertising," *New York Times* (Dec. 25, 1892): 17, col. 7. Walter Randt. Wolken als Projektionsfläche" *Das Licht* 2, 1932, 67–68.
12. Sir Isaac Newton. "Queries no. 12, 13, 14" *Opticks* (London, 1704)
13. Hermann von Helmholtz (1821–94) convincingly discredits all attempts at a direct analogy between color and sound: *Handbuch der Physiologischen Optik* (Leipzig 1867).
14. John Wellborn Root. "The Art of Pure Color," in: *The Meanings of Architecture; Buildings and Writings by John Wellborn Root* (New York: Horizon Press, 1967): 185.
15. This quotation has been sensitively highlighted most recently in George Heard Hamilton. *Painting and Sculpture in Europe 1880–1940* (Harmondsworth: Penguin Books, 1967): 192.
16. Champa, op. cit., 101–102.
17. A. Wallace Rimington. *Colour-Music. The Art of Mobile Colour*. (New York: F. A. Stokes, 1911).
18. The first historical account of the project is Adrian Bernard Klein. *Colour Music. The Art of Light*. (London: The Technical Press, 1926). See especially the enlarged third edition of 1937. See also: Kenneth Peacock. "Instruments to Perform Color-Music: Two Centuries of Technological Experimentation," *Leonardo* 21, no. 4 (1988): 397–406.
19. "Raymond Hood predicts 'Architecture of the Night,'" *Architecture of the Night*. General Electric Company, *Bulletin* GED-375 (February 1930).
20. Louis Bertrand Castel. (1688–1757) *L'Optique des Couleurs* (Paris: Briasson, 1740): 473–485. See also David Brenneman. *Music of Colors in Early 18th Century Theories of Painting*. M. A. Thesis (Brown University, Providence, RI 1988).
21. Thomas Wilfred. "Light and the Artist," *Journal of Aesthetics and Art Criticism*, 5, no. 4 (June 1947): 247–255.
22. Klein: 256–261.
23. Champa. *The Rise of Landscape Painting in France. Corot to Monet* (Manchester, New Hampshire: Currier Gallery of Art, 1991): 23–63.

12 Eiffel Tower with St. Elmo Fire and Search Light, World's Fair, 1889. Contemporary illustration.

Light Architecture: A New Term's Genesis

Werner Oechslin

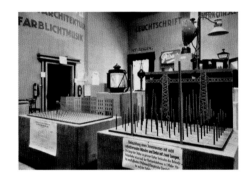

In 1927, Joachim Teichmüller (Fig. 1) published an article in the German journal *Licht und Lampe,* where—after previous articles about light technology—he used the term "light architecure" for the first time.[1] The scope of this new concept seemed so significant to the author that he explained its application in greater detail. "When I, almost exactly five months ago, dared to pronounce the words 'light architecture' for the first time, when I even dared to write these new words in big letters on a wall of my light technology section at the 'Gesolei' exhibition in Düsseldorf, I was somewhat afraid" (Fig. 2). While exhibitions would indeed occasionally "employ a powerful slogan," at that point it was impossible to determine if the development would in fact proceed as expected. Now, however, five months later, he felt more assured: "A light architecture exists. And by no means does it only exist as a seedling. Already it is sprouting and shooting everywhere, with such variety and richness that it is difficult to survey the whole field and bring order to the profusion of phenomena."

Was this more than rhetoric? What caused Teichmüller, after initial insecurity, to now profess such assurance? "The electric light bulb has brought in a new age"—this of course had long been obvious! Teichmüller had already stated in 1925 in *Licht und Lampe* that "a new epoch" in light technology had dawned. Rather, the decisive step now seemed to lie in the joining of the concept of light to that of architecture. That was the real risk. That was the real challenge.

"Architectural Light" versus "Light Architecture"

Considering this in 1927, Teichmüller recognized a twofold development. On the one hand, one had to deal with the "design of the light sources," with the lamps, which would complement the space, its forms and ornaments. On the other hand, it was important to realize the "space-shaping power of light" itself. For both developments, Teichmüller expected a future synthesis, which alone could justify the concept of "light architecture": "Both architecture and the lamps, in particular the light emanating from its source, are fused into an artistic unity, so intimate and inseparable, that one must speak of a light architecture."

The cooperation of light engineers and architects, he claimed, made sense in particular when it concerned the space-shaping power of light. The light engineer would first take into consideration only the image formed on the retina by light, the architect on the other hand would start with just the building. For the latter, light might simply "explain" architecture. This would perhaps produce architectural light, but not light architecture. "But this architectural light can lead to light architecture," Teichmüller concluded, "if with it, and only with it, specific architectural effects are produced, which appear and disappear simultaneously with the light."

Thus, in 1927, the task of light architecture is formulated: architecture itself should produce light-specific effects and use these as it would use any other structural elements. This is the essential requirement: light in architecture should no longer be simply provided indirectly by external conditions; rather, light should now be calculable—an instrument in the hand of the architect, and an essential component of his skill in determining spatial qualities.

This then was the debut that electricity , in the 1920s, made in modern architecture: a "modernism" that can be compared with the other blessings of industrial society and their relevant consequences for architecture and its desired renewal. What is comparable here is in fact the determination to fully integrate modern electric light. Walter Gropius, Le Corbusier, the spokesmen of the German Werkbund, had expressed similar intentions, regarding new construction materials and industrial production methods. The corresponding catchword, composed analogously, was "industrial architecture."

Under the title "The Development of Modern Industrial Architecture," Gropius formulated his thoughts in the Werkbund Yearbook of 1913. Financially supported by Karl Ernst Osthaus, he had developed them after his practical training with Peter Behrens and simultaneously with the construction of the Fagus works, the earliest example of a modern architecture based upon these premises.[2] In the wake of the convictions of the Werkbund and of the call for a "spiritualization of German labor" Gropius promoted the recognition of that integrative power, which he was willing to grant to the artist—and to no one else. What he described on the basis of the Werkbund's

1 Professor Joachim Teichmüller, photo, 1932.

2 Gesolei Exhibition Düsseldorf 1926, Lighting Technology Exhibit, Room 27, with sections on "Lichtarchitektur" and "Farblichtspiele."

3 Denis Diderot, Encyclopédie, *Lumière*, 1765.

demand for a synthesis of art, industry and trade, was simultaneously an artistic program of modernity: "Yet very gradually one recognizes in commercial circles which new values for the industry are conveyed by the intellectual work of the artist. As a result, one now attempts to secure the artistic quality of machine-made products from the start and to involve the artist early on in the creation of forms that are going to be mass-produced."[3]

This assumption was still valid at the moment when electricity got under way. According to this same ideal quest for synthesis, the modern forms of lighting design should be integrated with architecture. When much later, in 1956, a long overdue book with the title *Light Architecture* appeared, it was understood that this expectation had by now been met.[4] The publisher advertised the book by referring to the—presumably widely accepted—connection between modern architecture and its specific use of light, by day or by night. "Transparency, insubstantiality, weightlessness" as effects of daylight penetrating unhindered into rooms, the "beaming brightness" of the nocturnally illuminated buildings, "so that they resemble crystals, which radiate light by themselves"—these were the concepts used now to enthusiastically praise the advantages of "light architecture."[5]

Wassili Luckhardt, in the introduction to the suggestive sequence of images he had selected, once again pointed to the novelty of the concepts of "architectural light" and "light architecture."[6] Walter Köhler referred to Teichmüller's concepts and remarks and concluded by integrating them into a somewhat larger framework: "Light architecture is the logical advancement of the architectural ideas which had been the basis for the great architects of Antiquity and the Middle Ages, who used daylight as an architectural element in the sense characterized here."[7] Relative to light and electricity, the historical dimension is thereby established and the historical significance of technological innovations is once more identified, corresponding to the idea of progress, which is so characteristic of modernity.

Yet here at the latest, questions also appear. The process did not run seamlessly. A certain amount of time passed until the claim "light—a luxury for everybody"[8] was actually fulfilled. What had been known since the '20s regarding illuminated advertising and astonishing day / night effects had still to be integrated into residential construction—and would there degenerate all too easily into mere catchprases, as in "light with a special ambiance" at "fireplace and television," as if the idea of muted light and indirect illumination were already the final word of wisdom.[9]

On the other hand, it becomes obvious that despite the assumption of a rationally controllable principle of electricity, countless "residues" of a mystically transfigured notion of light could equally survive in modernity. "Logical progress" regarding light is more of a program than an architectural reality—not to the detriment of architecture, as is easily seen. In this respect, a short review could in fact be illuminating and enlightening.

A Historical Recourse

No one doubts that light has always played an important role in architecture. Paradoxically this subject, as well as other fundamental questions of architecture, has little or rarely been dealt with systematically. The textbooks of architectural theory pursue objectives other than the complete or systematic treatment of such questions; instead, they develop, with increasing frequency, the given theoretical premises (for example the Vitruvian orders) into progressively sophisticated design recipes. The reason why the topic of light has widely been omitted in architectural literature was probably, at least in part, due to the difficulty in correctly describing and defining light.

The Piemontese architect Bernardo Antonio Vittone (1705–70), for example, not only had knowledge of Newton's optical theories,[10] but, more importantly, developed almost systematically new and sophisticated solutions of light direction and design for his small churches in Turin and Piemont. Nevertheless, one searches in vain for a corresponding fallout in his extensive theoretical work from the 1760s. Only around 1800 did the art of constructing and drawing shadows (usually on the basis of a simplifying constant forty-five-degree angle) become part of general education.

4 Luckhardt / Köhler. "Lighting in Architecture." International Horticultural Exposition, Hamburg, 1954, fountain.

5 Luckhardt / Köhler. "Lighting in Architecture." Manhattan at Night, c. 1956.

6 Deification of Newton. Engraving by Giovanni Battista Pittoni, Domenico and Giuseppi Valeriani, 1730.

Surviving textbooks suggest that until then, one merely studied the correct graphic description and simulation of the incidence of light according to a geometrical abstraction, which had long become customary and was hardly questioned anymore.

Yet, Diderot's *Encyclopédie* of 1765, in its article on "Lumière," referred to the "sensation":[11] thereby, "instrumentalization" in the sense of the (possible and comprehensible) "effect on the soul" was at least addressed. And thus a great potential of artistic expression was revealed, which later, for instance with Etienne-Louis Boullée, consequently became a program: "Je fais la lumière," formulated the artist in his "remarks on the significance and utility of architecture."[12]

The *Encyclopédie* also addresses the distinction between "lumière naturelle" and "lumière artificielle."[13] Yet, characteristically, this distinction is encountered in the section in which the concept "lumière" is treated in relation to art. Not the physical problem (of light production) stands in the foreground, but rather the artistic device, with which this is simulated—as it is already common in painting. Obviously, art, especially painting, has long developed its own experience with light, which exceeds the narrowness of scientifically valid statements (Fig. 3). Jacques-François Blondel formulates a similar observation in relation to vault technology, another topic neglected by the systematic surveys of architectural treatises: "La Pratique a long-temps devancé la Théorie dans tous les arts."[14] Concrete experience precedes, theory follows behind and develops the rules. With light this is certainly the case.

For art there was only a limited need for scientific clarification of what in practice had long been utilized and operated in a differentiated way. The use of light was always an artistic matter, even when the artistic and architectural theory only left insufficient traces. We must therefore reconstruct the knowledge about concrete interaction with light indirectly. There is evidence, at least sporadically, for the assumption that light itself was noticed by architects beyond the philosophical fundamentals.

When, for instance, in 1926 Le Corbusier presented his changes to architectural principles in the "5 points," he argued as Claude Perrault had already argued 250 years before:[15] It is not a matter of simply denying the old in order to place the validity of the new in a better light. Rather, it is important to use familiar criteria to make the new appear plausible and advantageous. To make the "plan libre" palatable, Le Corbusier also—in part using the same concepts—formulated: "car nous aimons l'air, le jour et les dégagements." And so the "fenêtre en longueur" is naturally not simply a light-technical measure, but rather an ingenious architectural idea to improve upon the problem of illumination. Here, a synthesis is achieved—and fundamentally formulated—of the kind which Teichmüller also demanded for his "light architecture."

The qualities of new materials offer advantages that the architect must utilize: "Réduire les éléments portants à des dimensions moindres, c'est permettre l'accès libre de la lumière" is a formula, which Sigfried Giedion—on the basis of such assumptions—presents in his essay "Lumière et Construction."[16] The interaction of structural stipulations and light effects—from Henri Labrouste to Eugène Freyssinet—is here projected into history.

The value of this integrative method of argumentation, seemingly borrowed from history, only becomes clear when one compares it with the mere promises of the new technology. Le Corbusier speaks of light and not of electric illumination. However, André Lurçat, for example, deals with artificial light in his 1929 book, *Architecture*.[17] Even if he primarily stresses the adaptation of architecture to the new inventions, it is just these innovations from "Les techniques modernes et le machinisme" that he—analogously to the five points of Le Corbusier—designates as "Les Eléments Nouveaux": "pilotis," "terrasses," "fenêtre," "couleur," "lumière artificielle."

The accent—insignificant at first—has been shifted from the principles and their symbols to the "range of applications." Lurçat finds rhetorically convincing formulations in order to demonstrate the significance of electric light—and its barely foreseeable consequences: "Jusqu'à maintenant, dans la maison, presque toute vie disparaissait le soir en même temps que la lumière naturelle."[18] Now an event had occurred which, for the first time in centuries, could bring about a decisive change leading to improvement of life in the home. The euphoria surrounding this new technical achievement (amid mild reservations about constant exposure to magnetic fields!) predominates.

Such a positive position also explains the oppositional, skeptical statements regarding the thoughtless use of the new devices. Werner Hegemann, the urbanist, planner and professed opponent of the uncontrollably rising "metropolis," at the same time (1929) criticized the steadily decreasing sun exposure of New York's buildings and added, almost sarcastically: "Thus, professors now prove that artificial illumination is more advisable than sunlight."[19] Of course, criticism is and was always appropriate when electric light was treated as a mere makeshift. The conflict could not be avoided!

Hegemann had, at the same time, mentioned Hugh Ferriss as the "most successful lyrical poet" of skyscraper romanticism—and criticized him indirectly. The collision of the two arguments is symptomatic. Scientific research and artistic application of light clearly diverge repeatedly: enthusiasm over the new technical possibilities competes with the more cautious attempts to integrate relevant innovations! In this potential area of conflict there remains in any case sufficient space for all the transfiguring and mystifying relations of light, which only become more numerous with the dawning of the actual use of electric light.

Between Apotheosis and Luminous Advertising

Newton's separation of light with a prism was also not just celebrated as a breakthrough in physics, but rather was exalted and transfigured with images of divine, metaphysical symbolism. The chief elements of the physical experiment—light beam, prism, mirror—were portrayed in a sacred space in the *Apotheosis of Newton* (1730), painted by Pittoni and Valeriani, for example, in such a way that the parallel to the allegories of divine truth conveyed to men by (divine) rays is unmistakable[20] (Fig. 6). Thus, the physical discovery—quite in the sense of Voltaire—has been transformed into a "philosophy"!

One would misjudge modernity, if one wouldn't allow such possibilities of cultural self-assessment. With the technical incorporation of electric light into architecture, the question of electricity—and even more that of light—was by no means exhausted. Some time had to pass, though, before the new medium could create a new language for itself. From this speechlessness, the imagination derived a profit. For example, in order to represent and describe "light problems of medieval sacred architecture," architects would use terms such as "spirited chiaroscuro" or—"according to the time of day"—"impassioned undulations," and they discriminated between "still unformed and arbitrary" and "ordered and practically sculpted."[21] So many terms, then, for light, which one had just begun to utilize in a calculated and purposeful manner! Since attention had finally been directed to this "new achievement," it was now enjoyed and exploited thoroughly. For the aforementioned (late) publication on "light architecture" by Walter Köhler in 1956, a "series of pictures" still preceded the relevant explanation.[22] It was compiled by Wassili Luckhardt, whose early expressionist visions were well known. Luckhardt now celebrated light—beginning with a "Gas Nebula in Orion" and the "Explosion of the Atom Bomb"—in its universal breadth, from cosmic to apocalyptic. He presented a new world that light had recently begun to uncover ("inner stresses made visible by polarized light") and systematically demonstrated the corresponding applications. The catchwords now extended from "geometry" and "form of light" to the effects of transparency, weightlessness, space extension, and, finally to the "humanization of the factory environment." In tune with modern rhetoric and use of imagery, effects are introduced, contrasts are layed out—the illuminated Cologne cathedral in comparison with nocturnal Manhattan demonstrate the "mysticism of opposite worlds" (Figs. 4, 5). Thus, light has found its apotheosis in its modern, "electric" form as well.

By 1956, after a long period of work and experimentation, Wassili Luckhardt had gained a certain amount of experience with the new tool of articificial light. In 1927, though, one still stood at the beginning, according to Teichmüller's initially quoted views. In the same year, Walter Curt Behrendt had also talked about the new possibilities in his *Sieg des neuen Baustils*.[23] Clearly aware of the architectural potential, he talked explicitly about the "form problem of artificial light,"

7 Wassili and Hans Luckhardt. Commercial building at Tauentzienstrasse 3, Berlin, night view. (1925–27). Contemporary photo.

8 Arthur Korn, Berliner Wach- und Schliessgesellschaft, 1926. Collection Centre Canadien d'Architecture / Canadian Center for Architecture, Montréal.

and then immediately added that this was perhaps "one of the most interesting and exciting" problems that face architecture today: "moreover, it is also one that previously has barely been considered, not to mention dealt with practically."

Behrendt pointed to the use of electric light as "an effective instrument for interior decoration, for the interpretation of the role of space and the flow of space, or for the accentuation and strengthening of spatial relations and spatial tension." He wanted to be able to utilize light better, liberated by electricity, analogously to Le Corbusier's arguments in connection with the "plan libre." Yet Behrendt's assessment of the situation of 1927 confirmed how little had been done in this respect: "Nevertheless, the exploitation of these expanded possibilities has just begun. Until now, only illuminated advertising has made substantial use of the new freedom."[24]

To illustrate his observations, Behrendt used one of the buildings of the Luckhardt brothers: under the caption "Day- and Night-view," there appeared a commercial building, renovated in 1925 together with Alfons Anker, and located on Berlin's Tauentzienstrasse (Fig. 7, see also p. 122). Behrendt fully accepted illuminated advertising as "a new formal problem." A glance into the literature of the day immediately reveals that architects—foremost Erich Mendelsohn—recognized a new task important for their aesthetic goals. In those years, the journals were filled with pertinent articles. Under the title "Reshaping of Façades," Walter Riezler discussed the building on Tauentzienstrasse in the Werkbund journal *Die Form* in both its day and night exposure, and classified it as "more modern" than Mendelsohn's Herpich store.[25] The illuminated advertising here belonged "inseparably to the facade."

Adolf Behne selected the same example for his illustrated report "Berlin," which he published in *Das Neue Frankfurt* in 1928.[26] As early as 1925, Alfred Gellhorn had published the fundamental essay "Advertising and Cityscape" in *Die Form*, in which he rejected both petty criticism and half-heartedness and demanded that architects "compose and fashion the facades in such a way that they reveal the spatial possibilities."[27] In the same journal a few months later, Arthur Korn had presented the—also frequently cited—advertising in the facade of his Berlin Guard and Security Company (Wach- und Schliessgesellschaft), and defended it against official criticism[28] (Fig. 8).

The criticism here was directed against the growing chaos from increased advertising, which eventually would have to be overcome by artistic means. In 1927, Max Landsberg argued this point in *Der Städtebau*.[29] With the catchword "illuminated advertising in the city," he first professed to accepting the new situation, which had arisen through nocturnal illumination: "The most beautiful cityscape, the most beautiful edifice disappears at night behind its lights. The commercial city already has such a different appearance by day and by night, that one can speak of an urban architecture for the day, and must demand one for the night" (Figs. 9, 10).

The "architectural form of the modern commercial building" had in reality already been determined by advertising for quite some time. Consequently, he demands not only ordinances, but plans and competitions, "which ensure the quality of nocturnal urban architecture." Landsberg promises, "one night, out of the ugly hullabaloo of today, our commercial city [would] become a uniform spatial sequence of radiating illuminated beauty." From an architectural point of view, the "organization of illuminated advertising"—as demanded earlier—had thus become a pertinent issue, the tackling of which was an urgent task. At first barely recognized, within a few years the theme had attracted a huge amount of attention.[30]

In 1925, Ernst Cassirer, in his *Philosophy of Symbolic Forms*, had emphasized the contrast between day and night, between light and darkness as the embodiment of human cultural development.[31] Now all architectural journals were full of day and night variants of modern city facades. This double existence of architecture was systematically developed and increasingly organized—up to a nocturnal "display of the firm's signet via the interior lighting" in Düsseldorf's Thyssenhaus by Hentrich and Petschnigg (see p. 192).[32] Additionally, this new kind of architectural image found its glorification in the accompanying texts and books. "By day the city fills itself with energy, at night it emanates life away from itself. In the network of automobile headlights,

9, 10 Luckhardt and Anker. Office Building in Berlin, Kurfürstendamm 211, day view, *c.* 1927.

in the call of the illuminated commercial advertising, in the vertical rays of the skyscraper lights. A circus of light, rarely, as here, in tune with the rhythm of the architecture," read one of Erich Mendelsohn's captions under a photo from New York in his 1926 book, *Amerika. Bilderbuch eines Architekten.*[33]

In 1925, Ernst Cassirer stated: "The development of a feeling for mystic space proceeds everywhere from the contrast between day and night, between light and darkness."[34] So once more, the artistic interpretation—of the phenomenon of electric light—had caught up with the universal meanings and interpretations of light. How quickly and almost imperceptibly reality was exaggerated, Mendelsohn demonstrated in the same book. Mendelson described a picture that his friend, the German film director Fritz Lang,[35] had created by exposing the plate twice: "Weird. The contours of the houses are wiped out. But in our consciousness they still rise, run after each other, run each other down. That is the backdrop for the flaming script, the rocket fire of mobile illuminated advertising, emerging and vanishing, disappearing and erupting above the thousands of cars and the carnal whirlpool of people. Still disorganized, since exaggerated, yet still full of fantastic beauty, which one day will be perfected."[36] (See p. 43, Fig. 18)

Mendelsohn's description corresponds to what he had fundamentally expressed in 1923 in a lecture in Amsterdam.[37] "For one day we too will have to extend our technical ideas towards spiritual provisions," he formulated rather solemnly at the time.[38] Yet this fully matched his conception of an ideal synthesis of "function" and "dynamics," of reason and emotion. Light would occupy a prominent role in this ideal balance, "where emotional incidents can be related wonderfully to mathematical quantities and geometrical relationships." For architectural creation two components would be necessary: "The first, that of the intellect, of the brain, of the organizational apparatus..."; "the second, on the basis of the proposed organization, that of the creative impulse, of the blood, of the temperament, of the senses, of a feeling for organization." "Only the combination of both components," concludes Mendelsohn, "leads to mastery over the spatial elements: the physically tangible element of mass and the immaterial element of light." (Fig. 13)

This too is an apotheosis of light—in the sense of an ideal understanding of modernity, which claims to appropriate and incorporate all recent phenomena in a new synthesis. Mendelsohn can undoubtedly repeat what Boullée had formulated before him: "Je fais la lumière." He can claim, with Boullée and Le Corbusier, to have found the recipe: "L'art de nous émouvoir par les effets de la lumière appartient à l'architecture."[39] The topic of light is a chapter in the cultural history of modern architecture. Even a more realistic approach to the problem—in the by no means disdainful sense of "spaces in the proper light"[40]—cannot change this.

The actual significance of the discussion about light and electricity in architecture since the 1920s deserves further discussion. The somewhat exaggerated approach that Erich Mendelsohn had effectively presented in words and images can be complemented by the fundamental considerations put down on paper in 1781 by a physicist who—even among historians of science—is hardly a familiar figure. Vittorio Fossombroni from Arezzo, who later attracted attention through his investigations into questions of velocity, at that time published his *Saggio di Ricerche sull'Intensità del Lume.*[41] He preceded these mathematical explanations of light with an introduction, in which he fundamentally discussed the value of his investigations. Like Mendelsohn, he proceeds from the eternal battle between reason and fantasy, between the "tranquilla ragione paziente indagatrice della verità" and the "fervida immaginativa intollerante di freno." Fantasy would repeatedly win heart and minds, yet this does not extend beyond certain limits, as in the arts only the Borrominis would follow the Michelangelos. If there were an unlimited future for the sons of the intellect, then mathematics would have the greatest chance of success thanks to its alignment on the "astratte verità." One can also interpret this somewhat pessimistically: despite all the elevated thoughts and the exaggerated praise of the new possibilities of electric light in architecture, its banal, expedient utilization also predominates in our daily life. Light architecture, as protagonists envisioned it at the end of the '20s, is rare, yesterday as well as today.

11, 12 Brinkman and van der Vlugt. Van Nelle Tobacco Factory, Rotterdam, 1926–29.

13 Erich Mendelsohn, Schocken Department Store, Stuttgart, night view, *c.* 1928.

1. Joachim Teichmüller. "Lichtarchitektur," *Licht und Lampe*, 13 / 14 (1927): 421–522, 449–458. During the preparation of *Daidalos* 27 / 1988, Hans T. von Malotki drew my attention to the writings of Joachim Teichmüller. The following discourse is in many respects a continuation of the essay published there (Werner Oechslin, "Light: A Means of Development between Reason and Emotion," in: *Daidalos*, 27, 1988): 22–38). Compare also: Werner Oechslin, "Jour / nuit, clair / obscure: un thème architectonique," in: *Faces*, 10 (1988): 26 ff.

2. Walter Gropius. "Die Entwicklung moderner Industriebaukunst" in *Die Kunst in Industrie und Handel, Jahrbuch des Deutschen Werkbundes* (Jena: Diederichs, 1913): 17 ff.

3. Ibid., 17.

4. Walter Köhler and Wassili Luckhardt. *Lichtarchitektur, Licht und Farbe als raumgestaltende Elemente* (Berlin: Bauwelt Verlag, 1956). Published in English as *Lighting in Architecture: Light and Color as Sereoplastic Elements* (New York: Reinhold, 1959).

5. Ibid., blurb.

6. Ibid., 7.

7. Ibid., 125.

8. Cf. D. Hundertmark. "Räume im rechten Licht" (Spaces in proper light), *Bauwelt* 61, special edition (Berlin, 1964). This exposition also employed the motto: "The illumination is planned."

9. These are typical headlines (pp. 10 and 12) in the quite representative account, cited in note 8.

10. Vittone's library contained Algarotti's widely distributed popularizing exposition of Newton's theory of optics (*Newtonianismo per le Dame*). For an interpretation of this fact, which — in spite of the explicit profession of high regard "per i matematici moderni" — is still dependent on conjectures, cf. Paolo Portoghesi. *Bernardo Vittone* (Rome: Edizioni dell'Elefante, 1966): 20 and 250.

11. Cf. *Encyclopédie ou Dictionnaire raisonné des sciences, des arts, et des metiers*, IX (1765): 717 ff., article "Lumière"; the definition there: "est la sensation que la vûe des corps lumineux apporte ou fait éprouver à l'âme, ou bien la propriété des corps qui les rend propres à exciter en nous cette sensation. Voyez SENSATION."

12. Cf. Etienne-Louis Boullée. "Considérations sur l'Importance et l'Utilité de l'Architecture ...," in: same, *Essai sur l'Art*, published by Jean-Marie Pérouse de Montclos (Paris: Arts et métiers graphiques, 1969): 35 (fol. 54r). The question of light in regards to Boullée in conjunction with the doctrine of "expression" and "effet" as well as the theory of the sublime — would require its own extensive essay. Compare to this and to the consequences up to modernity: Werner Oechslin. "Emouvoir — Boullée and Le Corbusier," *Daidalos*, 30 (1988): 42 ff.

13. *Encyclopédie*, loc. cit. (n. 11): 724. The same difference can also be found e.g. in the relevant dictionary: cf. Roland Le Virloys. *Dictionnaire d'Architecture Civile, Militaire, et Navale, Antique, Ancienne et Moderne ...*, vol. II (Paris, 1770): 188: "Lumière ... Se dit, dans la Peinture, des parties éclairées d'un tableau: on la distingue en lumière naturelle & artificielle." It is of course significant that in this connection (see below) architecture is not the subject. Roland le Virloys refers (in this connection) to the article "Jour" (ibid., 125), in which "en général toute ouverture dans un mur, ou dans un comble, pour éclairer les différentes parties d'un bâtiment" is understood.

14. Jacques-François Blondel. *Cours d'Architecture ...*, Vol. VI (Paris 1777): 1.

15. Cf. also: Werner Oechslin. "5 Points d'une Architecture nouvelle," in: *Le Corbusier. Une encyclopédie* (Paris: Ed. du Centre Pompidou, 1987): 92 ff.; same, "A Cultural History of Modern Architecture, 1: The 'Modern': Historical Event vs. Demand," in: *A + U* 4 (1990): 50, especially 61 ff.

16. Cf. Sigfried Giedion. "Lumière et Construction. Réflexions à propos des ateliers de chemins de fer de Freyssinet," *Cahiers d'Art*, 6 (1929): 275 ff.

17. Cf. André Lurçat. *Architecture* (Paris: Au sans pareil, 1929): 107 ff., especially 147 ff.

18. Ibid., 149.

19. Werner Hegemann. "Cathedral or Secular Building," in: *Wasmuths Monatshefte für Baukunst*, (May 1929): 224.

20. Cf. (with ill.): Oechslin. "Licht: ein Gestaltungsmittel ..." loc. cit. (n. 1): 22 ff.

21. For an arbitrary, yet certainly representative example of art historical language on the subject of light, see: M. Escherich. "Lichtprobleme der mittelalterlichen Sakralbaukunst." in: *Deutsche Bauhütte*, 29 (1909): 233.

22. Köhler / Luckhardt. *Licht Architektur*, loc. cit. (n. 4); the cited figure captions to: B1, B3, B6, B9, B10, B37, B40, B61, B103, B19 / B20.

23. Cf. Walter Curt Behrendt. *Der Sieg des Neuen Baustils* (Stuttgart: Wedekind, 1927): 47 ff.

24. Ibid., 48.

25. Walter Riezler. "Umgestaltung der Fassaden" in: *Die Form*, 2 (1927): 33 ff.

26. "Berlin. Bilderbericht von Adolf Behne," in: *Das Neue Frankfurt*, II, 2 (1928): 37 ff.

27. Alfred Gellhorn. "Reklame und Stadtbild" in: *Die Form* (1925 / 26): 133 ff.

28. Arthur Korn. "Neuzeitliche Straßenreklame" in: *Die Form* 1, no. 12 (September 1926): 278–279.

29. Max Landsberg, "Lichtreklame im Stadtbild," in: *Städtebau*, XXII, 3 (1927): 35.

30. Cf. also, for example: E. Reinhardt. "Gestaltung der Lichtreklame," in *Die Form*, 4 (1929): 73, which refers to the relevant book by Wilhelm Lotz (*Licht und Beleuchtung*, Berlin: H. Reckendorf, 1928) and to the corresponding touring exhibition, which was organized at the time by the journal *Die Form*. An exhibition "Illuminated Advertising and Shop-window Illumination" also took place in Basel's Applied Arts Museum in 1928. The multiplicity of the light / architecture relation at this time is by no means exhausted with these references. The exhibition architecture and the especially impressive example of the German Theater Exhibition in Magdeburg, 1927 also deserves attention. Cf. *Neuere Arbeiten von Prof. Albinmüller* (Berlin, Leipzig, Vienna: Neue Werkkunst, 1928).

31. Ernst Cassirer. *Philosophie der symbolischen Formen* (Berlin: Bruno Cassirer, 1923–29) vol. 2 (1925): 122. Cf. Werner Oechslin. "Light: a Means of Development between Reason and Emotion," loc. cit. (n. 1): 22 ff.

32. Cf. Martin Mittag. *Thyssenhaus* (Essen, Detmold: Bauzentrum-Ring Verlag, 1962; H. Theissen. "Grundlagen für die lichttechnische Planung" ibid.): 93 ff.

33. Erich Mendelsohn. *Amerika. Bilderbuch eines Architekten* (Berlin: Mosse, 1926): 25.

34. Cassirer (see note 31).

35. Mendelsohn. *Amerika*, loc. cit. (n. 33), Fig. 44; the attribution of this photo, which also later became famous through El Lissitzky's use of it in a photo-collage, to Fritz Lang appeared in the 1928 reprint of Mendelsohn's book (Herbert Moldering, Nachwort: Mendelsohn, Amerika und der "Amerikanismus" in Erich Mendelsohn. *Amerika*, reprint 1991 (Braunschweig: Vieweg Verlag, 1991): 83–91.

36. Mendelsohn. *Amerika*, loc. cit. 44 (n. 33).

37. Cf. Erich Mendelsohn. "The International Correspondence of New Architectural Thought or Dynamics and Function" (1923, Lecture in "Architectura et Amicitia," Amsterdam), in: Erich Mendelsohn, *Das Gesamtschaffen des Architekten* (Berlin, 1933): 22 ff. (cited: 29, 31.)

38. In comparison with other, mystifying statements by architects regarding light, Mendelsohn's formulations seem indeed rather balanced and objective. That can hardly be said of Louis Kahn's poetic statements regarding the problem ("So light is really the source of all being"). Nevertheless, Kahn's reference to light — as one of the most prominent examples — must at least be mentioned here. Cf. also: J. Lobell. *Between Silence and Light. Spirit in the Architecture of Louis I. Kahn* (Boulder; 1979) (Kahn's text "Light": 22; A. Tyng. *Beginnings. Louis I. Kahn's Philosophy of Architecture* (New York: Wiley, 1984): 129 ff. It is left to the reader to decide which statements should be associated with the term "philosophy." It remains a fact, though, that until now a great chasm separates the "mystifying" and the "objective" method of observation of the problem of light in architecture. To the latter category belongs, for example, the book by I. L. C. Kalff, *Kunstlicht und Architektur* (Eindhoven 1943), which one may consult for comparison with Kahn's poetry!

39. Cf. above and note 12.

40. Cf. above and note 8.

41. Cf. Vittorio Fossombroni. *Saggio di Ricerche sull'Intensità del Lume* (Arezzo, 1781): III and V.

14 Night view of illuminated storefront showing electrical appliances, Zielona Góra, Poland, c. 1928. Collection Centre Canadien d'Architecture / Canadian Center for Architecture, Montréal.

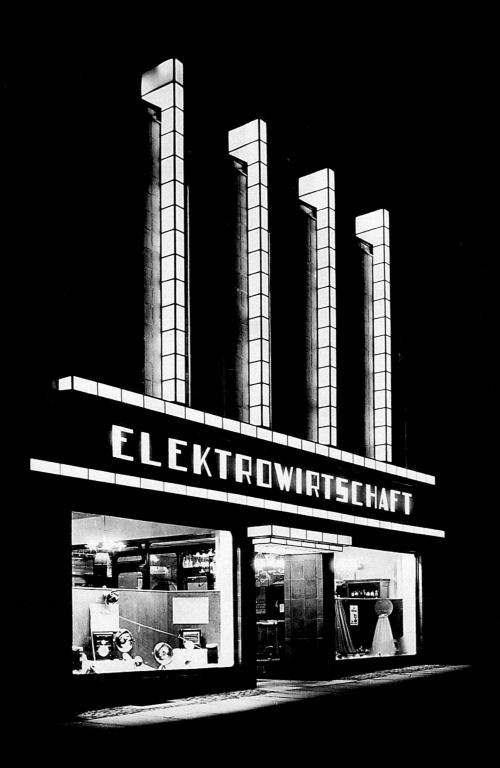

Lichtarchitektur and the Avant-Garde

Dietrich Neumann

1 Hans Scharoun, 1919 Gläserner Bau. Akademie der Künste Berlin, Sammlung Baukunst.

2 Hans Luckhardt, 1919, Kultbau. Akademie der Künste Berlin, Sammlung Baukunst.

3 Bruno Taut, *Alpine Architektur*, 1919.

"In the evening the lighted building will attract great attention. For a glass house you don't need to provide 'illumination' with added incandescent bulbs and such. You just need to light up the rooms of the glass house, and from the inside it will shine in the most beautiful light."[1] The crucial conceptual distinction that Bruno Taut made when he described the nocturnal appearance of his glass house at the Cologne Werkbund Exhibition in 1914 (Fig. 4), between a building's illumination from the outside and the glow of its own translucent architectural forms was going to assume a central position in the discourse about light and architecture after World War I. Taut had been in-fluenced by the ideas of the utopian writer Paul Scheerbart, who had frequently advocated glass architecture in his novels. Scheerbart himself had been inspired by the recent advances in public illumination at World's Fairs and the availability of glass blocks, which would, he predicted, allow buildings to "glow like lanterns." The most prominent recent example had been the 1907 extension of the Samaritaine Department Store in Paris (Fig. 5), where the architect Frantz Jourdain had introduced two bulbous domes of colored glass blocks crowning the building's corners and glowing at night due to electric lamps inside.[2] In the same year Scheerbart had introduced the term "Lichtarchitektur" (light architecture—see below), claiming later that "the abundance of electric light alone justifies glass architecture."[3] A few years later he added: "All we can say of those illuminated nights which glass architecture will bring us is that they are indescribable. Think of the searchlights on top of all glass towers and on all airships, and think of those searchlights in all painterly colors.... And add factories, in which at night light shines through colored glass panes. And then think about the great palaces and cathedrals out of glass ..."[4]

Scheerbart's writings and the great success of Taut's small 1914 Cologne exhibition pavilion helped to encourage a number of evocative architectural fantasies between 1919 and 1921 by Taut himself and his friends Hans Scharoun, the Luckhardt Brothers and others (Figs. 1–3). Their drawings would often show glass-enclosed buildings at night, glowing from within and present-ing centers for a new spirituality. Although these expressionist fantasies were hardly mentioned during the debates about architectural illumination in the 1920s (having not been as widely publicized yet as they are today), they undoubtedly provide an important source for the strong interest in luminous architecture in Germany throughout the 1920s.

Berlin was perhaps the most self-conscious of Europe's capitals in the 1920s, continuously concerned with its status, prestige and appearance. The comparatively young German capital

had recently become a city of more than three million inhabitants thanks to an administrative reorganization in 1920, and numerous articles wondered about the potential qualities that could truly characterize Berlin as not just a *Großstadt*—a big city, but a *Weltstadt* (world city). The intensive debates about future skyscrapers for Berlin during the 1920s were driven as much by these ambitions as jubilant reports about increased traffic, new power stations and modern housing projects. Photo reports from London, Paris and New York had long established the nocturnal appearance of a city as a central criterion for metropolitan qualities.

In September 1924, representatives of the German film and lighting industries had invited lawmakers and businessmen to a movie theater on Postdamer Platz and showed them documentary films about New York City and London by night. This screening was part of an ongoing effort to ease restrictions and win support for more *Lichtreklame* (luminous advertisements). All electric advertising had been switched off in 1916 in Berlin, and a hesitant reintroduction in 1921 had made little progress, partially due to regulations restricting advertising to the first floor.[5] While the initiative sprang from the immediate business interests of the lighting and film industry, it was generally welcomed as addressing a widespread concern.

The first palpable results after the initiative of 1924 were an enormous illuminated sign atop a power station of Berlin's Electricity Company (BEWAG) and the floodlighting of Osram's light bulb factory (Fig. 6) in early 1925. When Martin Wagner, in 1926, became city councilor for urban planning, restrictions were eased, and many observers noted that the nocturnal Berlin seemed more luminous (Figs. 7, 19, 20, 25). At the same time, an extensive debate began, which lasted for several years and is one of the most remarkable and least known architectural debates of the Weimar Republic. It soon went beyond luminous advertising to include the role of artificial light as a new building material, design problems in the nocturnal city, different approaches in Germany and America, and finally utopian visions of an immaterial, ephemeral architecture as the ultimate fulfill-ment of modernity. Numerous prominent representatives of modern architecture took part in the debate (among them Ernst May, Ludwig Hilberseimer, Hugo Häring, Marcel Breuer, Martin Wagner and Arthur Korn), in addition to journalists and representatives of the lighting industry. The fact that the debate was first initiated by the lighting industry and then joined by avant-garde architects is symptomatic for the entire development of ideas in this field.

Lichtreklame and Architecture

Progressive young architects in Europe, mostly politically liberal, usually welcomed the fast-paced life of the metropolis and its artistic potential as an expression of modernity. The Hungarian artist and writer Lajos Kassák wrote in a Swiss journal in 1926: "The *Lichtreklame* of our big cities … tells the visitors more, and more objectively, about us, than the reactionary flood of words in the heaviest Baedecker travel guide…. Advertising is *constructive* art. To create ad-vertising means to be a *social* artist."[6] At the same time the Berlin architect Alfred Gellhorn approached the topic in the spring of 1926 in the German Werkbund journal *Form*: "Everybody knows photographs of New York and Paris: while there is gray chaos during daytime, the wealth of luminous advertising provides an enchanted illumination at night. Where this is still lacking, we should hurry to catch up. The Potsdamer Platz still has too much unformed darkness." Gellhorn foresaw here great tasks for "architects, painters, illumination engineers" and a chance to identify a German position. "Instead of billboards in front of the windows as in America, where you sell an entire facade and work behind it with artificial light, we can design facades that fulfill their original spatial purpose."[7]

Shortly afterwards, the lighting engineer Joachim Teichmüller approached the topic (see Werner Oechslin's essay in this volume). As chair of Germany's first institute for lighting technology at the University of Karlsruhe, he was responsible for an exhibit at a large exposition in Düsseldorf between May 9 and October 17, 1926, which dealt with "health, social care and exercise" ("Gesolei")[8] (See p. 36). Thirty-three sections presented different lighting applications, culminating in the demonstration of *Lichtarchitekur* (light architecture) in a domed space at the end.[9] Here, Teichmüller presented "light as a new building material," demonstrated "painting with

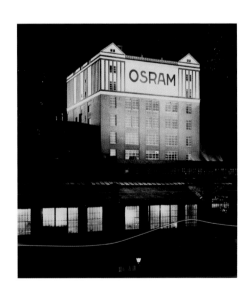

4 Bruno Taut, Glass Pavilion, Werkbund Exhibition, Cologne, 1914. Contemporary photo.

5 La Samaritaine Department Store with illuminated glass domes, architect: Frantz Jourdain, Paris 1907. Courtesy of Meredith Clausen.

6 Night view of the Osram factory, Rotherstraße Berlin, *c.* 1925. Collection Centre Canadien d'Architecture / Canadian Center for Architecture, Montréal.

7   Hans Poelzig, night view of Capitol Cinema, 1925. Collection Centre Canadien d'Architecture / Canadian Center for Architecture, Montréal.

8   "100% Lichtarchitektur": Mies van der Rohe's design for a skyscraper at Belin's Friedrichstrasse Railroad station (1921) from an essay by Ludwig Hilberseimer in *G – Material zur elementaren Gestaltung*, 1927.

light" by projecting images and abstract compositions onto the inside of the dome and showed how different building parts appear when subjected to different light sources.[10] Five months later, Teichmüller happily reported that his bold use of the term *Lichtarchitektur* had been an unqualified success. *Lichtarchitektur*, he claimed, was "… sprouting everywhere." It came about when "particular architectural effects are achieved exclusively with the help of the light, and come and go as a result of the light." This applied to interior illumination, in which Teichmüller was especially interested, as well as the "painting" with projected light, to the "luminous ornaments" of outline lighting and to *Lichtreklame*.[11] While Teichmüller had not invented the term *Lichtarchitektur* (as he seemed to believe) he popularized it in the exclusive sense of artificial, controllable light.[12] The above-mentioned utopian writer Paul Scheerbart first had introduced the term in 1906 in his novel "Münchhausen und Clarissa," describing imaginary festival lighting in the night sky high above a world's fair.[13] Ludwig Hilberseimer, on the other hand, had just recently presented Mies van der Rohe's famous design for a skyscraper at the Friedrichstrasse Railroad Station as "100% *Lichtarchitektur*"[14] (Fig. 8), referring to its emphasis on reflection, transparency and a flood of daylight inside the building. Nevertheless, the term was in general used solely for artificial light, which, given the modern movement's initial emphasis on *Licht, Luft und Sonne* (light, air and sun), denotes a significant paradigm shift in the second half of the 1920s.

The architect Hugo Häring, who was known for his radical functionalism and for his "organic" design of a dairy farm (Gut Garkau) in northern Germany in 1925, astonishingly, was one of the first to define the architectural potential of *Lichtreklame* in 1927, probably summarizing discussions held within the Werkbund. He predicted that the "nocturnal face" of architecture would soon be more important than the "diurnal face." "Advertising is about to replace the architecture …" he wrote. He actually welcomed the "destruction of architecture" through illuminated advertisements. "It is a fact that commercial buildings don't have an architectural facade anymore, their skin is merely the scaffolding for advertising signs, and lettering and luminous panels. The rest are windows."[15] Using Arthur Korn's recent remodeling of a Berlin security firm, Häring demonstrated how advertising served as the catalyst in the purifying evolution of a historicist facade towards a luminous work of abstract art. By way of comparison he included one of the abstract luminous reliefs by the contemporary Hungarian-German artist Nikolaus Braun (1900–50) (Fig. 9 a, b, c, d) with their hidden light sources and complex play of color, light and shade. At the same time, the German Werkbund commissioned a publication about the emerging field of architectural illumination, which was obviously appealing to an organization intent on furthering the collaboration between artists and industry. The publication appeared in 1928 under the title *Licht und Beleuchtung* (Light and Illumination) and contained essays by a number of Werkbund members.[16] Walter Riezler and Ernst May emphasized the potential differences between the German and American efforts. Ernst May, for example, cited the "luminous advertising on Broadway in New York" as a "classic counterexample." "The eye is unable to read any letters, or distinguish individual form, it is blinded instead by the overbearing amount of glimmering lights, countless luminous elements that cancel out each other's effects." Floodlighting should also be left to the Americans, both May and Riezler argued, to be employed "on towers and skyscrapers … where a building's mass will then, however, appear like a ghost against the night sky." Instead, Riezler argued, the building itself should cater to the artificial light by creating "bright, even, and large" surfaces, for the light to "develop its full potential" and to "calmly maintain its position in contrast to the liveliness of its surroundings."[17] Remarks like this are quite frequent in the 1920s and should not be underestimated: artificial illumination is recognized here as one of the major form-giving parameters along with function and materials. Ernst May cited concrete examples, such the "light cornices" in Erich Mendelsohn's and the Luckhardt Brothers' recent stores (see pp. 126, 130), which he found "discreet and artistically of excellent appearance."[18] While "light cornices" needed the reflecting surfaces of stuccoed wall areas, other solutions, like Erich Mendelsohn's Petersdorff Store in Breslau (see p. 134), applied lights within their actual window areas. Both of these approaches strongly suggested a horizontal facade layout. The next step—according to May "more expensive, but highly effective"—were panels of translucent glass lit from behind,

as in the "luminous facade" of the De Volharding Building in The Hague or the Luz lighting store in Stuttgart (see pp. 127, 132–133), which he considered "the most significant tool for nocturnal advertising...."[19] Luminous facades became so popular in Berlin in the following years that its "display lighting [of] glass brick and opal glass" made Berlin "the best-lighted city in Europe," according to the *New York Times*.[20]

It can hardly astonish that electricity companies happily joined the debate and commissioned architects to discuss the phenomenon: "At first luminous advertising merged continuously with the buildings that carried it. Soon, however, certain architectural elements were left out altogether in favor of artistically valuable light carriers. Entire buildings were designed for this luminous art.... And we already see beginnings pointing towards a great future: towards an absolute architecture of light. This pure luminous architecture would be the final imaginable step of our architectural development in general ...",[21] wrote state architect Hans Pfeffer in the AEG's journal.

In 1928, Hugo Häring applied similar arguments to urban planning. Due to the wealth of street lighting, of *Lichtreklame*, and *Lichtarchitektur*, "the square does not exist anymore as a space in the historical sense of urban planning." The coming struggle of "... light against stone, its conquest of open space, of the third dimension" was about to pave the way for "glass architecture."[22]

Martin Wagner adopted these predictions when he announced a major competition for a new urban design at Berlin's Alexanderplatz, a future *Weltstadtplatz* (world city square). Its essential purpose, Wagner suggested, was to be the support of traffic flow, which necessitated "clearest architectural forms.... A flood of light during the day and radiating light by night will create an entirely new appearance of the square. Color, form and light (advertising) are the three main elements of new world city squares."[23] Wagner also suggested that an architecture which was merely a background for advertising and lights and a container for rushing traffic could be short-lived: "Instead of designing ideal city plans for the next century ... it seems much more important to dynamically develop our urban system" in order to respond "to the fast succession of technical novelties [...] each generation [creates] the form of the city as needed."[24] Buildings at major intersections should "not be of any lasting economic and architectural value," and, after no more than twenty-five years, give way to the latest traffic requirements.[25] Several of the participants in the competition responded directly to Wagner's suggestions; the Luckhardt brothers for instance, whose winning entry showed facades entirely dissolved into horizontal bands for advertising, and Emil Schaudt, who presented two separate nocturnal perspectives[26] (Fig. 10). Mies van der Rohe had also taken

9 a, b, c: Arthur Korn, Renovation of Berlin Security firm, *c*. 1926; 9d Nikolaus Braun, "Lichtplastik," (Light Sculpture) *c*. 1926. Collection Centre Canadien d'Architecture / Canadian Center for Architecture, Montréal.

10 Berlin Alexanderplatz Competition. Design Emil Schaudt, nocturnal view, 1928. Collection Centre Canadien d'Architecture / Canadian Center for Architecture, Montréal.

11 Ludwig Mies van der Rohe, design for a department store in Stuttgart, 1928, model.

12 Erich Mendelsohn, Deukon House, Berlin, 1928. Contemporary photo.

13 Werner Mantz, Photo: Emil Riphahn, Exhibition Pavilion for *Kölnische Zeitung* at 1928 Pressa Exhibition, Cologne. Gelatin Silver Print. Collection Centre Canadien d'Architecture / Canadian Center for Architecture, Montréal.

part in the competition, but his stern assemblage of minimalist building blocks seemingly ignored Wagner's suggestions regarding traffic and advertising. The publication of two Mies van der Rohe designs for department stores in Berlin and Stuttgart in the same year facilitated an understanding of what the buildings for Alexanderplatz might have looked like in detail. Ludwig Hilberseimer, frequently acting as the public voice of his notoriously taciturn friend, presented Mies' minimalist, glass-wrapped boxes for "the new commercial street," as the ultimate step beyond the solution of the De Volharding building: "Mies van der Rohe has presented the possibility of *Lichtreklame* independently from horizontal bands in his latest designs for commercial buildings. The entire facade consists of a skin of plate glass, held by a metal structure, on which advertisements can be placed independently from the architectural structure" [27] (Fig. 11). In a note to one of his clients, Mies corroborated Hilberseimer's interpretation: "In the evening it represents a powerful body of light and you have no difficulties in affixing advertising [which] ... will have a fairy-tale effect." [28]

The new lighting technology seemed to provide the means to overcome traditional structures, and the nocturnal city was envisioned as the stage for the final, liberating act in the project of Modern Architecture. Walter Riezler, among many, was tempted by the prospect that the "fantastic world" of light in the nocturnal city was about to offer a vibrant alternative to "the sobriety of functional life."

But Riezler's text also revealed a certain uneasiness: "The fact that the redesign of facades has become a serious architectural task is not without fundamental implications. It seems to contradict all principles of sound architecture. But it also proves that in the continuum of an urban street, the facade has become distinct from the structure behind it, so that it can be treated independently." [29] Other critics emphasized, on the contrary, that only at night did the structure of the building behind its facade become fully comprehensible. About Erich Mendelsohn's Deukon House (Fig. 12), the magazine *Form* wrote: "The nocturnal view shows clearly and unmistakably that the facade is only the skeleton for the inner distribution of spaces and that its design is determined by the spatial organism within." [30]

On the eve of the Great Depression, a distinct vision of architecture's future direction had emerged from a debate that went beyond the central notions of functionalism and structural rationalism. In 1929, *Form* succinctly acknowledged the enormous potential of artificial light's influence: "Light provides us with a new formal element devoid of material firmness, stability, and organic definition. It seemingly stands in great contrast to the formal elements of our time. We have to ask if our traditional understanding of form, based as it is on material and measurable values, might not have to be replaced with a new, more comprehensive notion...." [31]. One year later, the magazine *Bauwelt* summarized: "It would be difficult to find any construction or new building material offering as many artistic possibilities, and thus challenges, as light." [32]

Light Festivals

In the second half of the 1920s, many "light festivals" were held across Europe, temporarily transforming nocturnal cities through coordinated communal and commercial lighting installations. In significant contrast to earlier urban illuminations, these events professed to celebrating light itself, the achievements of its technology, rather than a political or historical event. Of course, such festivals would hardly be free of political subtexts. One of the earliest German lighting festivals was held in Frankfurt in August 1926. About 1,800 display windows were illuminated electrically, 19 buildings floodlit, and individual advertising kiosks displayed spectacular lighting programs. Visitors from all parts of Germany came to Frankfurt in order to see from the Main embankment illuminated bridges, churches and historical buildings. Siegfried Kracauer described the illumination and the patriotic feelings it stirred: "Slowly there appear lines of light in red and blue, which continue along the imaginary house facades.... Suddenly, the cathedral shows signs of life, its buttresses become visible in front of the darker ground.... The crowd on the river is singing the National Anthem." [33] The *Frankfurter Zeitung* claimed: "The correspondent of one of the greatest American newspaper assures us that he has seen such an impressive light festival neither in America, nor anywhere in Europe, not even in the city of light, Paris." [34]

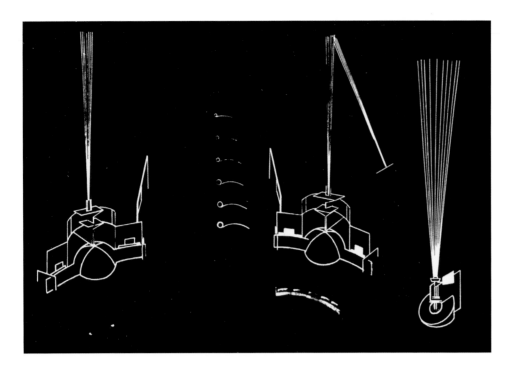

In 1928, the international press exhibition (Pressa) was held in Cologne, featuring both well-lit exhibition pavilions (Fig. 13) and extensive architectural lighting in the city, some of it continued afterwards.[35] In October 1928, a large scale illumination was organized in Prague, and Paris followed in November. In the following years, the newspapers mention events such as *Zwickauer Licht-Feiertage* (Zwickau's light holidays) or *Lichtwochen* (light weeks) in Austria, Switzerland and Italy.[36]

Joachim Teichmüller was in charge of the successful 1929 Karlsruhe Light Festival, where he tried to develop an artistic alternative to commercial lighting festivals by creating "cultural values" and city imagery for the refined, cultivated taste, and "indeed build with light, create light buildings."[37] The effects in Karlsruhe emphasized carefully composed, picturesque "luminous images," combining landscape lighting, colorful fountains and precisely planned building illumination, such as the outline lighting of Weinbrenner's pyramid on the market square.[38]

But the most important of all light festivals in Germany was "Berlin im Licht" from October 13–16, 1928.[39] Preparing for this "national event," Mayor Böss convened a committee of artists, architects and businessmen in order to develop significant light applications for art, architecture, urbanism and tourism beyond the customary luminous advertising. The nocturnal appearance of "Berlin, the 'heart of Europe' should not only equal, but surpass all other world cities."[40] While all major stores had special *Lichtreklame* installed, light sculptures without commercial purposes were installed, such as the "Berlin im Licht" Tower on Siegesallee (Fig. 15) and a *Lichtbaldachin* (light baldachin) of strings of incandescent bulbs criss-crossing above Friedrichstrasse. Hugo Häring, a member of the planning board, asked the Russian sculptor Naum Gabo to design lighting installations "... in larger scale ... beyond the ordinary" for Unter den Linden, Potsdamer and Pariser Platz.[41] "I have worked out several designs—none of them realized, however—because it is still very difficult to make a living with our kind of art ..." Gabo wrote shortly afterwards to Katherine Dreier. Among his proposals was a group of wooden constructions with outline lighting on Pariser Platz, covering existing sculptures and carrying the searchlights which would send their beams into the night sky[42] (Fig. 14). Instead of conventional architectural illumination, the light beams themselves would have provided formal and spatial configurations.

Kurt Weill (apparently with Bertold Brecht's help) composed and wrote the text for a song called "Berlin im Licht" to be performed at one of several "light balls": "Sunshine may be enough when you go for a walk, but the sun isn't enough to light up the city of Berlin. It's no little hick-town, it's one helluva city! If you want to see everything there, you've got to use a few watts ..."[43]

14 Naum Gabo, Searchlight Design for "Berlin im Licht," 1928. The works of Naum Gabo © Nina Williams.

15 Osram GmbH, "Berlin im Licht" Tower, 1928.

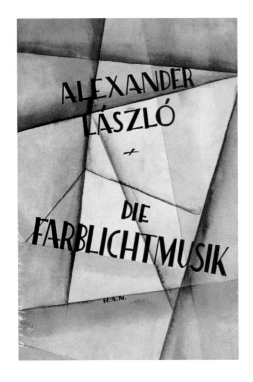

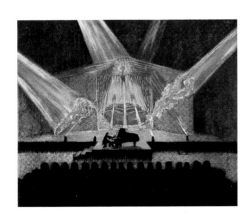

16 Alexander László, *Die Farblichtmusik*, (Leipzig: 1925). Cover.

17 Alexander László performing on the color organ. Illustration from László's *Farblichtmusik*.

While most newspapers were enthusiastic about the event's public success, the enormous municipal expenses also caused understandable criticism: "How will the organizers, how will the city government justify the waste of probably not insubstantial funds in the face of poverty and homelessness?.... Are there no dark streets and squares in Berlin which have been waiting for a long time to get even a meager gas light ...?"[44] The art journal *Kunst und Künstler* recognized other missed opportunities: "'Berlin in Light' should have been a wonderful experiment, a view into possible future developments, the fantasy image of a cosmopolitan city at night that Berlin will perhaps become. What was offered instead was a sad piece of cultural backwater."[45]

Nevertheless, of the many attempts to strengthen Berlin's metropolitan status, the nocturnal illumination of its architecture was probably the most successful in the eyes of contemporaries. "Berlin im Licht" had demonstrated that Berlin was not only "the capital of aesthetic *Lichtreklame*"[46] but that it had succeeded in its "Aufstieg zur Weltstadt" ("Ascent to a World City"), as the title of a book by newspaper critic Max Osborn announced.[47] Walter Curd Behrendt reported that "foreigners who come from Paris or London confirm that Berlin is, at the moment, the most vivacious city of Europe."[48] When, in 1929, the world advertising congress was held in Berlin, the tourism bureau called this event "the first great demonstration of a world power."[49]

The View towards America

Germany's complex "Americanism" of the 1920s embraced its main model and competitor with a mix of admiration and derision. While New York City's nocturnal imagery had provided much of the inspiration for the efforts to enhance Berlin's metropolitan qualities, many German architects took great pains to present their own approach as superior to the American.

The second half of the 1920s, with the lifting of travel restrictions and an economic recovery, gave many Germans the opportunity to travel to the United States and to develop a more differentiated picture. Film director Fritz Lang went to New York in 1924, and observed that "... the image of New York City by night would be sufficient ... as the center piece of a movie.... Streets are abysses full of light, of moving, twirling, circling light that is like a statement of happy life. And, sky-high above cars and elevated trains, skyscrapers emerge in blue and gold, white and purple, torn from the darkness of the night by powerful floodlights."[50]

These vivid and enthusiastic descriptions were transformed by his wife Thea von Harbou in her novel *Metropolis*, where, however, the city of the future emerged as a nightmarish extrapolation of things American, with enormous skyscrapers, traffic jams, slaves at gigantic machines, and the decadence of the ruling class. Here, the nocturnal spectacle is an "uncontained ocean of light, dissolving all forms by outshining them," with its "silent bickering of the luminous advertising" and "floodlights in the delirium of a battle of colors"[51] Lang's 1927 film, based on her book, featured a complicated trick sequence, in which beams of floodlights move across the "New Tower of Babel," the central skyscraper for the city's ruthless dictator (Fig. 19). Lang had captured the intensity of the luminous advertising on Times Square by exposing a photograph twice. His friend, the architect Erich Mendelsohn, who happened to be on the same boat to New York, would later include Lang's photograph in his book *Amerika* where he, not uncritically, described Broadway as: "A circus of light" that was "only very rarely ... in tune with architecture's rhythm."[52] Martin Wagner, Berlin's urban planner, traveled to New York City in the same year.[53] Although he would later express enthusiasm for a future ephemeral architecture dissolved into light and color, he had little sympathy either for the floodlighting installations on historicist skyscrapers in the United States or for his awestruck German colleagues. After seeing the Wrigley Building in Chicago (see pp. 108–109) he wrote: "When they stand in front of a skyscraper and admire the enormous boldness of the human spirit, then they should also know who has mastered this spirit, and they will come across one of the dollar kings, who can afford to have his fifty-story building illuminated by batteries of searchlights because he found innumerable men and women who bought his chewing gum from him and now go about their daily business chewing chewing gum."[54]

Wassili Luckhardt came to New York in 1929 after having designed several facades in Berlin with horizontal strip lighting—and ten years earlier, dreamed up nocturnal visions of towering glass cathedrals. He dismissed the colorful illumination of New York's skyscrapers as examples of a "female" sentimentality: "Just look at the way such a skyscraper design is presented: as a gleaming holy grail against the dark night sky. There are numerous skyscrapers which are illuminated in red or blue and look more like the dream castle of Valhalla then a modern functional building." But Luckhardt also found "the absence of any advertising on the large office buildings […] remarkable, especially since the buildings offer gigantic, widely visible wall areas." He offered two possible, albeit contradictory, explanations: "The ambition to be 'beautiful' is so strong that it even has an influence on commercial decisions.... and 'organic integration of advertising does not seem possible' on the typical historicist architecture."[55] Without having travelled to the United States, Hugo Häring came to similar conclusions: Contrary to the "utmost discipline" in Germany "the pure effect of these masses of light [in America] is giving a fairy-tale effect, and he thus achieves a result … which indeed contains the suggestive power that we basically expect from advertising … our regulated advertisements usually don't appear suggestive anymore."[56]

Indeed, the American fashion simply to illuminate commercial buildings without naming a product or company generously reframed the notion of advertising. While an illuminated movie theater, for instance, immediately invited customers, an office building, closed at night, could only hope to profit in rather circuitous ways from its presence in the nocturnal skyline. The civic pride that inspired urban communities in Europe to illuminate their historic buildings also guided American entrepreneurs when contributing to their city's nocturnal skyline.

Abstract Art and Color Music

Hugo Häring's above-mentioned sequence of images of a facade's evolution towards luminous abstraction examined architecture's relationship with the fine arts, which had been one of the predominant topics in the rise of modern architecture in Europe. The transgressions and redefinitions of conventional artistic genres so common in the 1920s often coincided with a fascination for new materials and technologies. While architects were debating the illumination of buildings and luminous architecture, many artists experimented with abstract color and film projection. Since its beginnings in the late nineteenth century in England and America (see Kermit Champa's essay in this volume), the idea of color music had spread throughout Europe in the 1910s and '20s. Be it the Italian futurist Bruno Corra with his "chromatic piano," the Russian artist Vladimir Baranoff de Rossiné, who performed on his "piano optophonique," or the "Color Light Plays" of Ludwig Hirschfeld-Mack at the Bauhaus—many artists were tempted by the prospect of a technologically infused synaesthesia between music and color or of an independent abstract art from color projection.[57] While several competing models existed, important inspiration came from the recent developments in the theater, where Alphons Appia and Gordon Craig had replaced traditional sets with colored light projection.

In our context, the occasional cross-fertilizations with architecture and spatial design are particularly important. While these rarely influenced actual building illuminations, they informed utopian visions of an ephemeral architecture and festival lighting. The Hungarian pianist, composer and inventor Sándor ("Alexander") László (1895–1970), for example, had considerable success performing color music in the 1920s in concert halls in Germany, (he also performed at the Bauhaus together with Ludwig Hirschfeld-Mack).[58] Joachim Teichmüller recognized the possibilities of a new ephemeral architectural decoration and invited him in 1926 to perform within the department of *Lichtarchitektur* at the Gesolei exhibition in Düsseldorf.[59] He was so successful that "his *Farblichtmusik* [color light music], unfortunately, gained considerably more attention than I would have deemed desirable for the general approach of the exhibition," as Teichmüller somewhat mournfully complained. A few years later, the results of Teichmüller's and László's experiments were adopted by Bonn's Metropol Cinema, whose dome ceiling in 1929 featured a "Space-Light-Color Symphony of lasting impression."[60] László published his ideas in the same year, and presented them as part of the pan-European project towards a new technologically inspired abstract art[61] (Fig. 16).

18 Fritz Lang, Photograph with double exposure: Times Square. 1924. From Erich Mendelsohn, *Amerika*, 1926.

19 Fritz Lang, *Metropolis* (1927), night view with searchlight illuminating the New Tower of Babel, film still.

The Dutch painter and theoretician Theo van Doesburg in 1929 demanded a "constructive, clear, elementary structure for a dynamic *Lichtarchitektur*. This kind of dynamic light design represents indeed the conquest of a new art form, which combines the sequential mode of music with the parallel mode of painting." Van Doesburg thought both of an extension of painting into three dimensions, as well as a combination with other media: "... as a pure work of art, film will be based on a much richer perception of space. Instead of a painterly attitude, we will need an architectural approach to it. This newly conquered material will make the new *Lichtarchitektur* possible and create unexpected dimensions ... the auditorium will became part of cinematic space."[62] While van Doesburg's explanations typically remain somewhat vague, he clearly intended light projection to be a new central element in spatial design.

The Berlin architect Hans Luckhardt (1890–1954), the above-mentioned designer of light-flooded, utopian religious buildings and a number of successful examples of *Lichtarchitektur* in Berlin, had, in 1921, patented a projection device for moving, abstract color composition. "With this device we will be able to create effects comparable to those of music," Luckhardt wrote in his patent application. He modified the idea in a second patent, in 1924, for the "creation of moving, luminous color advertisements."[63] Luckhardt's visions of a luminous architecture evolved along with technological progress. As late as 1945, he wrote in an unpublished manuscript, "Your Third Skin," of a utopian light building: "These walls can light up, just like neon and argon tubes, in the most beautiful colors of their diffuse lights. But they can also dim the daylight and shut out the external world, as if behind a veil [....] So I can be surrounded, as I please, by complete darkness, by all colors of the spectrum to whitest light."[64]

One of the most important, and to this day least known, artists who were fundamentally rethinking issues of light and architecture was the Czech architect Zdeněk Pešánek. Pešánek carried the common debates about how artificial light would help form a future architecture further by suggesting that the spherical cast of light from a central source would direct the choice of architectural forms: "As soon as the straight, vertical, flat areas have finished the war against Renaissance and Secession moldings, they will make room for the round, vaulted forms, which economically catch the light and reflect it.... The architect now also has to consider the nocturnal impression of a facade."[65] In competition with Alexander László, Pešánek developed a color piano, which could create about 700 color effects and contained moveable plastic elements. He planned to use this type of light projection in an urban context and after 1926 suggested a series of projects, such as the color illumination of Prague Castle with synchronized music accompaniment or citywide firework, illumination and advertising effects, which he intended to control and "play" with the help of his color piano. A new luminous urbanism would turn the entire city into a programmable, all-encompassing work of art. Pešánek's numerous designs for nocturnal advertising, often developed in collaboration with the Prague Electricity Company, realized such ideas on a much smaller scale, for instance, synchronizing the colors of a lit advertisement with an adjacent traffic light.[66] His best-known work was an abstract-kinetic sculpture on the flat roof of the Prague electricity station (1929–30), on which "symphonies of light and color" could be performed.[67]

The Hungarian Bauhaus teacher László Moholy-Nagy was familiar with many of these approaches, and included Alexander László's work in his own book, *Malerei, Fotografie, Film*, of 1925. As late as 1936, when Moholy-Nagy was struggling to survive as an emigrant in London, he published two essays on *Lichtarchitektur*, an art form he considered to be the ultimate goal of his artistic work.

"I dreamed of light-apparatus, which might be controlled either by hand or by an automatic mechanism by means of which it would be possible to produce visions of light, in the air, in large rooms, on screens of unusual nature, on fog, vapor and clouds. I made numberless projects, but found no architect who was prepared to commission a light-fresco, a light architecture, consisting of straight or arched walls ... which by turning a switch could be flooded with radiant light, fluctuating light symphonies, while the surfaces slowly changed and dissolved into an infinite number of controlled details.... The floodlighting of buildings has given the public the slightest hint of what is possible when frescoes of colored light become an architectural unit of buildings, interior or

20 Salamander Advertisement, Berlin, mid-1920s.
Collection Centre Canadien d'Architecture / Canadian
Center for Architecture, Montréal.

exterior.... The time has come for someone to make use of the third dimension and, by taking advantage of both materials and reflections, to create actual structures of light in space.... As a vision of the future we can imagine the play of light in community festivals of coming generations. From airplanes and airships they will be able to enjoy the spectacle of gigantic expanses of illumination, movement and transformation of lighted areas, which will provide new experiences and open up new joy in life."[68]

What Moholy-Nagy describes here seems to hint at both Albert Speer's contemporary light cathedrals (see below), and at the lighting installations that were currently being prepared for the Paris World's Fair of 1937 (see pp. 170–171). Moholy-Nagy had met with the painter Fernand Léger in Paris in 1935, who had just presented similar ideas to the committee for the preparation of that World's Fair: "I suggested Paris completely white; I asked for 300,000 unemployed to clean and scrub the facades. Create a white and luminous city—in the evening the Eiffel Tower, like an orchestra leader, playing the most powerful projectors in the world upon the streets (airplanes could have cooperated in creating this new fairyland)! Loud speakers would diffuse melodious music in key with this new colored world ... my project was thrown out."[69] When Moholy-Nagy reported for *Architectural Record* from the 1937 World's Fair, he must have realized that reality had caught up with his futuristic visions: "Sound effects and illumination were coordinated to produce a lighting composition. Fountains of water emerged directly from the river and from bases of bridges. Smoke was released and sent to a considerable height for screens on which light in color was projected. There were four broadcasting networks to provide the sound effects—from the Eiffel Tower, from the river, and from loudspeakers located in trees throughout the Exposition."[70] Even the architectural light frescoes suggested by Moholy-Nagy had had been realized convincingly on Robert Mallet-Stevens' Electricity pavilion, where a curved wall served as a projection screen for early cinemascope films and abstract color compositions.[71]

While the discussions about light architecture might have been particularly intense in Germany (probably thanks to its well advanced electrical industry), the examples above demonstrate that architects and artists all across Europe shared this fascination.[72] As an art heavily dependent on technology, it seems to have advanced due less to artists' initiatives, but rather to those of electricity companies and electrical engineers. Artists who had been widely considered members

21 Restaurant facade, Berlin, mid-1920s. Collection Centre Canadien d'Architecture / Canadian Center for Architecture, Montréal.

Unter den Linden bei Festbeleuchtung

22 Benno von Arent, Arthur Reiche (stage and lighting designers), decoration of Unter den Linden for Mussolini's official state visit to Berlin in 1937. Contemporary postcard.

23 Light Cathedral and procession celebrating Hitler's return from Prague, Berlin, 1939. Contemporary photo.

of the avant-garde in the early 1920s had to realize ten years later that technology and practice had long caught up with them, and that commercial lighting designers had realized ideas that surpassed their own visions.

Lichtarchitektur and National Socialism

The National Socialists were elected into power in Germany in 1933. In their unprecedented desire to control the aesthetics of daily life, they adopted or modified in some form or another all key ideas, topics and achievements that had recently emerged in the field of lighting. The compelling visual and metaphorical power of the notion of light penetrating darkness was given a central position in their rituals and ideology.[73] From torchlight parades and the revival of ancient "Germanic" rituals, such as summer and winter solstice, to dramatic nocturnal party rallies, the Nazi demagogues adopted the night as the realm for their religious-political manifestations.

Immediately after their assumption of power attempts were made at defining a new official position on *Lichtreklame*: "Millions are unhappy with the way in which exterior advertising spreads … a new law for exterior advertising has to be based on the … national socialist worldview, which holds decisive points of view towards questions of both economy and production and the protection of our heritage … any continuous exterior advertising is simply contrary to the state's philosophy…."[74] Legal limitations for luminous advertising had been suggested before (by Ernst May and Max Landsberg, for instance), but the tone of voice had clearly changed. This essay echoed Joseph Goebbels' hateful diatribe of 1928, where he had described the nocturnal spectacle on Kurfürstendamm as the "petrified heart of this city…. The eternal repetition of corruption and decay … of inner emptiness and despair …," for which "the Israelites" were responsible.[75] Eight months after the Nazis rose to power, laws were indeed passed placing permission for all outside advertising into the hands of a central commission (Werberat), but it seems that despite aggressive rhetoric, *Lichtreklame* continued to grow unhindered (Fig. 25). In fact, the Nazis recognized the importance of nocturnal advertising as a sign of metropolitan worldliness[76] and in the end arguments often differed little from those of the Weimar republic. In 1935, for example, the magazine *Licht* welcomed the "increasingly versatile application of light in order to produce pure architectural effects in restorations and new commercial buildings. While a few years ago, architecture and *Lichtreklame* seemed incompatible, we have responded to the need of the business world for *Lichtreklame* by integrating it into the architecture of the building's facade and thus created a new architectural value from it."[77] The techniques of *Lichtreklame* itself were usurped by the Nazis for political propaganda, for example in the preparation for the plebiscite on the annexation of Austria on 10 April 1938, when the capital glowed in its "luminous 'yes' decoration."[78] Two important essays about "Lichtarchitektur" and "Licht und Bau" (Light and Building) in the *Deutsche Bauzeitung* of 1934 intended to clarify the new positions.[79] The author, a Dr. Gamma (probably a pseudonym), agreed with the demand for a curtailing of *Lichtreklame* by demanding "a lighting police" and a lighting code in order to keep the street from becoming "a wild playground of all kinds of aberrations, different strengths of light, luminous appearances and figures." He continued: "What has not yet developed is an architecture that has honestly been devised and built for a decent daytime existence and will at night find its essential fulfillment by its metamorphosis into sheer luminosity." His proposals climaxed in an "urban mirage, a 'dream city Berlin'…. Designs that have never found their realization, and will not during daytime, could exist at night: one could in and above the existing city of Berlin, create one out of light and luminous relationships. Above the factual city, a tactical city would be built, one that is not graspable, but palpable and unfathomable…. A Light Space Architecture ("Lichtraumarchitektur")…. What about building and letting itself develop in grand gestures and great designs a Berlin-in-the-air, above the admittedly not very large Berlin. An entirely new Berlin. A "dream city Berlin" above the old one."[80]

This powerful vision of a city of pure light is not only reminiscent of Paul Scheerbart's 1906 definition of *Lichtarchitektur* and perhaps inspired by Friedrich Kiesler's 1925 *Raumstadt* project, it also provides a theoretical and urban context for Albert Speer's contemporary light cathedrals and reveals once more Berlin's perpetual quest for recognition as a world city. The article's illustrations from Japan, China and the United States underline the vision's international context.

While the lighting festivals of the 1920s were denounced as commercial enterprises, the tools developed for them were happily adopted for the increased festival culture that was part of the Nazi propaganda system. Enormous fountains with color illumination would, for example, become important centerpieces at large exhibitions such as Düsseldorf's "Schaffendes Volk" exhibition or the Stuttgart flower show in 1937.[81] In order to ensure the encounters of large parts of the population with powerful lighting displays, the number of regional installations was greatly increased. Between 1933 and 1938 alone, more than 100 temporary lighting installations were realized in upper Bavaria alone. Newly introduced summer solstice celebrations would come with floodlighting of buildings in Munich and in the countryside; "Days of German Art" in 1934, 1937 and 1938 saw increasingly elaborate street and building illumination. In Berlin, for the first time, a number of carefully selected historical structures were permanently illuminated, such as Schinkel's Neue Wache, now a memorial for the unknown soldier, the Brandenburg Gate, the cathedral, the Eosanderportal of the Royal Castle, the victory column and the Reich's ministry of education and propaganda.

Albert Speer has generally been given credit for the creation of the spectacular lighting designs for National Socialist party rallies and celebrations, and contemporary lighting engineers claimed "that the application of light has found in him a friend and supporter. He has proven to be not just be a master of architecture, but to the same degree a master of lighting application for the realization of heretofore unknown lighting effects."[82] On several occasions Speer worked with a prominent lighting designer Eberhard von der Trappen, whose contributions were crucial to both the Neue Reichskanzlei (see pp. 174–175) and the Lichtdom at the closing ceremony of the Berlin Olympics in 1936. Von der Trappen gratefully recognized this opportunity to apply his "skills when there is a task such as flooding with light a well organized formation of a nearly unfathomable number of people of all social strata or endless rows of men in brown shirts or a forest of venerable banners and standards"[83]

Since 1933, Speer had experimented with powerful searchlights for political events in the evening. The Party Rally (*Reichsparteitag*) in Nuremberg on September 7, 1934 saw the first application of vertical searchlights, which found a climax in 1936 with the Light Cathedral ("Lichtdom") at the closing celebration of the Olympic Games (16 August 1936) (Fig. 24), the swearing-in ceremony for 110,000 political leaders (Amtswalterappell) at Nuremberg's Zeppelin Field, and Mussolini's visit to Berlin (28 September 1937). On this occasion the vertical searchlights on both sides of the street were lowered towards the center, until they crossed and thus created a long baldachin above the street, or evoked crossed swords or fasces[84] (Fig. 23). Albert Speer later recalled the impression of the *Lichtdom* at the *Reichsparteitag*. "The actual effect far surpassed anything I had imagined. The hundred and thirty sharply defined beams, placed around the field at intervals of forty feet, were visible to a height of twenty to twenty-five thousand feet, after which they merged into a general glow. The feeling was of a vast room, with the beams serving as mighty pillars of infinitely high outer walls. Now and then a cloud moved through this wreath of lights, bringing an element of surrealistic surprise to the mirage. I imagine that this "cathedral of light" was the first luminescent architecture of this type, and for me it remains not only my most beautiful architectural concept, but, after its fashion, the only one which has survived the passage of time."[85]

To what extent the Nazis continued to use the popular culture of the Weimar Republic by attaching different contents to inherited forms is a question that defies easy answers.[86] While it has been argued that the heavy classicist facades used after 1933 were a counter-reaction to the increasingly dematerialized architecture of Weimar Germany,[87] it can also be shown that the classicism of Paul Troost and Albert Speer was considerably more current internationally than the still somewhat marginal modern style. Museum or government buildings in France or the United States (two of Hitler's most important cultural reference points) would in all likelihood employ comparable designs. Similarly, while the application of certain lighting techniques points

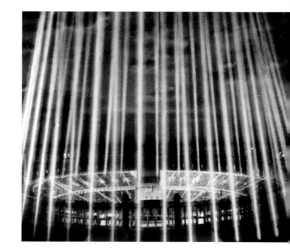

24 Speer, Albert, Eberhard von der Trappen, *Lichtdom* at the closing ceremony for the Olympic Games in Berlin, 16 August 1936. From Leni Riefenstahl, *Olympia*, 1936 © Ullstein Bilderdienst.

to predecessors in the Weimar Republic, the broader context provides an additional dimension. Lighting engineers were well informed about the international scene. A few examples: the sequences of large vertical flags attached to the building on either side of Munich's Ludwigstrasse and lit at night during the Days of German Art in 1937 and 1938 had been inspired by the decoration of London's Bond Street at the coronation of George VI in May 1937.[88] For Mussolini's official state visit to Berlin in 1937, stage designer Benno von Arent and lighting designer Arthur Reiche decorated Unter den Linden with 140 fluted, classical pylons, each one forty feet tall. Their illumination from the base made the columns appear translucent and glowing from within, just like the light columns at the Barcelona World's Fair that probably had provided the inspiration. The lights were equipped with yellow filters on one side and red filters on the other (Fig. 22). Contrary to what Albert Speer remembered, the dematerialized architecture of the *Lichtdom* not only had clear predecessors in some lighting and architectural concepts of the Weimar Republic, but also internationally. In Paris a comparable installation had been employed in 1919 above the Place de la Concorde,[89] and in the United States large festivals had experimented with searchlight installations since the Welcoming Celebration for Admiral Dewey in New York 1899, the Hudson Fulton Celebration of 1909 and the Panama Pacific Exposition of 1915. (see pp. 104–105). The most immediate model for Albert Speer might have been the vertical light beams that emerged in a circular formation from the Ford Pavilion at the 1933/34 Chicago World's Fair (see p. 164–165). While Speer's predecessors are not free from political subtexts either, of course, and the mind-numbing effects of the technological sublime have a long tradition, there were nevertheless important differences: Speer's light cathedrals were meant less as a spectacle to be viewed, than as an interior space of unfathomable size to be experienced by participants whose strictly choreographed positions were an important part of the arrangement. The rectangular space conjured up above Nuremberg's Zeppelin field and the oval form above the Olympic Stadium in Berlin, were illusionary *interior* spaces, carefully separated from the luminous city centers nearby, purged of color and movement and striving for a technologically infused modernity supposedly closer to Gothic Cathedrals than contemporary entertainment.

25 Askanischer Platz, Berlin. Nocturnal advertising,
1937. Contemporary photo.

1. Bruno Taut. *Glashaus, Werkbundausstellung Cöln 1914*, in: Wendschuh, Achim. (ed.) Bruno Taut 1880–1938. Exhibition Catalogue (Berlin: Akademie der Künste, 29 June–3 August 1980): 182. Taut follows almost verbatim Paul Scheerbart. Paul Scheerbart, *Glasarchitektur & Glashausbriefe* (1914) (Munich: Verlag Klaus G. Renner, 1988): 55.

2. Meredith Clausen. *Frantz Jourdain and the Samaritaine* (Leiden: E.J. Brill, 1987): 243, 288. I would like to thank Professor Clausen for informing me about the lighting of the Samaritaine Department Store.

3. Paul Scheerbart. Letter to Peter Scher, July 9, 1911. in: Rausch, Mechthild. 70 Trillionen Weltgrüße. Eine Biographie in Briefen 1889–1915 (Berlin: Argon, 1991): 426.

4. Paul Scheerbart, see n. 1: 91.

5. Gerhard Schmidt. "Licht-Reklame," *Licht und Lampe* (1924): 591; Schmidt, Gerhard. "Reklamebeleuchtung" *Licht und Lampe* (1924): 623. Gerhardt, "Das Wiedererwachen der Lichtreklame." *Licht und Lampe* 12 (1923): 578–579.

6. Lajos Kassák. "Die Lichtreklame," *Das Werk* 13, no. 7 (1926): 205ff. See also: Hannes Meyer. "Die Neue Welt," ibid.

7. Alfred Gellhorn. "Reklame und Stadtbild," *Die Form* no. 7 (April 1926): 133–135. Apparently there was no general agreement regarding the need for regulations. Ernst May and Max Landsberg, for example demanded strict guidelines. Max Landsberg. "Lichtreklame und Fassadenarchitektur" *Deutsche Bauzeitung* (12 October 1927): 677–678.

8. Joachim Teichmüller. "Moderne Lichttechnik in Wissenschaft und Praxis, dargestellt an den Darbietungen der Lichttechnischen Ausstellung auf der Gesolei in Düsseldorf" (Berlin: Union Deutsche Verlagsgesellschaft, 1928). "Gesolei" stands for: "Gesundheit, soziale Fürsorge und Leibesübungen."

9. H. Lux. "Das Licht auf der Gesolei." *Licht und Lampe* (1926): 559–560, 723–724.

10. Joachim Teichmüller. "Lichtarchitektur," *Licht und Lampe* (1927): 421–422, 449–458.

11. Joachim Teichmüller. "Gestaltung durch Schattenwirkung in der Lichtarchitektur." *Licht* (1930/31): 168–170. Teichmüller mentions similar experimental designs at the Compagnie des Lampes in Paris and at the World's Fair in Barcelona.

12. See also Werner Oechslin's essay in this volume. Werner Oechslin is the first to have written about Teichmüller. In the fall of 1928 Teichmüller traveled to the United States, and noted enthusiastic reports about the "abundance of light" in New York City in his travel diary. Teichmüller estate, "Studienreise in die USA 8.8.–8.11.1928," manuscript, Universitätsarchiv Karlsruhe 10/60/583, p. 108. Teichmüller clearly understood his work at the Karlsruhe Institute as a contribution to the development of modern architecture. Members of the institute published a positive evaluation of Walter Gropius' Dammerstock settlement in Karlsruhe, and as late as 1937 an institute's publication about successful light architecture did not mention the light cathedral at the Olympic games, but rather the Titania Palace Movie Theater in Berlin. Teichmüller took a position against National Socialism and left his professorship shortly after their assumption of power in 1933. His achievements in the field of illumination engineering and in particular his suggestions for a "light architecture" were either not mentioned after 1933 or others were given credit. In an obituary in 1939, he was called a "struggling mind … who was by no means always right." Walter Köhler. "Good Light—A Social Necessity." *Illuminating Engineering* XXXVI (March 1943): 148–151. Weigel, R.G. and W. Ott. "Eindrücke des Lichtingenieurs von der Dammerstock Siedlung in Karlsruhe." *Licht und Lampe* (1929): 1495–99. Weigel, R.G. and O.H. Knoll. "Das Licht als Mittel künstlerischer Gestaltung." *Das Licht* 7 (July 1937): 122–125. Lux, "Joachim Teichmüller." *Das Licht* 8 (July 1938): 141

13. Paul Scheerbart. *Münchhausen und Clarissa* (Berlin: Oesterheld und Co., 1906): 28. Scheerbart described a fictitious World's Fair in Melbourne, doubtlessly inspired by the sensations at recent fairs in Paris and St. Louis. He wrote: "The architectural stage set at the World's Fair lake in Melbourne was undescribably grand, but, when night falls, it was simply diminished by a light architecture (*Lichtarchitektur*), which slowly unfolded above us in the sky.... You will be able to imagine the light architecture (Lichtarchitektur) when I tell you that the 18 tethered balloons were connected by innumerable wires amongst each other and with the ground, and that these wires carried electric lights—so many in fact, that the number of stars visible through a telescope would not seem large in comparison— this is an image of the night sky, that should keep you awake for quite some time."

14. Ludwig Hilberseimer. "Amerikanische Architektur," *G – Material zur Gestaltung*, no. 7 (March 1926) Both Mies and Hilberseimer were members of the editorial board.

15. Hugo Häring. "Lichtreklame und Architektur," *Architektur und Schaufenster*, 24, no. 8 (1927): 5–8; and Hugo Häring. "Mitteilungen aus der Fachwelt: Lichtreklame und Architektur." *Moderne Bauformen, Monatshefte für Architektur und Raumkunst*, 27, no. 3 (March 1928): 2f. See also the very similar critique of Ludwig Hilberseimer, who wrote in 1929 that the "commercial building does not have an architectural facade anymore and his outer skin … is merely a scaffolding, penetrated by windows, for announcements, panels and luminous advertising." Ludwig Hilberseimer. "Die neue Geschäftsstrasse," *Das Neue Frankfurt* 4, 1929, quoted from: Hirdina, Heinz. Neues Bauen, Neues Gestalten. Das Neue Frankfurt/die neue stadt (Dresden: VEB Verlag der Kunst, 1984): 235–240.

16. Wilhelm Lotz (ed.) *Licht und Beleuchtung* (Berlin: H. Reckendorfer, 1928).

17. Walter Riezler. "Licht und Architektur" in: Lotz (ed.): 42–43.

18. Ernst May. "Städtebau und Lichtreklame" in: Lotz (ed.): 44–47.

19. Ibid.

20. Mildred Adams. "In their Lights the Cities are revealed." *New York Times* (11 December, 1932): SM 12, 15.

21. Hanns Pfeffer. "Im Anfang war das Licht," *Spannung. Die AEG Umschau*, II, no. 1 (October 1928): 1–5.

22. Hugo Häring. "probleme um die lichtreklame," *Bauhaus* 2, no. 4 (1928): 7. Hans H. Reinsch repeated Häring's formulation almost verbatim a year later in *Die Form*: "Both the corporeal and the ephemeral in the city's nocturnal image has been destroyed and has vanished, all surfaces are nothing, and instead, light fights against stone and boredom, soullessness, ghostlike darkness!" Reinsch, Hans H. "Psychologie der Lichtreklame." *Das Neue Berlin* 1, no. 8 (1929): 154. (reprint: Basel: Birkhäuser Verlag, 1988)

23. Martin Wagner. "Das Formproblem eines Weltstadtplatzes." *Das Neue Berlin*. 1, no. 2 (1929): 33–38. (reprint: Basel: Birkhäuser Verlag, 1988)

24. Martin Wagner. "Städtebauliche Probleme der Großstadt." (1929), quoted from: Martin Wagner 1885–1957. Exhibition catalogue (Berlin: Akademie der Künste, 1985): 104.

25. Ludovica Scarpa. *Martin Wagner und Berlin. Architektur und Städtebau der Weimarer Republik* (Braunschweig/Wiesbaden: Vieweg, 1986): 94.

26. The eventually executed design by Peter Behrens did not provide horizontal bands for future advertising, but featured tall luminous glass elements at each end of the building. The young Marcel Breuer adopted Wagner's ideas in his design of improved traffic patterns on Potsdamer Platz shortly afterwards, suggesting that its facades "… will only provide the basic rhythm underneath the constantly changing, suprising and individually-diverse forms and colors of the city. They are the naked body, which changing time will cover with current and diverse cladding." Breuer, Marcel. "Verkehrsarchitektur – ein Vorschlag zur Neuordnung des Potsdamer Platzes." *Das Neue Berlin* 1, no. 7 (1929): 136–141. (reprint Basel: Birkhäuser Verlag, 1988)

27. Ludwig Hilberseimer. "Die neue Geschäftsstrasse." *Das Neue Frankfurt* 4, 1929, quoted from: Heinz Hirdina. *Neues Bauen, Neues Gestalten. Das Neue Frankfurt/die neue stadt* (Dresden: VEB Verlag der Kunst, 1984): 235–240.

28. Ludwig Mies van der Rohe. "The Adam Building" in: Fritz Neumeyer. *The Artless Word, Mies van der Rohe on the Building Art* (Cambridge: MIT Press, 1991): 305.

29. Walter Riezler. "Umgestaltung der Fassaden," *Die Form*, no. 2 (February 1927): 33–40.

30. "Das Deukonhaus von Erich Mendelsohn," *Die Form*, no. 2 (February 1928): 43–48.

31. Ernst Reinhardt. "Gestaltung der Lichtreklame," *Die Form*, no. 4 (15 February 1929): 73–84.

32. "Das Licht in der Baukunst." *Bauwelt* 21, no. 1 (2 January 1930): 3.

33. Siegfried Kracauer, "Mainbeleuchtung," S.K. *Frankfurter Turmhäuser* (Zürich: Epoca, 1997): 61–64. Hanns Pfeffer. "Im Anfang war das Licht." *Spannung. Die AEG Umschau* 2, no. 1 (October 1928): 1–5.

34. Quoted from: G. Feissel. "Frankfurts Lichtversorgung," *Das Licht*, 6 (September 1936): 163–165.

35. C. Frangen, "Das leuchtende Köln." *Das Licht*, 7 (1937): 163–166.

36. H.Seeman. "Les illuminations de la ville de Prague en octobre 1928," *Revue Générale de l'Electricité* (14 September 1929): 409–412. Gerhard Schmidt. "Prag im Licht," *Licht und Lampe* (1929): 1241. Schn. "Zwickauer Licht-Feiertage," *Licht* 5 (1935): 125–126. Gerhard Schmidt. "Drei österreichische Lichtwochen Innsbruck, Bregenz, Klagenfurt," *Licht* 7 (1937): 29–31. J. Guanter. "Eine Lichtwoche in der Schweiz," *Der Werbeleiter*, no. 11 (1932): 225. J. Guanter. "Die Gotthard-Lichtwoche," *Das Licht 2* (1932): 193–194. J. Guanter. "Die Lichtwoche in der Schweiz," *Das Licht* 2 (1932): 214–217. J. Guanter. "Lichtwochen am Luganer See," *Das Licht*, 4 (1934): 127–129.

37. R.G. Weigel and O. Knoll. "Richtlinien für die lichttechnische Gestaltung eines Lichtfestes," *Licht und Lampe* (1929): 641.

38. Friedrich Herig. "Kritische Betrachtungen über ein Lichtfest." *Licht und Lampe* (1929): 188–189.

39. "Die Lichtparade," *Licht und Lampe* (1927): 840. See also: "Berlin Challenges Paris as Center of Light." *Electrical World* 92, no. 18 (3 November 1928)

40. "Berlin im Licht," *Licht und Lampe* (1928): 312. There are similar enthusiastic accounts in other papers, such as *Berliner Morgen Zeitung*: "For four days, all of Berlin, this ravishing, blossoming world city, will present a spectacle to its visitors and citizens, whose color and sparkle, beauty and elegance will surpass all centers of this world." "Berlin im Licht: Die Reichshauptstadt präsentiert ihr neues Gesicht." *Berliner Morgen Zeitung* 286 (14 October 1928). Quoted from: Janet Ward. *Weimar Surfaces: Urban Visual Culture in 1920s Germany* (Berkeley: University of California Press, 2001): 109. For the most extensive account of the Berlin im Licht Festival, see: Paul Paret. "The Crisis of Sculpture in Weimar Germany: Rudolph Belling, The Bauhaus, Naum Gabo" (Diss. Princeton University, June 2001), in particular 176–185. I am grateful that Dr. Paret has made his dissertation available to me.

41. Hugo Häring to Naum Gabo, 11 July 1928, (Beinecke Rare Book Library, Yale University). See also Paret, 176–193.

42. Paret. 183–184; Hammer, Martin und Christina Lodder. "Constructing Modernity. The Art & Career of Naum Gabo" (New Haven & London: Yale University Press, 2000): 170. The design was published in the Bauhaus' magazine. *Bauhaus* 2, no. 4 (1928): 6. The precise reasons why Gabo's proposal was not realized are not known.

43. Record cover text, "Berlin im Licht," *Kurt Weil Selections*, Record (Largo, 1990). The original text in German: "Und zum Spazierengehen genügt das Sonnenlicht / Doch um die Stadt Berlin zu sehn, genügt die Sonne nicht / Das ist kein lauschiges Plätzchen, ist 'ne ziemliche Stadt / Damit man da alles gut sehen kann, da braucht man schon einige Watt."

44. *Die Welt am Abend*, (26 April 1928) Quoted from: Bärbel Schräder and Jürgen Schebera. *Kunst Metropole Berlin: Die Kunststadt in der Novemberrevolution* (Berlin: Aufbau Verlag, 1987): 140. Paul Paret quotes a similarly scathing critique in Die Rote Fahne, 14 October 1982 (Paret: 181, 259).

45. Quoted from Paret: 181.

46. *Berlin im Licht. Festprogramm mit Lichtführer durch Berlin* (1928): 21–23 (quoted from: Bärbel Schräder and Jürgen Schebera. *Kunst Metropole Berlin: Die Kunststadt in der Novemberrevolution* (Berlin: Aufbau Verlag, 1987): 138.

47. Max Osborn. "Berlin 1870–1929: der Aufstieg zur Weltstadt" (1929; reprint Berlin: Mann, 1994)

48. Walter Curt Behrendt. "Berlin wird Weltstadt – Metropole im Herzen Europas." *Das Neue Berlin* 1 no. 5 (1929): 98–101. (Reprint Basel: Birkhäuser Verlag, 1988)

49. Karl Vetter. "Den Teilnehmer des Weltreklame Kongress, Berlin 1929. 11.–15. August." *Das Neue Berlin* 1, no. 8 (1929): 149.

50. Fritz Lang im *Filmkurier* 7, Nr. 151 (6.30.1925), quoted from: Gehler, Fred und Ulrich Kasten. *Fritz Lang, Die Stimme von Metropolis* (Berlin: Henschel Verlag, 1990): 9.

51. Thea von Harbou. *Metropolis* (Berlin: Scherl Verlag, 1926). (Reprint Frankfurt: Ullstein, 1984): 18, 21.

52. Erich Mendelsohn. *Amerika, Bilderbuch eines Architekten*. (Berlin: Mosse Verlag, 1926; reprint Braunschweig: Vieweg Verlag, 1991): 25. Many others wrote similarly enthusiastic accounts. See, for example: Adolf Behne. "Kultur, Kunst und Reklame." *Das Neue Frankfurt* 3 (1926–27), quoted from: Heinz Hirdina. *Neues Bauen, Neues Gestalten. Das Neue Frankfurt/die neue stadt* (Dresden: VEB Verlag der Kunst, 1984): 229–233; or the report by the conservative councelor of the city of Hannover, Paul Wolf. "Städtebauliche Reiseeindrücke in den Vereinigten Staaten von Amerika." *Deutsche Bauzeitung*, no. 102, 103 (22 December 1928): 861–873.

53. "Eine Studienreise nach Amerika." *Stadtbaukunst alter und neuer Zeit*, 4 (1924): 195.

54. Martin Wagner. *Amerikanische Bauwirtschaft* (Berlin, 1925), 14. (Martin Wagner's reaction might have been spawned by Leon Trotzky, who had accused Wrigley's spearmint of being an obstacle to the American revolution, as the continuous jaw movement of the American worker distracted him from the class struggle.) Ernst Lorsy. "The Hour of Chewing Gum," Anton Kaes, Martin Jay. *Weimar Republic Sourcebook*, (Berkeley: University of California Press, 1994): 662–663 (first published as "Die Stunde des Kaugummis." *Das Tagebuch*, no. 26 (26 June 1926): 913–915.

55. Wassili Luckhardt. "Stand der modernen Baugesinnung in Amerika." *Bauwelt* 20, no. 46 (1929): 1118ff.

56. Hugo Häring. "Lichtreklame im Städtebild," *Licht und Lampe*, no. 19 (20 September 1920).

57. For the most detailed survey of the history of color music see: Adrian Bernard Klein. *Colour Music. The Art of Light*. (London: The Technical Press, 1926) in particular the revised version of 1937. See also: Kenneth Peacock. "Instruments to Perform Color-Music: Two Centuries of Technological Experimentation," *Leonardo* 21, no. 4 (1988): 397–406 and Fred Collopys website: http://RhythmicLight.com. Baranoff Rossine. "L'Optophonie" (1926), available online (1 Mai 2002): http://perso.club-internet.fr/dbr/optophon.htm. For information about Ludwig Hirschfeld-Mack: *Ludwig Hirschfeld – Mack, Bauhäusler und Visionär*. Exh. cat., Andreas Hapkemeyer & Pier Luigi Siena (eds.) (Bozen, Vienna, Frankfurt 2000/01)

58. Alexander László had begun as composer for silent movies and developed his "Farblichtmusik" (color light music) since 1924. In 1938 he emigrated to the U.S., where he had a long career as composer for movies and television. Information on László available online: (8 May 2002) http://www.classic-themes.com/moodComposers.html. Moholy-Nagy, László. *Painting, Photography Film* (Cambridge, Mass.: MIT Press. 1969): 143.

59. Joachim Teichmüller. *Lichtarchitektur*. Ibid.

60. Ingeborg Flagge (ed.). *Jahrbuch für Licht und Architektur 1992* (Cologne: Müller, 1993): 106–107.

61. Alexander László. *Die Farblichtmusik*. (Leipzig: Breitkopf & Härtel, 1925).

62. Theo van Doesburg. "Film als reine Gestaltung" *Die Form*, no. 10 (15 May 1929).

63. Matthias Schirren. "Die Brüder Luckhardt und der architektonische Expressionismus – Ideologisches, Experimentelles und Monumentales," *Brüder Luckhardt und Alfons Anker. Berliner Architekten der Moderne* (Berlin: Schriftenreihe der Akademie der Künste, vol. 21): 42–51.

64. Hans Luckhardt. "Deine dritte Haut, eine Sehnsucht von jedermann." n.d., n.l. (carbon copy of typescript, *c.* 1945): 18; Archiv der Akademie der Künste, Sammlung Baukunst, Nachlass Luckhardt, quoted from: Schirren (no. 66): 50.

65. Zdeněk Pešánek. "Licht und bildende Kunst" *Das Licht* 1 (1930/31): 282–283.

66. Jiři Zemánek. *Zdeněk Pešánek 1896–1965* (Prague, Národní Galerie v Praze, 1996).

67. "Modelling in Light in Prague," *The Illuminating Engineer* (July 1931): 172.

68. László Moholy-Nagy. "Light Architecture," *Industrial Arts* I/1 (London: Spring 1936) and "Letter to Fra. Kalivoda," *Telehor, International Revue* (Brno: 1936). reprint in: Richard Kostelanetz, *Moholy-Nagy* (New York: Praeger, 1970): 37–42, 155–159.

69. Fernand Leger. "Modern Architecture and Color," *American Abstract Artists* (New York: 1946), quoted from: Edward F. Frey (ed.), *Functions of Painting by Fernand Léger* (London: Thames and Hudson, 1973): 149–154.

70. László Moholy-Nagy. "The 1937 International Exhibition, Paris," *Architectural Record* 82 (October 1937): 81–93.

71. Mallet Stevens had worked both as set designer and architect and published a number of important essays on the theory of set design. In a 1928 essay, "Illumination and modern architecture," he reported on his extensive lighting experiments with the engineer André Solomon, and suggested architects could learn about lighting from the cinema, in search of an even and not blinding facade illumination, similar to daylight and without distorting shadows. Robert Mallet-Stevens. "L'Éclairage et l'Architecture moderne," *Lux; la Revue de l'Éclairage* (January 1928): 6–9. He wrote: "The cinema is a great educator, for all those who are interested in light: it has learned to research to light surfaces. The modern theatre has shown the architects the endless resources of electricity as a decorative medium; it has shown the effects, especially the effects of color, which one can achieve with simple methods."

72. The Italian architect Piero Bottoni, for instance, reported about the newest ideas regarding the "Illumination of Architecture" and an "Architecture of Illumination" in 1929, in the Italian magazine *Illumintotechnica*. Due to a lack of Italian examples he used the Berlin Titania Palast movie theatre and the Volharding Cooperative in The Hague as examples. As late as 1932 he had to defend himself against accusations that he was planning to disfigure the hearts of Italian cities with lighting installations after the fact – just as a silent movie would suffer from a soundtrack added later. Piero Bottoni. "Illuminazione dell'architettura," *Illuminotecnica*, no. 3 (March 1929): 6–9; "Architettura dell'Illuminazione," *Illuminotecnica. Rivista Italiana Di Technica Dell Illuminatione*, a.I, nos. 5–6 (March–June 1929): 18–27. "Note sull''Architettura della Luce'" in: *L'Illuminazione Razionale* 5, no. 1 (1932): 6–11. Reprint in: Piero Bottoni. "Una Nuova Antichissima Bellezza. Scritti editi e inediti 1927–1973." Graziella Tonon (ed.) (Rome: Laterza, 1995). See also: *Piero Bottoni. Opera Completa*, Exh.cat., Giancarlo Consonni, Lodovico Meneghetti, Graziella Tonon (eds.) (Milan: Rotondo dell Besana, 21 November 1990– 21 January 1991): 13.

73. For discussions about the use of artificial light in Nazi politics, see: Albrecht W. Thöne. *Das Licht der Arier: Licht-, Feuer- und Dunkelsymbolik des Nationalsozialismus* (Munich: Minerva, 1979);

Dieter Bartetzko. *Illusionen in Stein. Stimmungs-architektur im deutschen Faschismus* (Reinbeck: Rowohlt, 1985); Christian Kosfeld. *Das elektrische Licht im Nationalsozialismus.* Masters thesis (Berlin: Academy of Fine Arts, 1997); Wolfgang Schivelbusch. *Licht, Schein und Wahn – Auftritte der elektrischen Beleuchtung im 20. Jahrhundert* (Berlin: Ernst und Sohn, 1991); Klaus Vondung. *Magie und Manipulation. Ideologischer Kult und politische Religion im Nationalsozialismus* (Göttingen: Vandenhoek & Rupprecht, 1971).

74. W.M. Kersting. "Ein Beitrag zum Neuen Reklame-gesetz: Abwehr oder Aufbau?" *Die Form* 3, no. 9 (1933): 283.

75. Joseph Goebbels. "Around the Gedächtniskirche" (1928); Anton Kaes, Martin Jay, Ed Dimendberg. *The Weimar Republic Sourcebook* (Berkeley: University of California Press, 1994): 560–561 (first published as: "Rund um die Gedächtniskirche." *Der Angriff* (23 January 1928).

76. Janet Ward. *Weimar Surfaces* (Berkeley: University of California Press, 2001).

77. W. Kircher. "Lichttechnik und Reklame," *Das Licht*, V (July 1935): 156–158.

78. C. Saatmann. "Die Reichshauptstadt im 'Ja' – Leuchtschmuck," *Das Licht* 8 (1938): 95–96.

79. Dr. Gamma. "Lichtarchitektur," *Deutsche Bauzeitung* (1934): 789–798; "Bau und Licht," *Deutsche Bauzeitung* (1934): 996–1004. For other suggestions to regulate the use of light for advertising, see also: C.G. Klein. "Das Licht als Mittel architektonischer Gestaltung von Innenräumen," *Das Licht* 11, (1941): 25–28.

80. Dr. Gamma. "Bau und Licht," *Deutsche Bauzeitung* (1934): 1001/1003.

81. Eberhard von der Trappen. "Die lichttechnischen Aufgaben der neuzeitlichen Festgestaltung." *Licht* 7 (1937): 5–8, 23–26. J., H.L. "Spectacular Lighting Installations in Germany," *Light and Lighting* 30, no. 12 (December 1937): 360–361. Fr. Ernst. "Das Licht auf der Düsseldorfer Ausstellung 'Schaffendes Volk.'" *Das Licht*, 7 (July 1937): 129–131.

82. Philip Schmitt. "Die Beleuchtungsanlage des Zeppelinfeldes auf dem Reichsparteitaggelände zu Nürnberg." *Das Licht* 7, no. 4 (10 April 1937): 61–65. Speer's interest in nocturnal illumination might have influenced some of his architectural choices as well. The light-colored limestone and granite were good reflectors, the simplified classical forms could not be distorted by shadows cast by light sources from below, and the spatial layering of a colonnade would allow the dramatic effects of background lighting. Any blinding of the audience was avoided by placing the floodlights in light troughs.

83. Eberhard von der Trappen. "Die lichttechnischen Aufgaben der neuzeitlichen Festgestaltung." *Licht* 7 (1937): 5–8, 23–26.

84. See the compilation of dates in: Christian Kosfeld. "Das elektrische Licht im Nationalsozialismus." (Diss. Berlin, 1997).

85. Albert Speer. *Inside the Third Reich. Memoirs by Albert Speer.* (New York: MacMillan, 1970): 59.

86. Janet Ward. *Weimar Surfaces* (Berkeley: University of California Press, 2001): 133.

87. Henri Levebvre, *The Production of Space* (Oxford, Cambridge: Blackwell, 1991): 125.

88. J. Reiser. "Das Licht und seine technischen Ein-richtungen bei Feiern und Festlichkeiten in München." *Das Licht* 8 (1938): 189ff. W. Kircher. "Lichttechnisches im Rahmen der englischen Krönungsfeierlichkeiten." *Das Licht* 7 (July 1937): 131–134.

89. "Light, Illumination and Architecture." Address delivered at the American Institute of Architects Convention, 25 September 1939 by Jean Labatut, Professor of Architecture at Princeton University. 1939 (TM Jean Labatut papers, Princeton University Library, Special Collections, Box 13, Folder 8): 10.

Overleaf:

26 Engelhardt Brauerei, across from Bahnhof Friedrichstraße Berlin (on the site of the Friedrichstraße Skyscraper competition, for which Mies van der Rohe and others had provided designs), *c.* 1930. Design: Rudolf Fränkel. Braun Photo Dienst. Gelatin Silver Print. Collection Centre Canadien d'Architecture / Canadian Center for Architecture, Montréal.

"Architecture of the Night" in the U.S.A.

Dietrich Neumann

The success of the nocturnal illumination at great exhibitions and the continuous growth of lighting applications had made it clear that the production of light was about to become central to the public recognition and future growth of the electrical industry. While the *Illuminating Engineering Society of North America,* founded in 1906, included firms and individuals from the fields of gas lighting and day lighting, it was dominated by those involved in the promotion and application of electric light. While the members of this young profession were conscious of the fact that their relationship "to the several industries with which [they are] naturally connected is not yet fully settled,"[1] they recognized early on the crucial importance of a collaboration with architects, and questions of architecture and illumination were addressed almost immediately in the society's main publication, the *Transactions of the Illuminating Engineering Society (TIES).* The architects on the other hand seem to have been rather hesitant to work with (and pay for) yet another group of consultants; in fact they displayed, as one lighting designer put it in 1908, a "passive or active antipathy ... toward illuminating engineering...."[2] The relationship between the two groups remained somewhat contentious for many years to come and architectural lighting design initially was hardly covered in the architectural press, while a wave of lighting installations swept the country and made headlines in magazines, newspapers and the technical journals of the electrical industry.

Discussions had begun in 1907, when MIT architecture professor C. Howard Walker (his firm of Walker and Gillette had played a major role at the 1898 Transmississippi Exhibition in Omaha, Nebraska) lectured to illuminating engineers about "Electric Light as Related to Architecture." Walker was the first to identify and critically examine three major forms of architectural lighting, which were to remain dominant throughout the twentieth century. As others had before him, he found that outline lighting reduced the "masses, surfaces and details" of the architecture it adorned: "The lamps might as well be erected as a framework in the air. They are merely set pieces of permanent fireworks." In particular, vertical lines of light bulbs, he felt, disrupted the spatial perception and should be avoided. Walker praised the newly emerging "diffused lighting through translucent materials" both for future advertising and as an architectural element. His favorite form of lighting was that of projected light, as it had the potential of enhancing the architecture, rather than just being spectacular. The results could be predicted and planned, as they were comparable "to a photographer's negative": areas usually in shade would be brightly illuminated by the floodlights from underneath. Walker's arguments and categories set the pace for the debates to come and had a major influence on General Electric's chief lighting designer, Walter D'Arcy Ryan (Fig. 1), who was in the audience. Walker's final remarks, however, must have disappointed the engineers: Only buildings of architectural merit should be illuminated, he argued, while the vast majority "were not worthy of having light thrown on them."[3] Other architects expressed reservations about the impact that electric light had on their work, citing "new artistic difficulties" due to "shadows from opposite directions" and asked for restrictions on illuminated advertising signs.[4]

In the meantime, the electricity companies made a point of demonstrating how architectural illumination could be applied successfully in the urban context. The 1910 Gas and Electric Building in Denver (see pp. 98–99), which was covered by thousands of light bulbs, responded to the critique of the blinding and reductive appearance of linear outline lighting. Here, the well-planned distribution of light bulbs enhanced rather than obscured the architecture, and formed simple geometric ornaments on an otherwise flat facade. Walter D'Arcy Ryan's own philosophy evolved while he gathered practical experience with all forms of architectural illumination. He used strong light projectors at the temporary illumination of Niagara Falls in 1907[5] and was in charge of New York's 1909 Hudson Fulton Celebration. While celebrating Henry Hudson's journey of 1609 and the invention of the steam boat by Robert Fulton in 1807, the achievements of electricity were presented as equal in national importance. A broad range of electric illuminations was employed, from temporary outline lighting of all bridges across the East River, of major public buildings (Fig. 2) and the entire coastline to the floodlighting of the Singer building (see pp. 96–97) and the Plaza Hotel (Fig. 3). Several streets were turned into new urban spaces by glowing baldachins

1 Walter D'Arcy Ryan, director of the illuminating engineering laboratory of General Electric, *c.* 1934.

2 Hudson Fulton Celebration, Outline Lighting of Soldiers and Sailors Arch, 1909.

of incandescent lights (Fig. 4). Steam engines and smoke bombs provided clouds as fleeting screens for projected advertising and color plays, offering effects similar to those of fireworks, but lasting considerably longer. Ryan for the first time presented his "Scintillator," a multiple searchlight display, which became one of his trademark installations. [6]

When illuminating the General Electric Building in Buffalo in 1912 (see pp. 100–101), Ryan declared that outline lighting was "out of the question … for a building of such monumental character" and instead used mainly white light from floodlight projectors. Irked by the recent debates with architects, Ryan proudly pointed out how much his advice had influenced the "finish and decoration" of the building's architecture.[7] When planning the illumination at the 1915 Panama Pacific Exhibition in San Francisco (see pp. 104–105), he followed Howard Walker's argument against outline lighting and stated: "… the building merely serves as a background upon which to display lamps and when the lamps are lighted only a skeleton of light appears and the building is obscured by the glare."[8] Instead, his comprehensive lighting concept was based entirely on floodlighting and became a triumphant success. Following his advice, the architects had used something akin to a rough travertine finish as an ideal "diffuser and reflector,"[9] and Thomas Hasting's "Tower of Jewels," bedecked in 100,000 glass prisms, also reflected Ryan's ideas.

The exhibition's success not only elicited more calls for a close cooperation between architects and lighting engineers[10] but also helped to encourage the wave of architectural floodlighting in American cities during the 1920s and 1930s, as did the fact that electricity prices dropped continuously (by more than 50% from the second half of the 1920s into the early 1930s)[11]. The floodlighting of the Woolworth Building on January 1, 1915 (see pp. 102–103) was followed after World War I by the Wrigley Building in Chicago and then by innumerable lighting projects all over the country.

In 1925, the *New York Times* jubilantly noticed that the city's appearance at night had changed significantly: "There is a new Manhattan skyline—a new city of light and color rising above an old one …" the paper noted, a "fairyland of night" presenting "forerunners of a new order … a huge city of illuminated castles in the air." Apart from the Woolworth Building, the Bush Terminal, the Radiator, Metropolitan Life and Standard Oil Buildings had all been touched by the brush of "light impressionists."[12] This "modern architecture with its blazing building tops, has no counterpart throughout the world …"[13] and, quoting the architect Raymond Hood,[14] the paper suggested, in the near future "New York would be a riot of color and might look more like a dream city than a real one."[15]

3 Hudson Fulton Celebration, Floodlights at the Plaza Hotel.

4 Hudson Fulton Celebration, Court of Honor by Night, 1909.

Indeed, since 1924, beginning with the San Joaquin Power and Light Building in Fresno and the McJunkin Building in Chicago (see pp. 112–113), the immensely popular color floodlighting had at night continued the much talked about "chromatic revolution" that had recently swept the country and changed the appearance of everything from cars to crockery, thanks to new dyes, lacquers and chemical processes.[16]

Raymond Hood had been one of the few architects who actively sought the advice of lighting designers. His winning project for the Chicago Tribune Competition (see pp. 142–143) had emphasized its future illumination in response to the Wrigley Building vis-à-vis. Hood and the lighting designer Bassett Jones had tried theatrical lighting designs for this and Hood's next project, the American Radiator Building in New York (1924) (see pp. 114–115). (In both cases a much tamer version was eventually selected.) The latter building in particular was a major critical and public success, seen as a harbinger of a new architecture thanks to its pinnacle shape, its unusual black and gold color, and especially its lighting. Jones, while still working as a lighting designer for the theatre, had argued early for a close cooperation with architects.[17] He had been the first in 1912 to introduce electric floodlights on stage for Maud Adam's "Peter Pan" at the Washington Square Players and now applied his experiences to the illumination of buildings. As artificial light could never compete with daylight, he rejected any "attempts to give at night a forced daytime appearance of buildings." Instead, "the appearance of objects by day and by night should be correspondingly different." In addition, each building deserved individual attention: "Each is a problem in itself.... It is like the lighting of a stage, each play, each set, each scene calling for that which is suitable for itself alone."[18]

In the second half of the decade such theatrical installations were made easier by the invention of simpler dimmers, which lead to numerous examples of "mobile color floodlighting," the consecutive fading in and out of separate colors, or at least a repetitive washing out by white light. As was often the case, a building for an electricity company pioneered the novelty: here it was the Philadelphia Electric Company Edison Building (see p. 124), where, in 1928, lighting designer Arthur Brainerd placed different color floodlights on the top three setbacks and had them washed out by white light on different dimmer circuits. Only months later, the four-story McClatchy building in a suburb of Philadelphia, Upper Darby, would respond with a more complex color changing system, allowing for 30 color changes within a 10-minute cycle[19] (Fig. 6). Among the most popular color sequences (used for example at the Rand Building, Buffalo in 1930 and the Los Angeles City Hall in 1931), were a blue and a red section, periodically washed out by white light.

Energy providers, as well as lamp and light bulb manufacturers advertised extensively in the 1920s and 1930s. Often, their brochures would contain colorful visions of illuminated skyscrapers (Fig. 5). Floodlighting was suggested both for new buildings and for existing monuments and civic structures: "This intensive illumination of civic structures has a value that cannot be computed in terms of finance. Its educational worth in fostering an appreciation of architectural merit—its enhancement of municipal distinction—the quiet persistence with which it emphasizes important elements in the city's business and political prestige—all these contributions, and many others, mark a distinction of service and entitle floodlighting to a recognized place among the fine arts."[20]

Promoting floodlighting to business owners and city officials as a form of advertising, the brochures presented the wordless, imageless flow of color as a sophisticated alternative to the much maligned illuminated billboards, letters and signs, continuously threatened with restrictions.[21] "Properly designed lighting of this character attracts attention and comment, but is not in the least blatant. Banks, conservative business houses, high-grade office buildings, public buildings and factories may employ this medium for publicity as more subtle and dignified than some other forms of advertising."[22] Contrary to billboard structures and light bulbs for outline lighting, floodlighting had the great advantage of not leaving traces during daytime, as the projectors were usually hidden from sight.

Nevertheless, accepting this form of advertising required a certain amount of adjustment on the part of the clients, and it speaks for the persuasive powers of the companies that so many adopted their ideas. While, for instance, the illumination of an electricity company showcased the product it sold, and a brightly lit movie theatre could attract immediate business, the impact of an office tower's color illumination was not always that obvious. Instead, the motives behind it might have been more complex, as David Nye argued: "spectacular lighting had become a sophisticated cultural apparatus. The corporations and public officials who used it could commemorate history, encourage civic pride, simulate natural effects … and edit both natural and urban landscapes."[23] Thus, a selective nightscape emerged, "a new kind of visual text, one that expressed an argument or view of the world without writing, solely through suppressing some features of a site and emphasizing others. This new rhetoric of night space edited the city down to a few idealized essentials…."[24]

Research

By 1911, General Electric had established "the first laboratories in all American industry devoted to basic research."[25] In Schenectady, New York, Cleveland, Ohio or Harrison, New Jersey,[26] one explored such issues "as glare and visibility, eye fatigue, visual acuity, accuracy, color-vision and certain psychological effects of light and color as they influence the efficiency, the production, the welfare and the happiness of individuals."[27] Especially Matthew Luckiesh, who had worked for General Electric since 1910 and served as director of its light research from 1924–1950, saw light in its broadest cultural context.[28] Apart from his technical research, he was interested in the psychology of color and the potential connection between color and sound. Color music had been discussed and performed in the United States since the 1880s (see Kermit Champa's essay in this volume) and became an important component in the public acceptance of abstract art. In 1915, General Electric had a color organ built for a performance of Alexander Skriabin's Prometheus Symphony at Carnegie Hall (see p. 25, Fig. 11). Preston S. Miller developed the "Chromola" at the Edison Testing Laboratories in New York, capable of produ~ing 12 different hues synchronous with the music played.[29] While the performance was generally not considered very successful, the critical response kindled a wider interest in the synaesthesia between music and color. Matthew Luckiesh himself developed a "color organ" during the 1920s and presented his "Byzantine Jewel Box" in 1931 and supported the efforts of the prominent light artist Thomas Wilfred for many years.[30] Apart from regular performances of "Lumia" compositions on his "Clavilux" color organ, Wilfred also installed "luminous decoration" for interiors, such as the Sherman ballroom in Chicago in 1928, imitations of which soon became standard at movie theatres and performance spaces across the country.[31] Compared to such complex light projections, the "mobile color" on highrise buildings in the nocturnal skyline were comparatively simple. Wilfred apparently intended to change this when, in 1929, he patented Lumia projectors to be used on the top of skyscrapers. Years later, General Electric commissioned him to perform color projection pieces at their headquarters in New York City.[32]

Since only a few architects were interested in collaborating, the General Electric laboratories tested all aspects of architectural lighting installations and published the results. Building materials would be categorized according to their reflective qualities: brick or brown stone were almost impossible to floodlight, whereas marble and glazed terracotta had the best reflecting surfaces.[33] If color lighting was applied, the absorption in the filter needed to be taken into consideration: an amber filter absorbed 40–50%, a green screen 95–97% and a blue screen 95–97%. General Electric would recommend different lighting strategies for different building types: simple buildings should be floodlit uniformly, emphasizing solidity, strength, and mass. Setback towers in particular allowed for "magical and unusual" effects when steep grazing lights only illuminated the lower parts of the setbacks, leaving the upper parts dark.[34] This became one of the most popular lighting models, repeated throughout the 1920s and '30s all over the country (Figs. 13, 23).

Regarding the design of ornamental or sculptural details, great care had to be taken to avoid distorting their features as a result of floodlight from below, contrary to natural daylight (Figs. 7, 8). In a much published lighting experiment on Daniel Chester French's portrait of Abraham Lincoln, General Electric demonstrated how "natural shadows bring out forcefulness, kindness and life-like appearance," while "reversed shadows give the appearance of fear or startled surprise"—

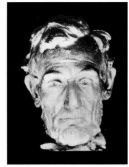

7 Daniel Chester French, Abraham Lincoln, c. 1920. Floodlighting Experiments by General Electric, mid-1920s.

8 Corinthian Capital, lit from above and lit from underneath. Floodlighting Experiments by General Electric, mid-1920s.

9 "A Guide to the Selection and Location of Equipment" General Electric, 1936.

an effect that stage lighting designers had struggled with since the introduction of lime lights at the foot of the stage in the nineteenth century. As architectural ornaments suffered similarly from such distortions, a great simplification of architectural features was recommended. [35] The numerous suggestions resulting from General Electric's research helped to promote architectural modernity and began to form a framework of rules, a theory for an architecture of the night.

General Electric's research facility at Nela Park in Cleveland began in the late 1920s to put miniature buildings on display, in order to demonstrate the appearance of street lighting, electrical advertising and architectural illumination, which were "probably remembered much longer than all of the other displays ..." and would "go a long way toward improving the nighttime appearance of our cities."[36] In 1927, chief designer E.F. Lumber created "The World's Most Miniature White Way," a detailed model for Nela Park's public exhibition spaces with a six-foot-wide street and 10-foot-tall buildings on either side, realistic street lamps and car lights, an illuminated marquee and a floodlit setback skyscraper[37] (Fig. 10). Nela Park also produced models for other Lighting Bureaus, such as the Electrical Association in Philadelphia and the Kansas City Light and Power Company in 1931. In Philadelphia, the model combined a setback skyscraper in the back and a number of different lighting schemes in a streetscape at front. While the stylistic range mirrors the potential diversity of facades in an American city, one particularly modern movie theatre in the foreground turns out to be a close copy of J.J.P. Oud's Café de Unie in Rotterdam of 1925–1927, hardly known in the United States before it was shown in the Museum of Modern Art's "Modern Architecture" Exhibition (Fig. 11). E.F. Lumber continually updated and modernized his models at Nela Park and in 1934 even added an entire new "business street of the future"—reflecting European modernism with luminous panels and simplified vertical and horizontal forms.[38]

In addition, both Westinghouse and General Electric had theatres built at their Lighting Bureaus in order to present individual buildings and entire skylines on stage to be lit in different ways for an audience of prospective clients[39] (Fig. 11). The imagined theatricality of the urban spectacle has hardly been more pertinently displayed then here.

"Architecture of the Night"

Architects, apparently, continued throughout the 1920s "to exhibit a peculiar reluctance to be educated,"[40] as the trade magazine *Light* complained in 1929, and new efforts were launched by the electrical industry to establish better working relationships. General Electric invited architects and illuminating engineers to its research laboratories "to launch a movement for cooperation in obtaining artistic effects in the exterior lighting of buildings in New York, Chicago and other big cities."[41] The Westinghouse Lighting Institute and General Electric's Chicago branch followed in 1930 with similar invitations,[42] and the illuminating engineers finally noticed certain improvements: "In the early days some architects were of the opinion that the furnishing of this lighting service was detrimental to the best interests of the architectural group. However, this feeling is gradually being eliminated as architects become convinced of the sincerity of company representatives in developing the art of illumination without expecting all the credit for the entire design of the installation. The company representative on the other hand needs the advice and guidance of the architect who, after all, is responsible for the final effect that is produced."[43]

In February 1930, General Electric published a booklet celebrating the collaboration between architects and lighting engineers: "Architecture of the Night" with texts by Raymond Hood (who had coined the title), Harvey Wiley Corbett, George Rapp and Walter D'Arcy Ryan.[44] Many of the arguments and facts cited by the architects repeated what had been formulated earlier in the publications of the electrical industry. Corbett, "one of the first to give serious consideration to the exterior illumination of buildings," was quoted as saying: "Night illumination of buildings has become a very popular and effective element in design, particularly in buildings of the skyscraper type." It confronted the architect with "beams of night light shooting upward at a dozen different angles, completely reversing his entire design problem so that every carefully studied shadow becomes a highlight and every studied proportion is turned upside down."[45] While the cornice had already widely disappeared in modern architecture, he pointed out, and "mass, proportion,

10 Electrical Association at Philadelphia, 1931. Lighting model, designed by E.F. Lumber of Nela Park, Cleveland. The Sylvania Theatre in the foreground left is modeled after J.J.P. Oud's Café de Unie, Rotterdam (1925/26).

11 Skyscraper Lighting Model on Stage at the Chicago Lighting Institute, 1930.

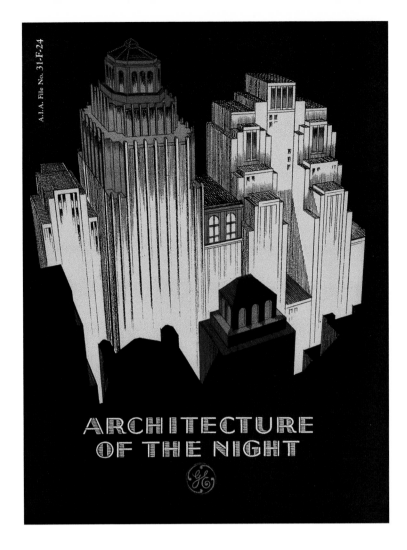

silhouette and color have become the commanding factors," making lighting easier than before, it was still too often just an afterthought.[46] Corbett suggested carefully planning for the transition between the lighted and non-lighted parts of a building. "The form of the illuminated portion should be so tied in with the rest of the building that it should appear as a jewel in a setting, forming a coherent part of the whole structure."[47] Corbett had achieved this when he created lower corner setbacks on the Pennsylvania Power and Light Building in Allentown, PA (see pp. 124–125), a solution widely adopted for skyscrapers across the country.

Recalling his early experiments with Bassett Jones, Raymond Hood placed the artistic potential of architectural floodlighting in a broader context: "... the possibilities of night illumination have barely been touched," he wrote. "There lies in the future a development even more fantastic than anything that has ever been accomplished on the stage. Eventually, the night lighting of buildings is going to be studied exactly as Gordon Craig and Norman Bel Geddes have studied stage lighting. Every possible means to obtain an effect will be tried—color, varying sources and direction of light, pattern and movement.... Anyone who has seen the color organ that has been played in some of our concert halls can realize that the illumination of today is only the start of an art that may develop as our modern music developed from the simple beating of a tom-tom."[48]

Hood suggested avoiding illuminating classical architecture altogether[49] and, similarly to Corbett, found the forms of the modern setback skyscraper "most easy to illuminate successfully ... as the lights can be arranged to stream up the vertical forms of the building, gradually disappearing into the night, and the setbacks and terraces provide ideal places for the operation of the lights." In addition, "vertical lighting from below adds the element of mystery, as the fading out of lights from the bottom to the top exaggerates the perspective, and seeing the building disappearing up into the night gives it increased height."[50]

John Mead Howells and Wallace Harrison seconded their friends in the *Transactions of the Illuminating Engineering Society* only a few months later. Howells emphasized how carefully

12 "Architecture of the Night." General Electric Company, *Bulletin* GED-375 (February 1930). Photograph courtesy of the Burndy Library at the Massachusetts Institute of Technology (Fagan Collection).

13 John Mead Howells, Panhellenic Tower, 1927–28 (now Beekman Tower Hotel) New York City. Day and night view.

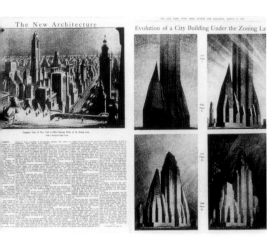

he had studied materials and the application of floodlights on his Panhellenic Tower (Fig. 13) in order to "accentuate the architectural form of the building" at night, in conscious contrast to buildings whose illumination was merely imitating daylight.[51] Wallace Harrison, who had worked with Howells and Corbett on the Pennsylvania Power and Light Building (see pp. 124–125), summed up the recent achievements: "Up to a few years ago, after nightfall, the building ceased to exist…. For centuries the architect has done nothing but study buildings in the daytime, and has worked only on that basis…," but now "we are really starting an entirely new art in architecture with modern lighting." Harrison estimated, however, that only "fifteen or twenty architects" were seriously involved in designing for the night, and suggested that the illuminating engineers had to "bring their knowledge to the attention of the architects…. You have given us a new architecture, a thing that works twenty-four hours a day."[52]

Despite such statements and increased lighting activitiy in the early 1930s, the somewhat difficult relationship between architects and lighting engineers did not improve substantially. William van Alen, for instance, architect of the Chrysler Building, complained in 1930, that the lighting designers he had worked with were "too anxious to please and … short on both facts and imagination."[53] The *New York Times* summarized the situation in 1932: "Between the lighting men who want architects to build with flood-lights in mind and the architects who demand that lighting men solve existing problems before asking that the world be rebuilt there is a gulf that yawns in everyone's face."[54] A few years later, there was still a "disturbingly large number of badly lighted buildings and badly designed luminous signs," threatening "an architect's finest composition."[55] But architects still had "not learned to handle light as part of architecture" while the illuminating engineers had "failed to help others apply their knowledge."[56]

The Metropolis of Tomorrow

The cover of the 1930 *Architecture of the Night* brochure had a certain resemblance with popular architectural renderings by the draughtsman and visionary Hugh Ferriss, whose work had achieved notoriety when he illustrated the effects of the setback regulation for the skyscrapers in Manhattan in a series of highly evocative drawings in 1922 (Fig. 14). Curiously, he depicted his four-step metamorphosis in an increasingly darker environment, so that its completion (supposedly assuring daylight in the streets) was shown at nighttime. Hugh Ferriss' style, made highly popular through his frequent publications, had a great influence on architectural rendering in the 1920s and 1930s.[57] In 1929, Ferriss assembled a number of his drawings (some of them had appeared previously in newspapers and magazines) into a poetic vision of the urban future, entitled "Metropolis of Tomorrow" (Fig. 15. Most of the images also showed the city at night with powerful floodlight illumination from below. Philip Johnson was among the few pointing this out at the time, describing the drawings as "falsely lighted renderings that picture fantastic crags rising above dark caverns."[58] The prominent architecture critic Douglas Haskell took quite the opposite view, embracing Ferriss' vision as an expression of an American modernity. He wrote in the *Nation*:

"It is the habit to speak of a "modern manner" as if there were just one, but already it is divided right down the middle. The Europeans get the Day; we get the Night…. The best way is to look at the pictures. A favorite architectural illustration abroad is of a sunny summer afternoon.

There are some bathing girls about, in one-piece suits. They are on a broad terrace, and behind them is a wall of pure glass through which you can see a few tables and chairs. Of "building" there is as little as possible, as if it were meant to stay out of the way like the bathing suits.

Compare this with pictures by our own Hugh Ferriss, whom our architects consider the "greatest renderer in the world." In his "Metropolis of Tomorrow" are sixty stations, among which a bare ten seem to represent daylight…. There are a few sunsets and mists and the rest is solid night.

Here is modernism indeed. Thousands of years went by with their changes of style, but not until this century was there electric light, which, far, far more than the familiar triad of steel, glass, and concrete, has changed the basis of all architecture. This is us.

By comparison, European Modernism looks a bit lazy. Not only does New York City probably build more cubage in a year than all Germany, but in the building that they do the Europeans

14 Hugh Ferriss. The New Architecture. New York Times *Book Review and Magazine*, March 19, 1922

15 Hugh Ferriss, "Projected Trends: Verticals on Wide Avenues," in: *Metropolis of Tomorrow*, 1929.

seem to lean too much on mere Nature.... Not the least advantage of course, is that there will be plenty of work for everyone to do: the illuminating engineers will be busy, and the power companies will shovel coal by the thousand tons for the lights, drawing on unsurpassed natural resources."[59]

While the idea that nocturnal illumination provided at times glimpses of the architectural future had been pronounced before (for example by Julius Meyer-Graefe at the Paris World's Fair of 1900), Haskell was perhaps the first to identify an American nocturnal modernity as distinctly different from that of Europe.

Luminous architecture

While there were indeed clear distinctions between Europe and the United States regarding their approach to architectural lighting, they were different from Haskell's analysis (see the chapters about *Lichtarchitektur* in this volume). By the end of the 1920s, the American interest in the European situation seems to have increased considerably. The lighting magazines report frequently about the latest "architectural" and "modernistic" lighting discussions and developments in London, Paris and Berlin.[60] Often earlier than architecture magazines, the electric trade journals reported, for instance, about Berlin's Titania Palace or The Hague's Volharding Cooperative.[61] The Germans were singled out as "more advanced than we are in their attitude of mind towards the relationship between illumination and architecture.... Lighting is not regarded as an addition to the building after the principles of its design have been laid down, but as an integral part of the basis upon which the whole design is built up." [62] In particular, "the use of glass paneling to bring light and color into the body of modern structures" was going on more "more rapidly in Europe than here."[63] Matthew Luckiesh, chief lighting designer at General Electric, even claimed that "Berlin is the best lighted city in Europe. Modern lighting is more prevalent there than anywhere else...."[64] He named Berlin "the city of opal glass" as its electric signs with incandescent bulbs were "rapidly giving way to translucent glass signs. The use of opal glass is extending to borders of store fronts, vertical strips on the faces of buildings, horizontal cornices and other elements. The overall effect is excellent. The streets have a finished and refined appearance...." [65]

The lighting industry recognized that this new European fashion had the potential of finally bringing architects and lighting engineers closer together, as luminous panels by necessity had to be integrated into the architectural design from the beginning. General Electric immediately commissioned a report about the possibilities of "Luminous architectural elements," which was successful enough to require a second print run.[66] Praising the logical simplicity of *Lichtarchitektur*, and citing research by Berlin's Osram Company, the report claimed that "Architecture is in an active period of transition" and suggested that luminous elements could replace any architectural element, such as "pylons, columns, pilasters, panels, parapets, spandrels; as beams, coves, coffers, moldings, niches, and decorative patterns ..."[67]

The electricity companies again set early examples, with offices in Syracuse and Olean (see pp. 160–161), Philadelphia or Los Angeles (Fig. 17). A luminous Shell gas station designed by John Eberson on 124th Street in New York City consisted almost entirely of 6-inch-square tiles (³⁄₈th of an inch deep) held in a steel grid, which were coated on the inside with yellow or red color[68] (Fig. 16). These patented glass tiles had been developed in Germany, and were marketed in the United States by the Luxfer Prism Company. Perhaps their most striking application was the shimmering glass house by Lawrence Emmons on top of Murgatroyd and Ogden's Barbizon Plaza Hotel in New York (later covered by gold painted metal), a striking successor to Bruno Taut's glass pavilion in Cologne of 1914, for which the same material had been used.[69] For his house in New York City (1933/34, Fig. 18), William Lescaze used an early, solid version of the new glass block, a predecessor to the machine-made hollow glass blocks, which adopted an important role as a structural daylighting device in American architecture of the 1930s. While in most cases no special lighting devices were installed for their nocturnal appearance, buildings with expanses of glass blocks would often be photographed at night, with all interior lights turned on, thus using established aesthetic expectations to suggest a building's strong presence in the nocturnal cityscape.

16 John Eberson. Gas Station 124th Street and Morningside, New York City. 1933/34.

17 Bureau of Power and Light. Los Angeles, 1938.

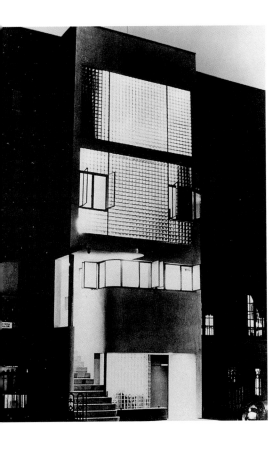

Lighting and the Depression

Astonishingly, the phenomenon of brilliantly illuminated skyscrapers lasted long beyond the onset of the Depression, creating a rather disturbing contrast to the poverty in the streets of urban America. One of the most talented American printmakers at the time, Martin Lewis, chronicled the striking contrast between the poverty in the streets and backyards of Manhattan and the shining tips of skyscrapers in the distance (see his "Manhattan Lights" 1931, p. 238). The high time of the lighting projects happened when electricity companies were in dire need of "load building," as slower sales of consumer goods (especially electrical appliances) had increased the availability of energy. The surge in lighting projects was thus directly connected to the economic situation. "In view of the lowered industrial load, floodlighting is timely, for it is a load builder of the first rank," explained a representative of the lighting industry; "one 500-watt floodlight operating all night equals 0.6 of a water heater, or 13 radios, or 28 ironers, or 3.5 average residences.... There are very substantial profits in the promotion of floodlighting."[70]

In 1931, General Electric started an advertising campaign promoting floodlighting as a means to counter the Depression. The campaign was humorously called "Get a load of it" and included brochures, sales activities and an eponymous film presentation (Fig. 19). And indeed, some of the most spectacular lighting installations (for example, the RCA building) happened during the Depression. H. Herbert Magdsick, a prominent lighting designer, envisioned a future "Prosperity Avenue" in which architect and engineer could create "...a new architecture which is responsive to the needs of our age, and increasingly aware of the progress in science and the art of lighting. Abundant, inexpensive, artificial light, flexible, and controllable in every quality is the incubating agency which is bringing the new street into existence." Electric signs would from now on be integrated by the architect, who "will cause projecting signs on Prosperity Avenue to grow naturally from their buildings. Roof signs, too, will be made an integral part of the structure, or given a satisfying unity with it."[71]

Apparently, the electrical companies were by no means the only ones who preferred to keep floodlights and signs aglow. During the World War I already, when the use of electric light for advertising and illumination had been curtailed to save fuel, the store and property owners on 5th Avenue protested, as they feared that this would diminish their public visibility and success.[72] Now, President Hoover lauded the psychological effects of the illuminations: "It enables our cities and towns to clothe themselves in gaiety at night, no matter how sad their appearance by day."[73] Similar opinions were voiced in Europe. "We firmly believe that this display has a psychological influence of considerable value, diverting the national mind and enabling it to take a judicious and dispassionate view of its difficulties."[74]

As David Nye put it, "If by day poor or unsightly sections called out for social reform, by night the city was a purified world of light, simplified into a spectacular pattern, interspersed with now unimportant blanks."[75]

To a certain degree, similar functions were fulfilled by the numerous fairs held during the economic crisis, which continued to act as showcases and testing grounds for architectural lighting ideas. In Europe, regional fairs in Antwerp, Liège and Stockholm in 1930, the Colonial Exposition in Paris 1931, or the Paris World's Fair of 1937 derived considerable fame from their nocturnal appearance. In the United States, apart from the impressive nocturnal spectacles at the large fairs in Chicago 1933/34, New York and San Francisco 1939/40 (see pp. 164–165, 176–177, 180–181), there were a number of smaller events, which also contributed to the evolution of architectural lighting. The 1936 Great Lakes Exposition in Cleveland (where General Electric's main research center was located), showcased the most sophisticated lighting techniques and the highest intensity of exposition lighting to date. A few months later, the Texas Centennial Exposition in Dallas followed with an elaborate mobile color floodlighting scheme and uniform modern architecture.

As electricity companies concentrated on development and research during the lean years of the Depression, a whole range of new lighting technologies became available, delivering more light for less wattage, and revolutionizing the nocturnal appearance of architecture by introducing

18 William Lescaze, architect's house (1934) New York City, 211 E 48th Street.

19 "Get a load of it!" Film still from General Electric promotional film, 1932.

20 Niagara-Hudson-Syracuse Lighting Company Building, Syracuse, NY (Architects: Melvin L. King, Bley & Lyman), 1932. Panel "Illumination."

new intensities and types of light. The extremely efficient low pressure sodium lamp was invented by Philips in 1932, but its characteristic strong golden light limited its applications mostly to street lighting. In the United States it was soon replaced by the similarly efficient high-pressure mercury vapor lamps that General Electric had developed. Its 400-watt model was as bright as a 1000-watt incandescent bulb and much truer to color. New colored fluorescent tubes decorated the Eiffel Tower at the World's Fair in Paris 1937 (see pp. 170–171). They were presented to the American public at the expositions in New York and San Francisco in 1939 and used on the General Electric Building in New York in 1940. The new water cooled mercury capillary lamp for flood- and searchlights significantly increased the lighting intensity and flexibility of illumination at the New York World's Fair of 1939.

In 1942, when the United States began to participate in World War II, "dimouts" and "blackouts" were instituted in cities across the country. In New York City the new regulations were applied to all "exterior lighting for advertising purposes… all upward beams of direct or reflected lights [and] lights above the fifteenth floor of buildings."[76] These restrictions remained in place until the end of the war. Searchlights meanwhile resumed their old role of detecting military ships and aircraft instead of conjuring up ephemeral architectural spaces or selecting highlights in the urban landscape.

1. E.L. Elliott. "Some Unsettled Questions in Illuminating Engineering." *Transactions of the Illuminating Engineering Society* 4, no. 3 (March 1909): 159–181.

2. Ibid.

3. Charles Howard Walker. "Electric Light as Related to Architecture." *Transactions of the Illuminating Engineering Society* 2 (October 1907): 597–602.

4. Emile G. Perrot. "Architecture and Illumination." *Transactions of the Illuminating Engineering Society* 3, no. 8 (November 1908): 619–626 and William Copeland Furber. "Illumination and Architecture." *Transactions of the Illuminating Engineering Society* 5, no. 8 (November 1910): 822–838.

5. Orrin E. Dunlap. "Illuminating Niagara Falls with Its Own Power." *Scientific American* 97 (19 October 1907): 273–274.

6. John A. Jakle. *City Lights* (Baltimore, Johns Hopkins, 2002): 129. Other sources of information: "City Illumined as Never Before." *The New York Times* (26 September 1909): pt. 2, 1–2. "The Illuminated City." *The New York Times* (27 September 1909): 8, col. 2. Hudson-Fulton Celebration Commission. *The Hudson-Fulton Celebration, 1909, the Fourth Annual Report of the Hudson-Fulton Celebration Commission to the Legislature of the State of New York,* 2 vols. (Albany: State of New York, 1910). David Nye. *American Technological Sublime (*Cambridge: MIT Press, 1996). James Grant Wilson. "The Hudson Fulton Celebration of 1909." *The Independent* 67 (15 July 1909): 114–120.

7. Walter D'Arcy Ryan. "The Lighting of the Buffalo General Electric Company's Building." *Transactions of the Illuminating Engineering Society* 7 (1912): 597–615. Walter D'Arcy Ryan. "New Light on an Exposition." *Sunset* 30 (March 1913): 292–298.

8. Walter D'Arcy Ryan. "Building Exterior, Exposition and Pageant Lighting." *Illuminating Engineering Practice* (1917): 547–556.

9. Walter D'Arcy Ryan. "'Night Architecture' will be perfected through the cooperative Efforts of Architect and Illuminating Engineer." *Architecture of the Night.* General Electric Company, *Bulletin* GED-375 (February 1930) n. p.

10. See for instance: Charles Rollinson Lamb. "The Architect and Illumination." *Transactions of the Illuminating Engineering Society* 11 (30 August 1916): 657–658.

11. Waldo Maitland. "Light and Architecture in England." *Transactions of the Illuminating Engineering Society (TIES)* (September 1937): 815–826.

12. Hollister Noble. "New York's Crown of Light" *New York Times* (8 February 1925): SM 2.

13. Hollister, ibid.

14. "Predicts New York as City of Color." *New York Times* (20 February 1927): RE 14.

15. "Gay Buildings seen in Artistic Trend. Brilliant Hued Materials Will Replace Present Types, Architects Predict." *New York Times* (10 July 1927): RE 12, 1. "Color Splashes the City's Drabness." *New York Times* (9 October 1927): SM 8, 9, 23.

16. Stephen Eskilson. "Color and Consumption." *Design Issues* 18, no. 2 (Spring 2002): 17–29.

17. Urging his fellow illumination engineers in 1908 to get involved in the architectural design process early on and to "appreciate and understand the architect's point of view," Jones provided a rather long-winded introduction into architectural aesthetics, which the president of the local chapter considered "the most important paper that has been presented before the New York Section of the Society." Bassett Jones. "The Relation of Architectural Principles to Illuminating Engineering Practice." *TIES* 3, no. 1 (1908): 9–66; See also his: "Indirect Lighting." *American Architect* 96, no. 1772 (8.12.1909): 245–249; "The Lighting of Churches." *American Architect* 96, no. 1761 (22.9.1909): 105–111.

18. Bassett Jones. "Structures in Light." *Light* (April 1924): 4–7.

19. "Thirty Color Changes in Floodlighting of Office Building." *Electrical World* 92, no. 16 (1928): 795. Arthur A. Brainerd. and John A. Hoeveler. "The Advertising Value of Mobile Color Lighting." *Transactions of the Illuminating Engineering Society* 24, no. 1 (January 1929): 40–60.

20. "Floodlighting." *General Electric Bulletin* GEA–161 (September 1926): 6.

21. See for instance: "New Electric Signs offending the eye." *New York Times* (10 September 1910): 4; "Broadway Signs: Electric Art." *New York Times* (12 February 1928): 37; "Insists Shop Signs are Business." *New York Times* (1 May 1929): 39; "Call Mass Meeting in Defense of Signs." *New York Times* (9 May 1929): 39.

22. "Mobile Color Lighting." Ward Leonard Electric Co. Mount Vernon, NY. *Bulletin* 74, (September 1928): 19.

23. David Nye. *Electrifying America. Social Meanings of a New Technology,* 1880–1940. (Cambridge, Mass.: MIT Press, 1990): 73.

24. Ibid., 60.

25. James A. Cox. *A Century of Light.* (Benjamin Company and General Electric: New York, 1979): 59.

26. The name referred to the National Electric Light Association, a conglomerate of smaller firms, controlled and eventually wholly owned by General Electric. See: Cox. 194–212. See also: Walter D'Arcy Ryan. "The Illuminating Engineering Laboratory of the General Electric Company, Schenectady, N.Y." Reprint from *The Digest* (March 1921): 2–7.

27. Matthew Luckiesh. "Contributions of Science to the Lighting Art." *Science* 65, no. 1692 (3 June 1927): 531–535.

28. "Dr. Matthew Luckiesh is Dead; G.E. Lighting Expert was 84." *New York Times* (3 November 1967).

29. "Color Music" in "The Poem of Fire." *New York Times* (21 March 1915): 12. "Color Music' tried here for the first time." *New York Times* (28 March 1915): SM 15.

30. A. L. Powell. *The Coordination of Light and Music.* General Electric Publication I. P. 101, Nela Park, Cleveland (August 1930). See also the efforts of architect and critic Claude Bragdon, whose compositions and designs for color music, developed since 1910, have survived in Bragdon Family papers at the Rush Rhees Library at the University of Rochester, NY. See also his arrangements for color ornaments at choir festivals: Claude Bragdon. "An Art of Light." *American Architect* (13 June 1917): III: 363–368; Claude Bragdon. "Song and Light." *Architectural Review* 4 (September 1916): 169–171; Claude Bragdon. "Song and Light." *House Beautiful* 42 (June 1917): 31–33, 54–58.

31. "Thomas Wilfred, Artist and Inventor, Dead at 79." *New York Times* (16 August 1968). F. J. Cadenas. "Colorama Lighting in the Ballroom of the St. George Hotel, Brooklyn, N.Y." *Transactions of the Illuminating Engineering Society* 25, no. 3 (1930): 282–291.

32. Rafael Lozano-Hemmer (ed.). *Vectorial Elevation* (Mexico City: Ediciones San Jorge, 2000).

33. Naturally, the National Terra Cotta Society was delighted about these results, and thanked Walter D'Arcy Ryan for his research, as "no more valuable contribution has been made to the possibilities of American architecture than the discovery of those factors in the action of light upon materials...." Substantial cost reductions would result from this knowledge, "placing magnificent night lighting effects within easy reach of the average property holder." See: "Building Floodlighting and Its Possibilities with Terra Cotta." (New York: National Terra Cotta Society, 1927).

34. "The Practical Side of the Floodlighting Art: A floodlighting lesson from the Nela School of Lighting." *Light* (February 1926): 30; H. E. Mahan. "The Central Station and Illumination." *General Electric Review* (June 1918): 441–448; H. E. Mahan. "Floodlighting: An Effective Advertising Medium." Reprint by General Electric from *Real Estate Record* (21 August 1937). H. E. Mahan. "Flood Lighting Possibilities for Public Buildings." *Architectural Forum* 55 (September 1931): 401–402. "Floodlighting" Edison Lamp Works of General Electric Company. Index 95, *Bulletin* LD-159 (ca. 1929): 5.

35. O. F. Haas and K. M. Reid. "Floodlighting." General Electric Company, *Bulletin* LD-16 (June 1931): 7. Christopher A. Thomas has dealt with the lighting problems in Henry Bacon's Lincoln Memorial Washington, which had caused GE's experiments, in: Christopher A. Thomas. "The Lincoln Memorial and Its Architect, Henry Bacon (1866–1924)." Diss. (Yale University, 1990): vol. 2: 629–633. Regarding the history of stage lighting, see: Wolfgang Schivelbusch. *Disenchanted Night: The Industrialization of Light in the 19th Century* (Berkeley: University of California Press, 1995): 195.

36. L. C. Kent. "Cities in Miniature." in: *The Magazine of Light* (October 1931): 7.

37. "The World's Most Miniature White Way." *Light* (April 1927).

38. H. H. Magdsick. "Two Lighting Opportunities." *The Magazine of Light* (1934): 20–24.

39. D. W. Atwater. "Suggestions on the Design and Installation of Lighting Demonstrations." *Transactions of the Illuminating Engineering Society* 24, no 10 (December 1929): 963–989.

40. C. E. Weitz. "Light and Architecture Merge Resources." *Light* (April 1929): 7–9.

41. "Architects ask for Aid in Illumination Field. Discuss Exterior Lights for Buildings at Session of the Edison Institute." *New York Times* (17 February 1929): II, 2:1. C. E. Weitz. "Light and Architecture Merge Resources." *Light* (April 1929): 7–9.

42. "Architectural Conference Held at Chicago Lighting Institute." *Transactions of the Illuminating Engineering Society* 25, no. 4 (1930): 435; "Architectural Courses for Illuminating Engineers." *Transactions of the Illuminating Engineering Society* 25, no. 9 (1930): 748–749; "Architectural Lighting Conference to be Held at Westinghouse Lighting Institute." *Transactions of the Illuminating Engineering Society* 25, no. 1 (1930): 118–119; "The Illuminating Engineering Society Lecture Courses on the Fundamentals of Architecture." *Transactions of the Illuminating Engineering Society* 25, no. 5 (1930): 447–450;.

43. "A Basis for Cooperation between the Architect and the Illuminating Engineer." *Transactions of the Illuminating Engineering Society* 25, no. 5 (1930): 461–469.

44. "Architecture of the Night." General Electric Company, *Bulletin* GED-375 (February 1930). "Architecture of the Night." *The Magazine of Light* (May 1930): 22–23, 39.

45. "Corbett Advises Designing Buildings for Night Illumination." *Architecture of the Night.* General Electric Company, *Bulletin* GED-375 (February 1930) n. p.

46. Ibid., 39.

47. Ibid., 39.

48. "Architecture of the Night." *The Magazine of Light* (May 1930): 22–23, 39.

49. "Raymond Hood predicts 'Architecture of the Night.'" *Architecture of the Night.* General Electric Company, *Bulletin* GED–375 (February 1930).

50. Ibid., 22.

51. John Mead Howells. "Fundamentals of Architecture as Related to Lighting." *Transactions of the Illuminating Engineering Society* (May 1930): 474–475.

52. Wallace Harrison. "The Importance of Artificial Light to Architecture." *Transactions of the Illuminating Engineering Society* (May, 1930): 475–478.

53. "Cooperation as One Architect Sees It: An Interview with William Van Alen." *Electrical World* 95, no. 11 (1930): 539-540.

54. Mildred Adams. "In their Lights the Cities are revealed." *New York Times* (11 December 1932): SM 12, 15.

55. Tyler Stewart Rogers and Alvin L. Powell. "Exterior Illumination of Buildings." *American Architect Reference Data* 18 (1935): 1–36.

56. Tyler Stewart Rogers. "Light Minded Architecture." *Transactions of the Illuminating Engineering Society* 31, no. 6 (1936): 576–582.

57. See for example the drawings by Gilbert Hall for Holabird and Roche and Holabird and Root, in: Robert Bruegmann. "Holabird and Roche, Holabird and Root."

58. Philip Johnson. "The Skyscraper School of the Modern Architecture." *The Arts* 17, no. 8 (May 1931): 433–35.

59. Douglas Haskell. "Architecture: the Bright Lights." *The Nation:* 132, no. 3419 (14 January 1931): 55–56.

60. "Architectural Lighting." *Transactions of the Illuminating Engineering Society* 24, no. 5

(December 1929): 487–488. "Continental Lighting." *Transactions of the Illuminating Engineering Society* 25 (December 1930): 905.

61. H. Maisonneuve. "Modern Art Lighting – The Development in Europe." *Transactions of the Illuminating Engineering Society* 24, no. 5 (1929): 456–472. H. H. Magdsick. "Building Prosperity Avenue." *Transactions of the Illuminating Engineering Society* 25, no. 5 (1930): 451–460.

62. "Continental Lighting." *Transactions of the Illuminating Engineering Society* 25 (December 1930): 905.

63. H. H. Magdsick. "Pointing the Way to Prosperity Avenue." *Light* (March 1930): 6–10.

64. Matthew Luckiesh. "Lessons from Europe." *The Magazine of Light* (December 1931): 11–13.

65. Ibid. See also: Mildred Adams. "In their Lights the Cities are revealed." *New York Times* (11 December 1932): SM 12, 15.

66. Wentworth M. Potter and Phelps Meaker. "Luminous Architectural Elements." *The Magazine of Light* (December 1931): 17. Wentworth M. Potter and Phelps Meaker. "Luminous Architectural Elements." *GE Company Brochure* (December 1931): 5–49. "Luminous Architectural Elements." *Transactions of the Illuminating Engineering Society* 26, no. 10 (1931): 1025–1049.

67. Ibid., 1025–1026.

68. A. L. Powell. "A Gas Station in Glass and Color." *Magazine of Light* (Summer 1934): 24.

69. Robert Stern, Gregory Gilmartin, Thomas Mellis (eds.). *New York 1930* (New York, 1987): 222; Eugene Clute. "Designing for Construction in Glass." *Pencil Points* 13 (November 1932): 741–742; "A New Beacon", *Architect* 14 (June 1930): 243.

70. A. C. Roy. "Get a Load of This." *The Magazine of Light* (November 1931): 7. See also: "Southeastern District Reports Progress in Floodlighting Load Promotion Campaign." *The GE Monogram* (March 1932): 5. W. A. Bowe. "Going ahead with the 'Get a Load of This' Campaign." *The GE Monogram* (February 1932): 5.

71. H. H. Magdsick. "Pointing the Way to Prosperity Avenue." *Light* (March 1930): 6–10.

72. "Plead to Maintain Broadway's Lights." *New York Times* (30 October 1917): 10.

73. Quoted from: H. H. Magdsick. "Building Prosperity Avenue." *Transactions of the Illuminating Engineering Society* 25, no. 5 (1930): 451–460.

74. "The Floodlighting of London." *The Illuminating Engineer* 25 (April 1932): 1

75. David Nye. *Electrifying America* (Cambridge, Mass.: MIT Press, 1990): 60.

76. "Drastic Dimout of All City Lights Effective Tonight." *New York Times* (18 May 1942): 1, 2.

21 "The World's Most Miniature White Way" 1927, lighting model, designed by chief designer E. F. Lumber at Nela Park, Cleveland.

Overleaf:

22 "Jewels in the Sky." Advertising publication with samples of floodlight illumination. Crouse-Hinds Company, August 1928.

23 Carew Tower, Cincinnatti (1929, Walter W. Ahlschlager), night view. Contemporary postcard.

Photography of the Night: Skyscraper Nocturne and Skyscraper Noir in New York

Mary Woods

Introduction

"Night photography, so termed because pictures are taken out-of-doors at night by either gas or electric light, has been the novelty of the year," photographer Alfred Stieglitz announced in 1897.[1] Although not quite as new as Stieglitz seemed to suggest, urban night photography under artificial light was widely discussed and remained an important trope in the years to come. Avant-garde photographers had to negotiate their position as artists in the face of an enormously growing production of urban imagery, created to satisfy an unprecedented demand for illustrated magazines, books and picture postcards beginning in the late nineteenth century. In the ensuing debate and photographs we can identify two competing impulses in depictions of the city and eventually the skyscraper at night: skyscraper nocturne, indebted to nineteenth-century romanticism and impressionism, and skyscraper noir, expressive of twentieth-century abstraction and dissonance. Photographing the architecture of the night posed, and continues to pose, formidable technical challenges. Focusing on the city at night, photographers have sometimes discovered new visual languages. But these photographers of the night have also conflated both the modern and anti-modern, looking backward to romanticism and the landscape and forward to abstraction and performativity.

Photographers in the Night

From the beginnings of photography in the 1830s and '40s, artificial light was used to reduce the lengthy exposure times of the early photographic processes. After first experimenting with pyrotechnic compounds, photographers burned magnesium in ribbons, wires, and cartridges to create a flash for exposures as brief as thirty seconds.[2] Igniting the magnesium was sometimes dangerous. Jacob Riis, the muckraking photojournalist of New York tenements, set a room on fire while photographing it with a magnesium flash during the late nineteenth century.[3]

Even today, photographing illuminated buildings remains a daunting assignment. In past and present discussions one repeatedly encounters the simile of the photographer as a hunter stalking an "elusive prey." One early critic celebrated nocturnal camera work as "conquests in night photography." Early articles in the 1890s and 1900s cautioned that one needed, like a hunter, a "good stock of patience and perseverance."[4] Exposures lasting from half an hour to three hours tested such qualities in a photographer. Focusing in the dark was also a problem. Although snow-covered and rain-slick streets enhanced reflectivity, reducing exposure times, moist weather also caused problems inside large format cameras.[5] This equipment, typically used for urban and architectural photography, was not watertight. Some photographers, for this reason, preferred the new, handheld cameras, which had become widely available since the 1880s.[6]

Magnesium flashes provided additional illumination, but their range was limited. Depicting urban life (moving figures and vehicles) also proved difficult. Forms in motion became blurred and shadowy because of the long exposure times. Even the faster lenses and films of today have not solved all the problems of night photography. Artificial illumination inside and outside buildings creates extremes of light and dark, making correct exposure difficult.[7]

Gas and electric lights hindered as well as helped photographers of the night. When photographed at too close a range, artificial lights flare. Called halations, these bursts of light on the print are caused by reflections on the glass plates or film emulsions inside the camera (see, for example, Fig. 8). To avoid halations, Paul Martin, a pioneering night photographer, recommended using rapid isochromatic plates with extra backing and keeping all artificial lights in the middle- and backgrounds well out of the foreground space[8] (Fig. 1).

The technical difficulties of photographing at night were so daunting that many amateurs and professionals resorted to fakery in order to achieve nocturnal effects. They simply shot what filmmakers call "day for night," taking daylight exposures when direct light was cut off by a cloud and then underexposing the prints in the darkroom. If they wanted to include artificial lights in their night views, they waited until dusk when street and office lights came on but the afterglow of the setting sun still provided illumination.[9]

1 Paul Martin, Piccadilly Circus at Night. 1896. Gernsheim Collection. Harry Ransom Humanities Research Center. The University of Texas at Austin.

2 Metropolitan Life Tower at night. Contemporary postcard.

Dramatic nocturnal views of skyscrapers like the Metropolitan Life Insurance Tower were especially popular during the golden age of postcards from 1900 to 1930 (Fig. 2).[10] Located at Madison Square and Twenty-third Street, The Metropolitan Life Tower was an ideal subject for an enterprising commercial photographer on assignment for a postcard manufacturer. Its light-colored facade faced west, reflecting the setting sun. Slight halation, from the street lamps of Madison Square, is visible in this postcard view. The uniformly black sky and brilliant highlights in the illuminated loggia and pinnacle of the tower were the results of retouching a test print with opaque paints, re-photographing it, and then applying black and yellow inks to the printing plate.

Art photographers like Alvin Langdon Coburn also retouched their views of skyscrapers at night. In his photogravure entitled *The Coal Cart* of 1911, a nocturnal view of the Metropolitan Life Tower, Coburn intensified the highlights of electric lights burning in offices by applying opaque paint (Fig. 3).[11]

The Aesthetics of the Night

Alfred Stieglitz, Coburn's mentor, is key in the development of both the techniques and aesthetics of photographing the modern metropolis at night. He made some of the first night views of New York in the 1890s (Fig. 4). Although he worked with a view camera, Stieglitz also used a handheld camera, taking mass-market equipment and transforming it into an instrument of art. Constantly testing himself and his equipment, he reduced the exposure times necessary for night photographs from three hours to thirty minutes and even to fifty-eight seconds. Furthermore, Stieglitz truly worked at night, photographing the Savoy Hotel depicted in *Reflections, Night* at precisely nine in the evening.[12]

Stieglitz was an artist, critic, editor, impresario, and mentor of the American avant-garde. Although he introduced Americans to successive waves of European modern artists—Auguste Rodin and Paul Cézanne, then Pablo Picasso and Henri Matisse, and finally Francis Picabia and Marcel Duchamp—he was committed to a distinctly American modernism promoting the works of Edward Steichen, Alvin Langdon Coburn, Marsden Hartley, John Marin, Georgia O'Keeffe, and Paul Strand. His passion was photography, and he saw himself as its savior, redeeming the medium from the degrading commercialism of George Eastman's "point and shoot" Kodak cameras and recasting it as the preeminent art form of modern life. Wealthy, educated, and refined amateurs like himself—he contended in his publications *The American Amateur Photographer* (1893–96), *Camera Notes* (1897–1902), and *Camera Work* (1903–17)—were key to photography's rejuvenation as a fine art. He exhibited photography with painting, sculpture, and other works on paper at his 291 Gallery on Fifth Avenue. But Stieglitz was also a master of the science of photography. While studying mechanical engineering in Berlin, he took his first photographs. There, he also explored the physics and chemistry of the medium with scientists like H. W. Vogel. After his return to the United States, he became a master printer after his father bought him a partnership in a photographic business. Charles Caffin, a critic and friend, wrote that "Stieglitz's prominent characteristic is the balanced interest which he feels in science as well as art."[13]

As a critic, Stieglitz wrote extensively about the technical and artistic challenges of night photography. Like Paul Martin, the British photographer whom he credited with pioneering night photography, Stieglitz intuitively recognized the potential that large cities offered for night photography, with their abundance of artificial light reflecting off building facades or wet pavements.[14] While he acknowledged that photographing city lights without creating halations was a technical accomplishment, he found such perfectionism "a decided shortcoming from a pictorial point of view." "A certain amount of halation," he continued, gives "a more sincere and picturesque rendering of the object itself." Such imperfections introduced, Stieglitz argued, life into nighttime images and recreated what the photographer saw as he exposed the image. This was "real picture-making," as opposed to a mere topographical view.[15] Shortly afterwards, in 1900, the critic and poet Sadakichi Hartmann identified potential urban motives for the artist: "Have you ever dined in one of the roof-garden restaurants and watched twilight descending on that sea of roofs, and seen light after light

3 Alvin Langdon Coburn. *The Coal Cart*. 1911. Courtesy George Eastman House.

4 Alfred Stieglitz. *Reflections, Night, New York, 1896*. Courtesy Museum of Fine Arts, Boston. Reproduced with permission. © 2000 Museum of Fine Arts, Boston. All Rights Reserved.

flame out, until all the distant windows began to glimmer like sparks, and the whole city seemed to be strewn with stars? If you have not, you are not yet acquainted with New York."[16]

Hartmann saw the photographers of urban scenes as pioneering the field for painters: "This should be painted," he declared, "but as our New York artists prefer to paint Paris and Munich reminiscences, the camera can at least suggest it."[17]

Skyscraper Nocturnes

Stieglitz photographed New York both at day and night and in the fog, rain, and snow. He was one of the first to photograph weather, standing for three hours in the 1893 blizzard to capture a stagecoach struggling up Fifth Avenue in the storm.[18] He also enveloped the skyscraper into the natural rhythms of time and season.

Photographing the Flatiron Building after a snowfall, he dissolved this American Renaissance skyscraper into what one critic called "a column of smoke"(Fig. 5).[19] Stieglitz paradoxically married the skyscraper, a symbol of American industrialization and capitalism, to pictorialism, a rarefied aesthetic of impressionism and hand-worked images. Moreover, he associated the skyscraper with the American landscape, visually rhyming the building's distinctive flatiron shape with the bough of a snow-encrusted tree in Madison Square. But Stieglitz also gave the Flatiron Building a dynamic identity; it was simultaneously light and solid, emerging and dissolving, natural and man-made, modern and timeless. He called the Flatiron Building both America's Parthenon and the "bow of a monster ocean steamer." It was, he continued, "a picture of a new America still in the making."[20]

Inspired by impressionism and symbolism, Stieglitz and his protégés Edward Steichen and Alvin Langdon Coburn created subtle explorations of form and tone[21] (Figs. 6, 7). Their urban compositions also recalled James MacNeill Whistler's London nocturnes;[22] Coburn even referred to himself as the "Whistler of photography."[23] While Whistler adored the London fog that veiled the "riverside with poetry" and turned "warehouses into palaces in the night,"[24] Stieglitz, Coburn, and Steichen found an electrified Manhattan mesmerizing. "It is only at twilight," Coburn wrote in 1911, "that the city reveals itself to me in the fullness of its beauty, when the arc lights of the avenue click into being." Beginning at Twenty-sixth Street, the street lights, Coburn continued, were like "the stringing of pearls" until they burst into a "diamond pendant at the grouping of hotels at Fifty-ninth Street."[25] In his photo of the Flatiron Building of 1913, Coburn documented the first of these lamps on Twenty-sixth Street (see Fig. 6).

Skyscrapers were especially appealing subjects as Stieglitz and his circle redefined pictorialism. Eschewing the landscapes, interiors, and portraits that had been staples of pictorialism during the 1890s,[26] they embraced the skyscraper as a vital, male, and modern form in the early 1900s. Coburn wrote in 1911 that photography was an art "born of the age of steel," that "must live in skyscrapers."[27]

The Stieglitz circle photographers searched for an organic modernism like the architects Louis Sullivan and Frank Lloyd Wright. Their modernism was tinged with romanticism and, as Jan-Christopher Horak and Wanda Corn have noted, they were often ambivalent about the modern city. While living and working in New York, Stieglitz and his circle often retreated to the country around Lake George, New York or Taos, New Mexico. Nature was a constant in their art and life.

There was a romantic longing for a harmony with nature and discovery of the spiritual that infused their depictions of the modern city.[28] Stieglitz's New York photographs, Lewis Mumford wrote, were "nature in its most simple form, the wonder of the morning and night." Somehow, Mumford marveled, Stieglitz always found the sky "in the cracks between buildings," and the trees "in the surviving cracks of the pavement."[29]

Skyscraper Noir

As these critics and photographers made attempts at embracing the modern life, they confronted the harsher aspects of a changing New York as well. The first two decades of the twentieth century saw a great ambivalence about skyscrapers, and many artists and writers rejected them on aesthetic grounds. While Henry James called the skyscrapers on the lower Manhattan skyline "extravagant pins in a cushion," William Dean Howells likened them to a "horse's jawbone with the teeth broken or dislodged."[31] New Yorkers had to learn how to perceive the vertical as modern and monumental. Photographers helped by discovering the skyscraper as a subject.

Sadakichi Hartmann had written in 1900: "Wherever some large building is being constructed, the photographer should appear. It would be so easy to procure an interesting picture, and yet, I have never had the pleasure to see a good picture of an excavation or an iron skeleton framework. I think there is something wonderful in iron architecture, which, as if guided by magic, weaves its networks with scientific precision over the rivers or straight into the air. They create, by the very absence of necessary ornamentation, new laws of beauty, which have not yet been determined and are perhaps not even realized by the originators. I am weary of the everlasting complaint that we have no modern style of architecture....The iron architecture is our style."[30] Alfred Stieglitz followed Hartmann's suggestion a few years later with his famous *Old and New New York*, a 1910 image showing the astonishingly transparent and lightweight steel frame of a skyscraper under construction. Simultaneously, photographers of the night were crafting a visual language for illuminated skyscrapers, while facing the appropriate technical challenges, which simultaneously suggested new aesthetic directions.

In 1909, Hartmann had identified a "new style of night photography" that followed his suggestion to deal "almost exclusively with the bewildering confusion of light as seen from high viewpoints...all sorts of artificial lights, vast vistas of lit-up skyscrapers...pictures that are perhaps less pictorial than a deserted street or a church in moonlight, but which are more realistically true of the restless flimmer and flare, the blaze and radiance of nocturnal life. They are not mellow harmonies, these night pictures."[32]

Although not usually taken from high vantage points, Hartmann presented the photography of William M. Van der Weyde in the same essay as "strikingly realistic" (Figs. 9, 10). Van der Weyde was one of the very few photographers to capture the Singer Tower, the first skyscraper bathed in searchlights, somewhat realistically in its nocturnal illumination in a photograph taken from the New Jersey shore of the Hudson River. Commercial photographers of the Singer Tower resorted to retouching and even piecing several negatives together to overcome the vast differences in exposure that the comparatively weak searchlights and street lights in the foreground required (Fig. 8 and pp. 96–97).

Beginning in 1913, some of Stieglitz's nocturnal photographs give a harder and edgier cast to New York. An angst and dissonance, the look and feel of what I term skyscraper noir, emerge simultaneously as Stieglitz begins to abstract his image of the city. In 1914, Steichen wrote that progress at Stieglitz's gallery 291 was due "not to a gradual process of evolution but to sudden and brusque changes caused by eager receptivity to the unforeseen."[33] Stieglitz's own work reflected these "sudden and brusque changes" at the gallery. Reinventing his photographic persona in the 1890s, Stieglitz moved away from his early intimate portraits and romantic landscapes to scenes of modern urban life and the machine age. Eventually a new style would accompany this change of subject matter as Stieglitz abandoned the impressionist forms and handworked plates of pictorialism for the crisp focus and high contrast of so-called straight or new vision photography before 1910.[34]

But Charles Caffin saw what he called "straight photography" even in Stieglitz's early pictorialist images of New York. Stieglitz, Caffin wrote, was not just imitating impressionism with his camera. He was "working chiefly in the open air, with rapid exposure, leaving his models to pose for themselves, and relying for results upon means strictly photographic."[35] Stieglitz embraced the very technical imperfections conventional photographers struggled to overcome when shooting at night: the blurring of moving forms, halation of street lamps, light streaks shimmering on wet pavement, and extreme contrasts of lights and darks. This New York was not a mellow, romantic fairyland. These images were, Sadakichi Hartmann wrote in 1909, "a new style of night photography," where: "The greatest extremes meet. Blinding light and absolute darkness. Vague spots here and there accentuated by vivid spots, flickering sheen, and unsteady scintillations. It is an impressive

<<
5 Alfred Stieglitz. *Flat Iron Building*. Photogravure, 1902. Herbert F. Johnson Museum of Art, Cornell University. Bequest of William P. Chapman, Jr., Class of 1895.

6 Alvin Langdon Coburn. *Flat Iron Building, Evening, New York, 1912*. Courtesy George Eastman House.

7 Edward Steichen. *The Flatiron—Evening*. Courtesy George Eastman House. © Barbara Morgan.

8 Singer Building, night view, 1908. From Otto Semsch, *A History of the Singer Building Construction* (Shumway & Beattie, 1908).

9 William M. Van der Weyde. *The Plaza New York*, 1909.

10 William M. Van der Weyde. *The Singer Building*, 1909.

drama of conflicts. The lighted objects issue painfully out of shadow, they surprise us with their vehemence of lustre, and the eye is startled from them to noticing gradations of obscurity in the universal duskiness that surrounds them. We have to discipline our eyes for these surprising contrasts."[36]

Night photography, he concluded, was one medium that could "most powerfully address the modern mind." *From the Back Window – "291"* (Fig. 10), one of several photographs Stieglitz shot from the rear window of his Fifth Avenue gallery between 1915–16, is a cubist collage wrought from the architecture of the night. It is a vision of a modern architecture that had not yet developed in America. In 1903, Sadakichi Hartmann had written that he preferred these raw, unfinished rear walls to the ornamented facades of buildings. "In the rear view," Hartmann stated, "the laws of proportion, the comparative relation of large flat surfaces, broken by rows of windows, create the aethetical impression."[37] This was indeed an organic modernism, but one distilled from the harsh realities of an overheated New York real estate market. The buildings behind Stieglitz's gallery are reduced to ghostly, skeletal frames. Skyscrapers tower over the brownstone buildings. In the Stieglitz print, lights flare from windows and doorways. An illuminated garland crowning the Vanderbilt Hotel is a grace note Stieglitz inserts into an otherwise austere geometrical composition. It functions like the curvaceous wine glasses and table tops Picasso and Braque introduced into the cubist still lifes that Stieglitz had exhibited at 291.

Coburn's *Times Square* of 1912 (Fig. 12) is another skyscraper noir image.[38] Here, lights flare and burst like rockets behind a subway entrance. The tonal scale is one of extremes. The buildings are reduced to thin planes punctured by rectangles of light. Outline lights strung across a dome seem a pathetic attempt at festivity. In photographs like *From the Back Window – "291"* and *Times Square* Stieglitz and Coburn have moved away from late nineteenth-century nocturnes toward a more abstract and harsh aesthetic of the twentieth-century city.

A Room with a View

Night was an ideal working time for the Stieglitz circle, artists determined to redeem photography and skyscrapers from American materialism and commercialization. Stieglitz and his circle shunned the other illuminated New York, Broadway's White Way and Coney Island, with crowds intent on the commodities and pleasures of consumer culture. Their quest was an elite and rarified calling to make art from the deserted and illuminated skyscrapers of lower Manhattan.

Eventually, they viewed the skyscraper from rooftops, balconies, and rooms. Coburn ascended to the Singer Tower's observation balcony to gaze down on the Liberty Tower, calling his image *The House of a Thousand Windows: A Cubist Fantasy*. Stieglitz viewed the changing city first from within his Fifth Avenue gallery near Madison Square and then from the midtown skyscrapers in the forties and fifties. Now the skyscraper became a form not only to see but also to see from. When Georgia O'Keeffe and Stieglitz in 1925, one year after their wedding, moved to the Shelton Hotel, a thirty-three-story skyscraper hotel in midtown, they were pioneers. (A decade earlier, fellow artist Marcel Duchamp had failed to find an apartment in a skyscraper because of restrictive zoning laws.) In a letter to his friend playwright Sherwood Anderson, Stieglitz wrote: "New York is madder than ever. The pace ever increasing.—But Georgia & I somehow don't seem to be of New York—nor of anywhere. We live high up in the Shelton Hotel—for a while— maybe all winter.—The wind howls & shakes the huge steel frame—We feel as if we are out at midocean—All is so quiet, except the wind—& the trembling shaking hulk of steel in which we live—It's a wonderful place."[39]

Living on first the twenty-eighth and then the thirtieth floor of the Shelton with Alfred Stieglitz, Georgia O'Keeffe inspired and challenged him to return to the nocturnal views of the city that he had last photographed between 1913 and 1920. It was O'Keeffe who depicted the first skyscrapers transforming midtown Manhattan around Grand Central Station from a neighborhood of low-rise brownstone shops and residences into a vertical city of offices, hotels, galleries, and stores. Stieglitz, Lewis Mumford, and others in her circle discouraged her.

According to O'Keeffe, Stieglitz initially refused to exhibit her skyscraper paintings in his gallery, encouraging her to paint instead the flowers and landscapes he believed were appropriate for her gender.[40] But she persisted. "I realize," she told a critic in 1928, "it's unusual for an artist to work way up near the roof of a big hotel in the heart of the roaring city, but I think that's just what the artist of today needs for stimulus. He has to have a place where he can behold the city as a unit before his eyes." This was especially true at night when, as historian David Nye has observed, darkness and electricity "edited, simplified, and dramatized" the urban landscape.[41]

Georgia O'Keeffe's American Radiator—Night (1927)

O'Keeffe's nocturnal views of Manhattan[42] drew on what Stieglitz had identified and produced technically and artistically in his photography: the flimmer and flare of halation, the abstraction of form, and the extremes of light and dark. She even introduced the converging lines that small, handheld cameras produced as they were focused on tall buildings. Her paintings, however, push his discoveries to a more radical abstractionism. In her *American Radiator—Night* of 1927, O'Keeffe engaged in an intense dialogue with Stieglitz and his art[43] (Fig. 14).

Raymond Hood's American Radiator Building had created a sensation in New York when it was finished in 1924. During the daytime its black brick surface and golden ornaments at the top were striking contrasts to the neighboring buildings, usually clad in gray limestone, and inspired lively discussions about a future architecture of color.[44] At night, the floodlight illumination at the top was considered so sensational, that it caused traffic jams on Fifth Avenue.[45]

Just as they shunned the typical nocturnal hunting grounds of commercial photographers, like Coney Island or Times Square, Stieglitz and his circle also had avoided depicting the Art Deco skyscrapers of the 1920s because they considered them vulgar and crass icons of popular culture. Georgia O'Keeffe had no such hesitations. Struggling to break free from the gender-laden stereo-types of flower painter, O'Keeffe embraced Art Deco skyscrapers precisely because they were vulgar. These building, for her, were infused with real life.

11 Alfred Stieglitz. *From the Back Window – "291."* Platinum print, 1915. Courtesy Museum of Fine Arts, Boston. Reproduced with permission. © 2000 Museum of Fine Arts, Boston. All Rights Reserved.

12 Alvin Langdon Coburn. *Times Square, New York* (?), Platinum print, 1912. Courtesy George Eastman House. Contrary to Coburn's title, the image seems to show the illuminated dome of the World Building on Lower Broadway.

13 "The Great Lantern, Bryant Park." Photograph by Ben Judah Lubschez, 1927.

14 Georgia O'Keeffe. *American Radiator—Night.* (1927) © VG Bild-Kunst, Bonn, 2002.

As mentioned previously, O'Keeffe's painting of the American Radiator Building (and in fact many of her city views in those years) appropriates the photographer's view and experiences: lights in the foreground show the typical coronas, the halation resulting from the photographic process, which her husband had identified in 1897 as introducing life into the art of night photography.[46] O'Keeffe seems to be demonstrating to Stieglitz that, yes, these motifs could and should be captured by a painter as well as by a photographer. But with equal conviction O'Keeffe demonstrated the freedom that painting, her medium, enjoyed. She placed the Radiator Building squarely in the center of her composition, assuming a viewpoint about the height of its tenth floor, which would have been difficult, if not impossible, for a photographer standing across from the building in Bryant Park to obtain. In the upper left of the painting, presumably on some Fifth Avenue rooftop, a large, red illuminated sign flashes the name of her husband, mocking his dislike for the blinking spectaculars of Times Square and resistance to advertising his gallery. The intense red color was typical for the early years of the most recent and then much talked about innovation in advertising, the neon light, which the French inventor George Claude had introduced in the United States in 1923.

While Georgia O'Keeffe might have witnessed the color experiments that Raymond Hood conducted with his lighting designer Bassett Jones at the top of the Radiator Building in 1924 and '25 (see pp. 114–115), she in fact depicted the illumination as pure white and less colorful than the amber light that was actually used. Radiating beams of distant floodlights are visible behind the building, and a billowing cloud from a smoke stack on an adjacent roof catches ambient light from an unseen source. But O'Keeffe went a step further. In her painting, she did what both nocturnal photography and architectural illumination had promised: to render a vision of a future urban and architectural aesthetic. Compared with any contemporary commercial photograph (Figs. 13, 17), the building appears greatly simplified due to her omission of almost all its ornamental features and one of its two setbacks. The facade now seems dissolved into windows, almost completely eliminating the wall area in between. Instead of the row of ten windows in the original building, O'Keeffe's version depicts fifteen and adds about eight additional stories, resulting in an image eerily close to the nocturnal appearance of postwar skyscrapers of the 1950s.

Stieglitz's Last Skyscraper Photographs

O'Keeffe's skyscraper paintings of the 1920s apparently challenged Stieglitz to photograph the city again after more than a decade. Two years after O'Keeffe began to paint from the Shelton Hotel in 1925, he photographed the city framed by the windows of their apartment for the first time. O'Keeffe though, as Anna Chave notes, disliked sharing subjects with Stieglitz[47] and stopped painting the changing cityscape after Stieglitz took up the subject in earnest. While her twenty paintings of New York had sold extremely well, she turned to other subjects after 1930.

Since ill health made Stieglitz give up photography altogether in 1937, the ninety skyscraper views he made for ten years beginning in 1927 represent his final comment on New York City. These images, which he exhibited only in groups of two or three photographs, captured the transformation of midtown Manhattan that O'Keeffe had first explored.[48]

Stieglitz no longer prowled the streets of New York at night. He withdrew into the interiors of the Shelton apartment or his Intimate and An American Place galleries. European modernism, which he had introduced at his 291 Gallery in the early 1900s, was now on the ascent at the Museum of Modern Art. Yet the American modernists like John Marin, Max Weber, Paul Strand, Arthur Dove, and Georgia O'Keeffe, whom Stieglitz had nurtured, were overlooked there. Moreover, he became estranged in these years from many of the artists he had championed. Set against what Stieglitz decried as the relentless pace of American capitalism and materialism, the changing cultural politics and personal turmoils made the 1920s and '30s a difficult time for him.[49] Nevertheless, Stieglitz looked out with his camera onto a changing city that he could still aestheticize. This, as the writer Jean Toomer observed, was fundamentally what Stieglitz was about: "the inside looking out unhindered…with a permanent intensity to perceive, feel, and know the world which it inhabits, to give a sheer record of experience."[50]

From the Shelton Looking West, taken perhaps in 1933, brings to a close the photography of the night that Stieglitz had first explored in the 1890s (Fig. 15). Following O'Keeffe's lead in the American Radiator Building, here, Stieglitz depicts the RCA Building, the most strikingly floodlit of all New York skyscrapers, in the center of the future Rockefeller Center. Like the Radiator Building, it too was the design of Raymond Hood. Floodlights mounted on smaller buildings in the complex play across the lower stories of the slender tower. But the crown of the building is inexplicably black, with only a few lights burning in the office interiors. Darkened buildings surround the proud and soaring shaft of the RCA tower. While commercial photographers like Samuel H. Gottscho captured a fully illuminated RCA Building at the same time (Fig. 16), Stieglitz's image casts the building as a dying star, going dark from its crown downward. This image of the RCA Building becomes a symbol connecting Stieglitz and New York, both buffeted by the turmoils of the 1920s and '30s. Although Stieglitz creates a cubist composition of cropped and splintered forms, he also masterfully manipulates light and shadow, casting a romantic but melancholy mood over the skyscraper in the darkening sky. He sees beauty but also despair in the architecture of the night, a despair that Stieglitz's friend Louis he had attributed to the unbridled ego and greed of men like John D. Rockefeller. This was, he prophesied, the self-destructive beauty of the megalopolis.[51] In this quintessential image, one of the very last New York images of his career, Stieglitz intertwined both strands of the photography of the night, the romance of the "nocturne" with the realism of "noir." These two aesthetics had defined both the modern and anti-modern in urban photography for him and others since the beginning of the twentieth century in New York.

15 Alfred Stieglitz. *From the Shelton Looking West*, Gelatin silver print, *c.* 1933. Courtesy Museum of Fine Arts, Boston. Gift of Miss Georgia O'Keeffe. Reproduced with permission. © 2000 Museum of Fine Arts, Boston. All Rights Reserved.

16 RCA Building, Rockefeller Center, New York, 1935. Contemporary photo.

1. Alfred Stieglitz. "Night Photography with the Introduction of Life." *The American Annual of Photography and Photographic Times. Almanac for 1898* (1897): 204.

2. Helmut and Alison Gernsheim. *The History of Photography* (New York: McGraw-Hill, 1969): 426–27.

3. Luc Sante. Introduction, *How the Other Half Lives* by Jacob Riis, (1890) (New York: Penguin, 1997): xviii.

4. E. Manny Abraben. *Point of View: The Art of Architectural Photography* (New York: Van Nostrand Reinhold, 1994): 134; Sadakichi Hartmann. "Recent Conquests in Night Photography," (1909) in *Valiant Knights of Daguerre: The Writings of Sadakichi Hartmann*, eds. Harry Lawton and George Know (Berkeley: University of California Press, 1978): 128; and Paul Martin. "Nocturnal Photography," *American Annual of Photography and Photographic Times for 1898*, 12 (1897): 60.

5. A view camera is a large format camera, often 8 x 10, mounted on a tripod to ensure stability during long exposure times. Ducking under a focusing cloth, the photographer sees the image full size, albeit upside down. Basically a lens mounted in a box with bellows, the view camera can swing and tilt, keeping the film plane parallel with the subject. This is essential in architectural photography to correct perspectival distortions. Buildings photographed with a view camera do not appear to topple over. The negative from a view camera is printed full size, retaining maximum detail in the photograph. The photographer sacrifices the speed and flexibility of a small camera for the added detail and control of the view camera.

6. F. M Needham. *Complete Instruction in Photography* (Chicago: Sears and Roebuck Company, n.d. 1900s?): 85. I am grateful to Michael Radow for suggesting this reference.

7. Michael Harris. *Architectural Photography* (Oxford: Focal Press, 1995): 90.

8. Martin. "Nocturnal Photography": 60, 67.

9. Hartmann. "Conquests of Night Photography": 127–28; and Needham. *Complete Instruction in Photography*: 85. Today professional architectural photographers also prefer to photograph buildings between sunset and total darkness, calling this the "magic hour," or between dawn and daylight. See Abraben. *Point of View*: 125 and Norman McGrath. *Photographing Buildings Inside and Out* (New York: Whitney Library of Design, 1993): 183, 186.

10. Photomechanical printing processes and rotary presses made mass production of photoprint postcards possible beginning in 1900. See Howard Woody. "International Postcards: Their History, Production, and Distribution," in *Delivering Views: Distant Cultures in Early Postcards*, eds. Christraud M. Geary and Virginia Lee-Webb (Washington, D.C.: Smithsonian Press, 1998): 16 and 42.

11. This image is now in the Coburn Collection at the George Eastman House, Rochester, New York. It is identified as a test print for New York, a portfolio of photogravures of Manhattan Coburn published in 1910 for which H. G. Wells wrote the introduction. See Alvin Langdon Coburn and H.G. Wells. *The Photographer and the Novelist* (Urbana-Champaign, Ill.: University of Illinois Press, 1997). Coburn also retouched a print of the Singer Tower at night. See *Alvin Langdon Coburn, Photographer, 1900–1914* (Zurich: Edition Stemmele, 1998): 98.

12. Alfred Stieglitz. "Introducing Life into Night Photography." *American Annual of Photography and Photographic Times 1898*, 12 (1897): 206.

13. Dorothy Norman. *Alfred Stieglitz: An American Seer* (New York: Random House 1960); William Homer. *Alfred Stieglitz and the American Avant-Garde* (Boston: New York Graphic Society, 1977); and

14. Paul Martin. "Nocturnal Photography," in: *The American Annual of Photography and Photographic Times Almanach*. 1897 / 1898: 59–62. Stieglitz. "Introducing Life into Night Photograph": 206.

15. Stieglitz. "Introducing Life into Night Photography": 204–06.

16. Sadakichi Hartmann. "A Plea for the Picturesqueness of New York." (1900) in: *Valiant Knights of Daguerre: The Writings of Sadakichi Hartmann* eds. Harry Lawton and George Know (Berkeley: University of California Press, 1978): 56–64.

17. Ibid.

18. Stieglitz. "The Hand Camera – Its Present Importance," (1897) in: Alfred Stieglitz. *Photographs and Writings*, eds. Sarah Greenough and Juan Hamilton (Washington, D.C.: National Gallery of Art, 1983): 183.

19. John Corbin. "The Twentieth-Century City." *Scribner's* 33 (March 1903): 261. Stieglitz's New York photographs were illustrations for the Corbin article.

20. Norman. *Stieglitz: An American Seer*: 45.

21. Wanda Corn. "The 'New' New York." *Art in America* 61 (July–August 1976): 60–1.

22. "Night gained a deeper pictorial significance with Whistler's nocturnes, and the various delineations of street scene painters. Most of us who dwell in the larger cities must have been struck some time or other with the charm which certain places display after daylight has taken its departure and artificial lighting reigns supreme ...." Sadakichi Hartmann, 1926. "Recent Conquests in Night Photography." (1909) in: *Valiant Knights of Daguerre: The Writings of Sadakichi Hartmann*, eds. Harry Lawton and George Know (Berkeley: University of California Press, 1978): 128.

23. Alvin Langdon Coburn. *An Autobiography*, eds. Helmut and Alison Gernsheim, 1966 reprint (New York: Dover Books, 1978): 14 and 18.

24. James MacNeill Whistler. *Ten O'Clock Lecture* (London 1888): 15.

25. Alvin Langdon Coburn. "The Relation of Time to Art," *Camera Work*, 36 (1911): 600.

26. Sadakichi Hartmann. "A Plea for the Picturesqueness of New York." *Camera Notes*, 4 (October 1900): 91–92.

27. Coburn. "The Relation of Time to Art": 72.

28. Jan-Christopher Horak. "Paul Strand: Romantic Modernist," in: *Making Images Move: Photographers and Avant-Garde Cinema* (Washington, D.C.: Smithsonian Press, 1997): 79–80; and Wanda Corn. *The Great American Thing: Modern Art and National Identity, 1915–1935* (Berkeley: University of California Press, 1999): xiv–xvii.

29. Lewis Mumford. "Metropolitan Milieu." in: *America and Alfred Stieglitz: A Collective Portrait*, eds. Waldo Frank et al. (Garden City, N.Y.: Doubleday, Doran, and Company, 1934): 48 and 49.

30. Sadakichi Hartmann. "A Plea for the Picturesqueness of New York." (1909) in: *Valiant Knights of Daguerre: The Writings of Sadakichi Hartmann*, eds. Harry Lawton and George Know (Berkeley: University of California Press, 1978): 56–63

31. Quoted in Merrill Schleier. *The Skyscraper in American Art 1890–1931* (New York: Da Capo, 1986): 6–11.

32. Hartmann. "Recent Conquests in Night Photography": 130–31.

33. Steichen. "291." *Camera Work*, 47 (July 1914): 63.

34. Schleier. *Skyscraper in American Art*: 41–68; Geraldine Wojno Kiefer. "Alfred Stieglitz, Camera Work, and Cultural Radicalism." *Art Criticism*, 7 (1992): 3; and John Szarkowski. "Alfred Stieglitz."

in *Looking at Photographs* (New York: Museum of Modern Art, 1973): 74.

35. Caffin. *Photography as Fine Art*: 39.

36. Hartmann. "Recent Conquests in Night Photography": 130–31.

37. Hartmann. "The Flatiron Building – An Esthetical Dissertation." *Camera Work*, 1 (October 1903): 39.

38. Although identified in Alvin Langdon Coburn as Time Square, this is a view looking east across City Hall Park toward Newspaper Row. The illuminated dome on the right is the World Building, and the glowing clock face belongs to the New York Tribune Tower. Coburn extensively photographed the skyscrapers around City Hall Park (the Woolworth and Park Row buildings) and lower Broadway (Liberty Tower and the Singer Tower). Coburn did not photograph, as far as I know, in the Times Square area.

39. 9 December 1925 Letter to Anderson from Stieglitz, reproduced in Alfred Stieglitz. *Photographs and Writings*, eds. Greenough and Hamilton: 214.

40. See also Elizabeth Duvert. "Georgia O'Keeffe's Radiator Building: Icon of Glamorous Gotham." *Places: A Journal of Environmental Design: 2*, no. 2 (1985): 3–17.

41. Chave. "O'Keeffe and the Masculine Gaze": 92–100, 179, no. 41; and Nye. *Electrifying America: The Social Meanings of a New Technology, 1880–1940* (Cambridge, Mass.: MIT Press, 1990): 47, 58.

42. Among them: *New York with Moon*, 1925, *City Nights*, 1926, *East River from the Shelton*, 1927 / 28, *Radiator Building – Night, New York*, 1927, *New York Night*, 1929.

43. Duvert. "Georgia O'Keeffe's Radiator Building....": 4

44. "Gay Buildings seen in Artistic Trend." *New York Times* (10 July 1927): RE12; "Architect Predicts New York as a City of Color." *New York Times* (20 February 1927): RE 14.

45. "Editorial Comment." *American Architect* 126 (19 November 1924): 487.

46. Stieglitz. "Introducing Life into Night Photography": 206.

47. Anna Chave. "Who Will Paint New York: The World's New Art Center and the Skyscraper Paintings of Georgia O'Keeffe." *American Art*, 5 (Winter / Spring 1991): 100.

48. Joel Smith. "How Stieglitz Came to Photograph Cityscapes." *The History of Photography* 20 (Winter 1996): 320–21.

49. Corn. *The Great American Thing*: 33–39.

50. Jean Toomer. "The Hill" in: *America and Alfred Stieglitz: A Collective Portrait*: 143.

51. Mumford. "The Metropolitan Milieu," in: *America and Alfred Stiegliz: A Collective Portrait*: 34. In his review of the building in the *New Yorker*, Mumford had written, that "The best time to see the Center is at night," when the building could appear "large, exciting, romantic" as only "at night one can forget that every touch of bad ornament is bad with an almost juvenile badness; ... one can forget that the broad face of the main building, running from east to west, and seventy stories high, permanently cuts off sunlight from a large swath of buildings to the north;" Lewis Mumford. "The Sky Line: Mr. Rockefeller's Center." *New Yorker* (23 December 1933). Quoted in Robert Wojtowicz. *Sidewalk Critic. Lewis Mumford's Writings on New York* (New York: Princeton Architectural Press, 1998).

17 American Radiator Building at Night, New York City, 1926. Samuel H. Gottscho photographer.

Architectural Illumination since World War II

Dietrich Neumannn

Most major trends of Western art and architecture in the second half of the twentieth century continued or responded to developments in the first half. To a certain degree the same is true for the approaches to architectural illumination, where key applications, artistic solutions and theoretical debates are remarkably similar in the early and later years of the century. While classic modernism in art and architecture, however, had ceaselessly been discussed, defined and celebrated since the 1950s, the ephemeral art of illumination temporarily fell into oblivion after World War II and again after the energy crisis of 1973.

"Nine points for a new monumentality"

In 1943, the French painter Fernand Léger, the Spanish architect José Luis Sert and the Swiss architectural historian Sigfried Giedion, all living on the American East Coast at the time, collaborated on a manifesto entitled "Nine Points on Monumentality" in response to an invitation from the *American Abstract Artists* for a publication about contemporary artistic activity. In their text, which was not immediately published,[1] the three authors regretted the fact that modern architecture had not yet successfully addressed the question of monumentality. They suggested that a new, contemporary monumentality could arise from "modern light materials, mobile elements" and a collaboration between urban planner, architect, painter, sculptor and landscapist: "During night hours, color and forms can be projected on vast surfaces. Such displays could be projected upon buildings for purposes of publicity or propaganda. These buildings would have large plane surfaces planned for this purpose, surfaces, which are nonexistent today. Such big animated surfaces with the use of color and movement in a new spirit would offer unexplored fields to mural painters and sculptors."[2] This was an astonishing proposition in the middle of the World War II, while searchlights were associated with air raids, and only a year after black outs in New York and other American cities had extinguished all floodlights and advertising signs. This part of the proposal seemed to show the handwriting of Fernand Léger, who had on several occasions expressed his fascination with American floodlighting, luminous advertising, and future light frescoes, and who was familiar with László Moholy-Nagy's similar ideas about the topic[3] (see p. 44–45). While none of the rich previous developments in the field were mentioned in the text, Giedion clarified their position a year later in a text called "The Need for a New Monumentality." Instead of the "pseudo-monumentality" of "lifeless schemes," such as Munich's "Haus der Deutschen Kunst" or the "Mellon Institute" in Pittsburgh (both 1937), "spectacles of water plays, light, sound and fireworks" like those at the recent World's Fairs in Paris and New York should fulfill art's task of "shaping the emotional life" of the masses and equip the modern architecture in future civic centers with monumental qualities. In considerable detail, Giedion analyzed the qualities of a future "Ephemeral Architecture," which he considered "one of the rare events where our modern possibilities are consciously applied by the architect-artists."[4] These ideas resurfaced in modified form when the 8th CIAM congress in Hoddesdon, England, discussed the core of the modern city in 1951 (both Giedion and Sert attended).[5] Although none of their suggestions had any influence on postwar urban planning, the fact that such colorful "ephemeral architecture" was now taken seriously by modern architects, who probably would have dismissed it a decade earlier, is remarkable. Simultaneously, formerly European ideas of luminous architectural parts were gaining ground in the United States.

Victory Celebrations

Immediately after the war, the well-developed vocabulary of nocturnal spectacles was used everywhere for joyful celebrations. In Los Angeles a veritable "Lichtdom" of one hundred strong converging searchlights was installed above the Los Angeles Memorial Coliseum for the Victory Celebration on October 27, 1945 (Fig. 1). To avoid any similarities with Albert Speer's installations, the organizers had 16-foot-wide color wheels built for each searchlight, which made it possible to produce a changing, multicolored "crown of light."

Despite "present restrictions affecting labor and materials," London's "Victory Lighting" in the summer of 1946 transformed the center of the city into a luminous "fairyland" combining the floodlighting of buildings with illuminated fountains and fireworks. Here as well, lighting designers

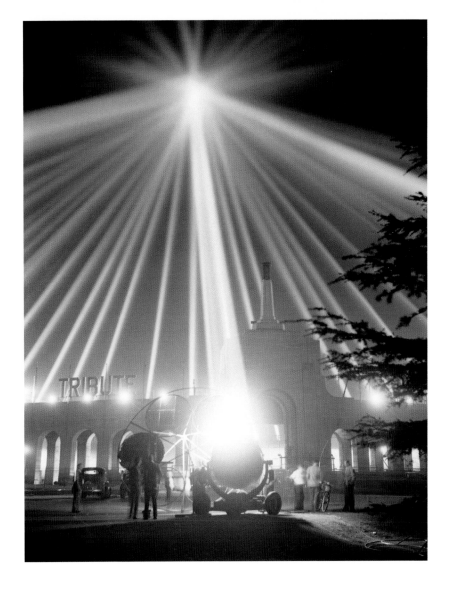

found that the searchlight had not lost its appeal for peaceful nocturnal displays, "…in spite of its ominous implications." Indeed, they explained, "it was perhaps most fitting that at least one implement of war should be employed to demonstrate the arts of peace." It was considered equally appropriate that the searchlight displays above the river were operated by the Anti-Aircraft Command of the Royal Artillery, which now could show its "skill in a happier way by suggesting patterns of royal colours."[6] The beams of light were kept in constant motion and employed various colors. Two stationary blue searchlight beams formed a gigantic "V" for "Victory" above Buckingham Palace, whose facade was floodlit in red, white and blue.

The rebuilding efforts in German cities began in the following years, and lighting soon played an important part there as well. "The reconstruction of lighting has outrun the reconstruction of the actual buildings so far that only at night does one become consciously and subconsciously aware of the plan underlying the rebuilding of the city," explained the British architect Gerhard Rosenberg after a visit to Cologne in 1953. "Lights outline the streets, replace the non-existent upper floors of buildings, create squares and define open spaces, outline and emphasize the buildings that are reconstructed and make one feel secure and at home in a town that, in daytime, still looks more like a shanty town or a huge bomb site than a thriving city."[7]

Son et lumière

The lighting of historical structures, which had already been immensely successful before the war, continued in response to the growth of tourism with the invention of "son et lumière" in the early 1950s.[8] Paul-Robert Houdin, who is generally credited with the idea, began staging his first sound and light performance at Chambord on May 30, 1952, under the title of "Les très riches Heures de Chambord,"[9] initiating an epoch of "nocturnal tourism." Houdin apparently had been inspired by

1 Colored Light Beams converging above the Los Angeles Memorial Coliseum as a "Tribute To Victory" on October 27, 1945. ©Bettmann / CORBIS

a visit to the Paris World's Fair of 1937 (see pp. 170–171) and by the illuminated monuments of Paris. The enormous success, which continues to this day, inspired spectacles at tourist sites all over the world, often incorporating elements of the long established festival and architectural lighting culture, such as smoke, fireworks and film projection.

At the Brussels World's Fair of 1958, the first after the war, Le Corbusier and the Greek composer Yannis Xenakis transported the notion of "son et lumière" from the historical spectacle for tourists into the realm of high art. Inside the Philips Exhibition pavilion, colors and sequences of images were projected simultaneously onto several interior walls, accompanied by contemporary music by Edgar Varèse. Commentators like Michel Butor once again envisioned a synaesthetic confluence of music, projected light, and architecture: "And now imagine future cities where at the main intersections buildings (of which this one is only a first prototype) play like instruments, or allow you play ... and the variety of our mental landscape will be heightened by a luminous dimension."[10]

The 1950s and 1960s

While traditional luminous advertising resumed its prewar role almost immediately after World War II in Europe and the United States, the intense debates about artificial light and architecture were not taken up again, and the floodlighting of buildings did not assume the same intensity as before the war. Stylistic preferences had begun to change in the late 1930s; the European influence had brought about buildings with wide openings, smooth, reflective surfaces, and setbacks —once such an efficient base for floodlighting—were employed less frequently.

In New York City, new approaches became manifest in buildings like the Manufacturers Hanover Trust on Fifth Avenue (see p. 184), with its impressive glass walls and its translucent luminous ceiling. Enthusiastic critics like Louis Mumford and Ada Louise Huxtable seemed to evoke architectural visions of 1920s Germany when they declared that "The whole, viewed from the outside, is no longer architectural in the traditional sense: it is a design, not of substance, but of color, light and motion."[11] Gordon Bunshaft repeated the success of this system immediately afterwards at the Pepsi-Cola headquarters on Park Avenue (1956–60), and Richard Kelly and Mies van der Rohe applied a similar approach, turning the Seagram Building on Park Avenue (1956–60) into a "tower of light."

It was the simultaneous completion of the Seagram Building and the Tishman Building at 666 5th Avenue (see pp. 188–191) that helped to re-ignite a debate about architectural lighting, as both structures came with a carefully designed lighting scheme, each one reinterpreting earlier traditions, and showcasing the talents of the two most prominent American lighting designers, Abe Feder and Richard Kelly. As the first independent lighting designer, Feder revolutionized the professional profile and argued for the "recognition of light as a building material, which can form space directly."[12] Richard Kelly also had early experiences with stage lighting but went on to study architecture in order to better advise architects in lighting matters. By 1947 he had established his own office and was soon working with Richard Neutra, Mies van der Rohe, Philip Johnson and Louis Kahn.[13] Referring to the two illuminated skyscrapers, the *New York Times* declared (obviously with little remembrance of the earlier lighting discussions in the 1920s and 1930s): "One of the big advances in recent years in architecture is the use of lighting ... lighting is now an art that combines function and decoration."[14] *Progressive Architecture* devoted an entire issue to the topic of "*lighting is architecture.*" The newly developed interest in architectural lighting caused an increase in illumination projects. The Waldorf Astoria Hotel was lit soon after, the top thirty stories of the Empire State Building were illuminated in 1964, as well as the controversial Pan Am Building on Park Avenue by Walter Gropius and Pietro Belluschi (again floodlit by Abe Feder).[15] While this building owed a great deal to the form of Gio Ponti's Pirelli Tower in Milan of 1960 (see pp. 196–197), the most elegant European skyscraper at the time, its lighting scheme had not been adopted. Gio Ponti had carefully studied the appearance of luminous ceilings and vertical lines of light on either side of his tower. "Lighting will become an essential element of spatial architecture .... By a predesigned self-illumination this architecture will present formal night effects never yet imagined—illusions of spaces, of voids, of alternations of volumes, weights, and surfaces,"

2 Helmut Jahn, Southwest Center (project), Houston 1982. © Helmut Jahn.

Ponti wrote in 1957 and predicted "a fantastic new architecture.... We are only at the beginning of this era of illumination." He said that floodlighting had nothing to do with architecture ... that it was primitive and barbaric. Instead, "...we artists will create luminously corporal entities of form. We will create a new nocturnal city."[16]

Just as this passionate, almost futuristic battle cry reminds us of the debates in the 1920s, certain questions and problems were formulated again and again, usually without knowledge of earlier debates. An American lighting designer, Derek Philip, wrote in 1964, "The appearance of buildings from outside at night is another dimension of architecture that hardly bore consideration until this decade when, with the freedom given by modern structures and the possibilities of artificial lighting, the synthesis between inside and outside appearance could become a reality.... There are few disappointments as real as entering some towns after dark and experiencing the sense of scale and vitality given by the facades of neon signs, only to find the following morning one has been in a shanty town of huts at low level, above which large sign frameworks have been erected. The nighttime appearance need not be the same, but it should bear sufficient correlation with the day appearance to be appreciated as the same building."[17]

Derek Philip probably was thinking of Las Vegas, which was being discovered as a cultural phenomenon around this time. The writer Tom Wolfe had been one of the first, in February 1964, to point out the strange contrast between the enormous, colorful signs and the one-story casinos —the "signs have become the architecture of Las Vegas" he exclaimed.[18] A few years later he coined the term "Electrographic Architecture" for their combination of "lighting, graphics and building structure in a single architectural form," stating that commercial designers had shown considerably more creativity and skill than the "avant-garde" of contemporary light artists, such as Dan Flavin, Robert Rauschenberg, Apple etc.[19] Nevertheless, the importance and lasting influence of non-commercial kinetic-luminous experiments by a number of artists in those years (among them Nicolaus Schöffer, Frank Malina, Lucio Fontana) should not be underestimated.[20]

While Las Vegas was little affected, elsewhere most floodlighting and architectural lighting came to a halt between 1973 and 1975 as a result of the international energy crisis. Many of the lights were not turned on afterwards and their potential has long been forgotten. The city of Paris went so far as to allow members of the public to pay for special illuminations of the Eiffel Tower and other monuments.[21]

Architectural Illumination since the 1980s

From 1977 on, architectural lighting slowly regained its former popularity. Major public monuments were floodlit again.[22] The Empire State Building, whose top thirty stories had been bathed in white light from 1964 until 1973, received a new lighting installation allowing for the application of color to commemorate particular days and events. (Not everybody was happy. Architecture critic Paul Goldberger called it "...a total violation of the design...."[23]) By 1981, New York City had a new "crown of light" (including the Chrysler, Helmsley and Metropolitan Life Buildings), which was greeted with the same exuberance that had welcomed it for the first time in 1925.[24] Many of the lighting schemes for existing or new buildings during the 1980s nostalgically emulated the floodlighting achievements of the '20s and '30s.[25] Helmut Jahn's designs for the Southwest Center in Houston of 1982 (Fig. 2) or I. M. Pei's Bank of America Tower in Miami (1980–1987) (see p. 206–207) are typical examples of this. Today, a number of European projects seem like late responses to the earlier utopian visions of a pure, luminous architecture, such as Peter Zumthor's Kunsthaus in Bregenz of 1996 (see p. 215) or Rafael Moneo's Kursaal in San Sebastian of 1999.

The relationship between luminous advertising and architectural illumination (much discussed in the 1920s and '30s) is one of the reference points for recent installations at Orlando's Universal City Walk in Florida, connecting Universal Studios and the Islands of Adventure (Fig. 3). The artificial urban environment in the tradition of World's Fairs and amusement parks offers an assemblage of shops, restaurants and nightclubs, of passages and squares bordering a man-made lagoon, characterized by an absence of cars, dime stores or homeless people. Site architect John

3 John Johnston at Sussman Prejza. Universal City Walk, Orlando, Florida, 2001.

4 John David Mooney, "Lightscape '89" at Mies van der Rohe' IBM headquarters building, Chicago, 1989. © John David Mooney Foundation.

Johnston created a series of streetscape elements such as totems, towers and signs to "create a coherent civic presence."[26] Instead of carrying a message, the neon signs are colorful abstractions that are integrated into the architecture, and flash on and off to music. The light sculptures ("totems") serve as orientation points along the way. The artificial coherence of this environment made possible a lighting concept for signs, sculptures and buildings that could forego its commercial roots and instead explore its artistic potential, mindful of constructivist influences and the history of neon art.

Since the 1980s, computer-based technologies have allowed for color and light sequences far more complex than the "mobile color" system of the 1920s and '30s. By responding to the changing conditions of its environment (see pp. 204–205, 210–211, 214, 216, 222–223), luminous architecture has assumed a more engaging role in the nocturnal cityscape. Large-scale LED screens offer an equivalent of the "light frescoes" that had been predicted in the 1920s, but face the challenge of an integration with the architecture that carries them. The few successful examples, such as Renzo Piano's recent KPN Telecom Tower in Rotterdam (2000) or Rem Koolhaas' (unexecuted) 1989 design for the Center for Media Technology in Karlsruhe are outnumbered by projects where the application of such screens seems a mere afterthought, or whose architectural integration seems not yet fully developed, as in Fox and Fowle's Nasdaq Screen at 4 Times Square, in New York City. While there are successful examples of collaborations between architect and lighting designer, and a number of prominent lighting designers (such as Howard Brandston, Ross DeAlessi, Jonathan Speirs and Heinrich Kramer) have developed thriving practices, the early prediction of lighting designers in every architectural office and their routine involvement in every architectural design is still far from reality.

Festival Lighting

With the revival of architectural illumination in the late 1970s, the tradition of carefully choreographed searchlight displays was also rediscovered. Chicago-based artist John David Mooney was commissioned to develop "Light Space 1977," where he used 36 carbon arc searchlights on Chicago's lakefront and on barges on Lake Michigan. American Airlines commissioned a similar piece in 1990 to celebrate the opening of their new O'Hare terminal. Mooney has also created unique projects that temporarily transform modern architecture into colorful luminous sculptures, as in "Lightscape '89," which installed light sources and colorful screens in the 7,152 windows of Mies van der Rohe's IBM building in Chicago for the company's 75th birthday (Fig. 4). The Chicago Tribune's headquarter, which had been one of the earliest testing grounds for architectural illumination in the United States (see pp. 142–143), was transformed by Mooney's project "Light Muse'" in 1997[27] (Fig. 5). Such temporary building illuminations, along with a revived culture of light festivals, flourished during the 1980s and 1990s all over the world. Some of the most spectacular events with laser and light projection in urban surroundings were staged for music performances by Jean Michael Jarre, as in Paris' La Defense district (1990) or the skyline of Houston (1986).[28] The French designer Yann Kersalé has been responsible for some of the most memorable temporary (and permanent, see pp. 226–227) architectural lighting installations, such as "Lumières" at the Grand Palais in Paris in 1987, where blue fluorescent lighting under the building's glass dome rhythmically increased and decreased, suggesting the beating heart of the metropolis. In Kersalé's work in particular, experiences gathered at temporary festival installations inform the permanent architectural installations developed in collaboration with architects such as Jean Nouvel and Helmut Jahn.

During the summer of the year 2000, while the city of Hannover in Germany was hosting the World's Fair, the city's 1928 Anzeiger Hochhaus (architect: Fritz Hoeger), was illuminated by the German light artist Yvonne Goulbier (Fig. 6). Both owner and architect had planned for an illumination of the dome in the late 1920s, which was prevented by the world's economic crisis. Goulbier responded more than seventy years later with contemporary technology, and colorful moving light projections turned the outer shell of the planetarium into continuously changing views of an imaginary planet.[29]

The onset of the year 2000 inspired innumerable lighting projects around the world, their vocabulary usually dependent and in dialogue with that developed during the first half of the century. In Berlin for example, illumination artist Gert Hof had been commissioned to develop fireworks and a search-light display for the occasion. When he presented his concept, called "Art in Heaven," which included rows of 250 white xenon searchlights reaching thirty miles into the sky, creating a "pyramid of light, a cathedral for the millennium,"[30] a storm of protests arose, voiced by prominent German writers such as Günter Grass and Peter Rühmkorf, historians such as Hans und Wolfgang Mommsen, and others, who saw similarities with Albert Speer's "Lichtdom" installations under National Socialism (see pp. 50–52). The ensuing debates revealed how closely the iconography of such an installation depended on its time and place and that neither the artist nor his critics had sufficient knowledge about the medium's rich prehistory. That Gert Hof had not associated Albert Speer with his lighting installation, could, at least partially, be explained by the fact that he had grown up in the East German city of Leipzig. Critical debates about the legacy of Nazi Germany had been more intense in West Germany than in the communist dictatorship in the East, which was also less hesitant to adopt cultural strategies that had worked well in Germany under Hitler. "Lichtdomes" were installed regularly, in particular in Leipzig's large sports stadium at the closing ceremonies after major competitions (Fig. 7). Responding to the public criticism, Gert Hof added more color and movement.[31]

For the same night, Mexican/Canadian artist Rafael Lozano-Hemmer had staged a lighting spectacle above the Zocalo in Mexico City,[32] undisturbed by any such debates. From December 26, 1999 to January 7, 2000, Lozano-Hemmer maintained a website where anyone could submit designs for the eighteen robotic Zenon searchlights on the roofs surrounding Mexico City's historic central square, which were then executed in sequence, just long enough to be documented by three webcameras at different locations in Mexico City. More than 100,000 participants from all over the world submitted requests or watched the light spectacle unfold via videostream on their computer screens (Fig. 8). Lozano-Hemmer understands his projects as "'relational architecture,' altering the urban experience through technological interventions."[33] He sees himself in a tradition reaching back to the art of projected color in Thomas Wilfred's Lumia projects from the 1920s to the '40s (see pp. 23, 61) and other lighting spectacles in the public realm, and consciously responds to what he calls the "cathartic intimidation" of Albert Speer's *Lichtdom* with the "intimacy" of individual participation in his projects.[34]

It seems appropriate at the end to remember one of the most thoughtful responses to architectural illumination in the 1920s. After a visit to Times Square, the British writer G. K. Chesterton explained that artistically he had nothing against luminous advertising and illuminated skyscrapers. "When a child would see these colors, it would dance," he wrote. But he objected to the use of "colors and fire" in Times Square as a "vulgarization of the symbolic." While the former celebrations at royal weddings or church holidays deserved spectacular color and light, with today's commercialization, "the significance of such color and such light has been entirely killed," he explained, and thus, the "new illumination has made people weary of proclaiming great things, by perpetually using it to proclaim small things."[35] While Chesterton's critique is as valid today as it was in 1927, new projects continuously suggest a rethinking of notions such as representation, monumentality and the technological sublime.

Epilogue: The World Trade Center

Between March 11 and April 13, 2002, every evening from dusk until midnight, 88 custom-made Xenon searchlight projectors sent two shafts of light vertically into the New York sky. They had been installed next to the site of the World Trade Center, destroyed six months before in the terrorist attacks of September 11, 2001. This "Tribute in Light" developed by a group of New York architects and designers[36] served as a temporary and ephemeral memorial to those who died in the attacks and to the towers themselves, by evoking their form and position in the skyline. The conceptual clarity of this gesture gains complexity in the light of the long tradition of comparable applications and stands as a convincing response to Chesterton's critique quoted above.

7 "Lichtdom" above the Leipzig Sportstadium, July 1977. ©Ullstein Bild, Photographer Klaus Schlage

8 Rafael Lozano-Hemmer. Relational Architecture. Lighting Installation above the Zocalo in Mexico City, December 31, 1999. ©Rafael Lozano-Hemmer.

Shortly after the World Trade Center opened in 1975, New York Times architecture critic Paul Goldberger had described how its nocturnal illumination transformed its appearance. This hauntingly prophetic account is worth quoting at length:

"The World Trade Center remains largely lit for much of the night, and at night its vast towers undergo perhaps the most remarkable transformation of anything in the city.

The 110-story buildings, monstrous and cold as ice by day, become a stunning presence. The tight mesh of the center's "skin," with its narrow windows, by day is ugly from without and uncomfortably confining from within, but by night gives the building a soft texture that none of its neighbors can match. [...]

Up close, the center—which is still a construction site, although largely occupied—becomes surreal. The enormous metal shafts, which rise without setback or ornament, are always more like abstract forms than like buildings, and at night, they give up any pretense at all to being real. They stand, glowing, in an empty landscape, with silence all around, bigger than one had ever dreamed yet somehow, at night, able to be touched and perceived more clearly.

It is an image at once terrifying and moving—an architectural experience of genuine power."[37]

1. Christiane C. and George R. Collins. "Monumentality: A Critical Matter in Modern Architecture." *The Harvard Architecture Review*, no. 4 (1984): 15–35. The text was published much later by Sigfried Giedion, in: *Architecture, You and Me: The Diary of a Development* (Cambridge, Mass.: Harvard University Press, 1958): 48–51.

2. J.L.Sert, Ferdinand Léger, Sigfried Giedion. "Nine Points on Monumentality" reprinted in: *Harvard Architecture Review* IV (Spring 1984): 62–63.

3. After a visit to the office of Harvey Wiley Corbett (who was promoting color floodlighting at that time, see p. 59) Fernand Léger had written, for example: "A transparent, translucent New York, with blue, yellow, and red floors! An unprecedented fairyland, the light unleashed by Edison streaming through all that and pulverizing the buildings." Leger. "New York." *Cahiers d'Art*, Paris, 1931, quoted from: Edward F. Frey (ed.). *Functions of Painting by Fernand Léger* (Thames and Hudson: 1973): 84–90

4. Sigfried Giedion. "The Need for a New Monumentality." *The Harvard Architecture Review*, no. 4 (1984): 52–61.

5. J. Tyrwhitt, J.L. Sert, E.N. Rogers. *The Heart of the City: Towards the Humanization of Urban Life* (London, New York, 1952): 28, 65, 164–168. See also: Eric Mumford. *The CIAM discourse on urbanism, 1928–1960.* (Cambridge, Mass., 2000): 204–215.

6. Rollason W. Ames. "Public Lighting for the Victory Celebrations in London as Designed and Executed by the Ministry of Works." *Light and Lighting* 39 (July 1946): 117–130.

7. Gerhard Rosenberg. "The Architectural Use of External Lighting of Buildings." *Light and Lighting* 46, no. 7 (July 1953): 270–272.

8. "Yesterday in floodlights." *New York Times* (14 June 1959); For a history of "son et lumière" see: Bertrand Fillaud. *Les Magiciens de la Nuit* (Antony: Sides, 1993).

9. Fillaud: 15.

10. Michel Butor. in: *Le Poème électronique. Le Corbusier* (Editions de Minuit, 1958): 103–107.

11. Ada Louise Huxtable. "Banker's Showcase." *Arts Digest* 29 (1 December 1954): 12–13.

12. Abe Feder. "Light as an Architectural Material." *Progressive Architecture* (September 1958): 124–131.

13. Richard Kelly. "Lighting as an Integral Part of Architecture." *College Art Journal* (Fall 1952): 24–30. The most exhaustive scholarly treatment of Kelly to date is to be found in Margaret Maile. *Richard Kelly, Defining Modern Architectural Lighting Design: from Philip Johnson's Glass House to Seagram's Glass Box.* Master's Thesis (The Bard Graduate Center: June, 2002).

14 Thomas W. Ennis. "Lighting, Once Mere Utility, Has Become an Important Element of Design." *New York Times* (26 October 1958): RE 1, 8.

15. "Lights Embellish City Skyscrapers." *New York Times* (27 December 1964): 202.

16. Gio Ponti. "In Praise of Architecture." (New York: F. W. Dodge Corporation, 1960); originally published as *Amate l'Architettura*, 1957.

17. Derek Philips. *Lighting in Architectural Design* (New York: McGraw-Hill, 1964): 208.

18. Thomas K. Wolfe. "Las Vegas (What?), Las Vegas (Can't hear you! Too noisy), Las Vegas!!!" in: *Esquire* 61, 2 (February 1964): 97–106, 121.

19. Tom Wolfe. "Electrographic Architecture." *Architectural Design* (7 / 1969): 379–382.

20. Hannah Weitemeier. "Lichtchoreographien" in: Michael Schwarz. *Licht und Raum.* (Cologne: Wienand Verlag, 1998): 46–59.

21. "City to Turn Off Lights in Money-Saving Move." *New York Times*, (2 November 1975): 61; Terry Robard. "British seek 10% Fuel Cut by Heat and Speed Curbs." *New York Times* (10 December 1974): 1.

22. "Washington Restores Lights at Monuments." *New York Times* (6 March 1977): 29. Due to the natural gas shortage that winter, several floodlights had been switched off, that had been re-illuminated as a result to the energy crisis in 1974.

23. Paul Goldberger. "Design Notebook." *New York Times* (8 December 1977)

24. "Crowns of Light Grace the Skyline." *New York Times* (26 November 1981): B 1; cf.: Hollister Noble. "New York's Crown of Light." *New York Times* (8 February 1925): SM 2.

25. Thomas Fisher. "Night Lights." *Progressive Architecture* 68, No. 9 (September 1987): 150–155.

26. Catherine McHugh. "Lighting Projects: Universal City Walk, Orlando Florida." *Architectural Record* 11 (November 2001): 195–198. John Johnston of Sussman / Prejza & Co. worked in collaboration with Kaplan lighting design.

27. I would like to thank Barbara Jones at the John David Money Foundation for providing this information.

28. Alessandro Rocca. "Against Las Vegas. The Return of the Sublime by Night," in: *Lotus International* 75 (1993): 32–44.

29. http://www.poesia-hannover.de/index_eng.html

30. Christa Hasselhorst, "Lichtbahnhof am Himmel" *Die Welt*, (9 November 1999)

31. Rainer Haubrich. "Kleine Taschenlampe brenn." *Die Welt* (21 December 1999)

32. See: http://www.lozano-hemmer.com and Rafael Lozano-Hemmer (ed.). *Vectorial Elevation* (Mexico City: Ediciones san Jorge, 2000.)

33. Daniel Canogar. "Spectral Architectures" in: Lozano-Hemmer (Ed.), 77–93.

34. Geert Lovink. "Interview with Rafael Lozano-Hemmer," in: Lozano-Hemmer (ed.): 49–67.

35. Quoted from: William Leach. "Land of Desire: Merchants, Power, and the Rise of a New American Culture." (New York: Pantheon, 1993): 347.

36. The principal creators of the project were the architects John Bennett and Gustavo Bonevardi of Proun Space Studio, artists Julian LaVerdiere and Paul Myoda together with the architect Richard Nash Gould and lighting designer Paul Marantz. The main supporters of the project were General Electric, the Deutsche Bank AG and AOL Time Warner.

37. Paul Goldberger. "At Night, City Comes Out of Hiding." *New York Times* (9 November 1975): 1, 10.

9 "Tribute in Light" at the site of the former World Trade Center, New York City, March / April 2002. © dpa

Overleaf:

Forty-Second Street Studios and Paramount Theater Building, see p. 120, 222. Originally published in the *New Yorker*. © Robert Polidori 2000

Selected Projects

Exposition Universelle · Paris · 1900

Dates: **April 15–November 12, 1900**

Selected Architects:

Joseph-Antoine Bouvard: Architect in Chief

Charles-Louis Girault: Petit Palais

Albert-Félix Thomas, Henri Dèglane & Albert Louvet: Grand Palais

René Binet: Monumental Gate

Eugène Henard: Palace of Electricity, Waterworks, Hall of Illusions

Marie-Joseph Cassien-Bernard & Gaston-Clément Cousin: Pont Alexandre III

Gustave Raulin: Festival Hall, Waterworks

Henri Sauvage: Loie Fuller Theater, Pavilion Marjorelle

René Dulong & Gustave Serrurier-Bovy: Pavilion Bleu Restaurant

Eliel Saarinen: Finnish Pavilion

Lighting Designer: **Henry Beau and others**

Monumental Gate (design René Binet) by night, watercolor, 1900

Palace of Electricity and Waterworks by night, contemporary postcard

Ilumination from the Eiffel Tower, contemporary print, 1900

Selected Bibliography:

"A Revolving Palace." *Canadian Architect and Builder* 10, no. 3 (1897): 50.

"Electrical Palace and Fountain at the Exposition." *Scientific American* 83 (13 October 1900): 225, 231.

"Electricity at the Paris Exhibition." *Review of Reviews* 21 (March 1900): 347–348.

"The Crest of the Palace of Electricity." *Scientific American Supplement* 50, no. 1280 (14 July 1900): 20518–20519.

Mandell, Richard D. *Paris 1900: The Great World's Fair.* Toronto: University of Toronto Press, 1967.

Meier-Graefe, Julius, ed. *Die Weltausstellung in Paris 1900 mit Zahlreichen Photographischen Aufnahmen, Farbigen Kunstbeilagen und Plänen.* Paris, Leipzig: F. Krüger, 1900.

Shaw, Albert. "Paris and the Exposition of 1900." *Review of Reviews* 21 (June 1900): 679–688.

The Exposition Universelle of 1900 was the fifth international exposition to be held in Paris during the latter half of the nineteenth century. The exposition was situated on the Champ de Mars, but also included land on the opposite bank of the Seine, across the new Pont Alexandre III to the Avenue Triomphale with the Petit and Grand Palais. In contrast to the 1889 exposition with its exposed iron structures, the 1900 fair saw a return to highly decorated plaster facades. The iron and glass Galerie des Machines of 1889 vanished behind the ornate trimmings of the Palace of Electricity, while its interior was completely redesigned as the Salle des Fêtes. An effort was made to present contemporary design in such eclectic Art Nouveau structures as the Pavillon Bleu Restaurant and the Porte Monumentale.

The 1889 Paris fair had seen the rise of electric light as an artistic and urban medium in architectural contour lighting. Due to recent technological advances, the lighting scheme for 1900 was not only more spectacular than that of any previous fair, but also for the first time several buildings were designed particularly for their nocturnal appearance. The tripod form of the Porte Monumentale was brought to life with 3,100 colored incandescent bulbs and twenty-six arc lamps. Five hundred incandescent bulbs lit the Pont Alexandre III. The Eiffel Tower, which had somehow escaped the refurbishment plans that had made the Galerie des Machines nearly unrecognizable, was illuminated by 7,000 incandescent lights of ten candlepower each. Electric lamps now totally replaced the gaslights that had partially illumined the famous tower in 1889. Again, the bright beams of moveable arc lights at the top picked out individual buildings on the fairgrounds and in Paris at night. Gas had not completely disappeared by 1900, however, and the 1878 Trocadéro exhibition palace, whose terraces alone had been lit in 1889, was now outlined with thousands of gaslights, which provided a softly glowing contrast to the harsher and more brilliant electric lamps.

The American dancer Loie Fuller had colored light projected onto her white, expansive costumes in a special theatre by Henri Sauvage. The outside displayed stucco ornament mimicking the flowing movement of her dress and colored lights at night. The most discussed installation was probably that of the Palace of Electricity. An elaborate crest of *repoussé* zinc topped the facade, its form outlined by 5,700 incandescent bulbs. Red, yellow, blue and white bulbs were employed, alone and in varying combinations. Ships and figures appeared in color for a few seconds, and were then replaced by other motifs. At the apex of the crest, behind a statue of the Genius of Electricity, a huge, multi-pointed gilt iron star was strung with wires holding glass fragments that reflected the lights of six arc lamps in a shimmering display. Additional arc lamps projected a soft rainbow of colors through the stained glass inserts in the zinc framework. In the center of the facade, stood the Chateau d'Eau, a grotto from which a grand cascade of water flowed in stages down to the central basin. Incandescent lamps alongside and behind the water used the same four colors found on the Palace of Electricity.

A 377-foot-tall revolving hexagonal tower of steel had been proposed for the fair, its surface and interior walls covered with multi-colored glass that was to be illuminated from within by 20,000 incandescent and 200 arc lamps. In concert with the light show, organs and chimes, operated by steam, electricity or air, were to be installed in the upper stories. This extravagant structure was unfortunately never built.

For the German art historian and critic Julius Meier-Graefe, who noted with enthusiasm that the palaces whose eclecticist architecture he had denounced were, at night, turned into "carriers of light," the nocturnal scenery contained hints about an architecture of the future: "Today already we can dream ourselves into the future, if we wander through the exhibition grounds by night. Then the little putti and cornices, all the small and small-minded embellishments, vanish, ghost-like, in the dark. What remains are the large outlines, the enormous masses of this creation. All by itself, the night presents what we expect from the new architecture: concentration and greatness."

(Meier-Graefe, p. 40)   K. B. / D. N.

Pan-American Exposition · Buffalo, New York · 1901

Dates: **May 1–November 2, 1901**

Architects: **John M. Carrère, Chairman of Board
of Architects: Triumphal Causeway and Pergola
John G. Howard: Electric Tower
Richard S. Peabody: Horticultural Building,
Graphic Arts Pavilion
Green & Wickes: Electricity, Machinery and
Transportation Buildings
J. Knox Taylor: United States Government Building
George F. Shepley: Manufactures, Liberal Arts &
Agriculture Buildings
Esenwein & Johnson: Temple of Music**

Color Scheme: **Charles Y. Turner**

Lighting Designers: **Luther Stieringer
and Henry Rustin**

"McKinley's Entrance," photograph, 1901

Electric Tower, photograph, 1901 >

Temple of Music and Machinery Building,
photograph, 1901 >

Selected Bibliography:

Brush, Edward Hale. "Electrical Illumination at the Pan-American Exposition." *Scientific American Supplement* 51, no. 1307 (19 January 1901): 20943–20944.

Davis, Hartley. "The City of Living Light." *Munsey's Magazine* 26 (October 1901): 116–128.

Dunlap, Orrin E. "Searchlight Signaling at the Pan-American Exposition." *Scientific American Supplement* 51, no. 1321 (27 April 1901): 21169.

Grant, Robert. "Notes on the Pan-American Exposition." *The Cosmopolitan* 31 (September 1901): 450–462.

Gray, David. "The City of Light." *Century Magazine* 62 (September 1901): 673–685.

Knaufft, Ernest. "Artistic Effects of the Pan-American Exposition." *Review of Reviews* 23 (June 1901): 686–693.

Page, Walter H. "The Pan-American Exposition." *World's Work* 2 no. 4 (August 1901): 1014–1048.

Rydell, Robert W. *All The World's a Fair: Vision of Empire at American International Expositions 1876–1916.* Chicago, University of Chicago Press, 1984: 126–153.

Thomas Edison's films about the fair available online at: http://memory.loc.gov/ammem/ammemhome.html

"The most magnificent and artistic nocturnal scene that man has ever made." This is how writer Walter Page described the illumination of the Pan-American Exposition in Buffalo. Organized in 1901, three years after the United States had bolstered its dominant role in the Americas by defeating Spain in the Spanish-American War, the exposition was proclaimed as a celebration of unity among the countries of the two continents. The exhibition was overshadowed by the murder of President McKinley by the anarchist Leon Czolgosz on September 6, 1901 during a reception at the Temple of Music. The organizers decided to continue the exhibition especially given its theme of civilization's triumph over barbarism.

The Columbian Exposition in Chicago of 1893 had greatly influenced the general layout and selection of building types. But, whereas that exposition was known for its White City of Beaux-Arts buildings, the Pan-American was fashioned as a "Rainbow City," its buildings based on the style of the Spanish Baroque in recognition of the importance of the Latin American countries among its exhibitors, and its color scheme a bold mélange of tints ranging from bright orange to violet to a subtle ivory. At the same time the exhibition was a showcase for North American technological superiority with an outline lighting scheme that surpassed anything that had previously been done. Thomas Edison, a pioneer in the development of both electric light and motion pictures, made his first successful night films at the fair.

The plan of the grounds was that of a cross, its main axis beginning at the southern end with the Triumphal Causeway. Arranged in a symmetrical pattern along this axis were the principal exhibition buildings, connected by colonnades and pergolas, and culminating at the northern end with the most popular building of the exposition, the 400-foot-tall Electric Tower. The general conception of the architecture, sculpture, and even the color scheme was that of man's evolution from barbarism to civilization and his triumph over nature. The apogee was reached with the Electric Tower, with its subdued hues of ivory, gold, and green. This tower, based on Seville's Giralda, symbolized man's dominion over Niagara Falls, whose power was harnessed to provide the electricity for the exposition itself. At the base, a miniature version of the falls flowed from the tower, and on the very top of the building an eighteen-foot-tall statue of the Goddess of Light was displayed, holding aloft an image of the sun.

The lighting design utilized up to 500,000 incandescent bulbs (35,000 on the Electric Tower alone), which outlined not only the outer edges of the turrets and domes but also the surface decorations, thereby retaining a sense of the three-dimensionality of the buildings. In place of the standard sixteen-candlepower, eight-candlepower bulbs were used, creating a soft, diffused glow far removed from the brilliant and overpowering arc lamps used in the first illuminated expositions or even the brighter bulbs used at the last great exposition in Omaha, Nebraska just three years before (Transmississippi Exposition, 1898). The gently glowing lights allowed the colors of the buildings to remain visible, though softened. Ninety-four searchlights were placed under and around the cascade of water at the base of the Electric Tower, suffusing it with a green glow reminiscent of the real Niagara. Another searchlight was placed on the top of the tower, to be trained on the fountains and other objects below. There were some additional lighting installations outside of the main court, including an Electric Fountain lit by twenty-two searchlights of changing colors and a building illuminated by a brilliant white acetylene gas light. The illumination was turned on gradually at dusk:

"In a dim, uncertain way, those who have worked so hard to see things become conscious of a faint flush in the gloom, as if millions of fireflies sought to fight the coming darkness.... It deepens into pink, and then are formed long lines with sharp angles, sweeping curves, and curious twisted shapes. The pink deepens into red, and the rosy light swiftly melts into a soft, luminous yellow. Everywhere there is light; the whole world seems bathed in it.... This is the City of Living Light, and those who look upon it know that in their wildest flights of fancy they never conceived anything to which it can be compared...." (Davis, pp. 116–117)

K. B. / D. N.

Coney Island, New York · 1903

Dates: **Steeplechase Park: 1897–1964. Luna Park: 1903–46. Dreamland. 1904–1911**

Architects: **Unknown. Steeplechase founded by George Tilyou. Luna Park founded by Frederick Thompson and Elmer Dundy. Dreamland founded by William H. Reynolds.**

Lighting Designer: **Unknown**

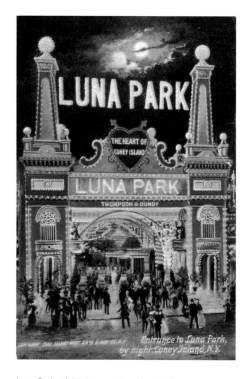

Luna Park, night view, postcard, c. 1905
Luna Park, night view, postcard, c. 1905

Dreamland, night view, photograph, c. 1905 >

Selected Bibliography:
"Luna Park First Night." *New York Times* (17 May 1903): 2, col. 4.
Gorky, Maxim. "Boredom." *Independent* 63 (8 August 1907): 309–317.
Koolhaas, Rem. *Delirious New York: A Retroactive Manifesto for New York*. New York: Oxford University Press, 1978.
Paine, Albert Bigelow. "The New Coney Island." *Century Magazine* 68 (August 1904): 528–538.
Pilat, Oliver and Jo Ranson. *Sodom by the Sea: An Affectionate History of Coney Island*. Garden City: Doubleday, Doran & Co., 1941.
Thompson, Frederick A. "The Summer Show." *Independent* 62 (20 June 1907): 1460–1463.

Coney Island, located on the southwestern tip of Long Island, was the largest and most famous amusement center in early twentieth-century America. The area had featured carousels and other rides since the 1870s, but by the 1890s had degenerated into a seedy district of gambling and prostitution. Entrepreneur George Tilyou changed this image when he erected the first of the three enclosed parks that would turn Coney Island into a haven for family entertainment. Tilyou had visited the 1893 Columbian Exposition and noted how fascinated people were by the world's first Ferris wheel. The following year he brought a smaller version of this famous ride, dotted with electric lights, to Coney Island, and in 1897, he opened Steeplechase Park. More interesting from both an architectural and a lighting standpoint, however, was Luna Park, opened in 1903 by Elmer Dundy and the architect Frederick Thompson. The two men had worked at both the Omaha 1898 and the Buffalo 1901 (pp. 90–91) expositions, as well as at Steeplechase. Together they created a park that was heavily influenced by the layout and design of the great expositions. The buildings of Luna Park were treated in a unified style, a highly romanticized Orientalist vision of orange, red, and white turrets, minarets and arabesques, with bridges and a lagoon. An Electric Tower, studded with in-candescent lights and with a small fountain at its base, was a focal point, providing a link to the great exhibitions, which had had similar towers. The entire park was lit by 250,000 colored electric bulbs, many of them used to outline the shapes and details of the buildings.

In 1904, former state Senator William H. Reynolds, who would become the developer of the Chrysler Building in 1929 (pp. 202–203), opened Dreamland, the last of the three great parks. In contrast to Luna, the architecture of Dreamland was all white and influenced more by European Baroque forms. Its central tower was based on Seville's Giralda and stood 375-feet tall, 200 feet taller than Luna Park's tower. Indeed everything about Dreamland was intended to surpass Luna. The tower alone was brilliantly illuminated at night by 100,000 lights, just a fraction of the million that were said to light the entire park. It also included a red and white searchlight beacon, which was taken down in 1906 because of its dangerous similarity to that of a nearby light-house. In 1907, Thompson claimed that the island held four times as many electric lights as any other place of comparable size on earth. These massive displays of luminosity were still a distinct novelty at the turn of the twentieth century. The advent of a trolley line to the island in 1895 had made the parks access-ible to millions of working-class New Yorkers, many of them immigrants who treasured the momentary escape from their daily lives. While amusement parks and pleasure gardens can be traced back to the sixteenth century, the arrival of electric lights immensely increased their popularity. The success of Coney Island inspired countless Luna Parks, White Cities and Electric Parks all over the world.

The Russian writer Maxim Gorky visited Coney Island in April 1906, when he was in New York trying to solicit support for the Russian revolution. His description of Coney Island is one of the most precise and clear sighted of the time:

"With the advent of night a fantastic city all of fire suddenly rises from the ocean into the sky. Thousands of ruddy sparks glimmer in the darkness, limning in fine, sensitive outline on the black background of the sky, shapely towers of miraculous castles, palaces and temples.... Fabulous and beyond conceiving, ineffably beautiful, is this fiery scintillation. It burns but does not consume.... From the very first moment of arrival at this city of fire, the eye is blinded.... The visitor is stunned; his consciousness is withered by the intense gleam; his thoughts are routed from his mind; he becomes a particle in the crowd. People wander about in the flashing, blinding fire intoxicated and devoid of will...." (Gorky, "Boredom")   K. B. / D. N.

Louisiana Purchase Exposition · St. Louis, Missouri · 1904

Dates: **April 30–December 1, 1904**

Architects: **Isaac S. Taylor, Director of Works
and President of Board of Architects
Emmanuel L. Masqueray, Chief of Design:
Colonnade, Cascades and several exhibition
buildings
Cass Gilbert: Festival Hall and Fine Arts Buildings
Eames & Young: Education Building
Carrère & Hastings: Manufacturers' Building
Van Brunt & Howe: Varied Industries Building
Walker & Kimball: Electricity Building**

Lighting Designer: **Henry Rustin**

Palace of Electricity, photograph, 1904

Festival Hall, photograph, 1904

Selected Bibliography:

"The Big Engine of the St. Louis Exposition and the
Illumination of the Buildings." *Scientific American Supplement* 58, no. 1489 (16 July 1904): 23853–23854.

"The World's Fair at St. Louis." *World's Work* 8, no. 4
(August 1904): 5052–5083.

Bennitt, Mark, Frank Parker Stockbridge et al. *History of
the Louisiana Purchase Exposition*. St. Louis: Universal
Exposition Publishing Co., 1905; reprint ed., New York:
Arno Press, 1976.

Francis, David R. *The Universal Exposition of 1904*, 2 vols.
St. Louis: Louisiana Purchase Exposition Co., 1913.

Grandeur of the Universal Exposition at St. Louis.
St. Louis: Robert A. Reid, 1904.

Love, Robertus. "Illumination of the World's Fair."
Scientific American 90 (21 May 1904): 399.

Lowenstein, M. J. *Official Guide to the Louisiana Purchase
Exposition*. St. Louis: The Official Guide Co., 1904.

Rydell, Robert W. *All The World's a Fair: Vision of Empire
at American International Expositions 1876–1916.*
Chicago: University of Chicago Press, 1984: 154–183.

The Louisiana Purchase Exposition in St. Louis was the last large-scale international exhibition in the United States to employ outline lighting as its chief form of illumination, although several smaller fairs and countless amusement parks continued the practice over the following decades.

Held in honor of the one-hundredth anniversary of the purchase of the Louisiana territory from the French government in 1804, the exposition occupied a site of 1,272 acres, nearly as big as the previous four largest American fairs combined. The main buildings, designed in the Beaux-Arts style of the Columbian Exposition in Chicago, were arranged around a central basin, fanning out on radiating plazas from the great domed Festival Hall by architect Cass Gilbert. From either side of this structure a Colonnade, fifty-two feet in height, ran down to the basin, while a set of three waterfalls flowed in the center. The color of the buildings was a uniform off-white, although some variations in color were allowed on the upper domes and towers of the structures.

The illumination of the Louisiana Purchase Expo was similar in many ways to that of the 1901 Pan-American Exposition in Buffalo (pp. 90–91). In both cases, the principal buildings were outlined with eight-candlepower incandescent bulbs. At St. Louis, however, there were some notable new developments. Colored light was used more fully here, not just to illuminate the Cascades as had been done at previous fairs, but also to animate the architecture. Festival Hall and its Colonnade were equipped with three separate lighting systems in different colors, whose sequential appearance was controlled by a rheostat. This effect was particularly impressive against the uniform white lights of the other exhibition buildings. An equally important innovation at St. Louis was the use of concealed lighting. Many structures were illumined by bulbs hidden behind columns, arches, and ornaments.

The nighttime appearance of the St. Louis Expo drew fascinated crowds and rhapsodic descriptions: "The first indication is a faint glow of red not unlike the last tinge of a summer sunset," noted one article, "which softly outlines the familiar forms of the various buildings. Slowly, these lines brighten, until the whole picture glows with fire, and then, as the full current begins to tell, the lines of light brighten into brilliant incandescence and the picture is complete." (*Scientific American Supplement*, no. 1489).

The official guide to the fair proudly noted that arc lights had been banished from the main exposition area because their brilliance would overwhelm the incandescent illumination. In all, a total of 120,000 bulbs were used throughout the fair. Its impressive lighting scheme is commemorated in the lyrics of the popular contemporary song, "Meet Me in St. Louis." Forty years later, the song and the nightly illumination ceremony would be nostalgically recalled in the Hollywood movie of the same name.   K. B.

Singer Building · New York, New York · 1908

Architect: **Ernest Flagg**

Location: **149 Broadway**

Construction Dates: **Original Building: 1896–98. Tower: 1907–08. Demolished in 1968.**

Installation Date: **1908**

Installation Type: **30 18-inch arc searchlight projectors lighting tower from base to 35th floor. 1,600 incandescent bulbs outlining the upper floors.**

Lighting Designers: **Walter D'Arcy Ryan and Charles G. Armstrong**

At 612 feet and forty-seven stories, the Singer Building was, upon its completion, the tallest skyscraper in the world. It had been added to the existing ten-story Singer administration building, when plans for the massive, 33-story City Investing Building (Francis Kimball) next door had become known. While the slender tower with its brick and limestone facing was influenced by the eclectic Beaux-Arts style, its central section of glass and steel also revealed the structural conditions of its existence. The building was illuminated immediately after its opening, the lighting scheme having been developed during the design phase. In 1908, outlining with small bulbs was still the norm for architectural

Singer Building, stereo photograph, 1908

Singer Building, retouched photograph, 1908 >

Selected Bibliography:

"City Illumined as Never Before." *New York Times* (26 September 1909): 2: 1–2.

Bacon, Mardges. *Ernest Flagg: Beaux Arts Architect and Urban Reformer.* New York: Architectural History Foundation, 1986.

Brainerd, Arthur A. and John A. Hoeveler. "The Advertising Value of Mobile Color Lighting." *Transactions of the Illuminating Engineering Society* 24, no. 1 (January 1929): 40–60.

Semsch, Otto F. *A History of the Singer Building Construction: Its Progress from Foundation to Flag Pole.* New York: Shumway & Beattie, 1908.

illumination. This type of lighting was seen on the Singer Building on its mansard roof, where 1,600 incandescent bulbs were placed to delineate the decorative details. The most spectacular aspect of the illumination, however, was a first, and short-lived, attempt at floodlighting the building with the employment of thirty specially-built searchlights (which still had little in common with later floodlight projectors). These were focused on the tower from its base to the thirty-fifth story and were powerful enough to allow the colors of the building materials to be seen at night. While the uneven lighting capacity of these early floodlights becomes evident in the stereo photograph, the company relied on heavily retouched nocturnal views for its own advertising. With this progress from outline

lighting to floodlighting, the lighting designer Walter D'Arcy Ryan anticipated the conceptual change with which he would triumph a few years later when he designed the lighting for the Panama-Pacific Exhibition (pp. 104–107) in San Francisco. One year after its completion, Ryan even installed a special design of colored lights for the weeklong Hudson-Fulton Celebration of 1909. "[W]hat every one of the visitors paused to gaze at was the Singer Building tower.... The main building was dark and gloomy, but from its center sprang a terra-cotta shaft set off with pale green pilasters rising to a golden cornice. The lights which illuminated it could not be seen, but it glowed against the sky...." ("City Illumined"). Photos of the time show a luminous, almost unearthly, pillar that was said to be visible for forty miles, a particularly dramatic sight at a time when most of the city still lay in darkness after sundown. Yet, this effect seems to have been short-lived. The northern facade of the tower was soon hemmed in by the immediately adjacent City Investing Building, and when the Woolworth Building (pp. 202–203) received its spectacular illumination in December 1914, only the old-fashioned outline lighting was visible on the Singer Building's upper floors and dome. Nevertheless, the earlier floodlighting scheme had been an inspiration for F. W. Woolworth, who was eager to continue his tower's dominance of the skyline into the night. The Singer Building, however, deserves to be remembered for its role in establishing color floodlighting as a means of architectural expression.   K. B. / D. N.

Gas & Electric Building · Denver, Colorado · 1910

Architect: **Frank E. Edbrooke**

Location: **910 15th Street**

Construction Dates: **1908–10. Extant**

Installation Dates: **1910–43, 1945–55. With reduced number of light bulbs: 1955–62, 1990–present. The building is currently illuminated with 6,998 5-watt bulbs.**

Installation Type: **1910: 13,000 incandescent light bulbs covering the surface of the building, ranging in power from 5–200 watts. Between windows of the 2nd, 9th and 10th floors, lights form a cross and diamond within a rectangle.
On 3rd to 8th floors, lights form crosses between, above and below windows. On top two floors, lights outline and form arch patterns above each window.**

Lighting Designer: **Cyrus Oehlmann**

Denver, 15th Street, postcard, *c.* 1913

City of Denver, postcard, *c.* 1913

Denver Gas & Electric Building, postcard, *c.* 1913 >

Selected Bibliography:

Anderson, O.P. "Sign Lighting." *Transactions of the Illuminating Engineering Society* 6, no. 4 (April 1911): 377–397.

"Denver Gas and Electric Company." Denver Landmarks and Districts webpage. Online. Available: http://www.denvergov.org/AboutDenver/today_landmarks_denvergas.htm. 13 July 2001.

One of the most remarkable early examples of a building especially designed with its nighttime appearance in mind, the Denver Gas & Electric Building was known for many years as "The Best Lighted Building in the World." The importance that architectural illumination was already beginning to take on in American cities in 1910 is evidenced by the fact that the mayor of Denver officially turned the lights of this building on for the first time and a crowd of 75,000 people was there to witness it. The glazed white terra-cotta and pressed brick facing of the ten-story rectangular construction served as a reflecting surface for an installation of 13,000 light

bulbs, arranged in various patterns on all four sides of the building, which is situated on a corner lot. Proud contemporaries called the building "a flashing diamond" within the business district of Denver. Cyrus Oehlmann's lighting design went beyond a mere outlining of the architectural features to create patterns on the surface that could be changed by varying the wattage of the bulbs. Special lighting designs were employed to mark important events, such as Charles Lindbergh's first trans-Atlantic flight, in honor of which the name "Lindy" was spelled out in lights on the four sides of the building. Although dimming equipment did exist even at this early date, it was not used to create the illumination

patterns here. Instead, workmen simply leaned out of the windows to remove the unneeded light bulbs.

The lights were temporarily turned off during World War II, and the number of bulbs was reduced by the year 1955 to 6,998, after adjacent structures had hidden the two facades not facing the street. They were turned off completely when the building was sold in 1962 (and came perilously close to being torn down). In 1990, in conjunction with efforts to revitalize Denver's downtown, the building was restored and illuminated again. The brilliant lighting was seen as an important incentive to bring other businesses back

to downtown. Today the building houses major facilities in the telecommunications and Internet sector and is the largest consumer of electricity in the Central Business District.

K.B./D.N.

General Electric Company Building · Buffalo, New York · 1912

Architects: **Esenwein & Johnson**

Location: **535 Washington Street**

Construction Dates: **1912. Additional stories added to main building in 1924 and 1927. Extant**

Installation Dates: **1912, 1927, 1963**
The building is currently illuminated by white floodlights, with red and green filters added in separate tiers at Christmas.

Installation Type: **1912: Arc lamps at curb line, top of main structure (4th-floor level), and on 14th, 15th and 16th floors of tower. 5 of the same lights on a 30-foot standard. Concealed blue-purple lights on tower. Revolving searchlight beams from three 30-inch projectors with color screens. 1927: Floodlights with white, green, and purple filters in three separate tiers. 1963: Holiday lighting: Thousands of different-size bulbs on 20-second cycle. Floodlights on each of top three tiers. Strands of flashing lights and Christmas trees. Red, green, amber and white lights used.**

Lighting Designer: **1912: Walter D'Arcy Ryan**

General Electric Building, night view, postcard, *c.* 1930
General Electric Building, night view, postcard, *c.* 1912

General Electric Building, photograph, 1914 >

Selected Bibliography:
"Buffalo General Electric Illuminates its Office Building." *Electrical World* 90 (31 December 1927): 1369.
"Holiday Lighting Brings Queries." *Electrical World* 160 (23 December 1963): 15.
Herko, Carl. "The Landmark in a New Light: Two-Year Renovation Sets Electric Building Aglow." *Buffalo News* (18 December 1992): 15.
Ryan, Walter D'Arcy. "The Lighting of the Buffalo General Electric Company's Building." *Transactions of the Illuminating Engineering Society* 7 (1912): 597–615.

The illumination of the General Electric Company (now Niagara Mohawk) Building in Buffalo demonstrated the transition from outline lighting to floodlighting, with the latter style soon to become the dominant form after its use at the Panama-Pacific Exposition (pp. 104–107) in 1915. Walter D'Arcy Ryan, who was in charge of the lighting for both this building and the later expo, wished to design a lighting system that would be representative of the latest developments of the time. Because of the large size of the building, which had been inspired by the Electric Tower of the 1901 Pan-American Exposition in Buffalo (pp. 90–91), Ryan decided to replace the usual small lamps used in outlining with white arc lamps. These were set around the foundation at the curb line, along the top of the main building, and on the upper floors of the octagonal tower. Faced with glazed terra-cotta, the building appeared as a white shaft punctuated by yellow tungsten lamps that shone through the windows. The columns in the upper portion of the tower were lit by white arc lights shining on the outer faces,

while a blue-purple light towards the rear caused a shadow effect. At the apex of the building, in imitation of the lighthouse of Alexandria, upon which the building was also modeled, a revolving searchlight was projected through colored filters, progressing through a variety of hues as it turned. This use of color and of a relatively few large lamps instead of numerous small white lights was a forerunner to the many spectacular multi-colored flood-lighting installations that were to come in the 1920s and '30s. It was also the first of several lighting designs that would be employed for this building. The tower has been regularly lit with different colored floodlights or with strings of incandescent bulbs on each of its three uppermost tiers, particularly during the holiday season.   K. B.

Electric Building at Night, Buffalo, N.Y.

Woolworth Building · New York, New York · 1914

Architect: **Cass Gilbert**

Location: **233 Broadway**

Construction Dates: **1911–13. Extant**

Installation Date: **1915. The tower of the building is currently lit with white lights, similar to the original installation.**

Installation Type: **600 automobile lamp projectors with 250-watt incandescent lamps and corrugated filters on the 27th, 30th, 43rd, 49th, 53rd and 54th floors. 24 1000-watt lamps on automatic dimmers in 60th-floor lantern.**

Lighting Designers: **1915: H. Herbert Magdsick. Current: Douglas Leigh**

Woolworth Building, night view, retouched photograph, c. 1916

Woolworth Building, night view, photograph, 1913 >

Selected Bibliography:

"55-Story Building Opens on a Flash." *New York Times* (25 April 1913): 20, col. 4.

"Spectacular Illumination of Woolworth Building." *Electrical World* 65 (9 January 1915): 132.

Cochran, Edwin A. *The Cathedral of Commerce.* New York: Munder-Thomsen, 1916.

Magdsick, H. H. "Flood Lighting the World's Tallest Building." *Electrical World* 68 (26 April 1916): 412–414.

Person, Charles W. "New York's Greatest Lighting Spectacle." *Scientific American* 112, no. 8 (20 February 1915): 1.

The Woolworth Building, at the time of its construction, was the tallest skyscraper in the world and President Wilson himself officially opened the building by telegraph from the White House on April 24, 1913. The button he pushed simultaneously turned on 80,000 lights throughout the structure, from the basement to the tower. Despite providing an undoubtedly impressive spectacle, the interior lighting would have been a rather impractical and costly way of securing a dominant role for the building in the city's nocturnal skyline. Woolworth therefore hired a team of engineers under the leadership of General Electric's H. H. Magdsick to work on an exterior lighting scheme. The sheer size of the sixty-story structure rendered outline lighting impractical, and since Walter D'Arcy Ryan's first experiments at the Singer Building (pp. 96–97) in 1908, floodlighting technology had made considerable progress. The new nitrogen-filled, tungsten filament lamps suddenly made floodlighting a much more practical means of illumination, and the Woolworth Tower thus became the first building in New York to be evenly and permanently illuminated solely by floodlights. These lights were focused on the thirty-story tower and were attached to the structure itself, hidden by screens from passersby below. Some of the lamps were arranged so as to cast their beams upwards while others faced down to cover the areas that could not be reached from below, thereby ensuring that the entire tower was evenly lit, and the gothic ornamentation was carefully emphasized. Faced with a reflective white terra-cotta and decorated with gold leaf, the Woolworth Building stood out on the New York skyline at night as none had ever done before. In order to create an even more brilliant beacon at the apex of the tower, much brighter 1000-watt lamps were placed within the lantern, which was encased in diffusing glass. These lights were set on an automatic dimmer so that they continually grew and faded in strength on an irregular cycle, from the deep red of the lowest intensity to the brilliant white of the highest and back again. "The color effects are brilliantly wonderful," wrote Edwin Cochran, after the lighting installation had been switched on at 11 p. m. on New Year's Eve, December 31, 1914: "The light, soft and mellow at its base, gradually increases in intensity as it reaches upward and, at the very top, the pinnacle, an immense ball of fire appears, giving the effect of a gorgeous jewel resplendent in its setting of gold … this dazzling illumination … is acknowledged to be the greatest triumph in flood-lighting ever achieved."

K. B. / D. N.

Panama-Pacific International Exposition · San Francisco, California · 1915

Dates: **February 20–December 4, 1915**

Selected Architects: **Edward H. Bennett and Ernest Coxhead: Exposition ground plan**
Thomas Hastings: Tower of Jewels
Bernard Maybeck: Palace of Fine Arts
Bakewell & Brown: Palace of Horticulture
McKim, Mead & White: Court of the Universe
Louis C. Mullgardt: Court of Abundance
Henry Bacon: Court of the Four Seasons
George Kelham: Court of Flowers and Court of Palms

Color Scheme: **Jules Guerin**

Lighting Designers: **Walter D'Arcy Ryan, A. F. Dickerson (assistant), J. W. Gosling (decorative designer)**

Tower of Jewels, postcard, 1915

Exposition at night, postcard, 1915

Selected Bibliography:

Barry, John D. *City of Domes*. San Francisco: J. J. Newbegin, 1915.

Bayley, G. L. "Illumination of Panama-Pacific Exposition." *Electrical World* 65, no. 7 (13 February 1915): 391–395.

Macomber, Ben. *The Jewel City: Its Planning and Achievement; Its Architecture, Sculpture, Symbolism, and Music; Its Gardens, Palaces, and Exhibits*. San Francisco: John H. Williams, 1915.

Markham, Edwin. "Edwin Markham on the Exposition." *New York Times* (17 February 1915): 10, col. 5.

Ryan, Walter D'Arcy. "Illumination of the Panama-Pacific International Exhibition." *Transactions of the American Institute of Electrical Engineers* 35, Part 1 (June 1916): 757–781.

Ryan, Walter D'Arcy. "Illumination of the Panama-Pacific International Exhibition." *General Electric Review* 18 (June 1915): 579–586.

Todd, Frank Morton. *The Story of the Exposition*, 5 vols. New York: G. P. Putman's Sons, 1921.

Wright, Hamilton M. "The Panama-Pacific International Exhibition at Night." *Scientific American* 112 (24 April 1915): 378, 389.

Just nine years after its devastating earthquake and fire, San Francisco was chosen to host the new exposition in honor of the completion of the Panama Canal. While none of the big exhibitions are without political meaning and reverberations, the timing and purpose of the Panama-Pacific Exhibition revealed a particularly strong political subtext. Taking place as World War I had begun in Europe and searchlights there filled the skies to detect enemy aircraft, the Panama-Pacific Exposition presented a spectacle of unprecedented splendor. As a celebration of American technological superiority, it helped to quell any criticism of the rather Machiavellian politics with which the United States had assumed control of the Panama Canal Zone.

The exposition site along San Francisco Bay was laid out in a sequence of palaces around three large and several smaller courts, with the Tower of Jewels serving as the entrance to this court area. The architectural theme was a mixture of Classicism and Orientalism, referring to the "wedding of two oceans" that the canal had accomplished.

Despite contemporary accounts to the contrary, this was not the first exposition to abandon the concept of a "White City," first seen at the Chicago exposition of 1893 (Buffalo's liberal employment of color had been much commented upon by the visitors to its 1901 exposition). San Francisco's "Jewel City," however, was the first in which the overall color scheme was enforced for every detail, even down to the guards' uniforms, trashcans, and the sand on the ground. Over a base of ivory, a subdued palette of greens, red, oranges and blues was used. This color scheme had been developed by Jules Guerin, a French painter and graphic artist whose moody perspectives for Daniel Burnham's Plan for Chicago had earned considerable attention. His role in articulating the oriental theme of the exhibition had been presaged by his recent book illustrations for Robert Hichens' *The Holy Land* (1910) and *The Near East* (1913).

The color scheme was complemented by the illumination of the grounds at night. In fact, the exposition marked a turning point in the history of architectural illumination as the first to use concealed floodlighting instead of outline lighting. A journalist wrote, "There is no blaze or glare. Light floods the Exposition, but from concealed sources. All-pervasive, seemingly without source, the illumination is rather a quality of the Exposition atmosphere than an effect of light." (Macomber, p. 134). Lighting Designer Walter D'Arcy Ryan went to great lengths to hide the light sources behind special decorative features. He believed that the outline lighting of previous expositions, though often beautiful, had detracted from the architecture by casting shadows and hiding details as well as causing eye fatigue. His plan was to eliminate most shadows with a combination of searchlights trained on the buildings and red-tinted incandescent bulbs hidden in the cornices and niches. The Tower of Jewels received the most attention for its unique design and illumination. This 435-foot-tall structure surpassed that of the 1901 Buffalo exposition (pp. 90–91) in height and was also based on Seville's Giralda, a structure then enjoying enormous popularity in the U. S. as a symbol of the confluence of eastern and western ideas. It was covered with 102,000 "Novagems," both colored and clear glass prisms, each backed by a mirror and suspended so that it constantly moved in the breeze. During the day, the cut glass refracted the sunlight. At night the effect was more brilliant as the prisms reflected the beams of fifty-four searchlights and created a diffused cloud of light around the tower.

The three main courts of the Exposition were illuminated in different colors: green for the Court of the Four Seasons, white for the Court of the Universe, and red for the Court of Abundance, which also was lit by gas flares, steam cauldrons and other theatrical effects. The two fountains in the Court of the Universe were capped by twin columns, ninety-five feet high and made of translucent opal glass. At night, incandescent lamps contained within the glass were turned on to create two softly glowing shafts. Inside the Palace of Horticulture, twelve floodlight projectors were arranged in a circle, their beams focused on the glass dome above. This "Electric Kaleidoscope" created a series of patterns such as revolving bars and rings and dissolving colors, which could be seen on the exterior of the dome. It was the largest projection of abstract color patterns ever attempted. This building and the Palace of Fine Arts were the only ones whose interiors were lit at night, but the doors and windows of all the main palaces glowed from the light of orange-tinted lamps.

Three times a week, the "Scintillator," a battery of forty-eight searchlights with changeable color filters, was set up in a corner of the harbor. Against the fog of San Francisco Bay or, on clear nights, steam from a stationary passenger locomotive, rays of light delighted the crowds with different motifs such as Scotch Plaid, Ghost Dance, and Fighting Serpents.

It comes as no surprise that the Panama-Pacific was most appreciated for its nighttime appearance. The poet Edwin Markham cabled the following to the *New York Times*: "I have tonight seen the greatest revelation of beauty that was even seen on earth. I say this, meaning it literally and with full regard for all that is known of ancient art and architecture, and all that the modern world has heretofore seen of glory and grandeur. I have seen beauty that will give the world new standards of art and a joy in loveliness never before reached. This is what I have seen—the courts and buildings of the Panama-Pacific Exposition illuminated at night." (Markham)

K. B. / D. N.

2010 TOWER OF JEWELS AND GENERAL VIEW OF THE GROUNDS, BY NIGHT, PANAMA-PACIFIC INTERNATIONAL EXPOSITION, SAN FRANCISCO, 1915.

Overleaf:

1 Palace of Horticulture, postcard, 1915

2 Tower of Jewels and Manufacturers' Building, postcard, 1915

3 Exposition, bird's-eye view, postcard, 1915

2004 PALACE OF HORTICULTURE, BY NIGHT.
PANAMA-PACIFIC INTERNATIONAL EXPOSITION,
SAN FRANCISCO, 1915.

1

2

Wrigley Building · Chicago, Illinois · 1921

Architects: **Graham, Anderson, Probst & White (designer: Charles Beersman)**

Location: **400 North Michigan Avenue**

Construction Dates: **1919–21, 1924–25. Extant**

Installation Dates: **1921, 1933, 1982. The building is currently floodlit with its most powerful installation to date.**

Installation Type: **Original installation: Incandescent floodlights. 198 500-watt lamps, 16 250-watt lamps. Revolving beacon on top. Later installations added to the number of projectors. 1980s installation: 118 1,000-watt halide lights on Wacker Drive. 17th and 19th floors and top: 16 500-watt quartz lights. River Plaza Building: 16 1,000-watt quartz lights.**

Lighting Designer: **Original installation: James B. Darlington, Superintendent of the Wrigley Building**

Wrigley Building with its 1924–25 extension and the Chicago Tribune Building in the background, postcard, c. 1929

Wrigley Building, floodlighting equipment, c. 1921

Wrigley Building, before the 1924–25 extension, photograph, c. 1921 >

Selected Bibliography:

"Architecture and Illumination: A Notable Example in the Wrigley Building, Chicago." *Architectural Forum* 35 (October 1921): 135.

"The Wrigley Building at Night." *Architecture and Building* 53, no. 12 (December 1921): 95–97.

"Wrigley Building Floodlighted Ten Times Former Intensity." *Electrical World* 102 (22 July 1933): 105.

Chappell, Sally A. Kitt. "As if the Lights Were Always Shining: Graham, Anderson, Probst and White's Wrigley Building at the Boulevard Link." *Chicago Architecture 1872–1922*, ed. John Zukowsky. Munich: Prestel, 1987.

Chappell, Sally A. Kitt. *Architecture and Planning of Graham, Anderson, Probst and White, 1913–1936: Transforming Tradition.* Chicago: University of Chicago, 1992.

Wagner, Martin. *Amerikanische Bauwirtschaft.* Berlin: Vorwärts, 1925: 14.

124—Wrigley Buildings and River by Night, Chicago

The new building for the Wrigley Company on Michigan Avenue marked the extension of Chicago's business district north across the river in accordance with Daniel Burnham's 1909 Plan for Chicago. Other firms soon followed and the Wrigley Company itself commissioned an extension only three years after the original building had been completed. The brilliant white illumination of the building was the result of William Wrigley Jr.'s desire for a lighting installation that would surpass anything that had been attempted up to that time. The installation also served to publicize an advertising campaign for his most important product, a peppermint flavored chewing gum, with which the qualities of freshness and health were associated. The tower became the first major building in Chicago to be floodlit at night and was touted as the world's most complete illumination of a single structure. Clad in terra-cotta, the thirty-four-story skyscraper's facade was finished in six shades of gray and cream, gradually growing lighter as it reached the top. This variation in tone was matched by the floodlighting, which increased in intensity at the upper stories. Banks of floodlights were installed on nearby buildings as well as on the setback and on three levels of the Wrigley Building itself, where special pockets were constructed solely to hold the lighting equipment. The ornamentation of the tower, one of the many references to Seville's Giralda that were popular on American skyscrapers during the 1920s, was brought out by bulbs of lesser wattage than those that shone on the facade. A revolving beacon was also located at this topmost part of the tower. The building's illumination was widely published around the world, not necessarily to universal acclaim. Berlin' socialist city planner Martin Wagner scolded his enthusiastic colleagues after a visit in 1927: "When they stand in front of a skyscraper and admire the enormous boldness of the human spirit, then they should also know who has mastered this spirit, and they will come across one of the dollar kings, who can afford to have his fifty-story building illuminated by batteries of searchlights because he found innumerable men and women, who bought his chewing gum from him and now go about their daily business chewing chewing gum." (Wagner)

The Wrigley Company had the entire building washed several times a year to keep it from being darkened and discolored by the

city's grime. In 1933, during the depths of the Depression, the floodlighting load was actually doubled as the illumination was found to be such an effective advertising tool. Except for a few short periods, the building has remained brightly illumined, with a new and more powerful lighting installation added in the 1980s.

K. B. / D. N.

Brazil Centennial Exposition · Rio de Janeiro · 1922

Dates: **September 7, 1922–July 31, 1923**

Selected Architects: **Carlos Sampaio (President of Exposition Commission): Layout
Memoria and Cuchet, Palace of Industries
Frank L. Packard: American Pavilion
Armando de Oliveira: Fisheries Building
Morales de los Rios Filho: Agricultural Building, Entrance to the Amusement Park.
Sylvio Rebecchi: Administration Building**

Lighting Designers: **Walter D'Arcy Ryan, A. F. Dickerson (assistant engineer), J. W. Gosling (decorative designer), all with General Electric.**

1922 Rio de Janeiro, Brazil Centennial Exposition. North Garden. Night view with Walter D'Arcy Ryan's "Scintillator," contemporary graphic

Photograph, 1922, by Bippus © Instituto Moreira Salles, Rio de Janeiro/São Paolo, Brazil >

Photograph, 1922, by Thiele-Kollien © Instituto Moreira Salles, Rio de Janeiro / São Paolo, Brazil >

The international festival and exhibition that celebrated one hundred years of Brazil's independence was the first of its kind in South America. It was also the first time that the newest achievements in exhibition lighting were presented outside of North America and Europe.

The fifty-five acres of exhibition grounds were divided into a Brazilian and an International section for the twenty-two participating foreign countries. Here, a rather broad range of historicist styles was used to signify the essential architectural characteristics of each country. The French Pavilion, a replica of the Petit Trianon, remained after the exhibition as the permanent home of the Brazilian Academy of Arts and Letters; the American Pavilion became the residence of the American Ambassador. The architecture of the Brazilian part referred stylistically to its own architectural development from Portuguese colonial architecture, alluding to the time period of Brazil's struggle for independence.

During the preparation for the exhibition, Rio de Janeiro embarked on an urban planning scheme that was as radical as anything Le Corbusier would suggest shortly afterwards. A densely built area in downtown Rio, Castle Hill, was entirely razed to make room for further development and to relieve traffic congestion. The material taken from Castle Hill was used to create additional new land in the bay. The exhibition took place partially on the newly created land in the bay, partially on the grounds of the former Castle Hill. (Ironically, fifteen years later, Le Corbusier would be involved, with Lucio Costa and Oscar Niemeyer, in one of the first modern high-rise projects in the former Castle Hill area, the Ministry of Education.) This adaptation of contemporary town planning went hand in hand with other gestures to demonstrate Brazil's embracing of modernity, especially a nocturnal lighting scheme at the exposition to equal any of its North American predecessors. The dean of American lighting designers, Walter D'Arcy Ryan, was invited, following his successful work at the Panama-Pacific Exposition (pp. 104–107). Ryan worked with the same team that had assisted him in San Francisco. A scintillator cast rays of colored light into the sky on special occasions, 40,000 "Novagem" Jewels graced the Palace of States, and the general lighting was based on Ryan's development of floodlighting from hidden sources. Rose, red and orange were used for relief lighting in contrast to white lights, and masses of solid color. The Ilha de Fiscal, a small island with a Neo-gothic customs house half a mile offshore, was bathed in soft colors, surrounded by scarlet colored palm trees. Contemporary visitors described the "charming vistas … at night when the buildings are set off by their brilliant illumination." (Curtis) Most buildings were predominantly white with only a few color accents. Walter D'Arcy Ryan himself claimed that the lighting features in Rio de Janeiro "surpass in certain respects any illuminated spectacle heretofore created." (Ryan)   D. N.

Selected Bibliography:

Bianco, Francesco. "La Celebrazione del Centenario Brasiliano." *Nuova Antologia* 219 (16 August 1922): 348–356.

Curtis, John P. "Architecture of the Brazil Centennial Exposition." *Art and Archaeology* 16, no. 3 (September 1923): 95–104.

Guia Official da Exposição do Centenario. Rio de Janeiro: Editado Pelo, 1922.

Ryan, Walter D'Arcy. "Illumination of the Brazilian Centennial Exposition." *Transactions of the Illuminating Engineering Society* 17 (October 1922): 475–477.

"American Engineers to Design Brazilian Centennial Lighting." *Electrical World* 78 (12 November 1921): 991.

"Brilliant Lighting Planned for Brazil's Exposition." *Electrical World* 80 no. 6 (5 August 1922).

Sisson, Rachel. "Rio de Janeiro, 1875–1945: The Shaping of a New Urban Order." *Journal of Decorative and Propaganda Arts* 21 (1995): 137–155.

McJunkin Building · Chicago, Illinois · 1924

Architects: **Marshall & Fox, Arthur U. Gerber**

Location: **4554 North Broadway (corner of Broadway & Wilson Avenue)**

Construction Date: **1923. Extant**

Installation Date: **1924. The building is currently not illuminated.**

Installation Type: **Incandescent floodlights. Balcony: 150 500-watt lamps, half with sanded blue lenses and half with clear red lenses; 43 250-watt lamps with white sanded lenses. Cornice: 60-watt amber lamps. Flashers to change the lighting effects.**

Lighting Designer: **Edwin D. Tillson**

McJunkin Building, balcony for floodlights, photograph, *c.* 1924

McJunkin Building, night view, photograph, *c.* 1924

Selected Bibliography:

"Color Lighting Makes Building Exteriors Attractive." *Electrical World* 84 (22 November 1924): 1090.

"The Flood Lighting of the New McJunkin Building, Chicago." *Light* (June 1924): 10.

Gerber, Arthur U. and Edwin D. Tillson. "Color Flood Lighting of Buildings." *Transactions of the Illuminating Engineering Society* 19, no. 6 (July 1924): 518–530.

Tillson, Edwin D. "Color Lighting for Building Exteriors." *Electrical World* 84 (22 November 1924): 1091–1094.

Tillson, Edwin D. "Why Did They Use Colored Lights?" *Light* (June 1924): 8–9.

The McJunkin Building, a long, low, commercial edifice with classically inspired details and cream-colored terra-cotta cladding, was un-remarkable as both a building type and a work of architecture. Today it stands entirely forgotten on a street corner in a somewhat uninviting part of Chicago. For the history of architectural illumination, however, this build-ing is of prime importance, as it was the "first permanent color-lighted building." W. D. McJunkin wanted to have the "best lighted building in the country" and initiated the early contacts between the architect Arthur U. Gerber and Edwin Tillson of the Edison Company. Extensive tests about color shadows with a large model were conducted. The lighting engineer Tillson explained that the use of different colors made it easier to illuminate a lively facade with niches and reveals and made the architectural details more pronounced and readable. Gerber stated that he had actually changed the architectural design in order to better adapt it to the floodlighting scheme of Tillson. A balcony was specially designed solely to hold the illuminating equip-ment and from it, very bright white lights were projected onto the pilasters. Between these pilasters, the recessed panels were lit at the bottom with blue lights that gradually merged with red in the upper portion, creating a sequence of purple shades which were further varied by flashers that turned on and off at varying intervals. Additionally, a string of amber bulbs outlined the cornice, lighting this section of the building more brilliantly than that below and thereby creating, along with a line of the same lights at the second floor level under the balcony, a bold delineation of the entire construction. The result was an installation that recalled the common use of outline lighting in the early years of illumination, yet also served as a harbinger of the color floodlighting effects that were to dominate the next decade and a half. The success of the building was recognized when it hosted in the year of its completion a joint meeting between the Chicago section of the Illuminating Engineering Society and the Western Society of Engineers. K. B. / D. N.

San Joaquin Light and Power Corporation Building · Fresno, California · 1924

Like many other utility companies of its time, the San Joaquin Light and Power Corporation used floodlighting both to call attention to its new building and to encourage other businesses to do the same. Together with the McJunkin Building (see opposite) and a few other examples, the San Joaquin Light and Power Corp. Building pioneered the application of colored floodlights in the United States. It was locally considered the "most beautifully illuminated building in the world" (Frost). Illuminating engineers H. H. Courtright and Carl F. Wolff used the colored lighting at the 1915 Panama-Pacific Exposition (pp. 104–107) in San Francisco as a model. In fact, the building was quickly dubbed the "Fresno Tower of Jewels," after the famous tower of the Panama-Pacific. The building's design readily divided into four zones, which could be illuminated individually. The lowest part was lit only from within by lights in the lobby and by colored illumination in the display windows. The lighting of the three upper

zones was accomplished by banks of floodlights concealed on the surface of the building itself, which was faced with terra-cotta and brick.

Forty-eight color schemes were developed, with such hues as magenta, emerald and mauve, and with the separately lit areas, several hundred combinations could be achieved. An eight-foot electric sign advertising the building was also fitted to the roof and could be set to flash on and off or to spell out the company's name one letter at a time. Finally, in the most attention-getting aspect of an already theatrically lit building, twenty-one cauldrons were set into the tenth-floor promenade, from which steam issued forth that could be lit in various colors. The building's stunning illumination drew raves from contemporary writers: "Fairy tales once convinced me that there was a pot of gold at the end of the rainbow. Facts ... have proven that the new home of the San Joaquin Light & Power Corporation is located at its long sought tip." (*Light*, p. 9) K. B.

Architect: **Raymond R. Shaw**

Location: **1401 Fulton Street**

Construction Date: **1923**

Installation Date: **1924. The building is no longer illuminated.**

Installation Type: **Incandescent floodlights. 84 1,000-watt and 250-watt lamps on roof of marquee above 1st floor, 112 250-watt lamps on colonnade above 8th floor, 21 250-watt lamps on 10th floor; lamps on all floors holding colored lenses. 21 urns with steam jets and 250-watt lamps on 10th floor. Four roof corners lit with 500-watt lamps.
680 25-watt bulbs in electric sign on roof.**

Lighting Designers: **H. H. Courtright, Walter D'Arcy Ryan, and Carl F. Wolff.**

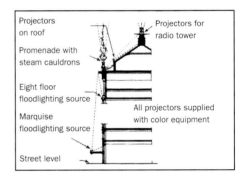

San Joaquin, lighting diagram, *c.* 1930

San Joaquin Light & Power Corporation, postcard, *c.* 1924
© Curt Teich Postcard Archives, Lake County (IL) Discovery Museum

Selected Bibliography:

"Spectacular Color Floodlighting." *Electrical World* 94, no. 3 (1929): 140–141.

Fellows, J. Worthington. "Fresno – At the end of the Rainbow." *Light* (August 1924): 9–10.

Frost, A. M. "Commercial Possibilities of Color Flood-Lighting." *Journal of Electricity* 54, no. 10 (15 May 1925): 351–355.

American Radiator Building · New York, New York · 1924

Architects: **Raymond Hood and André Fouilhoux**

Location: **40 West 40th Street**

Construction Date: **1924**

Installation Date: **1924. The building is currently illuminated with white lights.**

Installation Type: **56 incandescent floodlighting projectors: 8 1,000-watt units on the 21st floor, 15 500-watt units on the 22nd floor, 24 500-watt units on the 24th floor, and 8 1,000-watt units on the roof.**

Lighting Designer: **Bassett Jones**

Selected Bibliography:

"Editorial Comment." *American Architect* 126 (19 November 1924): 487.

"Raymond Hood Predicts 'Architecture of the Night.'" *Magazine of Light* (May 1930): 39.

Duvert, Elizabeth. "Georgia O'Keeffe's Radiator Building: Icon of Glamorous Gotham," *Places: A Journal of Environmental Design: 2*, no. 2 (1985): 3–17.

Hood, Raymond. "The American Radiator Company Building, New York." *American Architect and Architectural Review* 126 (November 1924): 466–474.

Hood, Raymond. "Let's Buy some Daylight Too." *Light* (April 1925): 8–9, 52, 54.

Jones, Bassett. "Structures in Light." *Light* (April 1924): 6.

Kroly, Herbert. "New Dimensions in Architectural Effects." *Architectural Review* 57 (January 1925): 94.

Stern, Robert A.M., *Raymond Hood: Pragmatism and Poetics in the Waning of the Metropolitan Era*. New York, Rizzoli, 1982.

Designed shortly after Hood's and Howells' Chicago Tribune Tower (pp. 142–143) and built at the same time, the American Radiator Building was a serious attempt at an architecture *parlante*. While still employing the Neo-Gothic forms of the previous building, the daring selection of black and gold colors ensured that this building stood out in the increasingly crowded Manhattan landscape and evoked the company's products.

Although Hood had already suggested nocturnal illumination for the Chicago Tribune Tower, and was to become an ardent promoter of an "Architecture of the Night" a few years later, he was equally aware of the need for natural light and in 1925 wrote an essay for a publication of the lighting industry defending daylight, and mildly poking fun at his illumination engineering friends, who were dreaming of windowless buildings artificially lit twenty-four hours a day (*Light*, 1925). Instead, he presented a vision of thin office towers for New York, slender enough to allow daylight at every desk. Typologically, the American Radiator Building is one of those slender towers. Nevertheless, it also became one of the first skyscrapers where detailed experiments for the artistic possibilities of architectural illumination were carried out, and it suggested to contemporary architects "bewildering possibilities as to the future use of surfaces with colors, glows, and lights in order to convert the high places of New York, as seen from distant streets, into a wonderland of elaborate, fanciful, and vivid masses and patterns." (*Architectural Review*, 1925). While the black brick was the least ideal surface for the reflection of floodlight, the golden ornamentation at the top stood out even more splendidly in contrast.

Hood remembered: "We tried multi-colored revolving lights and produced at one time the effect of the building's being on fire. We threw spots of light on jets of steam rising out of the smokestack. Then again, with moving lights, we had the whole top of the building waving like a tree in a strong wind. With cross-lighting, that is to say, lighting from different sources and different directions across the same forms, the most unusual cubistic patterns were developed. All of this, however, was experimental, as we did not feel that either our knowledge of the art or the perception of the public was at a point, where it would be wise to attempt extravagant and exotic effects." (*Magazine of Light*, 1930). The lighting designer Bassett Jones wrote: "My mental picture of this building at night would result from pouring over the structure a vast barrel of spectral hued incandescent material that streams down the perpendicular surfaces, cooling as it falls, and, like glowing molten lava, collects in every recess and behind every parapet." This was to be achieved with rose, scarlet and amber color screens. Slightly less dramatic, the eventually executed lighting scheme included uniform amber light from fifty-six incandescent floodlighting units placed in growing numbers from the twenty-first floor upwards. The result was still impressive enough to inspire Georgia O'Keefe's famous painting in 1927 (p. 74). The *American Architect* reported in 1924 that the illumination had attracted and held the attention of thousands who ordinarily give little heed to street architecture. "The appearance of the building at night is one of the sights of the city.... The vast throngs that crowd this district at night are blocking traffic...." (*American Architect*, 1924)   D.N.

American Radiator Building, painting by Birch B. Long, 1927

American Radiator Building, photograph by Samuel H. Gottscho, *c.* 1927 >

Exposition Internationale des Arts Décoratifs et Industriels Modernes · Paris · 1925

Dates: April 25–October 25, 1925

Architects: **Charles Plumet: General Plan, Palais des Métiers (with Michel Roux-Spitz), Exhibition Towers**
Le Corbusier and Pierre Jeanneret: Pavillon de l'Esprit Nouveau
Henri Sauvage: Pavillon Primavera du Printemps
Konstantin Melnikov: USSR Pavilion
Josef Hoffmann: Austrian Pavilion
Peter Behrens: Austrian Pavilion Conservatory
Josep Gocar: Czech Pavilion
Victor Horta: Belgian Pavilion
Robert Mallet-Stevens: Cubistic Garden, Tourism Pavilion
Louis-Hippolyte Boileau: Porte d'Orsay, Bon Marché Pavilion
P. Patout: Pavilion of the Sèvres Porcelain Manufacturing Co., Monumental Entrance at the Place de la Concorde
Tony Garnier: Pavillon de Lyon et Saint-Étienne
P. V. Bailly, G. Saaké & J. Lambert: Pavillon des Diamantaires
G. & A. Perret: Pavillon des Editions Albert Lévy, Théâtre (with André Granet)
René Lalique and Marc Ducluzaud: Lalique Fountain

Lighting Designers: **Dilly, Fernand Jacopozzi, Vedovelli**

Eiffel Tower with Citroën sign, photograph, 1925

Pavillon des Diamantaires, photograph, 1925

P. Patout: Pavilion of the Sèvres Porcelain Manufacturing Co.

Pavillon des Magasins du Bon Marché, photograph, 1925

Selected Bibliography:

Atherton, C. A. "The Present Lighting Renaissance in France." *Light* (December 1925): 13–15.

Boutteville, R. "La Distribution de l'Énergie Électrique à l'Exposition Internationale des Arts Décoratifs et Industriels Modernes." *Revue Generale de l'Electricité* 19, no. 1 (1926): 13–22.

Boyer, Jacques. "Les Fontaines Lumineuses de l'Exposition des Arts Décoratifs." *La Nature* 53, pt. 2 (5 September 1925): 150–154.

C., H. de. "A General View." *Architectural Review* 58 (July 1925): 3–19.

Curchod, A. "Les Illuminations 'Hydroélectriques' à l'Exposition Internationale des Arts Décoratifs et Industriels Modernes." *Revue Générale de l'Electricité* 18 (3 October 1925): 572–578.

Gronberg, Tag. "Cascades of Light: The 1925 Paris Exhibition as Ville Lumière." *Apollo* 142.1 (July 1995): 12–16.

Harriss, Joseph. *The Tallest Tower: Eiffel and the Belle Epoque*. Washington DC: Regnery Gateway, 1975.

Rather than a universal exposition of arts and industry, the Exposition des Arts Décoratifs et Industriels Modernes was an attempt to reestablish France as a leader in the world of art and design. (Its name was later adapted for the term 'Art Deco.') Located along the Avenue Alexandre III and the Esplanade des Invalides, the exposition was smaller in scope than previous ones held in Paris.

While a large number of prominent modern European architects were involved in the exhibition, and the starkly modern Pavillon de l'Esprit Nouveau by Le Corbusier and the Soviet Pavilion by Konstantin Melnikov are today perhaps the best known representatives of this fair, they were by no means typical. Although many of the buildings used simple shapes and avoided direct eclecticism, many commercial pavilions of French manufacturers and department stores indulged in rich layers of ornamentation, which seemed to draw upon Egyptian and Mayan motifs (due to spectacular recent archaeological discoveries) as well as trends in Austrian and French decorative art movements.

Instead of American-style floodlighting, the Paris designers developed a new form of indirect outline lighting where incandescent lamps, partially covered with reflective metal paint, were installed in curved reflectors and responded carefully to the architectural requirements. Even a representative of General Electric had to admit that this deliberately modest alternative to the rich American illuminations was "perhaps more suited to the general purposes of the Nouveau Art movement." (Atherton, p. 14).

Some structures, such as the Entrée de la Concorde, were partially lit by spotlights. In the case of the Pavillon de la Manufacture de Sèvres, a grazing light was used. Concealed under the cornice, incandescent lamps behind opal glass illuminated most of the facade in a gradual manner, gently fading from the top to the bottom.

Other buildings glowed from within, thanks to lights shining through semi-opaque glass, such as the small Pavillon des Diamantaires, whose faceted dome echoed Bruno Taut's Glass Pavilion of 1914. Colored glass, also illuminated from within, marked several exposition buildings, in particular the galleries on the Esplanade des Invalides. A set of pillars was erected in the formal gardens on either side of the main court. Painted a purplish-red, they were lit by neon lamps, while their glass tops were illumined from within by the stronger red light of incandescent lamps, to striking effect.

As was customary for Parisian expositions dating back to 1889, the Eiffel Tower was given a special lighting design, albeit one that appears oddly commercial to modern eyes. The Italian lighting designer Fernand Jacopozzi created an installation utilizing 250,000 lights in six colors, programmed to flash on and off in sequence. They made the tower come alive with moving depictions of stars and other celestial objects, as well as signs of the zodiac. Automobile magnate André Citroën paid for this installation in return for the inclusion of his company's name and logo as one of the displays. An enormous success, the lighting scheme would be revised and expanded upon continuously until 1935 when Citroën finally withdrew his funding.

Luminous fountains also played an important role at the fair. René Lalique designed a crystal tower composed of sculpted glass plates, illuminated from within by colored lights. In addition to fountains on pontoons in the Seine, lit by colored incandescent lamps, a particularly spectacular installation known as the Rideau d'Eau was to be found on the Pont Alexandre III. A system of pipes was installed on each side of the bridge, through which water was pumped from the Seine and then forced out through thousands of tiny holes. With colored incandescent lamps projected onto the falling water, the effect was that of a "luminous rain" (Curchod, p. 574). One architectural critic echoed the comments of Julius Meyer-Graefe at the 1900 fair: "The whole place is fairer at night for night, like trees, hides and unifies. The illumination is well done, throwing up simple and impressive masses where daylight would reveal a cheap ornament or a thoughtless moulding." (H. de C., p. 6)   K. B. / D. N.

Pacific Gas and Electric Company · San Francisco, California · 1925

Architects: **Bakewell and Brown. Renovation: Page and Trumbull**

Location: **245 Market Street**

Construction Dates: **1924–25. Renovation: 1995**

Installation Date: **1925. The building is no longer illuminated.**

Installation Type: **Incandescent floodlights. 14th floor: 27 1,000-watt lamps mounted on each side of bases of columns. 16th floor: 36 1,000-watt lamps on balustrade. 62 projectors were mounted on the roofs across Market and Beale Streets.**

Lighting Designer: **C. Felix Butte, Hunter and Hudson**

Pacific Gas and Electric Company on Market Street's "Path of Gold," *c.* 1925

Pacific Gas and Electric Company, photograph, *c.* 1925

Selected Bibliography:

"Floodlighting in the Old World and the New." *Electrical Record* (May 1929): 72–73.

"Selling Floodlighting." *National Electric Light Association-Marketing Electricity Series*, no. 1 (1930): 1–21.

Phelan, Roy N. "Details of Several New Floodlighted Buildings in San Francisco." *Journal of Electricity* 55, no. 11 (1925): 402–407.

Spencer, Clifford W. "Practical Floodlighting." *Architectural Forum* 53 (November 1930): 627–634.

The seventeen-story headquarters of the powerful San Francisco Pacific Gas and Electric Company was opened in 1925, in time for the seventy-fifth anniversary celebration of California's admission to the Union. The building's illumination was a key component in the spectacular urban lighting festival for this occasion. As at the Panama-Pacific Exposition in 1915 (pp. 104–107), Walter D'Arcy Ryan was invited to design the general concept, which included a special illumination of City Hall (built ten years earlier by the same architects), a Triumphal Arch covered in 40,000 Novagem Jewels, colored searchlight displays and a pair of radio panchromatic fountains, whose colored lights and movements could react to radio signals and accompany any music that was played.

The two main facades of the Pacific Gas and Electric Company, which is placed on a corner lot, were illuminated from neighboring structures with sixty-two floodlights. Lighting designer Felix Butte made sure that none of the floodlighting reached the street level to avoid blinding drivers and pedestrians. All floodlights were equipped with attachments for the occasional use of color screens. Above the fourteenth floor began the more dramatic lighting on the building itself. A shallow setback with a two-story columnar arcade allowed for the installation of twenty-six floodlights accompanying the columns with steep vertical lights. The next setback at the sixteenth floor held thirty-six floodlights behind its parapet. The classical details of the top floors had been greatly simplified in anticipation of the floodlighting from below.

The renovation in 1995, following the Loma Prieta earthquake, turned the building into one of the most energy efficient structures in California and it won not only a preservation award, but also an award for energy conservation. The original floodlighting has not been used in recent years.   K. B. / D. N.

Pacific Telephone and Telegraph Company Building · San Francisco, California · 1925

The elegant and slender twenty-six-story building was considered one of the premier skyscrapers to be built in San Francisco's boom time during the '20s and one of the crowning achievements of the rebuilding efforts after the devastating earthquake of 1906. It was also one of the first skyscrapers in the U.S. to adopt the rigorous verticalism that Eliel Saarinen had introduced with his second placed entry for the *Chicago Tribune* (pp. 142–143) Competition. "This skyscraper graphically indicates the trend of business architecture from the ornate and rococo styles of former years to designs in which simplicity is tempered with a rugged beauty essentially western in character," wrote the *San Francisco Newsletter* in September of 1925. Lighting engineers considered it "an ideal subject for floodlighting" and a splendid example of a successful collaboration between lighting designer, architect and the building industry. After extensive testing, the terra-cotta sheathing of the building had been carefully selected with the intended floodlighting in mind. As a result it was published again and again in the reports about new floodlighting applications.

In contrast to the Pacific Gas and Electric Company Building (see opposite), which went up at the same time in San Francisco, the entire facade of the building was not illuminated, but instead only setbacks above the nineteenth, twenty-third and twenty-sixth floors, isolating the top of the building at night. The lower corner setbacks, applied here in such clarity for the first time, served as platforms for a group of floodlights in order to visually tie the illuminated crown to the building—soon a very popular motive. All floodlighting equipment was installed directly on the building itself and shielded from view behind parapets, urns and finials, provided by the building's gothicizing style. Due to the asymmetrical form of the building, each side required a different number of floodlights.

D. N.

Architects: **James R. Miller and Timothy Pflueger, with AA Cantin**

Location: **134 New Montgomery Street**

Construction Dates: **1924–25**

Installation Date: **1925. The building is no longer illuminated.**

Installation Type: **Incandescent floodlights. 139 1,000-watt lamps, 33 500-watt lamps, and 111 200-watt lamps. Floodlights installed on three corners above the 19th floor, and on all four sides at the setbacks above the 23rd and 26th floors. Additional floodlights for the tower and flag illumination.**

Lighting Designers: **Simonson and St. John (electrical engineers). Arthur Fryklund, C. Felix Butte.**

Pacific Telephone and Telegraph Building, night view, photograph, c. 1925. Collection Centre Canadien d'Architecture / Canadian Center for Architecture, Montréal

Pacific Telephone and Telegraph Building, day view, photograph, c. 1925

Selected Bibliography:

"Building Floodlighting and Its Possibilities with Terra Cotta" National Terra Cotta Society: New York 19 West 44th Street, 1927.

Phelan, Roy N. "Details of Several New Floodlighted Buildings in San Francisco." *Journal of Electricity* 55, no. 11 (1925): 402–407

Smith, Richard C. "The News Letter and the Telephone." *San Francisco Newsletter* (Diamond Jubilee Edition, September 1925).

Paramount Theater Building · New York, New York · 1926

Architects: **Rapp & Rapp**

Location: **1501 Broadway**

Construction Date: **1926. Extant**

Installation Date: **1926. The glass ball and the flood-lights on the setbacks were re-illuminated in 1998.**

Installation Type: **473 incandescent floodlights on setbacks from the 19th story to the top, including 70 250-watt, 365 500-watt and 38 100-watt lamps. Stud lighting on hands and minute points of clocks in tower. Flashing white and red lights inside 19-foot glass ball at top.**

Lighting Designers: **Rapp & Rapp**

Paramount Building, postcard, *c.* 1926

Paramount Building, photograph, *c.* 1926 >

Selected Bibliography:

"Dome Atop Skyscraper Throws Light to Suburbs." *Transactions of the Illuminating Engineering Society* 22, no. 6 (July 1927): 601–602.

"Floodlighting the new Paramount Building." *Transactions of the Illuminating Engineering Society* 21 (November 1926): 959.

"Paramount Tower Adds 35,000,000 c.p. to the Great White Way." *Electrical World* 90, no. 20 (12 November 1927): 985.

Mumford, Lewis. "Magnified Impotence." *New Republic* 49 (22 December 1926): 138–140.

Rapp, George L. "Character in Architecture Emphasized at Night." In "Architecture of the Night." *General Electric Company, Bulletin* GED-375 (February 1930).

Stern, Robert A. M., Gregory Gilmartin and Thomas Mellins. *New York 1930* (New York: Rizzoli, 1987).

T-Square. "The Sky Line." *New Yorker* 2 (27 November 1926): 80–82.

With its distinctive ziggurat form the Paramount Theater Building instantly became a character-istic feature of the New York City skyline. It combined the most opulent movie theater of its day with a twenty-nine-story office building. The exterior lighting design had to compete with the flood of lights at Times Square as well as live up to the extravagance of the theater within. Architect George L. Rapp, who special-ized in movie theaters, was well versed in the art of interior illumination and included exterior floodlighting as a component of his designs. He argued that a building should "always be the same in composition, both night and day" (Rapp, 1930), and that the lighting design should complement the lines of the architec-ture. Here it even helped to shape the build-ing's form. While the many setbacks above the nineteenth floor might have seemed a rather literal response to the New York Zoning Code, they were in fact intended to hold and shield from view 473 floodlighting projectors, the largest installation of its kind.

In addition to the floodlighting, the tower included large clocks whose hands and minute points were studded with lights. The theater's most notable nighttime feature, however, was the sphere that surmounted the tower, suggesting the global reach of Famous Players Lasky Corporation. Consisting of ninety squares of glass and spanning nineteen feet in diameter, this ball was illuminated from within by high-intensity lamps that were used to indicate the time: a corresponding number of white flashes noted the hour, while red flashes marked the quarter hour. The globe could also be made to glow steadily for special occasions and was visible from as far as New Jersey and Long Island. The *New Yorker* ridiculed it as "an incinerator for the ashes of departed movies." (*New Yorker*, 1926)

While critics such as Lewis Mumford considered the building's architecture "a grandiose nightmare" (Mumford, 1926), the general public saw in it "a dream of gorgeousness." (Stern, 256) Rapp predicted the development of even more dramatic lighting effects, such as illuminated clouds of smoke in different colors, towers of light illuminated from within or "shafts equipped with mirrors and having colored light thrown on the mirrors from various angles." (Rapp, 1930)

K. B. / D. N.

Sesqui-Centennial International Exposition · Philadelphia, Pennsylvania · 1926

Dates: **May 30–November 30, 1926**

Selected Architects: **John Molitor, Supervising Architect: Tower of Light and most exhibition palaces. Ralph B. Bencker: Pennsylvania State Building**

Color Scheme: **W. DeL. Dodge**

Lighting Designer: **Samuel G. Hibben**

Tower of Light as originally planned (John Molitor), drawing, c. 1924

Palace of Liberal Arts & Manufactures, photograph, 1926 >

Liberty Bell replica, covered with 26,000 light bulbs, postcard, 1926 >

Selected Bibliography:

"A Luminous 'Liberty Bell.'" *Electrical World* 87 (5 June 1926): 1259.

"Fair to Celebrate Triumph of Invention." *Popular Mechanics* 45 (April 1926): 618–623.

Atwater, D. W. "Lighting the Sesqui-Centennial International Exposition." *Transactions of the Illuminating Engineering Society* 21 (December 1926): 1141–1152.

Austin, E. L. and Odell Hauser. *The Sesqui-Centennial International Exposition* (Philadelphia: Current Publications, 1929); reprint ed. New York: Arno Press, 1976.

Molitor, John. "How the Sesqui-Centennial was Designed." *American Architect* 130, no. 2508 (5 November 1926): 377–382.

The Sesqui-Centennial International Exposition, Philadelphia, June First to December First, 1926. Philadelphia: Franklin Trust Co., 1926.

The Sesqui-Centennial Exposition in Philadelphia was the first major American exposition to take place in over a decade, following the Panama-Pacific of 1915 (pp. 104–107). On a 450-acre site in South Philadelphia, this fair offered views of America's national past and encounters with its newest technological achievements such as a stadium for 100,000 visitors, the first talking motion pictures and radio announcements throughout the fair. Illumination played a vital role in the overall design, aiding greatly in the determination of the final appearance of its buildings.

As the fair was held in honor of the 150th anniversary of the signing of the Declaration of Independence, the architectural scheme took inspiration from the colonial period. A "High Street" showing colonial Philadelphia was a great success. As this style did not suit the large scale of the exhibition halls, however, supervising architect John Molitor, who designed all major buildings, developed a more modern approach that he considered to be distinctly American, employing elements of the setbacks seen in contemporary skyscrapers. Although turrets, columns and other embellishments were included, the overall scheme emphasized simplicity, with broad, unornamented walls that were relieved by a textured stucco surface and by pastel shades of yellow, pink, and salmon.

At night, the exhibition's nickname of "Rainbow City" held true as the main exhibition palaces were washed in floods of color. Because the exposition took place during the hot summer months, the lighting design emphasized cool and dark shades such as blue and green, with amber used for contrast, especially at building entrances. Brighter and more colorful lights were trained on corner towers, which were in turn topped by beacons of high intensity.

Advance publicity promoted the planned Tower of Light, a building type that had been the traditional focus of expositions for decades. Located at a central point, the tiered structure was intended to glow with a silver radiance at night and illuminate the entire grounds, according to one source, or it would be illumined by moving color, each tier being lit and washed out in sequence, according to another. Cost considerations, however, forced the abandonment of these plans when the tower was only half-built. At 150 feet in height, construction was stopped and a huge searchlight was placed on top of the steel structure.

Perhaps the most popular of the illuminated exhibits was the eighty-foot-tall sheet-metal replica of the Liberty Bell that was suspended over the main entrance. The largest electrical structure in the world at that time, the Liberty Bell was covered by 26,000 fifteen-watt colored light bulbs.

Lighting effects for the exposition were employed beyond the fair grounds to include some of the most important buildings in Philadelphia. City Hall was floodlit by 860 lamps in ruby red, with amber radiating from the windows. Cornices were then outlined in red and blue while columns were silhouetted from behind with colors graduating from red at the bottom through purple to blue. The statue of William Penn at the apex of the building was so strongly floodlit, its shadow could be seen superimposed on the clouds above. Independence Hall was also illuminated, but with a brilliant white light, color being judged unsuitable for the historic nature of this structure. Special lighting shows were presented using a battery of fourteen high-intensity searchlights that had been supplied by the United States Army. Furnished with color screens and arrayed along both sides of the exposition grounds, the lights created a display of "fantastic" effects, reminiscent of Walter D'Arcy Ryan's scintillator performances in San Francisco in 1915. The combined intensity of 6,300,000,000-candlepower was the greatest intensity of light ever found in one place up to then.

Philadelphia's Sesqui-Centennial Exposition, although little remembered today, played an important role in the development of the key concepts for urban and exhibition lighting. The use of colored light was just gaining popularity (Philadelphia's own "miracle of color lighting," the Electric Company Tower (p. 128) followed a year later), and the decidedly modern forms of the fair's buildings predated the spectacular combination of colored light and modern architecture at the World's Fairs in 1933 and 1939.

K. B. / D. N.

Pennsylvania Power & Light Company Building · Allentown, Pennsylvania · 1927

Architects: **Helmle, Corbett & Harrison**

Location: **9th and Hamilton Streets**

Construction Dates: **1927–28. Extant**

Installation Dates: **1928, 1983, 1990. The building is currently illuminated.**

Installation Type: **1928: 212 incandescent floodlights with red and amber lenses. 1983: Floodlights replaced by metal halide and high-pressure sodium vapor lamps. 1990 and 1991: Lit from inside through vinyl shades and, later, colored plexiglass with fluorescent tubing and colored reflectors for special holiday lighting designs on the 9th through 20th floors**

Lighting Designer: **Walter D'Arcy Ryan.**

Pennsylvania Power & Light, day view, photograph, c. 1930

Pennsylvania Power & Light, night view, postcard, 1930 >

Selected Bibliography:

"Allentown Trimmings, PP&L Tower to Light Up with Holiday Spirit." *Morning Call* (13 November 1991): 801.

"Allentown's PP&L Building Gets Decorative Lights Back." *Morning Call* (29 June 1991): 804.

"Architecture of the Night." *General Electric Company, Bulletin* GED-375 (February 1930).

"New Pennsylvania Power and Light Building Open for Public Inspection." *Morning Call* (17 July 1928).

"Selling Floodlighting." *National Electric Light Association-Marketing Electricity Series*, no. I-1 (1930): 1–21

Beck, Bill. *PP&L: 75 Years of Powering the Future: An Illustrated History of the Pennsylvania Power & Light Co.* Eden Prairie: Pennsylvania Power & Light Co., 1995.

The headquarters of the Pennsylvania Power & Light Company was Allentown's first skyscraper, a twenty-three-story tower that served as a particularly fine example of architecture and illumination designed in concert. In the typical fashion of the time, vertical piers underlined the upward movement of its facade, and setbacks at the ninth and twentieth stories provided a dynamic rhythm as well as room for the floodlighting equipment. The building was completely illuminated from top to bottom with a combination of red and amber floodlights. The crown was more brightly illumined than the main mass of the structure, producing a shining jewel at the top. This was set off by similar bright lights in the cutaway portion of the corners located at the first setback, effecting a transition from the somewhat darker lower section to the radiant summit. The building department of the Pennsylvania Power & Light Company Building insisted that all shades be drawn when employees left work in the evening, in order to preserve the uniform appearance created by the floodlighting scheme.

It speaks for the importance of this commission that General Electric's top lighting designer Walter D'Arcy Ryan became involved. His collaboration with the two architects Harvey Wiley Corbett and Wallace Harrison turned them both into convinced proponents of nocturnal architectural illumination, and two years later, in 1930, their essays about night lighting appeared next to Ryan's in a publication called "Architecture of the Night" (published by the *Architectural Forum* and General Electric). Corbett's essay especially reflected Ryan's suggestions and the recent experience of their collaboration.

It was vital, Corbett wrote, for architects to integrate floodlighting designs into their original plans: "The form of the illuminated portion should be so tied in with the rest of the building that it should appear as a jewel in a setting, forming a coherent part of the whole structure." The Pennsylvania Power & Light Company Building had utilized just such a design. Thanks to the beauty of the installation and its importance in providing publicity for the company, the tower continued to be floodlit until the energy crisis of the 1970s. In 1983, new energy-efficient lamps were installed, bringing the building back to its former nighttime prominence.   K. B. / D. N.

Renovation of a Commercial Building · Berlin · 1927

Architects: **Luckhardt Brothers and Alfons Anker**

Location: **Tauentzienstrasse 3**

Construction Dates: **1925–27. The facade was added to an existing 19th-century building. The building was destroyed during World War II.**

Installation Date: **1927**

Installation Type: **Incandescent lights behind horizontal metal screens, illuminating light colored strip of wall with advertisement above.**

Lighting Designers: **Luckhardt Brothers and Anker**

During the economically difficult 1920s, building activity in the center of Berlin was widely confined to modernization and enlargement projects of existing buildings. A very important example was the new facade for the business building in Tauentzienstrasse, executed in conjunction with an additional floor by the Luckhardt brothers and their collaborator, Alfons Anker. As with Erich Mendelsohn's contemporaneous Herpich store (p. 130), an illumination scheme was incorporated into the design of the facade as one of its form-giving elements.

Above each floor, incandescent lights were installed behind a metal screen, shining upwards against a light colored horizontal band with brass letters advertising the stores in the building. Thus, the entire facade was effectively divided into a sequence of bright and dark strips. This appearance was heightened by the fact that the horizontal bands were slightly inclined towards the light sources and so ensured that the windows above were kept in darkness.

The facade, which frequently appeared in publications, inspired many similar solutions and was cited by the critics as a positive example of the influence of nocturnal advertising on "a simplification and purification of the facades, especially from pretentious decoration … the recent transformation of business streets in Berlin proves that even advertisements can profit from order and organization, and from being integrated into a clear architectural organism: it loses its noisy aspects, but not its impact…." (Bier)   D. N.

Berlin, Tauentzienstrasse 3, photograph, *c.* 1927

Berlin, Tauentzienstrasse 3, night view, photograph, *c.* 1927

Selected Bibliography:

Bier, Justus. "Über Architektur und Schrift. Zu den Berliner Geschäftshausfassaden der Brüder Luckhardt und Alfons Anker." *Baumeister* 27 (November 1929).

Landsberg, Max. "Lichtreklame und Fassadenarchitektur." *Deutsche Bauzeitung* 61 (1927): 676–679.

Maitland, Waldo. "Modern Lighting." *Journal of the Royal Institute of British Architects* 3rd ser., 42, no. 13 (1935): 753–773.

Nowitzki, Dagmar. *Hans und Wassili Luckhardt: Das architektonische Werk*. Munich: Scaneg Verlag, 1992.

Wendschuh, Achim. *Brüder Luckhardt und Alfons Anker*. Berlin: Akademie der Künste, 1990.

Lichthaus Luz · Stuttgart · 1927

While the famous Weissenhof Settlement was being built on a hill at the edge of the city, the downtown of Stuttgart simultaneously got a number of modern buildings, such as Richard Döcker's Lichthaus Luz, or Otto Oswald's Tagblatt Tower. The strict horizontal layout of the facade, with its wide openings and a protruding bay window, represented a stark image of modernity among its conventional historicist neighbors. At night the horizontal bands of white glass between the windows were partially lit from behind over the full width of the first and second floors. Above those, the luminous bands appeared in the protruding bay windows only. The trademark of Hermann Luz's store, a star, rotated on the roof of the building, outlined in two-colored neon, while a smaller one in white light protruded into the street above the second floor. In many publications about light and architecture in the 1920s, this building was presented as a successful example. Ernst Reinhardt, for example, wrote in the Werkbund's magazine *Form* in 1929: "Döcker has built a commercial building in Stuttgart, where a bay window protrudes from the facade into the street. It consists entirely of transparent glass without any letters.... Light will assume an important role with such glass buildings, a role whose impact and artistic importance we cannot yet estimate today. Solid form will be dissolved, and the impression of such a glass building by night will be that of an overflowing luminous body without firm boundaries." After the National Socialist government assumed power in Germany, and immediately monopolized journalism everywhere, the installation was criticized: "The illumination is added on to the architecture. This has not become a light facade. One should really build towards light, and think with light's potential for appearances and impact." (Gamma). This simple solution, however, had an enormous influence on business architecture all over Europe and the United States in the 1930s.   D. N.

Architect: **Richard Döcker**

Location: **Königstrasse 48**

Construction Date: **1927 (destroyed in WW II)**

Lighting Installation: **1927**

Lighting Type: **Incandescent light bulbs behind white opalescent glass.**

Lighting Designer: **Richard Döcker**

Lichthaus Luz at night, photograph, *c.* 1927

Selected Bibliography:

Gamma, Dr. "Lichtarchitektur." *Deutsche Bauzeitung* (1934): 789–798.

Oechslin, Werner. "Lichtarchitektur." *Moderne Architektur in Deutschland 1900 bis 1950. Expressionismus und Neue Sachlichkeit*. Deutsches Architektur-Museum, Frankfurt / Main, eds. Vittorio Magnago Lampugnani and Romana Schneider. (Stuttgart: Verlag Gerd Hatje, 1994): 117–131.

Reinhardt, Ernst, "Gestaltung der Lichtreklame." *Die Form*, 4, no. 4 (15 February 1929): 73–84.

Schmidt, Gerhardt. "Das baulich modernste Beleuchtungsgeschäft Deutschlands." *Licht und Lampe* (1927): 852.

Philadelphia Electric Company Edison Building · Philadelphia, Pennsylvania · 1927

Architect: **John T. Windrim**

Location: **130 South 9th Street**

Construction Date: **1927. The building is extant and belongs today to Thomas Jefferson University.**

Installation Date: **1927. The building is not currently illuminated.**

Installation Type: **472 500-watt and 48 1,000-watt floodlights, usually placed in groups, one third equipped with white and one third each with different color filters. Mounted on the 15th, 18th and 22nd floors and on the 11th floor roof of an adjacent building. 14 200-watt prismatic vapor-proof units on 23rd-story ledges. 2 18-inch 1,500-watt incandescent searchlights. Dimmer on the 18th floor with 3-speed changes.**

Lighting Designer: **Arthur A. Brainerd, Philadelphia Electric Co.**

Reactive dimmer for floodlights, photograph, 1929

Edison Building, night view, photograph c. 1927
Collection Centre Canadien d'Architecture / Canadian
Center for Architecture, Montréal >

Selected Bibliography:

"Changing-Color Floodlighting for Philadelphia." *Electrical World* 91, no. 18 (5 May 1928): 923.

"Floodlighting the Quaker City Edison Building." *Electrical World* 91 (14 January 1928): 117.

"Philadelphia's 'Tower of Light.'" *Transactions of the Illuminating Engineering Society* 23, no. 3 (March 1928): 229.

"Philadelphia's Lofty Gem of Hue on Hue." *Light* (March–April 1928): 21.

The floodlighting for the Philadelphia Electric Company's Edison Building was turned on for the first time by Thomas Edison himself, who tapped a telegraph key from his home in West Orange, New Jersey on December 31, 1927. One of the earliest installations to use mobile washes of color, the upper nine floors of this twenty-six-story building were illuminated by projectors concealed on the balconies and setbacks of three sides, while those on the fourth side, which had only one narrow balcony, were lit by lamps placed on the roof of an adjacent building. Special caps and lenses were fitted to some of the lamps so that color changes could be easily made. The colors projected onto the building were made to grow and fade in intensity by using white lights on a dimmer that could be set to cycles of thirty seconds, one minute or two minutes. The lamps on each setback were connected to a separate pair of reactors, thereby allowing different cycles for

each section and a panoply of changing hues which included such varied shades as turquoise, purple, orange and pink. The initial lighting on New Year's Eve presented a red crown set on top of a green base in honor of the holiday season and from then on the lighting scheme was changed several times a year. This "miracle of color lighting" inspired one writer to observe, "... when seen at night it is more like a fantastic dream, a rose-red summit supported on green bastions, with long pillars of blue at the corners; like a giant opal, the fire-red glows, to burn slowly to a dazzling whiteness." (*TIES*, March 1928). So successful and novel was this installation, the Philadelphia Electric Company was forced to devise a standardized form to send out in answer to the many requests for information that they received from across the country.

K. B.

First Methodist Episcopal Church of Chicago · Chicago, Illinois · 1927

Many religious congregations in American cities during the 1920s and '30s bemoaned their churches' loss of prominence on the urban skyline against the growing number of commercial buildings. The response, in this case, was an unusual combination of functions ("the revenue church"). The actual church itself occupied the ground floor of Holabird & Roche's Chicago Temple Building, separated from its spire by over twenty stories of business offices, thereby giving it the highest steeple in the country. "Standing 556 feet from street level to the tip of its spire, the Chicago Temple is the second highest building in the world.... It is the highest church in existence, being taller by a liberal margin than any European cathedral. It is also one foot higher than the Washington Monument." (*Chicago Commerce*, 1923.) Behind the elaborate Gothic tracery at the foot of the spire was a "sky-chapel" to be reached by express elevator.

To secure attention at night as well, the church employed an elaborate scheme of architectural illumination. Rather than simply floodlighting this steeple, which might have washed out and overpowered some of its Gothic details, silhouette lighting was used from the roof of the main building to the base of the spire. The light was projected against the background of the structure, leaving the buttresses and pinnacles to stand out in picturesque shadows. Very bright floodlighting was then used for the upper portion, with the cross at the apex lit more brilliantly than any other part of the building. Underlining the significance of this new installation, President Calvin Coolidge was in attendance in Chicago to push the button that turned on the lights for the first time. Before the building was entirely surrounded by taller skyscrapers in the 1960s, its illuminated cross was visible at a distance of up to twelve miles.

The Methodists repeated the mixed-use concept of the Chicago Temple in several U. S. cities in the following years. The planned, gigantic Broadway Temple in New York City's Washington Heights neighborhood, however, remained unfinished due to the onset of the Depression. K. B. / D. N.

Architect: **Holabird & Roche**

Location: **77 West Washington Street**

Construction Date: **1924. Extant**

Installation Date: **1927. The building is currently lit with a similar installation.**

Installation Type: **196 incandescent floodlights, of which 124 were mounted on the tower, 72 on the spire.**

Lighting Designer: **W. A. Beile & Co.**

First M. E. Church, night view, postcard, 1938

First M. E. Church, day view, postcard, *c.* 1924

Selected Bibliography:

"A Flaming Cross Above a Great City." *Transactions of the Illuminating Engineering Society* 21 (January 1926): 5–6.

"Chicago Temple: Wonder of Churches." *Chicago Commerce* (8 September 1923): 9–10.

"Lofty Chicago Tower Becomes Pillar of Light." *Electrical World* 87 (16 January 1926): 166.

Paul, George F. "A Needle of Light Points Heavenward." *Light* (Summer 1927): 7.

Van Leeuwen, Thomas A. P. *The Skyward Trend of Thought.* Cambridge: MIT Press, 1988.

C. A. Herpich Sons, Furriers · Berlin · 1928

Architect: **Erich Mendelsohn, Felix Samuely (assistant)**

Location: **Leipziger Strasse 9–13**

Construction Dates: **1925–27, 1928. Destroyed in World War II.**

Installation Dates: **1928, 1930**

Installation Type: **1928: Incandescent lamps placed in horizontal troughs inside cantilevered windowsills. 1930: Blue neon outline lighting.**

Lighting Designer: **Erich Mendelsohn**

Herpich Store with blue neon outline lighting, photograph, c. 1930

Herpich Store, night view, photograph, c. 1928 >

Selected Bibliography:

Canesi, Giovanni and Antonio Cassi Ramelli. *Architetture Luminose e Apparecchi per Illuminazione*. Milan: Ulrico Hoepli, 1934.

Georgiadis, Sokratis. "Giedion and the 'Third Factor.'" *Daidalos* 27 (15 March 1988): 61–65.

James, Kathleen. *Erich Mendelsohn and the Architecture of German Modernism*. Cambridge: Cambridge University Press, 1997.

Kircher, W. "Lichttechnische Betrachtungen zur Licht-reklame" *Bauwelt* 1 (1930): 9, 19–20.

Landsberg, Max. "Lichtreklame und Fassadenarchitektur." *Deutsche Bauzeitung* 61 (1927): 676–679.

Riezler, Walter, "Umgestaltung der Fassaden." *Die Form* 2 (February 1927): 33–40.

Zevi, Bruno. *Erich Mendelsohn: The Complete Works*. Basel, Boston: Birkhäuser, 1999.

Among the much discussed attempts at integrating advertising and architecture in 1920s Berlin, Erich Mendelsohn's Herpich facade and the Luckhardt brothers' facade for a commercial building in Tauentzienstrasse (p. 126) were the most frequently cited. Mendelsohn's radically modern facade in front of three existing older structures consisted of a reinforced concrete frame covered with travertine and bronze and broken into long, horizontal lines by ribbon windows. The structure also included two new top floors that were set back from the main facade, following the local height requirements. On either side two protruding bay windows framed the four floors above the display windows. Both the design's uncompromising modernity and its size were in stark contrast to the surrounding architecture, and could be built only after a long and much publicized struggle with the building authorities.

In designing the windows of the facade's central section, Mendelsohn included troughs in the cantilevered windowsills, which held white incandescent lights behind opal glass, illuminating the travertine bands underneath. Just above the ground floor display windows, a band with the name of the company was illuminated.

Compared to much of the commercial lighting in Berlin in 1928, when the building was finished, Mendelsohn's solution was a model of restraint. Already in 1930, the lighting scheme was revised. Instead of the reflective light off the travertine bands in the central section of the first four floors, blue neon outline lighting now adorned the upper edge of the ribbon windows on all seven floors.

Mendelsohn's subtle illumination designs were in conscious contrast to the spectacular mobile color floodlighting that he had seen during his trip to New York City in the midtwenties. Mendelsohn continued to experiment with designs for the nighttime appearance of several of his commercial buildings in the following years (see for instance his Petersdorff Store in Breslau, p. 134).

K. B. / D. N.

Titania Palast Theater · Berlin · 1928

The Titania Palast was one of the premiere movie theaters in Europe and had the highest degree of night lighting of any cinema in Berlin. The cubic arrangement of its volumes at the corner, the subtle ornamentation and surface treatment had been developed with the nocturnal appearance in mind by the architects in close collaboration with lighting engineer Ernst Hölscher. The building employed both concealed color floodlighting and bands of translucent glass lit from behind. A row of bright lamps outlined the top edge of the building, below which blue neon tubes against a red background spelled out the name of the theater on both facades. Above the main entrance stood a one-hundred-foot tower of black-painted concrete, decorated with alternating bands of opal glass, lit from within by 4,000 light bulbs. Six long bands encircled the base of the tower while twenty-seven smaller ones rose in a vertical shaft to the top, lit in dark red with a lighter pink at the top. Concave moldings between each horizontal strip of light accentuated the contrast between the alternating dark and light bands.

Contemporary commentators were enthusiastic: "At no other movie theater in Berlin have the lighting effects been employed as an element of its exterior architecture. Usually the nocturnal illumination is a new, sometimes alien, element that is added to the architecture. Here it is an element of the architecture itself." (Zucker/Stindt, p. 86)

K. B. / D. N.

Architects: **Ernst Schöffler, Carlo Schloenbach & Carl Jacobi**

Location: **Schlossstrasse 4–5, (corner of Gutsmuths-strasse 28, Berlin Steglitz)**

Construction Dates: **1926–28. Interior rebuilt 1953 (Hermann Fehling), movie theater closed 1966, converted to a commercial building 1969. 1995: converted again to a movie theater with 5 screens, lighting restored to original colors and intensity.**

Installation Dates: **1928–c. 1942. 1995–present.**

Installation Type: **4,000 25-watt incandescent lamps in red behind opal plate glass lit from interior, blue neon tubes for letters of sign.**

Lighting Designer: **Ernst Hölscher**

Titania Palast, day view, photograph, 1927

Titania Palast, night view, photograph, c. 1928

Selected Bibliography:

"L'Éclairage du Titania Palast à Berlin." *Lux: La Revue de L'Eclairage* (April 1928): 62.

Boeger, Peter. *Architektur der Lichtspieltheater in Berlin: Bauten und Projekte 1919–1930.* Berlin: Willmuth Arenhövel, 1993.

Schmidt, Gerhard. "Das Licht als Bauelement." *Licht und Lampe* (1928): 126–129.

Zucker, Paul and Georg Otto Stindt. *Lichtspielhäuser, Tonfilmtheater.* Berlin: Ernst Wasmuth, 1931.

De Volharding Building · The Hague · 1928

Architects: **Jan Willem Eduard Buijs and Joan B. Lürsen**

Location: **Grote Markt 22–24**

Construction Dates: **1927–28. Extant**

Installation Dates: **1928–33. The building is not currently illuminated.**

Installation Type: **Incandescent lights behind opal glass spandrels, colored glass panes and glass blocks.**

Lighting Designer: **Jan Buijs in collaboration with the Osram Lichthaus, Berlin**

De Volharding Building, day view, photograph, *c.* 1928

De Volharding Building, night view, photograph, *c.* 1928 >

Selected Bibliography:

Howells, John M. "Fundamentals of Architecture as Related to Lighting." *Transactions of the Illuminating Engineering Society* 25, no. 5 (1930): 474–475.

Rehorst, Chris. "Jan Buijs and De Volharding, The Hague, Holland." *Journal of the Society of Architectural Historians* 45 (May 1985): 147–160.

Rogers, Tyler Stewart, and Alvin L. Powell. "Exterior Illumination of Buildings." *American Architect Reference Data* 18 (1935): 1–360.

Rothschild, Richard. "Zwei neue holländische Geschäfts-häuser." *Wasmuths Monatshefte für Baukunst und Städtebau* 9 (September 1932): 420–426.

Probably the most frequently cited example for the potential applications of a future "light architecture" in 1920s Europe, the building was designed to house the offices of the Dutch socialist cooperative, De Volharding ("The Perseverance"). Architect Jan Buijs, a member of the Dutch Socialist Party SDAP who had previously built only private residences, drew on formal ideas from *De Stijl*, Willem Dudok and Russian Constructivism as well as German discussions of Lichtreklame combining advertising, light and architecture. In fact, the lighting design was developed in conjunction with the Osram Lichthaus Berlin. In fulfilling his clients' demand for an edifice with a nighttime advertising component, Buijs created a structure that was soon called the "most famous of all luminous buildings" (Rogers, p. 69). Glass covered the entire exterior of the De Volharding building. The areas above the large plate-glass windows consisted entirely of opal glass panels, and glass bricks made up the elevator shaft and staircase tower, as well as the horizontal band above the ground floor windows. By day, the opal glass appeared as an opaque white. At night, interior lights silhouetted letters and other forms that were placed behind the glass (which could be accessed via twenty-eight-inch-wide gangways), turning the two street facades into a sequence of advertising panels. However, befitting a socialist cooperative, the texts in the facades did not advertise consumer products, but spelled out the benefits that the cooperative bestowed on its 16,000 members. How little the clients relied on advertising was demonstrated by the fact that they went along with Buijs' decision to place the letters behind the glass, even if that rendered the information visible at night only. While advertising on the outside of opal glass became common, Buijs' particular solution found no successors.

The cooperative's name was announced on the roof as part of a cubic assemblage of white, yellow and blue panes of glass, its illuminated shaft shooting upward into the sky, while a strip of blue glass panels reached downward to create a divider between the staircase and the elevator shaft. Buijs stated at the building's opening that he intended to create a structure "that seemed to consist of light" (Rehorst,

p. 159). Contemporary illuminating engineers believed that he had succeeded admirably and illustrations of the building were frequently shown in professional journals and helped to popularize the use of luminous panels.

Unfortunately, the De Volharding Building was illuminated for just a few years and its nocturnal potential was subsequently forgotten for decades. In 1996, one facade was partially lit in honor of the National Week of Architecture in the Netherlands, but the building has yet to return on a permanent basis to the stunning nighttime appearance that made it so famous in the 1920s.   K. B. / D. N.

Rudolf Petersdorff Department Store · Wrozław (formerly Breslau) · 1928

Architect: **Erich Mendelsohn**

Location: **formerly Ohlauerstrasse /
Schuhbrückestrasse**

Construction Date: **1928. Extant**

Installation Date: **1928**

Installation Type: **White neon lights on ceiling in
soffits between glass and curtains. Light reflected
from fabric.**

Lighting Designer: **Erich Mendelsohn**

The famous design for a clothing store in the former German city of Breslau was perhaps Erich Mendelsohn's most successful and most thoughtful integration of artificial light and architecture. The new building on a busy corner in downtown Breslau consisted of a steel skeleton, clad in travertine and bronze. Its most prominent element was a series of ribbon windows, which dynamically cantilevered into a semicircular corner section. This part, with its strong horizontal emphasis, contrasted sharply with the rest of the building and its individual large windows. It also contained the lighting installation for the store's nocturnal appearance.

Mendelsohn developed an entirely new system of integrating the lighting into the facade. The transoms in the ribbon windows, which stepped back behind the window surface and could be opened, consisted of translucent glass. Behind them the ceiling held neon lamps, whose light was reflected by white curtains out into the street, thus turning the ribbon windows into bright bands of illumination. Separated from the rest of the interior by the curtains, the sole task of the ceiling lights was to shine a bright light to the outside. Compared to the Herpich Store (p. 130) in Berlin, which, due to a number of delays, was eventually opened in the same year, the lighting design for the store in Breslau was more tightly integrated with its architectural features. Mendelsohn explained that the facade "would hang in the ceiling like a glowing curtain" (James, p. 155) and Wilhelm Lotz, a member of the German Werkbund, considered this building a key example of "Light Architecture," because light "had become a building material." (Lotz, p. 62)

K. B. / D. N.

Petersdorff Store, day view, photograph, *c.* 1928

Petersdorff Store, night view, photograph, *c.* 1928

Selected Bibliography:

James, Kathleen. *Erich Mendelsohn and the Architecture of German Modernism.* Cambridge: Cambridge University Press, 1997.

Lotz, Wilhelm. *Licht und Beleuchtung.* Berlin: H. Reckendorf, 1928.

Zevi, Bruno. *Erich Mendelsohn: The complete works.* Basel, Boston: Birkhäuser, 1999.

Filmtheater Lichtburg · Berlin · 1929

While commercial skyscrapers and power company buildings were often the subject of spectacular lighting designs in the United States, the most striking sights in European cities after dark were frequently the movie theaters, uniting two of the modern world's most popular technological achievements. The film and variety theater Lichtburg was not located in the center of town, but in Berlin's north, in the traditional working class neighborhood of Wedding. It was the central part of a new housing development, which had been planned around a new intersection of subway and suburban trains, called Gesundbrunnen. Architect Rudolf Fränkel designed the protruding half cylinder above the entrance to the theater as the final climax in the long curve of a block of shops and apartments at the intersection of Behm- and Brunnenstrasse. In striking contrast to the horizontal window ribbons of the adjacent apartments, this seventy-four-foot-tall tower was partitioned into fifteen vertical windows, each one thirty-nine feet in height, fitted with a double layer of opal glass between

dark brick pilasters. Between two layers of this glass, 1,000 incandescent lamps were installed, producing a luminous white glow through the windows at night. Above, four-foot-high letters in red neon announced the name, and from a roof pavilion above the tower, a searchlight sent out three rotating beams. Due to the elegant simplicity of the facade and the nocturnal lighting scheme, it was deemed un-necessary to follow the general fashion for large movie posters on the facade.

Rudolf Fränkel continued to apply his ideas for a luminous architecture with glowing semi-cylinders as pilasters in the lobby and indirect floods of light on the ceiling of the 2,000-seat auditorium. Central to the new idea of providing large-scale and attractive evening entertainment in close proximity to new working-class residential areas was the notion of bringing with it some of the visual excitement that the city center would offer. The architecture of the Lichtburg Theater and its spectacular lighting scheme were the key elements of this concept.

K. B. / D. N.

Architect: **Rudolf Fränkel**

Location: **Behmstrasse 7–9 (Berlin-Wedding)**

Construction Date: **1929. Heavily damaged during WW II. Demolished 1961.**

Installation Date: **1929**

Installation Type: **1,000 25-watt incandescent white lamps behind opal glass windows. 3,000-watt searchlight with triple lens. Red neon lettering on roof.**

Lighting Designer: **Rudolf Fränkel**

Lichtburg Theater, night view, photograph, c. 1928. Unknown photographer. Gelatin silver print. Collection Centre Canadien d'Architecture / Canadian Center for Architecture, Montréal

Selected Bibliography:

Berlin und seine Bauten. Teil V Bauten für die Kunst. Berlin: Ernst und Sohn, 1983.

Boeger, Peter. *Architektur der Lichtspieltheater in Berlin: Bauten und Projekte 1919–1930.* Berlin: Willmuth Arenhövel, 1993.

Posener, Julius. "Allemagne: Deux Théâtres de Rudolf Fraenkel." *L'Architecture d'Aujourd'hui* (September–October 1933): 45–52.

Schmidt, Gerhard. "The Castle of Light: A New Large Cinema Theatre in Berlin." *Illuminating Engineer* 24 (March 1931): 70.

Paul Zucker and G. Otto Stindt, *Lichtspielhäuser. Tonfilmtheater.* Berlin: Wasmuth, 1930.

Karstadt AG Department Store · Berlin · 1929

Architect: **Philipp Schaefer**

Location: **Hermannplatz 5–10 (previously Kaiser Friedrich Platz), Hasenheide 1–4, Urbanstrasse 77–81.**

Construction Dates: **1927–29. Partially destroyed 1945, rebuilt afterwards in a different style and without any provision for illumination.**

Installation Date: **1929**

Installation Type: **Luminescent tubes for the lighting of the display windows, outline lighting with incandescent lights framing each vertical bay of the seven-story facade. Two four-story setback towers above roof level lit by floodlights hidden behind parapets above their 2nd and 3rd floors. Above there are two 49-foot-high light columns of translucent opal glass, lit from within by incandescent lights.**

Lighting Designer: **Unknown.**

Selective Bibliography:

Heinz, Johannes. *Neues Bauen in Berlin, 1931* (reprint 1981): 66.

Berlin und seine Bauten, vol. VIII A.: 57ff.

Neue Warenhausbauten der Rudolph Karstadt A. G. von Architekt Philipp Schaefer Hamburg. Introduction by Werner Hegemann. Berlin, Leipzig, Vienna: Friedrich Ernst Hübsch Verlag, 1929.

Gamma, Dr. "Bau und Licht." *Deutsche Bauzeitung* (1934): 996–1004.

"Modern Lighting in Germany." *Electrical World* 94 (28 December 1929): 1275.

Oechslin, Werner. "Lichtarchitektur." *Moderne Architektur in Deutschland 1900 bis 1950. Expressionismus und Neue Sachlichkeit* Deutsches Architektur-Museum, Frankfurt / Main. eds. Vittorio Magnango Lampugnani and Romana Schneider. Stuttgart: Verlag Gerd Hatje, 1994: 117–131.

The largest department store in Europe (775,000 square feet of floor space) in Berlin's Neukölln area was realized shortly before the onset of the Depression, during a short period of economic prosperity in Germany partially caused by substantial American investment following the Dawes Plan. The Karstadt Company also had received a fifteen-million-dollar credit from the U. S. for its new building. While the vertical forms of the building's facade could be seen as a late response to the stylistic solution of department store architecture in Germany, the setback forms of the two towers and the illumination scheme were clearly influenced by American models.

The lighting was, in fact, a summary of the major approaches to architectural lighting developed so far. Above the brightly illumined display windows, the facade's bays were framed by incandescent outline lighting. The setbacks of the towers carried floodlights behind their parapets, whose intensity faded towards the edge of the next setback, and above were forty-nine-foot-tall light columns made of white opal glass and lit from within by innumerable incandescent lightbulbs.

Werner Hegemann, the German critic and urban planner, who knew the American situation well from his own long experience, was reminded of "the fantastic castle that Aladdin's lamp magically let rise from the sands of the desert. But even this comparison is not sufficient: when after dusk vertical strips of light entirely change the appearance of the building's gigantic mass, and when above its towers light columns thrust their silver shafts into the dark sky, then there seems to have been realized one of the utopian, technological worlds of which the novels by Jules Verne or Wells fantasize." (*Neue Warenhausbauten*). As late as 1934, an architecture critic expressed his enthusiasm: "How beautiful it is, when the wanderer in Berlin's street at night suddenly comes across the fairy tale towers of Karstadt." (Dr. Gamma)   D. N.

Karstadt Department Store, photograph, 1929

Karstadt Department Store, night view, photograph, 1929 >

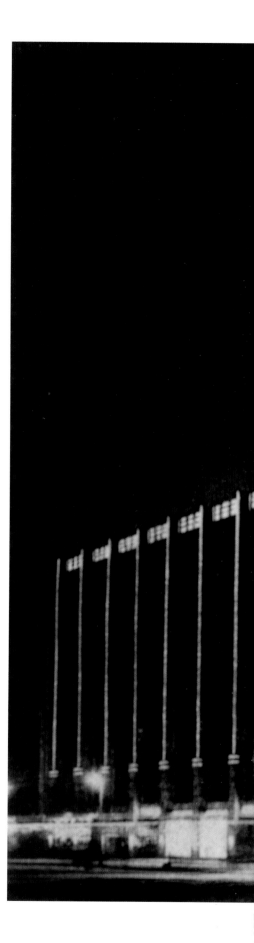

World's Fair · Barcelona · 1929

Dates: **May 19–September 1929**
(continued as "Barcelona Exhibition" in 1930)

Selected Architects:
Puig I Cadafalch (with Guillem Busquets): Plaza de Espana, Palau Nacional, Palace of Industrial Arts; Palace of Queen Victoria Eugenia, Palace of Alfons XIII
Jean-Claude Nicolas Forestier, Nicolau Maria Rubió y Tuduri: gardens and masterplan
Francesc Folguera and Ramon Reventós: Spanish Village
Amadeu Llompart y Alexandre Soler: Palace of Electricity
Ramon Reventós y Farrarons: Entrance Towers
Dragisa Brasovan: Yugoslav Pavilion
Ludwig Mies van der Rohe: German Pavilion (re-erected 1983–86 by Fernando Ramos and Ignasi de Solà-Morales)
Office of Mies van der Rohe: German Electricity Pavilion

Lighting Designers: **Carles Buïgas (fountains), Marià Rubió i Bellver (light columns), Charles J. Stahl, K. W. Johansson (Westinghouse Corporation)**

Selected Bibliography:
"Light Supreme at Barcelona." *Electrical World* 94 (7 December 1929): 1126–1130.
"The International Exhibition at Barcelona." *Transactions of the Illuminating Engineering Society* 25, no. 3 (1930): 302.
Cary, Walter. "Modern Tendencies in Illumination." *Electric Journal* 27, no. 3 (March 1930): 130–135.
Glassman, Don. "The Magic of Colored Light." *Popular Mechanics* 54, no. 1 (July 1930): 8–12.
Grandas, Carem M. *L'Exposicio Internacional de Barcelona de 1929*. Barcelona: Espluges de Llobregat, 1988.
Johansson, K. W. "La iluminación eléctrica de la Exposición Internacional de Barcelona." *Ingenieria Internacional* 17, no. 5 (1929): 236–238.
Mattie, Erik. *World's Fairs*. New York: Princeton Architectural Press, 1998.
Riggs, Arthur Stanley. "The Spanish Expositions." *Art and Archaeology* 27, no. 4 (April 1929): 147–164.
Stahl, Charles J. "The Colored Floodlighting of the International Exposition at Barcelona, Spain." *Transactions of the Illuminating Engineering Society* 24, no. 9 (1929): 876–889.

The only World's Fair to be held in the 1920s was of great importance for the city of Barcelona, whose recognition and cultural independence gained a significant boost from the enormous international success of the exhibition. In conjunction with the fair, urban projects were advanced, including a new subway and the tram above the harbor up to Montjuic Hill. Held three years after the death of Antoni Gaudí, the exhibition's architecture fell stylistically into a transitional phase between the late Catalan Art Nouveau, late eclecticism, and new alignments with the international modern movement. A "Spanish village" continued a tradition of earlier world's fairs and assembled copies of individual buildings from all over Spain into a picturesque, timeless collage.

In the end a somewhat restrained Beaux Arts style still dominated the great exhibition palaces, whereas more design freedom was to be found among the individual country pavilions, such as Mies van der Rohe's famous German pavilion, a key monument to the newly emerging architectural principles, his office's German Electricity Pavilion, Dragisa Brasovan's Yugoslav pavilion and the elegant Swedish Pavilion.

The fair owed much of its success to its great emphasis on nocturnal illumination. The exhibition organizers agreed to purchase a $250,000 custom-made apparatus from Westinghouse to synchronize the color changes (from yellow and red to light green) of 850 floodlight projectors installed near the exhibition palaces, creating a lighting spectacle on "a scale several times larger than any similar display hitherto produced." (Stahl, "The Colored Floodlighting …"). Puig I Cadafalch's exhibition palaces provided expansive windowless walls to be used as large reflectors. In order not to appear entirely dull during the daytime, sequences of flat *scraffito* pilasters had been applied in the outside stucco, vanishing under the nighttime illumination.

Mies van der Rohe had insisted that his pavilion be moved to the end of the main cross axis, next to one of the large exhibition palaces, where it served as a convenient vantage point for the nocturnal spectacle. The pavilion's materials reflected the colors of the exhibition's main lighting scheme and a single translucent wall with white interior light responded calmly to the noisy color symphony. The white, windowless cube of the German Electricity Pavilion shimmered at night from soft reflections of colored lights.

The park's architectural lighting was complemented by a well-coordinated sequence of fifty fountains and cascades, illuminated in color and designed by the Catalan "magician of light" Carles Buïgas. Especially the central cascades, almost half a mile long, gave the impression "that color seems to flow down like the water carries it; only more slowly." (Stahl, "The Colored Floodlighting …"). Blue, red, green and white sequences would change in a cycle of twelve minutes, for example, and twenty different variations could be arranged. The large fountain in the center of the exhibition sent a jet of water 200 feet in the air, lit in colors by a battery of twenty-four incandescent searchlights. Many additional jets in three concentric rings surrounded it, and more than 1,000 lamps were placed under glass beneath the water.

In addition, there were about two hundred illuminated glass columns and crystal elements lit in white, yellow, red and blue. The spectacle found its nocturnal climax in an 'aurora borealis' from twenty-four searchlight beams behind the dome of the National Palace, an idea that Westinghouse had clearly adopted from Walter D'Arcy Ryan's scintillator.   D. N.

German Electricity Pavilion, photograph, 1929

< German Pavilion, photograph, 1929

Palace of Queen Victoria Eugenia and fountain at night, illustration, 1929 >

Palau Nacional and Cascade No. 1 at night, contemporary postcard, 1929 >

Palmolive Building · Chicago, Illinois · 1929

Architect: **Holabird & Root**

Location: **919 North Michigan Avenue**

Construction Date: **1927–29. Extant**

Installation Dates: **1929. The building is currently floodlit and carries a stationary beacon.**

Installation Type: **389 incandescent floodlights: 25 1,000-watt, 230 500-watt, and 134 200-watt. A 2-billion-candlepower rotating beacon and 300-million-candlepower fixed beam installed at the top.**

Lighting Designer: **Unknown**

Palmolive Building, photograph, c. 1929

Chicago's nocturnal skyline including the Palmolive (background left) and La Salle Wacker Building (foreground), contemporary postcard, c. 1930.

Palmolive Building, night view, postcard, c. 1929 >

Selected Bibliography:

"To Light the Lanes of the Sky …" *Electric Journal* 28, no. 1 (January 1931): 6.

Bouman, Mark J. "'The Best Lighted City in the World': The Construction of a Nocturnal Landscape in Chicago." *Chicago Architecture and Design: 1923–1933*, ed. John Zukowsky. Munich: Prestel, 1993.

Bruegman, Robert. *Holabird & Roche & Holabird & Root: an illustrated catalog of works*. New York: Garland, Chicago Historical Society, 1991.

Essberger, E. "Flutlicht in Chicago." *Das Licht* 1, no. 10 (1931): 272–274.

Hoskins, Henry J. B. "The Palmolive Building, Chicago," "Structure and Equipment of the Palmolive Building." *Architectural Forum* 52 (May 1930): 655–666, 731–736.

The headquarters of the Palmolive Company, a prominent producer of cleaning products, was the first building erected at a considerable distance from Chicago's downtown area, at the northern end of Michigan Avenue. The floodlighting installation on Holabird and Root's building had been a crucial part of the design concept. While inspired by the floodlighting of the Wrigley Building (pp. 108–109) and the Tribune Tower (pp. 142–143), the Palmolive Building was the first in Chicago to employ an illumination scheme on a modern, setback skyscraper. The entire exterior of this thirty-seven-story structure was lit, with projectors placed on the setback roof decks on all four corners. The central section had three characteristic shallow indentations containing floodlights at the bottom, whose upward light was thus precisely framed, creating a striking sequence of bright and dark sections on the facade. (Holabird and Root would pursue a very similar lighting concept in the following year with the slightly taller LaSalle Wacker Building, also in Chicago.)

The Palmolive's off-white Indiana limestone cladding served as a perfect reflector, and underlined the firm's claim that the building was a "monument to cleanliness." The building served as headquarters for *Playboy* magazine from 1965 to 1989, a fact that does not seem to have elicited any changes in the lighting scheme.

Although color had been mentioned as a possibility in the plans for the lighting and had been used to spectacular effect on the McJunkin Building (p. 112) a few years earlier, clear lamps were used exclusively, giving the building a silver appearance that resulted in the nickname, "La Tour d'Argent" (The Silver Tower). Drawing further attention to the edifice was a brilliant revolving light at its top, originally named for the popular aviator Charles Lindbergh, but called the Palmolive Beacon after 1931. Mounted on top of a 150-foot-high mast and rotating at a rate of two times per minute, the beacon served as a navigational tool for airplanes and was purportedly visible from as far away as St. Louis and Cleveland. An additional stationary beam pointed toward the Chicago Municipal Airport (now known as Midway). Except for periods of darkness during World War II and the energy crisis of 1973, the rotating beacon was in use until 1981, when complaints from downtown residents forced it into temporary retirement. In the fall of 2001, a new beacon was installed. Unlike the old beacon, which made a 360-degree revolution, the new one moves in a 120-degree arc over Lake Michigan. Still floodlit today, the Palmolive Building remains one of the outstanding skyscrapers on the Chicago skyline.   K. B. / D. N.

Chicago Tribune Tower · Chicago, Illinois · 1929

Architects: **Raymond Hood and John Mead Howells**

Location: **435 North Michigan Avenue**

Construction Date: **1924. Extant**

Installation Date: **1929. Two levels of the crown (the very top and two stories below) are currently illuminated with floodlights.**

Installation Type: **174 incandescent floodlighting projectors with amber filters to light the crown.**

Lighting Designer: **Bassett Jones**

Night view of Grant Park Section of Chicago, 1929. Collection Centre Canadien d'Architecture / Canadian Center for Architecture, Montréal.

Golden Glow Floodlighting Projectors. Cover of sales brochure, 1932. Collection Centre Canadien d'Architecture / Canadian Center for Architecture, Montréal.

Top of Chicago Tribune Tower, illuminated, photograph, 1932. Collection Centre Canadien d'Architecture / Canadian Center for Architecture, Montréal.

Tribune Tower, night view, postcard, c. 1929 >

Selected Bibliography:

"Floodlighting a Famous Newspaper Building." *Electrical World* 93 (16 February 1929): 361.

Jones, Bassett. "Structures in Light." *Light* (April 1924): 6.

The International Competition for a New Administration Building for the Chicago Tribune MCMXXII. Chicago: Tribune Co., 1923; reprint ed., *Chicago Tribune Tower Competition & Late Entries.* New York: Rizzoli, 1980.

Hood and Howells' design for the Tribune Tower was the winning entry in a famous and controversial international competition of 1922, to which prominent European modernists such as Walter Gropius, Bruno Taut and Adolf Loos had submitted entries. Both Raymond Hood and John Mead Howells later wrote extensively about illumination and architecture, and their interest in floodlighting played a part in the composition of the thirty-four-story gothic-influenced structure (based on one of the entrance towers of Rouen Cathedral). In their accompanying description they called "attention to the fact that the upper part of the building has been designed not only for its own outline and composition, but for the possibilities of illumination and reflected lighting at night" (*International Competition*). In 1922, when floodlight illumination was still in its infancy, this short description suggested a sense of modernity and an awareness of the building's urban position across from the Wrigley Building (pp. 108–109) that might very well have contributed to the entry's success.

Before the building was completed, theatrical and architectural lighting designer Bassett Jones published plans for its illumination. As the Wrigley Building was lit with a brilliant white light, Jones suggested using color and a complex balance of luminous windows and floodlights. From each of the fifth-floor windows, floodlights with reddish filters would cast their beams down towards the sidewalk: "I think of this great tower as standing in a pool of rose-colored light, from which it rises like a wonder fountain—a Gothic tracery-work of light against the sky" (Jones, p. 7). The shaft of the building would remain dark from this level to the twenty-sixth story, where strip lights would be installed in the windowsills. Opal glass lit from within would enclose the windows of the next floor. The stone tracery of the first roof level would be silhouetted against the illuminated central tower behind it. Here, again, a rose-colored light would gradually fade as it reached upward. Finally, eight incandescent searchlights would serve as a beacon at the top. For special occasions, Jones imagined even more theatrical effects. Steam would be discharged from the upper tower, illumined by "fire-color" lights, and supplemented by smoke and fire-

works. "The whole effect will be that of Walhalla burning in the skies, bringing to mind, perhaps, the finale of the *Götterdämmerung*" (Jones, p. 7). The building seems not to have actually been illuminated, however, until 1929, by which time Jones' dramatic scheme had been reduced to 174 golden-colored floodlights on the crown. Although these lights were carefully arranged to set off the building's gothic tracery, one cannot help but regret the loss of Jones' dramatic proposal.

K. B. / D. N.

Union Trust Building · Detroit, Michigan · 1929

Architect: **Wirt Rowland**

Location: **500 Griswold Street**

Construction Dates: **1928–29. Extant**

Installation Date: **1929. The building is not currently illuminated but the equipment is still in place.**

Installation Type: **Automated scintillator employing 8 36-inch General Electric arc searchlights with four different color filters.**

Lighting Designer: **Walter D'Arcy Ryan**

Union Trust Building, night view, postcard, *c.* 1934

Union Trust Building in Detroit's nocturnal skyline, photograph, 1930 >

Selected Bibliography:

"500,000,000 c. p. of Colored Searchlights." *Electrical World* 96 (30 August 1930): 376.

Ferry, W. Hawkins. *The Buildings of Detroit: A History.* Revised ed. Detroit: Wayne State University Press, 1980.

The Union Trust Bank Building, now known as the Guardian Building (and owned by the neighboring Michigan Consolidated Gas Company), remains one of the most colorful examples of Art Deco architecture to be erected in the 1920s. The forty-story skyscraper was covered with a veneer of orange tinted brick and extensively decorated with multi-colored terra-cotta. Above the green, blue, cream and orange tiles, a short tower on the north side was topped with a golden crown. Architect Wirt Rowland strongly believed in the use of color to make an impression in a fast-paced world and to attract a broad range of investors. Inside, a richly ornamented banking hall inspired the building's nickname, "Cathedral of Finance."

The most spectacular element of coloring appeared each night at the top of the building's tower. A set of eight arc searchlights was situated on the roof, one at each of the points of the polygonal tower. Employing filters of magenta, green, orange and yellow, and attached to a motorized control, the lights produced moving beams of color that intersected each other and filled the skies above Detroit with brilliant, changing patterns. Designed by Walter D'Arcy Ryan, the scintillator

had first been used to great acclaim at New York's Hudson-Fulton Celebration of 1909 and then had become a mainstay at major exhibitions. Here, however, the rays' patterns were not cast vertically, but horizontally into the urban sky, symbolizing the bank's reach over the city and serving as a powerful focal point downtown. The Union Trust design was one in a series of fantastic illumination displays that were installed across the country in honor of the fiftieth anniversary of Edison's incandescent bulb. The beams of light, visible for up to fifty miles, continued to put on a nightly show until World War II forced American cities into darkness. Sadly, they were not restored at the end of the war, but the lighting equipment still exists on the tower, leaving open the possibility of a grand searchlight display once again topping this unique and striking skyscraper. K. B. / D. N.

Chanin Building · New York, New York · 1929

Architect: **Sloan & Robertson**

Location: **122 East 42nd Street**

Construction Date: **1928. Extant**

Installation Date: **1929. The building is not currently illuminated.**

Installation Type: **Total of 212 white incandescent floodlights; 156 arranged in batteries on the 52nd and 53rd story setbacks to light the crown, 28 arranged in groups of 7 at each corner to light the flagpole on top of the building.**

Lighting Designer: **Westinghouse Co. Electrical contractors: Edwards Electrical Construction Co.**

Chanin Building, day view, photograph, *c.* 1929

Chanin Building, night view, photograph, *c.* 1929

Selected Bibliography:

"A Golden Crown for a Skyscraper." *Transactions of the Illuminating Engineering Society* 24 (September 1929): 627–628.

"The Chanin Building, New York City." *Architecture and Building* 61, no. 2 (February 1929): 38–47.

"To Light New Skyscraper." *New York Times* (14 January 1929): 42, col. 2.

Agrest, Diana (ed.) *Irwin S Chanin, A Romance with the City.* New York: Cooper Union Press, 1982.

Klein, Dan. "The Chanin Building, New York." *Connoisseur* 186 (July 1974): 162–169.

Sexton, R. W. "A Theater on the 50th Floor." *Architectural Forum* 62 (May 1930): 727–30.

One of New York's great Art Deco skyscrapers, the Chanin Building was also one of the most prominent structures to have its illumination planned as an essential component of its design. The fifty-six-story tower, faced with brick and terra-cotta, was topped with a set of buttresses that were placed all around the fifty-third story setback and were pierced by a promenade. These buttresses gave the structure its distinctive crown, upon which the illumination scheme was centered. Batteries of floodlights were installed at this level, partially hidden behind a row of terra-cotta ornaments above the fifty-second-story windows. The white lights shining on the yellow terra-cotta facing gave the crown a golden glow, purported to be as strong as 30,000,000 candlepower, while the main body of the tower was left unlit. The idea was to present a night view that was the opposite of that seen during the day: the spaces between and behind the buttresses were highlighted while the buttresses themselves were left in darkness.

At the inauguration of the floodlighting installation, the client, Irving Chanin, a Broadway impresario who had a theater built on the fiftieth floor of the building right underneath its luminous crown, described his intent: "Instead of ornamentation in brick, stone, terra-cotta or other tangible materials, lights and shadows in various degrees of intensity, cast at numerous angles, create decorative schemes by optical illusion, much in the same manner that the theatrical producer secures a variety of effects through the manipulation of stage lights." (*New York Times*). The brilliant crown hovering high above Manhattan captured the imagination of artists, such as American printmaker Martin Lewis, who depicted it as a symbol of the complex contrasts in 1930s urban America (p. 228). K. B. / D. N.

Bata Store · Prague · 1929

The shoe store on Prague's Wenceslas Square employed an architectural lighting device similar to that used on the contemporary De Volharding Building (pp. 132–133) in The Hague and Lichthaus Luz (p. 127) in Stuttgart. Horizontal bands of opal glass separated the large windows in each floor of the store, their outside surfaces carrying dark letters for advertisements. The reinforced concrete construction on a twenty-foot grid deliberately celebrated the thin, almost ephemeral structures of modern architecture, while interpreting them with a different, but complementary rhythm at night.

Kysela's building and its lighting scheme inspired a number of immediate followers, such as Pavel Janak's Hotel Juliš of 1928–33, also in Wenceslas Square. The hotel, which included a café and a movie theater, had similar matte glass bands illuminated from behind. Vladimír Karfík, Bata's head architect from 1930 onwards (after working with Le Corbusier, Holabird & Root and F.L. Wright), made the gleaming white bands of opal glass into something of a trademark for Bata Stores, employing it in Bratislava, Liberec, Brno and Karlovy Vary (all 1930–31). The lighted buildings on Wenceslas Square were so popular that the Czech architect Joseph Chochol proposed in an enthusiastic essay about Prague's luminous architecture written in 1929 to demolish all buildings that could not contribute to the nocturnal scene. (Zemánek)   D.N.

Architects: **Ludvík Kysela, František L. Gahura and Josef Gočar**

Location: **Václavské náměstí 6, 774**

Construction Dates: **1927–29. Extant**

Installation Date: **1929. The building is partially lit again today after several interruptions since World War II.**

Installation Type: **Incandescent lightbulbs behind opal glass**

Lighting Designer: **Ludvík Kysela**

Bata Shoe Store, night view, photograph, c. 1935

Selected Bibliography:
Šlapeta, Vladimir, (ed.) *Czech Functionalism 1918–1938*. London: Architectural Association, 1987.
Šlapeta, Vladimir. *Bata: Architektura a Urbanismus 1910–1950*. Zlin, Statní galerie ve Zlíne, 1991.
Zemánek, Jiři, *Zdeněk Pešánek 1896–1965*. Prague: Národní Galerie, 1996.

Merchandise Mart · Chicago, Illinois · 1930

Architects: **Graham, Anderson, Probst & White**

Location: **222 Merchandise Mart Plaza**

Construction Dates: **1928–30. Extant**

Installation Date: **1930. The lighting was turned off between 1973 and 1984. The building is currently illuminated with the 1984 installation.**

Installation Type: **600 incandescent floodlighting projectors, mounted at 4th-floor cornice, 2 set-backs at top, corner towers and central tower. 1984: 426 150-watt high-pressure sodium lamps lighting upper setbacks and towers.**

Lighting Designer: **1930: Unknown. 1984: Charles Lorenz, electrical project engineer at Merchandise Mart.**

Constructed by Marshall Field & Company in collaboration with the North Western Railway, the Merchandise Mart was intended to serve as a central trade facility for manufacturers and distributors in the city of Chicago. The massive steel-frame structure covered two entire city blocks and was the largest building in the United States until the construction of the Pentagon. At night, an inspired illumination scheme made this structure one of the most memorable in a city that was known for its outstanding lighting installations.

The eighteen-story building was clad in limestone, its surface divided by vertical bands of windows. The spaces between the windows

were left dark. The resulting pattern of light and shade greatly de-emphasized the building's mass and solidity. Reflected in the Chicago River, the Merchandise Mart appeared to float above its darkened base. During a time of widespread popularity for moving color illumination, the uniform lighting of the Merchandise Mart extended a certain dignity to a building that had been constructed to serve the entire business community of Chicago. A German observer attested to its illumination: "an image of concentrated greatness." ("Anleuchtung")

K. B.

Merchandise Mart, night view, postcard, *c.* 1931

Merchandise Mart, night view, photograph, *c.* 1931   >

Selected Bibliography:

"Anleuchtung." *Das Licht* 1 (1930–31): 211.

"New Lighting Showcases Merchandise Mart." *Architectural Lighting* 1 (July-August 1987): 14.

Bouman, Mark J. "'The Best Lighted City in the World': The Construction of a Nocturnal Landscape in Chicago." *Chicago Architecture and Design: 1923–1933*, ed. John Zukowsky. Munich: Prestel, 1993.

Bruegmann, Robert "Relighting the Skyline." *Inland Architect* 26 (1982): 51–57.

Chappell, Sally A. Kitt. *Architecture and Planning of Graham, Anderson, Probst and White, 1913–1936: Transforming Tradition*. Chicago: University of Chicago, 1992.

Saliga, Pauline A., ed. *The Sky's the Limit: A Century of Chicago Skyscrapers*. New York: Rizzoli, 1990.

were illumined at a low intensity by lights placed along the cornice of the fourth floor and set above a base that was left largely in shadow. The upward shafts of light emphasized the vertical nature of the window bands, but allowed the intensity of the illumination to fall off gradually until the upper walls of the facade were returned to near darkness. In sharp contrast to the dark upper stories, the two setbacks at the top were bathed in light. The scheme culminated in the illumined central tower, which rose seven additional stories above the main structure. The tower's top three floors and roof as well as the upper edges of the corner turrets were lit to an intensity similar to that of the setbacks, while the floors below

Terminal Tower · Cleveland, Ohio · 1930

Architects: **Graham, Anderson, Probst & White**

Location: **50 Public Square**

Construction Dates: **1926–31. Extant**

Installation Dates: **1930, 1979, 1981, 1990s. The building is currently illuminated with the 1990s installation.**

Installation Type: **Original installation: Incandescent floodlights: 648 100-watt lamps and 228 lamps ranging from 200 to 1,000 watts on the 44th, 48th and 52nd floors. 6 Sperry gyroscope beacons and 6 1,500-watt lamps at the 49th floor. 1981 installation: 229 golden-white high-pressure sodium lights: 167 400-watt, 8 250-watt and 54 150-watt lamps. 1990s: 277 400-watt high-pressure sodium lights with colored gels.**

Lighting Designer: **1930: Designer unknown. 1981: General Electric Co., John J. Kennedy**

Built as part of a large railroad station complex that included offices and a hotel, the fifty-two-story Terminal Tower was for many years the tallest building west of New York. The new railroad station in the city center at Public Square, brought together all passenger and freight train lines, replacing nine existing passenger stations. Like Chicago's Wrigley Building (pp. 108–109) by the same architects, the tower is one of many variations on Seville's famous Giralda Tower (1184–98 and 1558) that could be found in the U.S. at that time.

The building's upper half was illuminated from the start with white lights that allowed it

the tallest in the U.S. to be illuminated from bottom to top with lighting at its base.

The 1990s saw yet another development in the lighting of the Terminal Tower. The sodium lights then in use were replaced in the late '90s by deluxe high-pressure sodium lamps that allowed for truer values in depicting the actual tones of the building. Different color effects could now be used for the first time as well, with plastic gels sandwiched between clear Lucite panels installed over individual floodlights and changed by hand as needed. For special events and holidays throughout the year the tower can be illuminated with

Terminal Tower, night view, postcard, c. 1930–40

Terminal Tower, night view, photograph, c. 2000
Courtesy of General Electric Lighting Institute
Cleveland © >

to be seen for many miles, yet still revealed details and shadows through a judicious employment of lamps with varying intensities. In the topmost lantern, a revolving beacon cast its beams across the city. World War II forced the discontinuation of this illumination, and the tower remained dark until 1979, when its owners had a new lighting system installed on the upper floors. This partial scheme was criticized for its timidity, and a new, more comprehensive plan was revealed in 1981 that washed the entire structure in a golden-white flood of light until midnight each evening. Floodlights were installed on roofs around the tower, hidden from view, making the tower

different color combinations and is kept lit continuously from dusk to dawn.

K. B. / D. N.

Selected Bibliography:

"Cleveland's Terminal Tower—Point-by-Point Illumination." *Lighting Design & Application* 13 (March 1983): 20–23.

Chappell, Sally A. Kitt. *Architecture and Planning of Graham, Anderson, Probst and White, 1913–1936: Transforming Tradition.* Chicago: University of Chicago, 1992.

Lacher, Walter S. "Dedicate New Cleveland Station Today." *Railway Age* (28 June 1930): 1553ff.

Leedy, Walter C. Jr. "Cleveland's Terminal Tower: The Van Sweringen's Afterthought." *Gamut* 8 (Winter, 1983).

Litt, Steven. "Lively Lighting Makes City Glow." *Plain Dealer* (29 December 1991): sec. H, 1.

A. E. Staley Manufacturing Company Administration Building · Decatur, Illinois · 1930

Architect: **Aschauer & Waggoner**

Location: **2200 East El Dorado Street**

Construction Date: **1930. Extant**

Installation Dates: **1930–42, 1945–73, 1989. The current installation is a computerized update of the original with additional sequences available and without the rotating beacon.**

Installation Type: **195 incandescent floodlights. White lights on facade, colored lights used at top, controlled by Thyratron tube dimmer. Rotating beacon in dome.**

Lighting Designers: **1930: F. D. Crowther, General Electric Company. 1989: Lutron Co., Bodine Electric & Staley Co.**

Staley Building, colored night view on a General Electric advertising brochure, 1931. Collection Centre Canadien d'Architecture/Canadian Center for Architecture, Montréal.

Staley Building, night view, postcard, c. 1930

Selected Bibliography:

"1991 Progress Report." *Lighting Design & Application* 21 (November 1991): 17–32.

"Control Equipment for Mobile Color Lighting." General Electric (1931) (GEA 1444).

"Interim Report-Committee on Light in Architecture and Decoration: Floodlighting and Architecture." *Transactions of the Illuminating Engineering Society* 25, no. 10 (1930): 857–863.

Liston, John. "Developments in the Electrical Industry During 1930." *General Electric Company*, 1931.

How much the enthusiasm for colored architectural illumination moved beyond the metropolitan centers in the early 1930s is shown by this administration building for a soy and corn processing company in Decatur, a small business community in central Illinois. The building was illuminated upon its completion with mobile color floodlighting effects, which were then rapidly rising in popularity throughout the country. The limestone and granite structure stretched out horizontally up to its sixth floor. Then it rose up in a central section for nine more stories, culminating in a cupola. The main facade of pale stone was lit only with white light. Contrasting with this rather reserved front, the top of the building from the eleventh floor up was lit by a system of colored lights set on timers that varied on all four sides. These colors ranged from red to blue, green, amber and white, and the wattage for each varied according to the brightness of the color, so that an even appearance of light was the result. The first of two cycles would hold one of the colors for a set period while the other cycle caused the rest of the tints to continue changing. Every fifteen seconds a complete change of color occurred, and it took twenty-two-and-a-half minutes until the same combination could be seen on all four sides of the tower. This was made possible by the first use of a new device that General Electric had just developed, the Thyratron tube dimmer. "The artistic illumination of A. E. Staley Company's administration building, at Decatur, Illinois, gives nightly evidence that mobile color floodlighting—a scientific innovation in exterior illumination—continuously revealing new and beautiful aspects of the structure, is in entire harmony with established canons of design," ("Control Equipment....") General Electric noted when marketing its new device.

Typically for its time, a revolving beacon was also added to the dome. The lighting was turned off for World War II, and when resumed in 1945, the changing effects were no longer employed. Shut down again for the energy crisis of 1973, the lights were turned on for the release of the American hostages by Iran in 1981, and again for the holiday seasons in the late 1980s. It was not until 1989, however, that the company decided to bring back the mobile color lighting on a permanent basis. A computer was installed that could reproduce the original color sequence as well as an endless supply of new ones. K. B. / D. N.

Richfield Building · Los Angeles, California · 1930

The Richfield Building was one of the most strikingly extravagant and metaphorically rich buildings of the 1920s in Los Angeles, especially after dark. It housed the headquarters of one of LA's largest oil companies, founded in the California Oil Fields in 1905 and in need of a new headquarters building by 1926. In order to bolster its public image, the company sponsored car races and aviation, and its architects aimed for "an expression of modern art and thought" (quoted in Gebhard) and carefully documented how countless models had guided their choice of black and golden terra-cotta tiles. While this color combination might have been influenced by Raymond Hood's American Radiator Building (pp. 114–115) in New York, it also symbolized the "black gold" of the oil industry. Its elaborate floodlighting scheme at night carefully emphasized the smooth, shiny quality of the black and the sparkling radiance of the golden surfaces.

A dense sequence of shallow ribs (c. two inches wide), along with narrow, vertical shafts of gold between each pair of windows, heightened the reflective qualities and sparkle of the facade. The Gothic design of the building allowed the integration of the floodlighting equipment within the facade's terra-cotta ornamentation. From the tenth to the fourteenth floors, windows were grouped in vertical recesses and floodlit separately, framed by illuminated corner setbacks.

Winged golden angels by San Francisco sculptor Haig Patigian adorned the upper edge of the facade and were lit by narrow spotlights. The illumination reached its pinnacle of brightness at the deeply setback penthouse and tower above the fourteenth floor. An openwork metal tower resembling an oil derrick crowned the building and served as both an aviation beacon and a structure to carry the firm's name, spelled out in neon letters on all four sides. The addition of this tower made the structure, at 372 feet, one of the tallest in Los Angeles. Similar, but smaller openwork structures with aviation beacons at the top adorned the company's numerous gas stations up and down the Pacific Coast.

Only a year after the lighting had been installed, price wars and the depression pushed the company into a five-year-long receivership during which the floodlighting was kept on.

The Richfield Oil Company merged with the Atlantic Refining Company in 1966 into the Atlantic Richfield Company (ARCO—now part of BP), and demolished the Richfield Building in 1969 in order to build the new ARCO headquarters in 1972 (AC Martin, Architect).

K. B. / D. N.

Architects: **Morgan, Walls & Clements**

Location: **6th and Flower Streets**

Construction Dates: **1928–29. Demolished in 1969.**

Installation Date: **1930**

Installation Type: **382 incandescent floodlights: 2nd and 10th floors: 500 250-watt lamps in special pockets within window reveals. 11th-floor corner setbacks with: 250-watt lamps behind sculptures, 500-watt upward beams on setback for illumination of angel sculptures. Floodlights on main roof and penthouse to light penthouse and tower. Neon letters, aviation beacon.**

Lighting Designer: **Ralph Phillips**

Richfield Building, photograph, c. 1930

Richfield Building, night view, photograph, c. 1930

Selected Bibliography:

"Richfield Oil Building." *Transactions of the Illuminating Engineering Society* 26 (March 1931): 218–219.

"The Richfield Building, Los Angeles." *Architectural Record* 67 (June 1930): 505–510.

"The Richfield Building." *American Architect*. vol. 139 (May 1931): 44.

Gebhard, David. *The Richfield Building*. Los Angeles: Atlantic Richfield Co., 1970.

Kansas City Power & Light Company Building · Kansas City, Missouri · 1931

Architects: **Hoit, Price & Barnes**

Location: **1330 Baltimore Avenue**

Construction Dates: **1930–31. Extant**

Installation Date: **1931. The building is still illuminated with a similar installation.**

Installation Type: **Incandescent floodlights with 500 and 1,000-watt lamps: 250 white lights on balconies above entrances and at 16th, 20th, 22nd, 27th, and 28th-floor setbacks. Red, green, amber and white lights at 31st, 32nd and 33rd floors, using Thyratron tube and telechron motor. 6 floodlighting projectors within opalescent glass in 34th-floor lantern. 32 red neon tubes in lantern tip.**

Lighting Designer: **General Electric Co.**

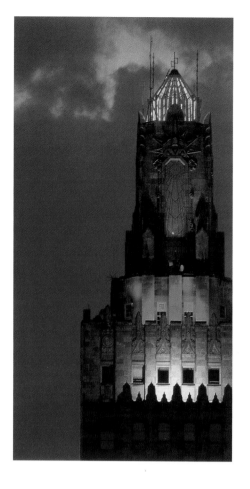

Kansas City, Power & Light Co. Building. Photo by David Pulliam. © Reprinted by permission of the Kansas City Star.

Kansas City Power & Light Co. Building, night view, photograph, *c.* 1946–59   >

Selected Bibliography:

"New Building to be a Triumph in Decorative Lighting Effects." *The Tie* (September 1931): 11.

"New Kansas City Power and Light Building: A Shining Example of Full Use of G-E Equipment for Modern Sky-scrapers." *GE Monogram* (March 1932): 13.

Engle, Tim. "Lighting the Way." *Kansas City Star Magazine* (29 April 2001): 14–22.

Hieronymus, T. G. "Utility Building Features Newest in Electrical Design." *Electrical World* 100 (27 August 1932): 270–271.

The thirty-one story Kansas City Power & Light Company Building was the tallest skyscraper in Missouri for many years. As with many utility company buildings of the time, nocturnal illumination was an important part of the initial design, and the combination of color flood-lighting with luminous panels and red neon outlining resulted in one of the most dramatic lighting installations of the 1930s. The structure was clad in limestone and floodlit entirely with white lights up to the twenty-ninth floor, the lamps increasing in intensity at each set-back and causing the building to shine more brightly at each successive level. Special balconies over the main entrances held the first banks of projectors above ground level. Above the main structure, mobile color lighting was used to illumine the tower, the first such installation in the city. As in the Staley Building (p. 152) in Decatur, Illinois, red, green, amber and white lights were connected to a Thyratron tube control. This allowed a sequence of colors to go through a complete cycle every thirty seconds. The cycle could be varied to last from as little as six to as many as 150 seconds. Projectors were placed both within the twenty-six-foot-high glass windows and on the exterior of the tower, allowing contrasting color combinations from the interplay between the two systems. The windows were embedded in dramatic relief images, which were part of the exciting new iconography that had developed along with the rise of electricity.

A cupola of opalescent glass topped off the tower and, in concert with the six floodlighting projectors contained within, emitted a luminous white glow above the panoply of colors below. Within the angled sides of the cupola's roof, thirty-two neon tubes were also placed, crowning the skyscraper with a blazing red tip. Although no longer owned by the company that built it, the Power & Light Company Building today remains a prominent feature of the Kansas City skyline. After a temporary halt to the moving colors during the 1970s and early '80s, it is again illuminated by the changing hues that were such a modern element in 1931.   K. B.

Empire State Building · New York, New York · 1931

Architects: **Shreve, Lamb & Harmon**

Location: **350 Fifth Avenue**

Construction Date: **1931. Extant**

Installation Dates: **1931, 1932, 1956, 1964, 1976. The building is currently illuminated with the most recent installation.**

Installation Type: **1931: Frosted glass panels in mooring mast lit from within by 1,872 5-watt incandescent lamps. 250-watt incandescent floodlights at tower base. 8 portholes at tip of tower each containing a 1,000-watt searchlight. 1932: searchlight beacon added. 1956: 4 counter-clockwise revolving beacons, each with a 2,500-watt short-arc mercury bulb, installed at the 90th floor. 1964: 278 1,000-watt incandescent floodlights on the 72nd, 81st and 90th-floor setbacks. 1976: Colored gels added to floodlights. Later replaced by 204 1,000-watt metal halide lamps and 310 fluorescent lamps with colored gels.**

Lighting Designers: **1931: Meyer, Strong & Jones. 1956: Raymond Loewy. 1976: Douglas Leigh.**

Selected Bibliography:

"Try Empire State Beacons." *New York Times* (2 September 1931): 37, col. 1.

Bracker, Milton. "Empire State Building Becomes Lighthouse as 4 Beacons Go On." *New York Times* (4 May 1956): 27, col. 5.

Clavan, Irwin. "The Empire State Building: IX: The Mooring Mast." *Architectural Forum* 54 (February 1931): 229–234.

Clute, Eugene. "Lighting the World's Tallest Building." *Electrical World* 98 (18 July 1931): 106–110.

Lelyveld, Joseph. "The Empire State To Glow at Night." *New York Times* (23 February 1964): 63, col. 3.

Tauranac, John. *The Empire State Building: The Making of a Landmark*. New York: Scribner, 1995.

Empire State Building Official Internet Site. Online. Available: http://www.esbnyc.com. 17 November 2001. (Contains a calendar with the color schedule.)

President Hoover himself pushed the button to switch on the lights of the world's tallest building on May 11, 1931, at the height of America's worst financial crisis. Although continuously lit since then, the fact that the Empire State Building was initially not as exuberantly illuminated as some of its contemporaries might have had to do both with its iconic status, and with its initial reputation as a symbol of the hubris that had caused the Depression: the enormous building stood almost entirely empty for a number of years. Initially, the lighting concentrated entirely on the supposed "zeppelin mooring mast" at the top, a futuristic idea of the designers that had never been tested and in the end turned out to be impractical.

Countless five-watt lamps were installed within the four 160-foot-high frosted glass panels of the mast, the base of which was lit by floodlights behind ornaments above the uppermost windows on the north and south sides of the main building mass. The windows of the eighty-sixth-floor observation rooms provided a band of light, while just above them, the tower stepped back in four levels, each band containing glass panels designed specifically to be illuminated from within, although they were not so employed at that time. At the very tip of the mooring mast, eight portholes were each backed with a searchlight. The beams were intended to radiate upward from the tower, but "the air at more than 1,200 feet above the street was so comparatively free from dust and soot that the light was not diffused and reflected sufficiently to be visible from below" ("Try Empire State Beacons"). However, a year later, a single, presumably stronger searchlight beacon was added when Franklin D. Roosevelt was elected president. In 1956, the "Freedom Lights" were installed. These four beacons were mounted at the ninetieth floor, one on each of the building's four sides. Each beacon revolved counterclockwise at an angle of five degrees above the horizon until it faced the building, at which point it swung to an upright position, before returning once again to the horizontal. The movement of the beams was coordinated in such a manner that one beam always pointed skyward at any given time. The design of this theatrical installation had been developed by

America's most prominent industrial designer, Raymond Loewy. Much was made in contemporary accounts of the comparison between the Statue of Liberty, who had welcomed with her torch earlier immigrants arriving by sea and the Empire State, now welcoming with its beacons the modern travelers arriving by air.

By 1964, when the building was about to lose its status as the city's tallest skyscraper to the World Trade Center, its owners looked for a way to reclaim its dominance of the skyline. The revolving beacons were turned off and, for the first time, the top thirty floors of the structure were floodlit. With the office lights turned off from the seventy-second story down, the effect of the white top hovering above the darkened building below was "like a chandelier suspended from the sky," as the *New York Times* noted. The eighty-sixth and eighty-seventh floors were left unlit, creating a black band for contrast between the lower levels and the upper.

Although the lighting designers had planned to use colored floodlights as far back as 1931, the first color installation came as late as 1976, when Douglas Leigh convinced the owner to add red, white and blue gels to the floodlights in honor of the Bicentennial. When the installation proved a popular success, he was asked to make the arrangement permanent, replacing the old incandescent bulbs with new energy efficient metal halide and fluorescent lamps. The upper floors of the building continue to be floodlit with white lamps until midnight every evening, except for holidays and special events, when a wide variety of appropriate color combinations is employed.   K. B. / D. N.

Empire State Building with Christmas Lighting
© Kim Steele / Getty Images

Empire State Building at night, *c.* 2000
© Peter Mauss / Esto >

Cities Service Building · New York, New York · 1932

Architect: **Clinton & Russell**

Location: **70 Pine Street**

Construction Date: **1932. Extant**

Installation Date: **1932. The building is currently illuminated with metal halide floodlights and a lighting installation in the lantern similar to the original.**

Installation Type: **Total of 90 incandescent floodlights: 59th-floor setback: 250-watt lamps with clear lenses and 500-watt lamps with clear and diffusing lenses. 63rd floor: cornice projectors, each with two 150-watt lamps. 200 100-watt and 150-watt Mazda lamps behind opal glass of lantern. 24 neon (hot cathode) tubes in beacon above lantern. One neon tube at tip of flagpole.**

Lighting Designers: **1932: Alfred Paulus, Westinghouse Lamp Co. Current: Horton Lees Lighting.**

The Cities Service Building was the last skyscraper to be built in New York's financial district during the Great Depression and was the third largest office building in the world at the time of its construction. The unusual design of the sixty-seven-story building included a glass-enclosed lantern that was and is the focal point for the tower's illumination scheme. Cities Service was, like many utility companies of the time, eager to use its new building to promote the use of electricity: "A slim tower of light and shadow springing upward almost 1,000 feet represents the power and purpose of electricity." (*Electric Journal*, p. 355). At the same time, the building's architects saw the lighting scheme as a component of the structure's design: "As a tool of the architect, [floodlighting] is more than just an advertising medium. Light and shadow lend a distinctive emphasis to the features of the design. They enhance the beauty and character of the facade to a degree rivaling that of daytime admiration" (Paulus & Sira, p. 1062). Lighting

for the building began at the fifty-ninth floor and grew gradually in intensity until it reached its high point at the pinnacle. Up to the sixty-fourth floor, only the corners of the building were lit, creating a strong contrast to the intervening areas that lay in shadow and anchoring the bright top to the un-illuminated floors below. The next three stories were lit in their entirety, and were topped by the twenty-foot lantern. Covered with an outer sheet of faceted, wired glass and an inner sheet of opal glass, the lantern was lit from within. This use of glowing, translucent glass, pioneered in Europe in the 1920s, was rarely seen on skyscrapers of the time. The tower was surmounted with a red neon beacon and supplemented by another tiny beacon at the very tip of the flagpole. Its lighting scheme has been updated over the years but has always retained the unique mixture of floodlighting and luminous glass that has made the building an unusual part of Manhattan's nighttime skyline.   K. B.

Cities Service Building, night view, 1965. Photograph by Evelyn Hofer. Courtesy Rose Gallery, Santa Monica

Selected Bibliography:

"Beleuchtete Turmspitze." *Das Licht* 2, no. 4 (1932): 199–200.

"Floodlighting World's Newest Skyscraper." *Electric Journal* 29, no. 7 (July 1932): 355, 357.

Paulus, Alfred and A. Sira. "Doherty Tower Floodlighted." *Electrical World* 99 (18 June 1932): 1062–1064.

Stern, Robert A. M., Gregory Gilmartin and Thomas Mellins. *New York 1930: Architecture and Urbanism Between the Two World Wars*. New York: Rizzoli, 1987.

Gaumont Palace Cinema · Paris · 1932

The original building was designed as a hippodrome in order to profit from the influx of visitors to Paris for the Exposition Universelle of 1900 (pp. 88–89). From 1908 onwards, films were shown, and in 1911 the building was remodeled to become the largest movie theater in the world with 3,400 seats. This record was soon taken by a movie theater in New York City, but came back to Paris in 1930 / 31 when the Gaumont Theater was remodeled once again, to now house 6,000 seats. At the same time an elaborate light installation was added both inside and on the exterior. The building itself was floodlit from forty projectors placed above the protruding canopy, under which the sidewalk reflected a gleaming brightness. The main attraction of the new design, though, was a light cascade that descended on the new corner tower from a height of 164 feet, and was possibly inspired by the light cascades at the Barcelona World's Fair (pp. 138–139) three years earlier. The firm in charge, Les Etablissements Paz e Silva, worked on the preparations for the lighting at the World's Fair in 1937 (pp. 170–173).

At the bottom of the stepped roof pyramid, ten-foot-high letters announced the name of the theater. An enthusiastic German journalist in 1932 described the effect as follows: "The tower with its four receding steps is covered with translucent opal glass and covered with thousand of low-voltage incandescent lamps, which form necklaces and garlands. The entire exterior illumination is slowly turned off, while on the dark front large red neon lights powerfully spell out 'Palace Gaumont Palace.' Then, at the top of the tower, the light cascade begins its performance, and gives the impression of a waterfall running down all three sides. The four steps are switched on in short sequence, and the moving, blinking lights provide the illusion of water tumbling down. The effect of this spectacle is heightened considerably by blue and green luminescent tubes, which are switched on in conjunction with the incandescent bulbs." (W. A. A.)   D. N.

Architect: **2nd restoration: Henri Belloc**

Location: **At the corner of Rue Caulaincourt and Rue Forest, near Place Clichy**

Construction Dates: **1900. 1st Restoration: 1911. 2nd Restoration: 1930 / 31. Demolished 1972.**

Installation Date: **1932**

Installation Type: **40 incandescent floodlights located above canopy. 5,000 incandescent bulbs, 2,000 meters of green and blue neon tubes. Letters in red neon tubes.**

Lighting designer: **Les Etablissements Paz e Silva**

Gaumont Palace, night view, photograph, 1931

Selected Bibliography:
Bidault des Chaumes, A. "Le Nouveau Cinéma Gaumont-Palace, à Paris." *Génie Civil* 99, no. 23 (5 December 1931): 565–570.
Soulier, A. "Les Installations électriques du plus grand cinema du monde 'Le Gaumont Palace.'" *Industrie Electrique* 40, no. 939 (10 August 1931): 341–351.
W. A. A. "Lichtfontäne auf dem Gaumont Palace." *Das Licht* 2, no. 4 (1932): 220.
Weil, Johann. "'Lichtblicke' aus Paris." *Der Werbeleiter*, no. 2 (1932): 41–42.

Niagara-Hudson-Syracuse Lighting Company Building · Syracuse, New York · 1932

Architects: **Melvin L. King, Bley & Lyman**

Location: **300 Erie Boulevard West**

Construction Date: **1932. Extant**

Installation Date: **1932. 1999. The building is currently illuminated with the 1999 installation.**

Installation Type: **1932: Luminous glass pilasters containing discharge tubing of rotating colors. Recesses lit by 75-watt Mazda lamps. Central spandrel lit by 8 1,500-watt floodlights. Glass corners of tower lit from within by hundreds of incandescent lamps. Marquee of chromium, opal glass and steel with indirect lighting and helium tube lettering. 1999: Glass corners lit by banks of 32-watt fluorescent strips with colored gels and dimming system. 6 glass pilasters on either side of entrance lit by red, green and blue neon with dimming system. Smaller vertical elements lit with 130-volt clear incandescent lamps. Brick sections lit by 100-watt metal halide lamps. Metal-halide and incandescent floodlights on building across the street. Metal halide projector on sculpture.**

Lighting Designers: **1932: Unknown. 1999: Howard Brandston and Kevin Simonson of Brandston Partnership.**

Niagara Hudson Building, Olean, NY, night view, photograph, 1932

Niagara Mohawk Building, night view, photograph, c. 1932–40

Niagara Mohawk Building, night view, photograph, 2000 >

Selected Bibliography:

"Niagara-Hudson-Syracuse Lighting Company." *Transactions of the Illuminating Engineering Society* 27 (November 1932): 680.

Linn, Charles. "A Restored, Relit Art Deco Icon Returns the Power of Light to Downtown Syracuse." *Architectural Record* 188, no. 11 (November 2000): 204–208.

Rivette, Barbara S. *Our Glorious Workplaces: Niagara Mohawk.* Syracuse: Onondaga Historical Association, 1998.

The Niagara-Hudson Electricity Company commissioned the firm of Bley and Lyman to design their headquarters in Syracuse and a number of showrooms in upstate New York, including a pair of small but brilliant jewel boxes in Olean and Niagara Falls. As was frequently the case with other electric company buildings, light became a major component of the design resulting in one of the key examples of luminous architecture in the United States.

The spectacular corporate headquarters building featured a stepped facade, culminating in a tower that reached a height of 114 feet and included glass corner panels illuminated

from within. Along the ground floor, luminous glass pillars produced an array of changing colors. A sculptural figure on the tower, dubbed the Spirit of Light, was constructed of stainless steel and glass and was lit by spotlights.

As with most illumination displays, its lights were turned off during World War II and the building remained dark until very recently, when the company, now known as the Niagara Mohawk Power Corporation, decided to commission a new lighting design. Brandston Partnership, designer of the new scheme, used updated equipment while never straying too far from the original lighting conception. The incandescent lamps in the glass corner panels and those behind the Spirit of Light were replaced with colored fluorescent strips, while red, green and blue neon lamps were

installed behind the six main pilasters on the facade. These lights, connected to a computerized timer, can now produce an almost infinite number of color combinations. The flagship building of the Niagara Mohawk Corporation was relit on November 26, 1999 as part of the annual "Light up Syracuse" festival, and has brought a new, and much appreciated, attraction to Syracuse's downtown at night.   K. B.

RCA Building · New York, New York · 1933

Architects: **L. Andrew Reinhard, Harry Hofmeister, Raymond Hood, Wallace Harrison, Harvey Wiley Corbett**

Location: **Rockefeller Center, 5th Avenue (between 48th and 51st Street)**

Construction Dates: **1931–33. Extant**

Installation Dates: **1933, 1960, 1984. The 1984 lighting is still in use, each night from dusk to 1:00 am.**

Installation Type: **1960: Mercury reflector lamps, 1984: 314 1,500-watt metal halide lamps (custom made by General Electric, to accommodate higher wattages in smaller bulbs) with an output of 160,000 lumens of white light at 11 different locations on adjacent buildings. Additionally: 28 high-pressure sodium lamps along the crown.**

Lighting Designer: **1984: Abe Feder (lighting designer), Aaron Chestnut (assistant)**

RCA Building, night view, postcard, c. 1933

RCA Building, night view, photograph by Samuel H. Gottscho, 1933 >

Selected Bibliography:

Allison, David. "Outdoor Lighting: An Expanding Technology." *Architectural Forum* 113 (July 1960): 128–133.

Balfour, Alan. *Rockefeller Center. Architecture as Theatre.* New York: McGraw Hill, 1978.

Fisher, Thomas. "Night Lights" 68, no. 9. *Progressive Architecture* (September 1987): 150–155.

Krinsky, Carol Herselle. *Rockefeller Center.* New York, Oxford University Press, 1978.

Mumford, Lewis. "The Sky Line: Mr. Rockefeller's Center." *New Yorker* (23 December 1933). Quoted in Robert Wojtowicz. *Sidewalk Critic. Lewis Mumford's Writings on New York.* New York: Princeton Architectural Press, 1998.

O'Mahony, Tom. "Rockefeller Center: Midtown Glows." *Lighting Design & Application* 15 (April 1985): 20–24.

Stern, Robert A. M., Gregory Gilmartin and Thomas Mellins. *New York 1930: Architecture and Urbanism Between the Two World Wars.* New York: Rizzoli, 1987.

The planning for a conglomerate of office buildings (today known as Rockefeller Center) in Midtown Manhattan began in 1928, during a time of unbridled belief in the future of the current building boom. Despite the economic crisis one year later, the planning for nineteen individual buildings went ahead and the buildings were executed between 1930 and 1940. The slender, seventy-story-tall tower for the Radio Corporation of America (RCA) was among the first to be finished (after Radio City Music Hall and another theater) in 1933. Le Corbusier called it the "temple of the machine age" and praised it as the representative of a new era. It was the result of a brilliant reinterpretation of the Zoning Code's setback ordinance, which mandated reduced sections in every high rise's upper stories in response to density and street width. Applying this rule to the entire width of the "superblock" made for freedom of design in the center and lead to the unprecedented elegance of the slender central tower.

Although the rest of Rockefeller Center was still under construction, floodlighting was installed for the RCA tower immediately, in order to revive interest in the project and attract investors at the height of the Depression. The fact that its architects Hood, Corbett and Harrison were among the most outspoken proponents of an "architecture of the night" might also have helped. Initially, only the eastern facade was floodlit. Nevertheless, the building was eighty percent rented by 1934, while the Empire State Building (pp. 156–157) had a vacancy rate of the same magnitude.

The prominent critic Lewis Mumford wrote in December 1933: "The best time to see the Center is at night. Under artificial lighting, in a slight haze, the group of buildings that now make up the Center looks like one of Hugh Ferriss' visions of the City of the Future. At night one can forget that every touch of bad ornament is bad with an almost juvenile badness; … one can forget that the broad face of the main building, running from east to west, and seventy stories high, permanently cuts off sunlight from a large swath of buildings to the north; … Here, at night, is what Ferriss meant: something large, exciting, romantic." (Mumford, 1933)

Since the mid-eighties, thanks to a new lighting installation, the RCA tower has become the best lit skyscraper in Manhattan and the only one that is illumined from top to bottom. Theater lighting designer Abe Feder designed an illumination concept for the central tower and proposed to light it evenly on all four sides for the first time. The different projectors have to spread their light over a distance of 600–800 feet. 342 lamps were installed at eleven different points on the surrounding roofs of ten buildings. As if responding to Mumford's criticism, Feder explained: "What I really wanted to do, was reveal Rockefeller Center and its RCA Tower as the magnificent piece of sculpture it was created to be … with Light." (Fisher). The sunken garden in front of the main entrance is turned by metal halide lamps into what Feder called, "an umbrella of light (Krinsky)," which exchanges a warmer light in the summer against a colder one in winter. The two red RCA signs at the top are lit by twenty additional 1,000-watt high-pressure sodium lamps with red filters. In response to a growing uneasiness about light pollution in the 1980s, Abe Feder very carefully aimed the narrow beams of the individual lamps to avoid light spill.   D. N.

A Century of Progress International Exhibition · Chicago, Illinois · 1933

Dates: **May 27–November 12, 1933;
June 1–October 31, 1934**

Architects: **Harvey Corbett, Chairman of the
Architectural Commission: General Exhibits
Buildings**
**John Holabird, Hubert Burnham and Edward
Bennett: Travel and Transport; Administration**
Raymond Hood: Electrical Group
Paul Cret: Hall of Science
Albert Kahn: Ford Building (1934)

Color Scheme: **Josef Urban (1933), Shepherd
Vogelgesang (1934)**

Lighting Designer: **Walter D'Arcy Ryan, General
Electric**

Hall of Science, postcard, 1933

Selected Bibliography:
"Discussion – Lighting A Century of Progress."
Transactions of the Illuminating Engineering Society 29,
no. 2 (February 1934): 143–49.
Cutler, C. M. "New Lighting Features of the 1934
Century of Progress Exposition." *Transactions of the
Illuminating Engineering Society* 30, no. 3 (March
1935): 255–265.
Ryan, Walter D'Arcy. "Lighting 'A Century of Progress.'"
Electrical Engineering 53, no. 5 (May 1934): 731–744.
Rydell, Robert. *World of Fairs: The Century-of-Progress
Expositions.* Chicago: University of Chicago Press, 1993.

Chicago's Century of Progress International Exposition sought to celebrate the centennial of the city's incorporation while reinventing the success of the World's Columbian Exposition of 1893. The exposition set the standard for 1930s American world fairs in both its dependence on private financing as well as its commitment to idealizing the achievements of science and industry. In terms of illumination, the exposition proffered innovative technology to the public, such as colored gas-tube lighting, as well as volume and intensity, becoming "The greatest flood of colored light that … any city of the world has ever produced." (*Official Guide Book*, p. 29).

The Century of Progress exposition occupied a narrow site over three miles long, incorporating eighty-two acres of landfill on Chicago's lakefront. The buildings were laid out in an asymmetrical plan designed by Raymond Hood after he visited the Barcelona World's Fair of 1929 (p. 138–139). The layout featured several themed clusters, but omitted any central axes or grand vistas. The buildings themselves were constructed of inexpensive, temporary materials, mainly asbestos-compressed cement board, sheet metal, and plywood. The most common exterior wall covering was gypsum board, coated with paper and primed with aluminum paint. The modern style of the temporary buildings, composed of an eclectic collection of rectilinear forms, was sharply criticized. The buildings were painted in 1933 using a palette of twenty-four bold colors chosen by the stage designer Josef Urban. Urban utilized "color geography," whereby the color scheme was related to the orientation of each building. Cool colors were used on northern exposures, warm colors on southern exposures, while neutral shades dominated the east and west sides of most structures. Even the flowerbeds and hedges were coordinated with the coloring of the buildings. Urban died in July 1933. In 1934, a second exterior color scheme was designed by Shepherd Vogelgesang, who utilized only ten colors clustered around different exhibit groups.

While the surface color of the buildings was enchanting, the major focus of visitors' amazement was the nighttime illumination. This illumination was ceremoniously introduced each night at the Arcturus ceremony in the courtyard of the Hall of Science at 9 p.m. This was the signature event at the fair, when light from a distant star was used to turn on the exposition's illumination. The exterior lighting of the fair drew 3,000 kilowatts of current, the illumination totaling twenty-one billion candlepower. The core of the illumination was 2,877 floodlights focused on the colorful buildings. These projectors produced the same color of light as the building's exterior paint because other colors were found to have a muddying effect. Further illumination was provided by various towers and pylons that were outlined with the new gas-tube lights. For example, the cascade on the Electrical Group, a feature which simulated water rushing down the side of the building, alone used 5,000 feet of blue gas-tube lighting. Finally, the walkways at the exposition were illuminated by 2,000 short 150-watt mushroom-shaped fixtures that cast light downward so as not to distract from the illuminated spectacles.

The exposition's light spectacles were concentrated in the South Lagoon. These included the "Aurora Borealis" on top of the Electrical Building that utilized seventeen searchlights. These lights intersected over a fountain in the court of the Electrical Building and then fanned out over the lagoon. (Throughout the grounds, illuminating engineers utilized the eighty acres of water at the fair as a reflecting device to magnify the lighting effects.) There were also three large fountains splashed with colored light in the South Lagoon. The climactic spectacle was called the "electric steam color scintillator." It consisted of a battery of twenty-four arc searchlights, creating a towering fan-shaped wedge of colored light each evening over the grounds of the fair. Some of the most memorable effects were attained by illuminating the patterns of smoke created by fireworks with the colored searchlights of the scintillator.

Private exhibitors were encouraged to add to the spectacle of the grounds. The Firestone building, for example, which housed a miniature tire factory, shone with both "pylons of brilliant glowing color" on the building itself, and, more spectacularly, the "Firestone Singing Color Fountain." This fountain consisted of six dome-shaped fountains shooting up twenty-foot streams of water. An eighty-by-twelve-foot gas-tube "Firestone" sign was placed behind the fountain, on the cornice of the pavilion. While the Singing Color Fountain's light changed with the intensity of the music, the sign ran through a cycle of different colors of varying intensity.

In 1934, the fair's illumination was increased by about fifty percent. A new fountain (the largest in the world) was added to the North Lagoon and framed by a second scintillator. Fountain technology was improved by fair engineers, who used a special nozzle (designed for spraying concrete roads) to split the water into smaller droplets with a higher reflecting capacity. In 1934, the Ford Building also featured a Pillar of Light projecting from its roof. This concentration of twenty-four searchlights, 200 feet at the base, projected one mile into the sky. The exposition closed on October 31, 1934 with a program entitled "The Festival of Illumination: The Apotheosis of Man-Made Light."   S.E.

Overleaf:

1 Electrical Building, tinted photo, 1933

2 Chrysler Motors Building, photograph, 1933

3 Ford Building with vertical searchlights, postcard, 1934

4 Libbey-Owens Glass Pavillon, postcard, 1933

1

2

Simpson's Department Store · London · 1936

Architects: **Joseph Emberton in collaboration with László Moholy-Nagy and Felix Samuely**

Location: **203–206 Piccadilly**

Construction Date: **1936. Extant**

Installation Date: **1936. The building is still illuminated.**

Installation Type: **Red, blue and green neon tubes concealed behind bronze screens on facade.**

Lighting Designer: **Joseph Emberton**

Selected Bibliography:

"Joseph Emberton: Design of a Modern Shop." *Industrial Arts* 1, no. 2 (Summer 1936): 88–94.

"Simpson's Store in Piccadilly, London: Mr. Joseph Emberton, Architect." *Architectural Review* 79, no. 475 (June 1936): 270–271.

"Store for Messrs. Simpson, Piccadilly, London." *Architectural Record* 80, no. 2 (August 1936): 120–129.

Ind, Rosemary. *Emberton.* Berkeley: Scolar, 1983.

James, Kathleen. *Erich Mendelsohn and the Architecture of German Modernism.* Cambridge: Cambridge University Press, 1997.

Moholy-Nagy, Sibyl. *Moholy-Nagy: Experiment in Totality.* Cambridge: MIT Press, 1969.

Moholy-Nagy, László. "Light Architecture" *Industrial Arts* 1, no. 1 (Spring 1936), reprinted in: Kostelanetz, Richard. *Moholy-Nagy.* New York: Praeger, 1970

Wainwright, David. *The British Tradition: Simpson – A World of Style.* London: Quiller Press, 1996.

Modern architecture gained ground in England later than in central Europe. Joseph Emberton's design for Simpson's new store in London was, in 1936, still considered a stunningly innovative construction of steel, glass and neon. Emberton's associate, Felix Samuely, had worked previously with Erich Mendelsohn, and a certain influence of the German architect's design for the Herpich Store (p. 130) in Berlin was apparent. The facade on Piccadilly featured five horizontal ribbon windows bordered on either side by vertical bands of portland stone and bronze. The top row of windows was set back under a canopy while the ground level was faced with black granite.

The lighting technology, however, had made great progress in the previous ten years, and the building's appearance at night was considerably more impressive than that of its German model. Concealed from view in the bronze troughs above each window were blue, red and green neon tubes that could be used singly or in any combination and that were all connected to dimmers. The resulting differences in hues and intensities allowed the building to be flooded by a wide range of colors that brought its serious modernistic facade to life. When all three colors were used at once, the mixture of tints even produced a white light. Light troughs at the vertical edges of the facade also created a rectangular frame of neon for the facade. As the lighting scheme had been an essential part of the building's conception, the surfaces of the facade were designed to incline slightly towards the light source in order to insure an even illumination. The store's name was eventually added in prominent neon letters. The rather restrained lighting of the building's facade was a conscious effort to stand out among the flashing lights of Piccadilly Circus nearby.

The Hungarian designer and former Bauhaus teacher László Moholy-Nagy had recently emigrated to London and was involved in the design of Simpson's. Although he had long thought and written about the use of light in architecture, his contributions here were apparently concentrated on interior decoration and display windows. Joseph Emberton seems to have worked out the design for the lighting of the facade himself. Nevertheless, Moholy-Nagy's essay on "Light Architecture" appeared in the magazine *Industrial Arts* while Simpson's was nearing completion, and only months before the same magazine reported on the finished building. Moholy-Nagy wrote about the potential of light as a new art medium. He predicted that current floodlighting practices would develop to the point where illumination —"colored light frescoes"—would become a key component of a future architecture.

Under new ownership, the building, which is on the National Register of Historic Places in Great Britain, continues to be lit.

K. B. / D. N.

Simpson's, night view, photograph, *c.* 1936

Simpson's, night view, photograph, 1996 >

World's Fair · Paris · 1937

Exposition Internationale des Arts et des Techniques appliqués à la Vie Moderne

Dates: **May 4–November 25, 1937**

Architects: **Jacques Gréber: Architect in Chief, Jacques Carlu, Louis-Hippolyte Boileau & Léon Azéma: Palais de Chaillot**
Albert Speer: German Pavilion
Boris Iofan: Soviet Pavilion
Alvar Aalto: Finnish Pavilion
Marcello Piacentini & Cesare Valle: Italian Pavilion
Josep Lluis Sert & Josep Lacasa: Spanish Pavilion
Robert Mallet-Stevens: Electricity Pavilion
Henri Favier: Triumphant Way of Light and Radio
Krejcar, Bolivka and Nicod: Czech Pavilion
Le Corbusier: Temps Nouveau Pavilion

Lighting Designers: **André Granet, Carles Buïgas, Eugène Beaudouin, Marcel Lods, André Salomon**

Italian Pavilion, photograph, 1937

Main axis at night, photograph, 1937

Overleaf:

1 Luminous towers at the entrance to the fair. Cover of the official fair publication, 1937.

2 Electricity Pavilion with film projection screen, architect: Robert Mallet-Stevens.

3 Fluorescent tubing underneath the Eiffel Tower, installed by André Granet.

4 German Pavilion, photograph 1937

5 Czech Pavilion, photograph 1937

Selected Bibliography:

"Lighting Effects and Luminous Decorations Planned for the 1937 Paris International Exposition." *Transactions of the Illuminating Engineering Society* 32 (April 1937): 346–351.

"Paris Exposition: Some of the Lighting Effects—Trocadéro and River Fountain." *Electrician* (25 June 1937): 839–841.

Chrétien, Henri, A. Gillett and Jean Tedesco. "The Panoramic Screen and Projection Equipment Used at the Palace of Light of the International Exposition (Paris, 1937)." *Journal of the Society of Motion Picture Engineers* 32 (May 1939): 530–532.

Granet, André. *Décors Èphémères: Les Expositions Jeux d'Eau et de Lumière*. Paris: Desfossés, 1948.

Harriss, Joseph. *The Tallest Tower: Eiffel and the Belle Epoque*. Washington DC: Regnery Gateway, 1975.

Moholy-Nagy, László. "The 1937 International Exhibition, Paris." *Architectural Record* 82 (October 1937): 81–93.

Powell, Alvin L. "Some Impressions of Illumination at the International Exposition, Paris, 1937." *Transactions of the Illuminating Engineering Society* 33 (June 1938): 566–587.

Schneider, L. "Der Internationale Beleuchtungskongress in Paris." *Licht* 7 (July 1937): 134–135.

Warnod, André. *Exposition 37: La Vie Flamboyante des Expositions*. Paris: Éditions de France, 1937.

Zemánek, Jiří. *Zdeněk Pešánek 1896–1965*. Prague: Národní Galerie, 1966.

The last in a long series of international expositions held in Paris, the Exposition of 1937 would later be mostly remembered for the ominous image of the neo-classical German and Russian Pavilions facing off at the heart of the exhibition grounds, two years before the outbreak of World War II. The turbulent planning of the exhibition, which was held during the short reign of the leftist Front Populaire, and frequent strikes during its construction, led to long delays in the opening of many pavilions. But the fair also deserves recognition for a number of striking works by Europe's leading modern architects and particularly for presenting a spectacular climax in the long development of exhibition lighting and architectural illumination.

The fair was situated like its predecessors on both the Champ de Mars and the Esplanade des Invalides, with the left and right banks of the Seine forming a link between the two axes. Architects and lighting designers used floodlighting more sparingly than at previous exhibitions. Boris Iofan's Soviet Pavilion, topped by gigantic Socialist Realist statues, was floodlit in its entirety. Albert Speer's German pavilion vis-à-vis also featured subtle but powerful floodlighting. Hidden lamps lit only the facade's recessed portions between the pilasters, resulting in a strong pattern of light and shadow. The neoclassical Palais de Chaillot (which had just replaced the Palais de Trocadéro of the 1878 exhibition) was illumined with a mixture of incandescent and sodium-vapor lamps, producing a golden glow.

Among the new approaches to lighting was the extensive employment of fluorescent tubing, used for the first time as a decorative element on a number of buildings, such as the Radio Pavilion, whose facade was ornamented by a pattern of green and blue lines. Many pavilions were composed largely of glass and illuminated mainly by their interior lights. The cubic Czech Pavilion, for example, featured an inner opaque and an outer transparent wall of glass. Lights installed between the walls lit up in a series of horizontal bands from bottom to top, until the entire building was illuminated, at which point the bands gradually returned to darkness—"a fragile poem of glass raised up into the air on the banks of the Seine" in the eyes of a contemporary critic (Zemánek). One of Marcello Piacentini's most modern buildings was the Italian Pavilion, whose facade was surrounded by an elegant steel skeleton carrying lights at night, and turning the windowless building into a luminous cube.

One of the exterior walls of the Electricity Pavilion consisted of a concave surface, 30 feet in height by 200 feet in length, on which movies were projected in Henri Chrétien's Hypergonar format, an early form of Cinemascope. The French director Jean Tedesco produced his film *Panorama au fil de l'eau* for this occasion. For the architect Robert Mallet-Stevens, who was also an important film set designer and theoretician, this building provided the synthesis of film and modern architecture that he had predicted in his writings. Between films, slide projectors were used to cover the building in changing patterns of color. In addition, an enormous searchlight rotated from a lighthouse at the top of the building. Le Corbusier's "Temps Nouveau" Pavilion, which housed an exhibition on his urbanistic concepts, consisted of a light steel constuction and translucent canvas. While not illuminated per se, it used strong colors of green, red and yellow, which fitted into the overall colorful exhibition scheme, and glowed softly at night, when the interior lights were on.

Along the Pont Alexander III stood twelve aluminum pylons with show windows in their lower portions. Mercury floodlighting gave the aluminum a greenish-blue tone. With music from loudspeakers added, the bridge was to represent a "Triumphant Way of Light and Radio."

The Eiffel Tower again featured a spectacular lighting installation, as had been the case at previous expositions. It had been modernized by removing the arches on its first platform. Thirty-two movable searchlight projectors were installed there, sending their beams upwards into the night sky. On the side facing the Palais de Chaillot, twelve additional projectors with mercury lamps were attached to pivoting mirrors, creating a huge fan pattern that opened and closed. In addition, green, red and yellow incandescent bulbs were placed throughout the structure. On the underside of the tower, in the dome formed between the four legs, lighting designer André Granet installed five miles of the new fluorescent tubing. The pastel shades of pink, blue and green were reflected by a pool set directly beneath, which itself was lit from below.

New fountains had been constructed in front of the tower and were lit by changing colored lamps as well as by ultraviolet lights that were projected onto fluorescent materials placed in the water. On fête nights, the "Gala de la Lumière" began with fireworks on the Eiffel Tower's various platforms, turning the entire structure into a pyrotechnic display. Additional illuminated fountains were towed into place on the Seine. Pontoons emitted clouds of smoke or steam, or sprayed water into the air, all illumined by colored lights, and also provided the bases from which fireworks were ignited. Searchlights along the shore projected patterns of color into the sky as loudspeakers transmitted music that had been especially composed for the fêtes, broadcast from the Eiffel Tower and apparently even from airplanes flying back and forth overhead. These effects, which a German visitor called "a fairy tale of lights, color and sound" (Schneider), were considered some of the most spectacular ever achieved at any exposition to that time.   K. B. / D. N.

PARIS 1937
EXPOSITION INTERNATIONALE

2

Neue Reichskanzlei · Berlin · 1939

Architect: **Albert Speer**

Location: **Vossstrasse**

Construction Dates: **1937–39. Destroyed 1945**

Installation Date: **1939–42**

Installation Type: **Illumination of main facade: 178 floodlights in 21 batteries on the roofs of adjacent buildings (173 kW, *c.* 3.6 million lumen). Hidden floodlights in glass-covered trenches in the interior courtyard, in front of the main entrance, between the two layers of glass at the windows of the Marble Gallery**

Lighting Designers: **Albert Speer, Eberhard von der Trappen**

"Lichtdom" (light cathedral) at the swearing-in ceremony political leaders at Nuremberg's Zeppelin Field, 1936

Berlin Reichskanzlei, news photograph taken during tests of the floodlighting equipment, 1939
© Ullstein Bilderdienst >

Selected Bibliography:

Bartetzko, Dieter. *Illusionen in Stein: Stimmungs-architektur des Deutschen Faschismus.* Reinbeck: Rowohlt Taschenbuch Verlag 1985.

"Beleuchtungseinrichtung in der Reichskanzlei." *Das Licht* 9, no. 3 (March 1939): 50–53.

Lotz, Wilhelm. "Repräsentationsbau und Lichttechnik: Zu dem Thema der Vorliegenden Heftes." *Das Licht* 9, no. 3 (March 1939): 47.

Schönberger, Angela. *Die neue Reichskanzlei von Albert Speer.* Berlin: Gebrüder Mann Verlag, 1981.

Speer, Albert. *Inside the Third Reich. Memoirs by Albert Speer.* New York: MacMillan, 1970.

Perhaps more than any other regime before them, the National Socialists understood architecture as an instrument of politics. They immediately usurped the notion of "Light Architecture," introduced strict controls for commercial advertisements, but also organized light festivals and initiated the permanent illumination of historic or politically important buildings, especially in Berlin. When Hitler asked Albert Speer to plan and build the New Reichschancellery, there were precedents for the illumination of contemporary monumental architecture, such as Werner March's bell tower at the Olympic stadium, or Speer's Zeppelin-field in Nuremberg and his German Pavilion at the Paris World's Fair (pp. 170–173).

Nevertheless, the illumination of the Neue Reichskanzlei was celebrated as a break-through in illumination engineering. Lighting designer Wilhelm Lotz (who, in 1928 had published a volume on architectural lighting for the Werkbund) wrote: "The first monumental building in the redesign of our capital opens a new chapter in contemporary lighting. For the first time, light has been used as a design element in representational architecture." Speer's interest in the topic, Lotz wrote, was a "signal, that lighting design is about to encounter new and grand tasks, especially with the redesign of Berlin, which he is organizing...." (Lotz, *Repräsentationsbau und ...*) Indeed, the nocturnal appearance was carefully planned and tried out with the help of illuminated models.

The lighting of the building's 1,200-foot-long main facade in Vossstrasse was developed by the prominent lighting designer Eberhard von der Trappen, who had been responsible for the illumination of historic monuments in Berlin. Floodlights were placed at the roofline of buildings across the street, about sixty feet high. This arrangement was intended to render the nocturnal appearance similar to that of daytime and at the same time made lampposts in front of the facade unnecessary. In the interior courtyard, hidden floodlighting from low, glass-covered trenches contrasted the columnar niches against the neighboring walls in a theatrically dramatic fashion. The main entrance was also lit from sunken light trenches. In the interior of the Reichskanzlei as well, the nocturnal illumination strove to mimic the appearance during daytime. Additional lights were hidden in the cornices. Perhaps the most telling innovation was the window lighting in the Marble Gallery, the most important representational space of the building. "Between the two layers of glass, which have a distance of eighty centimeters, there will be a number of hidden floodlights behind the window sill, which illuminate a white curtain.... As the inner window is translucent and the actual lights are hidden from view behind screens, the effect is that of incoming sun or daylight."

("Beleuchtungseinrichtung in der ...") While no visual connection to the outside could be established, there was an appearance of continuous daylight, and from outside, the row of brightly lit windows might have suggested continuous activity. Although the desire for a realistic appearance of the architecture at night seems a far cry from Speer's temporary light cathedrals, in many of its details the Reichskanzlei also had elements of a theatrical, illusionary architecture, here suggesting the timelessness that stood at the heart of the demagogic concept of a "1000-year Reich."   D.N.

New York World's Fair · New York, New York · 1939

Dates: **April 30–October 31, 1939;**
May 11–October 27, 1940

Architects: **Stephen F. Vorhees, Chairman of the Board of Design**
Wallace K. Harrison & J. Andre Fouilhoux: Trylon and Perisphere Theme Center, Consolidated Edison
Shreve, Lamb & Harmon: Glass Center
Skidmore & Owings, and John Moss: Westinghouse; Continental Baking
Aalvar Aalto: Finnish Pavilion
James Gamble Rogers: Chrysler Pavilion
Albert Kahn, and C. C. Colby and R. R. Kilburn: Ford Motor

Color Scheme: **Julian E. Garnsey**

Lighting Designers: **Bassett Jones, J. S. Hamel, Richard C. Engelken**

World's Fair poster by Nembhard N. Culin, *c.* 1939

Selected Bibliography:

"How New York World's Fair Exhibitors Use Light." *Transactions of the Illuminating Engineering Society* 34, no. 8 (September 1939): 855–880.

"Illumination Spectacle at New York World's Fair 1939." *Transactions of the Illuminating Engineering Society* 33, no. 5 (May 1938): 407–408.

"New York Fair." *Architectural Forum* 70, no. 6 (June 1939): 393–462.

"New York Fair: Flexibility, Circulation, Light Control." *Architectural Record* 86, no. 2 (August 1939): 40–47.

Cohen, Barbara L, et al. *Trylon and Perisphere.* New York: Harry N. Abrams, 1989.

Drawing the Future: Design Drawings for the 1939 New York World's Fair. Exh. cat. New York: Museum of the City of New York, 1999.

Official Guide Book of the New York World's Fair. New York: Exposition Publications, 1939.

Owen, Russell. "Symphony in Light at New York World's Fair 1939." *New York Times* (7 May 1939, VIII): 8.

Zim, Larry and Lerner, Mel, and Rolfes, Herbert. *The World of Tomorrow: The 1939 New York World's Fair.* New York: Harper & Row, 1988.

Commemorating the 150th anniversary of President George Washington's inauguration in New York City, the New York World's Fair of 1939–40 emphasized the technological achievements of the United States. As the United States emerged from the Great Depression, the fair's theme, "Building the world of tomorrow," was meant to present a hopeful view of a future, based on science, technology, and industry. Like the other American fairs of the 1930s, the New York exposition expressed this scientific idealism partly through the work of illuminating engineers. In terms of lighting technology, the most significant innovation was the extensive use of fluorescent and mercury-capillary tubes.

The New York World's Fair was constructed on 1,200 acres of reclaimed wetland, Flushing Meadows, in the borough of Queens. Under the leadership of Stephen Vorhees, the site was organized according to a symmetrical beaux-arts scheme that emphasized three avenues radiating from the fair's centrally located Theme Center, the 700-foot-tall Trylon and the 180-foot-diameter Perisphere, which housed an elaborate exhibition about the future of Urban America.

The architecture of the fair featured approximately forty mainly windowless exhibition buildings framed in wood and sheathed in gypsum coated with stucco. The buildings' designs—many of which had been rendered in dramatic chiaroscuro by Hugh Ferriss—relied on the streamlined modern forms popular in American commercial architecture. When criticized for lacking a coherent style, fair officials cited the building's "democratic character" and honesty, which "frankly expresses the temporary nature of the buildings." (*Official Guide Book*, p. 31). While the Trylon and Perisphere were painted pure white, the remaining buildings all had off-white as a base. Color was used only to articulate specific features of a building, like the ribs on the U. S. Steel building's aluminum dome, rather than as a broad surface treatment. In order to facilitate orientation, on each of the three avenues only a single color was used: red, blue, and gold, respectively, their intensity progressing from a pale tone at the center towards a deeply saturated one at the fringe of the site. However, because of the spare use

of color on the buildings themselves, the organizing function of the color was barely perceptible.

Important to an understanding of the fair's illumination is the fact that the engineers tightly restricted the use of floodlighting, which consulting engineer Bassett Jones called "archaic" (Owen, p. 4). Only the Trylon and Perisphere at the heart of the exhibition were floodlit. This illumination focused on the Perisphere, commencing at dusk with an amber glow, and then cycling through a sequence of reds, and finally changing to an intense blue. This saturated blue light was only possible because of the invention of mercury-capillary lamps. Thirty projectors, each with nine 400-watt mercury-capillary lamps, were required to illuminate the three acres of the Perisphere's exterior. Finally, another thirty 2,500-watt tungsten lamps fitted with aluminum disks projected clouds onto the globe's blue background. In order to emphasize the center's brightness, the rest of the grounds were illuminated through diffuse light sources. Hundreds of trees, for example, were lit by a 250-watt mercury-capillary lamp located directly underneath them. The trees glowed with such intense light that the veins in each leaf were visible to passersby and this light sufficed to illuminate the walkways. Many of the buildings also provided indirect lighting for the walkways.

The fair's nocturnal appearance was characterized through the frequent use of new low-intensity fluorescent tubes. These lamps were hidden in troughs directly on the facade, like those on the Petroleum Industries building, or placed behind sculptures. Some of the exterior walls of the buildings were pierced with opalescent glass or glass bricks, which had just been developed. Most notably was the Glass Center by Shreve Lamb and Harmon, whose tall walls consisted entirely of glass blocks.

Finally, light also diffused off of the many illuminated pylons, fountains, gateways and sculptures, many predictably sponsored by utilities and electrical appliance manufacturing corporations. Notable among these were the Westinghouse building's Singing Tower of Light and the Consolidated Edison building's forty-two-foot-high, 9,000-square-foot Wall of Water. The Edison building's architects,

Harrison & Fouilhoux (who also designed the Trylon and Perisphere) optimistically predicted that: "In the World of Tomorrow lighted water will rank with marble in the adornment of great public buildings." (Quoted from *Transactions of …*, p. 881)

The fair also featured the usual assortment of large-scale illuminated spectacles. The spectacle in the Lagoon of Nations at the end of the main axis, designed by architect Jean Labatut, was performed at 9 p.m. each night. It consisted of a synchronized medley of music, water jets, pyrotechnics, and colored lights. The 585 light projectors produced over two million candlepower through a combination of one tungsten and one mercury-capillary lamp. These two lamps enabled a more complete color spectrum than in past fairs. Labatut also designed the spectacle at Fountain Lake in the amusement zone, which, while somewhat smaller, added an element of mobility, as the projectors and water pumps were mounted on moving barges. The third major spectacle, a searchlight canopy above the Federal Building's Court of Peace, was located on the fair's central axis, adjacent to the Lagoon of Nations. Designed to close off the view down Constitution Mall from the Theme Center, the canopy consisted of twenty-one searchlights directed to create the effect of a coffered ceiling. The fair's illumination was deemed such a success in 1939 that it was left essentially intact in 1940.   S. E.

Overleaf:

1 Court of Power with the Wall of Water, photograph, 1939

2 Illuminated spectacle at the Lagoon of Nations, postcard, 1939

3 Italian Pavillon at night, photograph by Samuel Gottscho

2

Golden Gate International Exposition · San Francisco, California · 1939

Dates: **February 19–October 29, 1939;
May 25–September 29, 1940**

Architects: **George W. Kelham (d. 1937), First Chair
of Planning Committee, Court of the Seven Seas,
Court of the Moon and Stars. Administration
Building, Aviation Hangars.**
**Arthur Jr. Brown, Court of Honor, Tower of the Sun.
Second Chair of Planning Committee**
**Lewis Parsons Hobart, Court of Reflections, Arch of
the Winds, Court of Flowers, Rainbow Fountain.**
**Bernard Ralph Maybeck, and William G. Merchant:
Redwood Empire Building, Temples of the East and
East Facade.**
**Timothy Pflueger: Court of Pacifica, Court of Nations,
Federal Building, Facade of the California Building,
California Auditorium**
**Weihe, Ernest E.: West Facades, including the
Portals of the Pacific with the Elephant Towers
(with Donald Macky)**
**William Wurster: Buena Vista Clubhouse, assoc.
Architect: (with Armando D'Ans) Pavilion of
Argentine.**

Director of Color: **Jesse Stanton**

Lighting Designer: **A. F. Dickerson**

"Temple Compound," postcard, 1939

"Tower of the Sun," postcard, 1939 >

Selected Bibliography:
"A New Style of Architecture, Designed by Californians."
Official Guidebook. Golden Gate International Exposition
1939.
Bear, William P., William R. van Bokkelen and Wayne
Snowden. "Electricity for Treasure Island." *Electrical
Engineering* 58 (April 1939): 149–151.
Dickerson, A. F. "Color, Light and Structure at Golden
Gate Exposition." *General Electric Review* 42 (July 1939):
291–306.
Dickerson, A. F. "Color: New Synthesis in the West."
Reprint by General Electric from *Architectural Record*
(1939).
Dickerson, A. F. "The Exterior Illumination of the Golden
Gate International Exposition, San Francisco, California."
Transactions of the Illuminating Engineering Society 34
(July 1939): 681–708.
Neuhaus, Eugen. *The Art of Treasure Island*. Berkeley:
University of California Press, 1939. (Contains a list of
all the architects and artists involved.)

The exhibition was held in the same year as
the World's Fair in New York City (pp. 176–177)
and celebrated the completion of two gigantic
engineering projects, the Golden Gate Bridge
and the Bay Bridge. As had its predecessor, the
1915 Panama-Pacific Exposition (pp. 104–107),
the 1939 fair invited the countries around the
Pacific Ocean to contribute, and references
to their cultures served as an architectural
leitmotiv, underlining the U.S. western trade
connections and hopes for their further ex-
pansion. This electrically unified fantasy of the
Asian Orient happened only months before
the outbreak of World War II, and three years
before the attack on Pearl Harbor.

The exhibition site was outside the city on
Treasure Island, to which the new Bay Bridge
connected, and was surrounded by water on
three sides. The layout within the roughly
square exhibition area was determined by a
grid of major and minor axes that opened up
to a sequence of courts. The large majority of
the thirty-five architects involved had studied
at the Ecole des Beaux Arts in Paris. While
the architectural design concept claimed to
purposely avoid the "'modernistic' cubistic
extravagances" and the "utopian style"
(Neuhaus) of the fairs in Chicago (p. 164–167)
and New York, a supposedly new style, called
"Pacifica," was created: "Mingling Oriental,
Cambodian and Mayan styles in the lesser

masses and details, an effect of basic beauty,
refinement and richness is interwoven with a
mystical touch of yesterday," according to the
official guidebook.

Perhaps most convincing in this regard
were Ernest Weihe's staggered piles of Mayan-
inspired elephant towers and Arthur Brown's
slender, slightly Gothic "Tower of the Sun"
in the center of the Court of Honor. Bernard
Maybeck was commissioned to design two
simplified Cambodian towers (with William
G. Merchant).

One memorable exception to the overall style
was William Wurster's outstandingly modern
Buena Vista Clubhouse, whose facade was
entirely dissolved in a rhythmic sequence of
glass and structure.

The elaborate color scheme aimed at combining the lessons from the 1915 San Francisco
Fair with Jules Guerin's tonal harmonies and
the striking "chromatic stimulants" of Chicago
in 1933. Here nineteen different colors
(dominantly ivory, gold, browns, and blues)
were applied, their effect heightened by a
special new treatment of the stucco surface
that rendered it sparkling and reflective due
to small flakes of mica. Each court was given
a dominant color, such as a light green-blue
in the Court of the Moon and Stars and a coral
red in the Court of Reflections. An attempt at
reviving the long-standing experiments with

synaesthesia was made by tuning the sound of the forty-three bells in the tower to colors at the fair.

As had other exhibitions before, this one's popularity profited from the qualities of a powerful nocturnal lighting scheme. For the distant view of the island across the bay white floodlights were used around the outside walls. The lighting application was a central part of the designs, which provided spaces for hidden floodlights on setbacks and behind parapets or overhangs to give the effect of buildings magically glowing from within. Primary colors were carefully avoided and the effect of projecting color onto an already tinted surface was taken into account. All of the fountains in the grounds were illuminated. One, in the Court of Pacifica, was equipped with a shifting color cycle. The lighting designer, A. F. Dickerson, who had a great deal of experience as Walter D'Arcy Ryan's long-time assistant, and eventual successor at General Electric, saw his lighting scheme for San Francisco as a unique, new achievement. He claimed that the lighting served as a psychological stimulant: "Emotions are excited toward gaiety by shades of red, rose, orange, and yellow—while greens, blue greens, and blues are used as tranquilizers." (A. F. Dickerson, "Color: New Synthesis …")

More than ever before, light was used to create its own independent forms of ornament. Cross currents of light projected upward on a setback building would show striking "cubistic" patterns, and heightened in the eyes of contemporary observers the spatial rhythm of the architecture. Dickerson also employed the scintillator that his predecessor Ryan had invented: here a battery of twenty-four searchlights, each with a set of five different color screens, was operated by members of the U. S. Army during light spectacles.

The lighting industry used the exhibition as a showcase for its most recent developments: the fluorescent lamp allowed designers for the first time "to mix lights as the artist mixes paints, producing theatrical results" (Dickerson, "Dividends"). Also for the first time, ultraviolet light sources were used on a large scale outdoors and carefully calibrated in conjunction with luminescent paint. Finally, and once again for the first time, high-intensity

mercury lamps were used for the illumination of bushes and trees.

After a substantial deficit, the fair opened for a second season in 1940, during which the color treatment of the buildings was intensified in order to match by day the appearance by night.   D. N.

General Electric Building · New York, New York · 1940

Architects: **Cross & Cross**

Location: **570 Lexington Avenue**

Construction Dates: **1930–31. Extant**

Installation Dates: **1932, 1940, 1965. The building is currently illuminated with golden lights.**

Installation Type: **1932: white 1,000-watt incandescent floodlights. 1940: additional 159 15-watt blue fluorescent floodlights, 85 at the crown and 74 under the windows of the 45th through 49th floors. 24 750-watt red floodlights in crown. 4 mercury searchlights at ground level corners, each with 3 1,000-watt high-pressure mercury capillary lamps. 1965: 55 1,500-watt floodlights each on east and west facades, 54 on north facade, 75 on south facade. 1,500-watt lamps on 4 curved tower corners. 48 1,500-watt tungsten halogen lamps with dichroic gold filters in front of crown tracery and 528 PAR-38 100-watt blue-white, yellow and pink reflector lamps on programmed sequence controller.**

Lighting Designers: **1932: Unknown.
1940: A. F. Dickerson, General Electric Co.
1965: Robert E. Faucett, General Electric Co.**

General Electric Building, night view, photograph, 1965

General Electric Building with skyline, photograph, 1937

Soon after its completion in 1931, the fifty-story building for the Radio Corporation of America (R. C. A.) was sold to General Electric and subsequently illumined with white floodlights. This lighting scheme was entirely overhauled in 1940, by which time the "interest in building floodlighting … has been more or less dormant since 1930 …" as the lighting designer Dickerson wrote. He was convinced "that floodlighted buildings, perhaps more than any other thing, are most responsible for giving cities their night character." Dickerson turned it into a showcase for a new technology that General Electric was in the process of promoting: fluorescent lighting. After his great success at the San Francisco Golden Gate (pp. 180–181) exposition in the previous year, he was eager to apply these lights to a permanent installation and integrate them into an elaborate color scheme.

The top of the skyscraper included an allegorical representation of radio waves and was ornamented with a delicate gothic tracery, inside which red lights were placed. The new blue fluorescent lights were installed on the exterior of the crown, and, as a result, the edges where the two colors met were outlined in purple. The original installation of 1932 had included white lights that were used in coordination with the colors to create changing tones. Placed on a timer, the white lights were set to intensify periodically and wash out the blue tints as well as part of the red. When the white lights were at their brightest point, the top of the skyscraper was visible for miles and contributed greatly to the city's silhouette. On each side of the crown, terra-cotta sculptural details were highlighted with separate spotlights. Below the apex, the upper floor windows were also illumined in a unique manner. Blue fluorescent bulbs were placed in boxes underneath so that their rays projected only onto the glass and not to the areas in between, making the windows stand out in ghostly appearance against the background of the structure. At each of the ground-level corners of the building a mercury capillary searchlight was installed, its bluish-white beams projecting upwards to light both the building itself and the air space above.

Although its designers believed that the new cost-effective fluorescent bulbs and the popularity of illumination at the two recent expositions in San Francisco and New York would presage a revival in floodlighting, in fact the General Electric installation was destined to be one of the last for some time. The onset of World War II brought an abrupt halt to the art of illumination that lasted, in many cases, for decades afterward. In 1965, the company decided to add a new installation. The entire building was now floodlit, its east and west facades to an intensity thirty percent brighter than its north and south facades. In addition, the crown was lit from within by a set of golden lights, while lamps in blue-white, yellow and pink sparkled in random order, giving the impression of glimmering jewels. Added shortly after the Empire State Building (pp. 156–157) had received its own extensive new lighting installation, the theatrical effects at General Electric helped to revive the idea of architectural lighting in Manhattan in general.

K. B. / D. N.

Selected Bibliography:

"Floodlighting for New York's Skyline." *Illuminating Engineering* 60 (August 1965): 475–477.

"Fluorescent Floodlighting." *Architectural Forum* 72 (June 1940): 418.

"New Floodlighting for New York Skyscraper." *Illuminating Engineering* 35 (March 1940): 192.

Dickerson, A. F. "Revival of Building Floodlighting with Better Load Factor." *General Electric Review* 43 (March 1940): 139.

McIntyre, H. N. "What Every Engineer Should Know About Architectural Floodlighting." *General Electric Review* 58 (July 1955): 44–47.

Nash, Eric P. *Manhattan Skyscrapers*. New York: Princeton Architectural Press, 1999.

Blau Gold Haus · Cologne · 1952

This modern six-story office and commercial building next to Cologne Cathedral was typical of the rebuilding efforts in Cologne's heavily destroyed center. The facade consists entirely of vertical and horizontal structural members and vast expanses of glass. The transparent corners hint at Walter Gropius' Fagus Factory as a model.

The nocturnal lighting scheme was part of the original design and integral to the concept of the entire building as an advertisement for its builder, a prominent and long-established producer of perhaps the quintessential eau de Cologne, "Ferdinand Muehlhens 4711 Kölnisch Wasser." The trademark colors turquoise and gold were reproduced in the facade above a first floor with display windows surrounded by black wall cladding. White neon cove lighting was installed underneath the building's cornice as well as incandescent lighting at selected points in the vertical piers between the wide windows.

A contemporary British architect remarked in 1953: "This building in Cologne is an example of a way of incorporating lighting effects to form part of the architectural design of a building. The lighting consultant takes his place with the architect from the start.... Color, intensity, silhouette, texture, sparkle, contrast—the whole range of effects that are at the disposal of the lighting engineer could be enlisted under the guidance of an architect or designer with a vision of the possibilities of the final result, both of an individual building and of its effect on the whole scene of which his building only forms a part." (Rosenberg)   D. N.

Architect: **Wilhelm Koep**

Location: **Dornkloster 2**

Construction Date: **1952**

Installation Date: **1952. The building is currently illuminated.**

Installation Type: **Neon lights and hidden incandescent lights integrated into the facade in order to reflect from its gold and turquoise aluminum surface.**

Lighting Designer: **Wilhelm Koep**

4711 Building, night view, photograph, 1992

Selected Bibliography:

Flagge, Ingeborg. *Jahrbuch für Licht und Architektur 1992.* Berlin: Ernst und Sohn, 1993.

Rosenberg, Gerhard. "The Architectural Use of External Lighting of Buildings." *Light and Lighting* 46, no. 7 (July 1953): 270–272.

Manufacturers Trust · New York, New York · 1955

Architects: **Skidmore, Owings and Merrill. Design by Gordon Bunshaft**

Location: **510 Fifth Avenue**

Construction Date: **1952–54. Extant**

Installation Date: **1954, lighting extant**

Installation Type: **Cold cathode fluorescent tubing behind corrugated vinyl plastic, supported on an aluminum grid.**

Lighting Designers: **Gordon Bunshaft with Syska & Hennessy, Fischbach & Moore**

In contrast to the heavy walls found on most bank buildings, the glass exterior of the Manufacturers Hanover Trust on Fifth Avenue in New York provided an impression of brightness and openness. At the same time, a sense of supervision was provided by displaying the safe prominently through the enormous windows on Fifth wich featured the largest pieces of glass ever placed in a building: ten-by-twenty-two feet, five inches thick, weighing 1,500 pounds each.

The light from the luminous ceiling was a key element of the building's appearance at night. Practically the entire ceiling of the 6,000-square-foot second-floor banking hall was visible from the street, owing to the fact that the hall was set back twelve feet from the exterior wall. On the third and fourth floors, the luminous ceiling is restricted to L-shaped areas bordering the Fifth Avenue and Forty-third Street fronts. Remaining areas on these floors are illuminated by rows of individual fluorescent units. The luminous ceiling was brought right to the edge of the windows, and was supposed to de-emphasize glare on bright days by diminishing contrast. Gordon Bunshaft repeated the success of this system immediately afterwards at the Pepsi-Cola headquarters on Park Avenue (1956–60) and Richard Kelly and Mies van der Rohe applied a similar approach in order to turn the Seagram Building (pp. 188–190) on Park Avenue (1956–60) into a "tower of light."

The Manufacturers Hanover Trust became one of the most widely discussed buildings in the architectural press in the fall of 1954. Lewis Mumford famously called it "a crystal lantern … a paradoxical combination of transparence and solidity—crystalline, yes, but not in the slightest frail or film-like, for if anything it is both rugged and monumental. Viewed from the outside, this building is essentially a glass lantern, and, like a lantern, it is even more striking by dark than by daylight." (Mumford) Ada Louise Huxtable wrote: "In the Manufacturers Trust Building the glass is colorless and clear, and because of the even illumination inside, material walls disappear. Spandrels and mullions become mere frames for the arrangement of the interiors. The whole, viewed from the outside, is no longer architectural in the traditional sense: it is a design, not of substance, but of color, light and motion." (Huxtable, quoted in Stern) D. N.

Manufacturers Trust, photograph, *c.* 1954

Manufacturers Trust, night view, photograph, *c.* 1954

Selected Bibliography:

"1954 Building News: A Glass Bank and Two New Office Buildings." *Architectural Record* 114 (October 1953): 10–11.

"Manufacturers Trust Company Builds Conversation Piece on Fifth Avenue." *Architectural Record* 116 (November 1954): 149–156.

"Modern Architecture Breaks Through the Glass Barrier." *Architectural Forum* 101 (December 1954): 104–111.

"New Concept in Bank Design." *Illuminating Engineering* 49 (December 1954): 564–565.

Mumford, Lewis. "Crystal Lantern." *New Yorker* (13 November 1954): 197–204.

Stern, Robert M., Thomas Mellins and David Fishman. *New York 1960: Architecture and Urbanism between the Second World War and the Bicentennial.* New York: Monacelli, 1995.

Indianapolis Power & Light Company, Electric Building · Indianapolis, Indiana · 1956

Following a trend of the time, the Indianapolis Power & Light Company remodeled its Electric Building in the late 1960s, constructing a new addition and covering its existing facade with a new stone cladding. The building in its original state had already been floodlit in its entirety with provisions for colored lighting included. Believing that a floodlighting installation was an essential element of the renovation, the architects insisted that a lighting design be presented at the same time as that of the architecture. In the new design, the illumination scheme was focused upon the recessed windows that now almost entirely covered the facade. Each windowsill was fitted with a tungsten halogen lamp, which illumined the frame from below, but left the glass and the intervening stonework unlit. This produced the effect of a series of glowing rectangles against a dark backdrop. The lights could be set to a bright or dim voltage, and these differences in intensity were employed in both stationary and moving designs. Color filters were installed for further decorative effects. One setting turned off all the lamps in the first floor windows, producing a dark band, which then moved from the bottom to the top of the structure in twenty-one seconds, momentarily blacking out each story in turn. Suitable designs were presented for holidays and other special events, such as a cross for Easter or a flag for Memorial Day, and this tradition of special holiday lighting continues today. At other times, all of the building's windows could be lit with the same color and intensity. With its many combinations of different hues and changing patterns, the illumination of the Indianapolis Power & Light building was in fact an updated version of the mobile color-lighting concept that had been popular thirty years earlier, adapted to compliment the architecture of a new decade.   K. B.

Architect: **1924: Unknown. 1963–66: Lennox, Matthews, Simmons & Ford**

Location: **1 Monument Circle**

Construction Dates: **1924. 1968: Remodeled and new addition constructed. Extant**

Installation Dates: **1956, 1968. The building is currently illuminated using 350-watt quartz lamps with colored filters.**

Installation Type: **1956: 315 300-watt floodlighting units. 1968: 500-watt tungsten halogen lamps, one sunk in each exterior windowsill. Complex dimmer control, motor-driven rheostat, dichroic color filters.**

Lighting Designers: **1956: George E. Ransford, Indianapolis Power & Light Co. 1968: Norman F. Schnitker, Indianapolis Power & Light Co.**

Indianapolis Power & Light, night view, photograph, 1968

Selected Bibliography:

"Exterior Floodlighting." *Illuminating Engineering* 51 (May 1956): 376.

"Lighting Progress 1967." *Illuminating Engineering* 63 (January 1968): 1–16.

"Teamwork is Key to Integrated Floodlighting Design." *Illuminating Engineering* 63 (April 1968): 227–232.

Exposition Universelle et Internationale de Bruxelles · Brussels · 1958

Date: **April 17–October 19, 1958**

Architects: **Le Corbusier and Yannis Xenakis: Philips Pavilion**
Edward D. Stone: United States Pavilion
R. & J. Polak, André Waterkeyn, engineer: Atomium
Reima Pietilä: Finnish Pavilion
Howard V. Lobb & John C. Ratcliffe: British Government Pavilion
Edward Mills: British Industries Pavilion
Guillaume Gillet: French Pavilion
J. Van Doorselaere & J. Moeschal: Civil Engineering Pavilion
Sverre Fehn: Norwegian Pavilion
Kunio Mayekawa: Japanese Pavilion
Egon Eiermann & Sep Ruf: West German Pavilion
J. H. van den Brock, J. B. Bakema, Gerrit Rietveld & J. W. C. Boks: Dutch Pavilion
Werner Gantenbein: Swiss Pavilion

Lighting Designers: **Andre Boereboom, Rollo Gillespie Williams (U. S. Pavilion)**

Selected Bibliography:
"Brussels Light-Up Time." *Life* 44 (12 May 1958): 47–50.
"Expo 58." *Architectural Review* 124 (August 1958): 74–118.
"Lighting for the United States Pavilion." *Illuminating Engineering* 54 (January 1959): 6–8.
"The Brussels Exhibition, 1958." *Light and Lighting* 51 (June 1958): 202–206.
"The Philips Pavilion at the 1958 Brussels World Fair: I: The Architectural Design of Le Corbusier and Xenakis." *Philips Technical Review* 20, no.1 (20 September 1958): 1–8.
Boereboom, Andre. "Lighting at the Brussels 1958 Exhibition," *Transactions of the Illuminating Engineering Society* (London) 23, no. 3 (1958): 148–162.
Le Corbusier Le Poème électronique. Editions de Minuit, 1958. (Includes essays by L. C. Kalff, Michel Butor, Jean Petit and others.)
Walker, Howell. "Belgium Welcomes the World." *National Geographic* 113 (June 1958): 794–837.

The Universal and International Exposition of Brussels, or Expo '58, was the first World's Fair since 1939. A showcase for postwar modernist architecture and engineering, the 1958 expo occupied the Heizelplateau, the site of a previous World's Fair in 1935, and in addition, the park of the Laeken royal estate, for a ground area twice that of 1935. Several of the earlier buildings in Art Deco, Classical, and International Style forms had survived and were reused for the new exhibition, although a great many more were added. Simple, glass-enclosed boxes with slender support elements predominated as a building type, although a number of designers employed steel and reinforced concrete for such eye-catching forms as cantilevered arms and hyperbolic paraboloids. The latter could be seen in Le Corbusier's and Yannis Xenakis' design for the Philips Pavilion, a concrete structure with three peaks rising above a freeform floor plan. The pavilion was designed for the purpose of a son et lumière show that took place inside. Dubbed "An Electronic Poem," the show utilized colored lights and pictures projected onto the inner surfaces in concert with sound effects and music specially composed by Edgar Varèse and Xenakis.

The centerpiece of the fair, and a perfect symbol of 1950s obsessions, was the Atomium, a hugely magnified representation of an iron molecule, over 300 feet tall and consisting of nine spheres connected by steel tubes. Covered with an outer skin of aluminum, the spheres glinted in the sunlight and reflected the colored lights of the fair at night. In addition, each sphere was lit by 320 ten-watt bulbs that turned on and off in sequence, representing the movement of electrons across the surface of the atoms. Leading up to the Atomium was the Water Ladder, which ran from the Place de Belgique to the Porte Benelux. This staircase of water alternated calm and running basins, the former illuminated by white and blue cold cathode tubes, the latter by white and yellow. The effect of the colored lights and the differences in water movement caused the ladder to appear to flow uphill and was a unique variation of the usual exposition fountains.

Many of the glass pavilions were lit from within with little additional lighting on the exterior, the transparent nature of the walls creating warmly glowing boxes of fluorescent luminescence, as exemplified by the British Industry Pavilion. More imaginative lighting could be found on some of the other pavilions. The British Government Building, composed of three multi-faceted crystals, was illuminated on five of its faces with over 4,000 blue-green and white lamps, and floodlights trained on the upper portions producing a green tint. The underside of the entrance canopy was composed of 108 squares of rose and green acrylic panels, each one lit from behind by a one-hundred-watt bulb.

One of the more successful architectural designs was the United States Pavilion, a circular building 380 feet in diameter with transparent walls and a roof of translucent plastic. A metal mesh, draped from the ceiling, covered the exterior walls. 432 concealed floodlamps were placed above and below the ceiling mesh to create a scintillating pattern. The center of the structure consisted of a circular element that was left uncovered to catch rain. Reflector lamps were arranged around the inner drum, creating a pillar of light that was most impressive during rainstorms, when the individual water drops would glitter as they fell past the lamps. All of these lighting effects could be seen from the exterior by virtue of the transparent walls so that the entire building stood bathed in a soft, yellow interior glow.

The older buildings from the 1935 exposition had been remodeled and were also illuminated at night. The Grand Palais, which served as the Reception Hall, had a parabolic arch attached to its facade. Underneath the arch, a large bronze depiction of the exposition motif, along with a dove of peace, dominated the facade. Surrounding these were one hundred smaller versions of the motif, each one lit from behind by light blue fluorescent tubes. The arch itself was also outlined with fluorescent tubes, as were the colonnades that lined the other sides of the Place de Belgique.

More than ever before, the Brussels exposition saw the emergence of fluorescent lighting as a replacement for floodlighting in architectural and decorative illumination. Its International Style buildings with their reliance on interior lighting designs behind their transparent facades marked the fair as a prime example of the state of architecture and lighting in the 1950s. K. B.

< United States Pavilion, photograph, 1958

Atomium, photograph, 1958

Grand Palais, photograph, 1958

Seagram Building · New York, New York · 1958

Architects: **Ludwig Mies van der Rohe, Philip Johnson, Ely Jacques Kahn**

Location: **375 Park Avenue**

Construction Dates: **1954–58. Extant**

Installation Date: **1958. The special perimeter lighting was turned off in 1973.**

Installation Type: **Fluorescent tubes (*c.* 100 foot-candle) behind corrugated vinyl plastic, supported on an aluminum grid.**

Lighting Designer: **Richard Kelly**

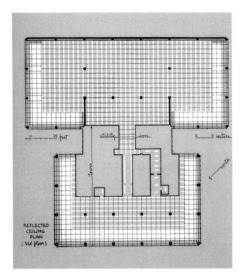

Selected Bibliography:

"Lightolier Ceiling to Keep Bronze Skyscraper Aglow." *New York Times* (7 April 1957): 10, advertisement: "A special report on 375 Park Avenue."

"Lighting is Architecture: Definition of Structure." *Progressive Architecture* 39 (September 1958): 115–180.

"Lighting, Once Mere Utility, Has Become an Important Element of Design." *New York Times*, 26 October 1958.

"New Progress in Light." *Architectural Forum* 106 (February 1957): 152–155.

Lambert, Phyllis. *Mies van der Rohe: The Difficult Art of the Simple*. Montreal: Centre Canadien d'Architecture, 2001.

Stern, Robert M., Thomas Mellins and David Fishman. *New York 1960: Architecture and Urbanism between the Second World War and the Bicentennial*. New York: Monacelli, 1995.

T. H. C. "A Critique of Critiques: Seagram House Re-Reassessed." *Progressive Architecture* 40 (June 1959): 140–145.

Mies van der Rohe's famous thirty-eight-story Seagram Building is prototypical in many respects—it provided an alternative to the setback tower that had been the legal standard for high-rises in Manhattan since 1916, while offering at the same time a new urban paradigm: a plaza opening from Park Avenue's tightly defined canyon of similar office towers. It was often compared to other postwar towers in New York City, such as the U. N. Building of 1947 and Lever House of 1952 across the street. While the thin slabs of these buildings ensured daylight throughout their interiors, the deep spaces of the Seagram Building relied on a large amount of electric light. Tinted window-panes together with black structural elements, gave the building the appearance of a dark monolith. In great contrast to this, however, the building was designed for a striking appearance at night. Mostly forgotten today, this fact garnered considerable attention at the time, and the tower was frequently published in nocturnal photographs.

Richard Kelly, one of the most prolific lighting designers of his time, had studied both architecture and illumination engineering, and previously worked on Louis Kahn's Yale Art Gallery and Richard Neutra's Kauffman House in Palm Springs. He developed a uniform lighting system inside the building to produce its outside appearance at night. A twenty-foot-wide band of luminous ceiling extended from the windows along all facades of the building, adopting and modifying an idea that Gordon Bunshaft had tried out at his Manufacturers Trust Bank (p. 180) on Fifth Avenue. During the daytime, its one-hundred-foot-candle level of illumination was supposed to counter sky glare. At night, on every story the luminous ceiling would be lit by a second lighting circuit of about one quarter the brilliance of that during the day, giving, especially from a street level perspective, the appearance of a "tower of light." Kelly felt that the ground floor had to be much brighter than the upper floors and talked Mies into exchanging the marble from dark green to highly reflective white travertine. "Black slots" in the ceiling hid the projectors for the illumination of those walls. The night-time brightness at ground level was designed to be about four times the level of the upper floors. One critic described the result: "One

of its glories as a spectacle is its floating-above-the-street quality at night." (T. H. C. "A Critique of Critiques").

Not surprisingly, the lighting industry hoped that this exuberant use of electric energy "may start a trend that will change the nighttime appearance of skylines in cities all over the country." ("Lightolier Ceiling") Instead, the costly installation was only used until the onset of the energy crisis in 1973 and has not been employed since. For Richard Kelly, who saw his role as a close collaborator with the architects, the lighting of the Seagram Building was certainly one of the key moments of his career. He had developed a specific nomenclature for his philosophy of lighting in the early 1950s, which differentiated between "Ambient Luminescence," "Focal Glow" and a "Play of Brilliants." At the Seagram Building all three of these approaches could be found.

The lighting of the Seagram Building was often compared with that of the Tishman Building (p. 191) at 666 Fifth Avenue, designed by Broadway lighting designer Abe Feder. Both buildings received awards from the Fifth Avenue Association in the same year, and in both cases their night lighting was cited. Their entirely different approaches represented two major trends in architectural lighting, both of which had a significant history: theatrical floodlighting from the outside, which had had its premiere at the Singer Building (pp. 96–97) in 1908 and afterwards enjoyed a long career in the U. S., and the transformation of the building itself with the help of interior illumination, which had been developed in Europe in the 1920s.   D. N.

Seagram Building, plan, ceiling, luminous panels

Seagram Building, night view, photograph by Samuel H. Gottscho, 1958

Seagram Building, lower portion, night view, photograph by Samuel Gotscho, *c*. 1958

Seagram Building, corner office with luminous ceiling panels

Seagram Building, plan, lighting diagram, "tower of light"

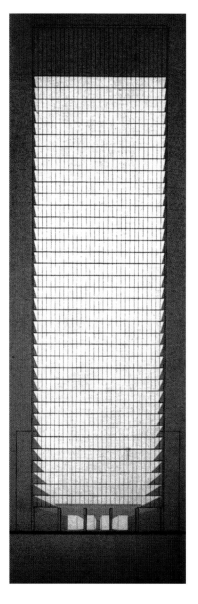

Tishman Building · New York, New York · 1958

An office tower with more than one million square feet and thirty-nine stories, the building owned by the Tishman Realty & Construction Co., between Fifty-second and Fifty-third Street, boasted the largest aluminum facade ever with a surface area of eight acres. The building had the typical setback section that had become the standard approach to high-rise buildings in New York since the early 1920s. On the first floor was an open shopping arcade with a central fountain designed by Isamu Noguchi. The building's success seems to have been greatly indebted to the nocturnal lighting scheme by probably the most prominent lighting designer of the day, Abe Feder, who owed this commission to his recent illumination of the United Nations and Lincoln Center. Here he had to respond to the reflective surface of the folded aluminum panels in the facade, which had been used in a similar fashion on Harrison & Abramowitz' Alcoa Building in Pittsburgh (1954) and New York's Socony Mobil Building of 1956. Since his Pennsylvania Power & Light building (pp. 124–125) in Allentown (1928), Wallace Harrison had been an ardent supporter of designs for the nocturnal appearance of buildings, and had helped to pioneer the new aluminum and stainless steel facades with their reflective qualities in mind. His influence is clearly palpable at 666 Fifth Avenue.

Instead of the repeated fading hues of color so typical for the setback skyscrapers of the 1920s and '30s, new technologies (partially developed by Abe Feder) allowed him to bathe almost the entire facade in the cold white light of mercury vapor lamps, counterbalanced by the numbers 666 in red neon at the top of the building. The impression was thus quite different from the sequence of quickly fading washes of light above each floodlight battery on the old setback skyscrapers.

The Fifth Avenue Association awarded the building a prize for the best new commercial building on Fifth Avenue for 1956–57, praising it for being "simple in form and rich in its patterned, textured, aluminum panels. Between windows and panels, a vertical emphasis is achieved by porcelain-enameled mullions. Exterior lighting makes the design equally effective at night...."

Just like the contemporary Seagram Building (pp. 188–190), this building was nicknamed "A Tower of Light" (*Real Estate Record and Guide*), although their illumination was quite different. The system used here gave the building a comparable appearance at night as in daytime, while the Seagram Building was entirely transformed from a dark monolith to a glowing and almost translucent tower.

D. N.

Architects: **Carson, Lundin & Shaw**

Location: **666 Fifth Avenue**

Construction Date: **1957. Extant**

Installation Date: **1958. The building is currently illuminated.**

Installation Type: **72 mercury vapor floodlight reflectors on neighboring buildings and setbacks at the 10th and 15th floors. The 9-foot-tall red neon numbers at the top were replaced in 1999 by a new logo.**

Lighting Designer: **Abe Feder**

Tishman Building, floodlights on setback, photograph, 1958

Tishman Building, night view, photograph, 1958

Selected Bibliography:
"666 Fifth Ave. Building." *Architectural Record* 121 (March 1957): 237.

"Lighting is Architecture: Assertion of Purpose." *Progressive Architecture* (September 1958): 145–149.

"Lighting, Once Mere Utility, Has Become an Important Element of Design." *New York Times* (26 October 1958).

"New Building for Tishman." *Architectural Record* 117 (April 1955): 210.

Allison, David. "Outdoor Lighting: An Expanding New Technology." *Architectural Forum* (July 1960): 128–134.

Stern, Robert M., Thomas Mellins and David Fishman. *New York 1960: Architecture and Urbanism between the Second World War and the Bicentennial.* New York: Monacelli, 1995.

Thyssenhaus · Düsseldorf · 1960

Architects: **Helmut Hentrich, Hubert Petschnigg**

Location: **August-Thyssen-Strasse 1**

Construction Dates: **1955–60**

Installation Date: **1960. The lighting was terminated in 1966 and has not been used since.**

Installation Type: **Ceiling lights with double fluorescent tubes close to windows on separate circuit for nocturnal appearance. 276 65-watt blue fluorescent tubes installed on each side of the vertical window frames of 138 windows in order to produce 13-story-tall signet.**

Lighting Designer: **Unknown**

Hailed as one of the most elegant skyscrapers in postwar Germany, the building was planned as the headquarters of a new firm, Phoenix-Rheinrohr AG, the result of a recent merger, and in large part owned by the Thyssen Family. The building consists of three slabs nineteen-and-a-half fee wide, a wider and taller one (twenty-six stories) in the center accompanied by smaller ones (twenty-three stories) at each side. Where all three overlap, the central slab contains the elevator and sanitary core of the building. The depth of the resulting office spaces is never greater than thirty-nine feet and can be lit by daylight from both sides. While somewhat influenced by the elegant slab of the U. N. building in New York City, the building provided an alternative to the deep spaces common in American sky-scrapers, such as in Mies van der Rohe's Seagram Building (p p. 184–186), built at the same time. The ends of the narrow slabs consist of concrete panels with metal cladding, while the long sides are aluminum curtain walls.

The building was conceived for two different nighttime appearances. All fluorescent tube ceiling lights close to the windows could be switched on together but separately from other ceiling lights. At night the facade would thus be translated into a sequence of gleaming ribbon windows, a solution similar to that of the Seagram Building in New York. Alternatively, 138 windows on each side were equipped with additional blue fluorescent lights on both vertical sides of their outside frames, in order to display the Phoenix-Rheinrohr AG firm's signet of a blue circle with three blue central horizontal bands. The sign would be displayed over a height of thirteen stories and be widely visible. However, since the merger of Phoenix-Rheinrohr with Thyssen in 1966, it has not been used.

D. N.

Thyssenhaus, night view with signet, photograph, 1962

Thyssenhaus, night view, photograph, 1962

Selected Bibliography:

Hitchcock, Henry Russell and Hans-B. Adams. *HPP: Bauten und Entwürfe / Buildings and Projects. Hentrich-Petschnigg & Partner.* Düsseldorf: Econ Verlag, 1973.

Mittag, Martin. *Thyssenhaus: Phönix-Rheinrohr-AG Düsseldorf.* Essen: Bauzentrum-Ring-Verlag, 1962.

Las Vegas, Nevada · 1960

In the history of nocturnal architecture, Las Vegas occupies a unique position. Its monoculture of hotels and casinos in the Nevada desert is so unusual that neither comparisons with amusement parks or world's fairs, nor other urban environments provide fitting categories. While Las Vegas' success is too young to have taken part in the architectural lighting boom of the 1930s, it has continually provided an intense display of new ideas for advertising and architectural illumination since the 1950s. Perhaps more than anywhere else the design of its nocturnal appearance is given highest priority, as considerably more guests populate its urban areas at night than during daytime. What we usually mean when we refer to Las Vegas is a section of Fremont Street downtown and the "strip" outside of the city limits.

Las Vegas was discovered in the 1960s as a subject for study and serious debate. The American writer Tom Wolfe described how its signs had become its architecture, and suggested a more serious consideration of its formal richness. He inspired the American architects Robert Venturi, Denise Scott Brown and Steven Izenour in September 1968 to take fifteen Yale students on a field trip to Nevada in order to "learn from Las Vegas." They claimed that it represented "a new form of Urbanism" and that the "biggest strip in the world" provided a paradigmatic architecture of color and light, signs and symbols. While their analysis and the ensuing publication helped to support the growing appreciation of the popular culture of advertising signs, motels and fast-food restaurants, there was little in the strip's monoculture that was applicable elsewhere. Somewhat ironically, the architectural development in the city had just begun to embark on a new path. In addition to the "decorated shed," a simple, nondescript building with a sign in front, which Venturi and Scott Brown had identified as the strip's most paradigmatic type, the 1966 Cesar's Palace started a tradition of architecturally expressive casino hotels that eventually lead to creations such as the Luxor, the Paris, New York, New York and others.

The clear distinction between the building and the sign in front of it that Venturi and Scott Brown suggested had been blurred long before. Since the 1950s, there had been many examples where signage and illumination had become an integral part of the architecture itself. When, in 1953, the Flamingo Hotel—built in 1947 for Bugsy Siegel by the architect George Vernon Russell—underwent a dazzling makeover by Pereira and Luckman, the Young Electric Sign Company (YESCO) added a free-standing, cylindrical metal tower "covered from top to bottom with neon rings in the shape of bubbles that fizzed all eight stories up into the desert sky all night long like an illuminated soda tumbler filled to the brim with pink champagne." (Tom Wolfe,

Freemont Street from Second Street, postcard, c. 1969. Curt Teich Postcard Co.

quoted in Hess), The *New York Times* saw "a palpitating sea of electric illumination." For the architectural historian Alan Hess, the Mint hotel casino on Fremont Street "blurred the line between two-dimensional signs and three-dimensional architecture." Its one-hundred-foot-wide block was dominated by "a swooping line that began on the edge of the sidewalk, swept up through the canopy, arched down, and then shot skyward." This feature was up to eighteen feet wide and eighty-two feet tall at the end. It was studded with incandescent lights, which performed a wave towards the top, where it burst into a bright neon star from 300-watt signal lamps and neon lights. The 216-foot-long and twenty-seven-foot-wide sign at the Stardust hotel

Dates: **1939 (birth of the strip)–present**

Selected Architects:
George Vernon Russell: Flamingo Hotel I (1947)
Pereira and Luckman: Flamingo Hotel II (1953)
Walter Zick, Harris Sharp: The Mint
Melvin Grossman: Cesar's Palace (1966)
Jon Jerde: The Fremont Street Experience (1995)

Lighting Designers: **Hermon Boernge (YESCO): The Mint. Kermit Wayne (YESCO): Stardust, Golden Nugget. Jeremy Railton: Fremont Street Experience**

Selected bibliography:

Hess, Alan. *Viva Las Vegas: After Hours Architecture.* San Francisco: Chronicle Books, 1995.

Anderton, Frances and John Chase. *Las Vegas, The Success of Excess.* Cologne: Könemann, 1997.

Wolfe, Thomas K. "Las Vegas (What?) Las Vegas (Can't hear you! Too noisy.) Las Vegas!!!" in: *Esquire* 61, no. 2 (February 1964): 97–106, 121.

Wolfe, Tom. *The Kandy-Kolored Tangerine-flake Streamline Baby.* New York: Farrar, Straus and Giroux, 1965.

Wolfe, Tom: "Electrographic Architecture" *Architectural Design* 7, no. 6 / 7 (1969): 379–382.

and casino covered the facade so completely, that it "became the architecture" (Hess).

Since the 1980s, the strip has become continually more attractive to pedestrians, who walk the distance between hotel casinos or wait in large crowds for the Mirage's volcano to explode or for the nautical battle at "Treasure Island." Recent hotel complexes have come with extensive shopping arcades,

to the successful strip, YESCO was hired to introduce a new concept. The architect Jon Jerde worked with set designer Jeremy Railton on the concept of a light canopy, a long screen attached to a ninety-foot-high, 1,400-foot-long semi-circular space frame, supported by sixteen columns along a section of Fremont Street that had been converted into a pedestrian zone. On its inner surface, nearly 2.1 million small LED lights are installed in combination with 180 strobe lights and sixty-four color lighting fixtures. Computer programs generate animated images with more than 300 colors, synchronized with music and sound effects.

Many of the former staple designs for large exhibitions, be they illuminated fountains or translucent light columns with changing colors, have recently been employed at the Bellagio and Bally's Hotel Casinos, for example. With an architecture that is firmly geared towards its mainstream clientele, Las Vegas' nocturnal appearance has typically relied more on sheer size and dazzle than on innovation and sophistication.   D.N.

Las Vegas, Fremont Street, contemporary postcard. Curt Teich Postcard Co.

View from the New York, New York Hotel, with a replica of the Chrysler Building in the foreground, towards the Paris Hotel, with its half-scale replica of the Eiffel Tower, 2000. © Richard Cummins / Corbis 2000 >

Fremont Street with the "Fremont Street Experience." © Picturenet / Corbis 1999. >

and have replaced the earlier monoculture with greater variety. Two exhibition spaces have opened in recent years. In 1995, the Luxor Hotel opened, a dark, black pyramid with a thirty-five-billion-candlepower beam reaching vertically into the night. Since then a sequence of large theme hotels, among them the Paris and New York, New York, have followed. While the replicas of each city's buildings can hardly ever pretend to be more than an oversized stage set, its illumination at night helps to provide a more credible rendering. The lighting of the Eiffel Tower comes close to the contemporary version while the replicas of both the Empire State (pp. 156–157) and Chrysler Building (pp. 202–203) convincingly employ the original's current lighting schemes.

When the downtown section of Las Vegas was in danger of losing its attractiveness

Grattacielo Pirelli · Milan · 1960

Architects: **Gio Ponti with Antonio Fornaroli, Alberto Rosselli, Structural engineers: Pier Luigi Nervi and Arturo Danusso.**

Location: **Piazza Duca d'Aosta, Via Fabio Filzi**

Construction Date: **1955–60**

Installation Date: **1960**

Installation Type: **Fluorescent lights in luminous ceilings; white, incandescent floodlights behind parapet reflected from cantilevered roof above.**

Lighting Designers: **G. Ponti, A. Fornaroli, A. Rosselli**

Selected Bibliography:

Banham, Reyner. "Pirelli Criticism." *Architectural Review* 129 (1961): 194–200.

Cappelini, Lorenzo. *Guida di Architettura Milano*. Milan: Umberto Allemandi & C., 1990.

McQuade, Walter. "Powerful tower, delicate shell: the Pirelli Building in Milan," *Architectural Forum* 114 (February 1961): 90–93.

Philips, Derek. *Lighting in Architectural Design*. New York: McGraw-Hill, 1964.

Pirelli: *Nuova Sede in Milano*. Milan: Pirelli S. p. A., 1958.

Ponti, Gio. "Espressione dell'edificio Pirelli in Construzione a Milano." *Domus* 316 (1956): 1–16.

Ponti, Gio. "Pirelli Building, Milan." *Architectural Design* 30 (December 1960): 490–496.

Ponti, Gio. *In Praise of Architecture*. New York: F. W. Dodge Corporation, 1960; originally published as *Amate l'Architettura*, 1957.

Ponti, Lisa Licitra. *Gio Ponti: The Complete Work, 1923–1978*. Cambridge, Mass.: MIT Press, 1990.

The skyscraper, which the critic Rayner Banham called "certainly the most impressive, probably the best, building put up in Milan since the war" (Banham, 194), announced the economic prowess of the Pirelli Company and gave visual presence and economic incentives to a newly developing business district next to the Central Railroad Station. Seen by many as an important European response to the American skyscraper, the slender thirty-four-story structure was firmly anchored between two rigid, windowless, tapered corner towers containing auxiliary rooms, and two additional concrete piers interrupting the taught glass skin of the office floors in between. Thanks to the collaboration with Pier Luigi Nervi, the structural qualities of reinforced concrete became a formative part of the design.

When Ponti published the building, he emphasized his careful planning for its nocturnal appearance: "Only recently have the fantastic possibilities of the creation of self-illuminating architecture been realized. This implies the creation of a simultaneous second architecture, the nocturnal, determined by the lights on or behind the building's own surfaces, lights which not only reveal the mass of the building (extracting it from the darkness of the night) but which create new volumes of light, the effect of new volumes, of broken surfaces, of eliminated weight and of hidden elements or supports, etc. It is not a case of illuminating architecture, but rather of making use of light 'in the architecture' to create unusual effects." (Pirelli: *Nuova Sede in Milano*) Ponti was opposed to any form of floodlighting ("child's play") but wanted his building to glow from within as "self-lighting architecture" (Ponti, Pirelli Building). He worked with a model that could be thus illuminated and showed the building as a shining shaft of light. He had envisioned the thin vertical openings on each side as an unbroken fissure of light, and the facade less horizontally structured than it eventually appeared. In the roof section, Ponti applied a lesson he had learned from the nocturnal "self-illumination" of his Villa Planchart (1955) in Caracas: white light from invisible sources was reflected from the cantilevered roof plane.

Ponti had already addressed the issue of nocturnal architecture in broader terms a few

years earlier, when he published his loose collection of thoughts about architecture *Amate l'Architettura* in 1957 and predicted "… luminous spatialities, luminous apparitions. We are only at the beginning of this era of illumination." (Ponti, *In Praise of Architecture*)

D. N.

Pirelli Building, model at night, photograph, 1959

Pirelli Building, model at night, photograph, 1959

Pirelli Building, night view, photograph, c. 1960 >

Michigan Consolidated Gas Company Building · Detroit, Michigan · 1961

Architect: **Minoru Yamasaki**

Location: **1 Woodward Avenue**

Construction Date: **1961. Extant**

Installation Date: **1961. The building is no longer illuminated.**

Installation Type: **Floodlights with red, green and blue filters installed in banks on the 27th and 29th floors. Automatic dimmer system. 3-lamp and 4-lamp 40-watt fluorescent lighting elements in first two interior perimeter lighting modules of the 2nd through 26th floors.**

Lighting Designers: **John J. Andrews and James McDonald**

The Michigan Consolidated Gas Company's new building of 1961 was the immediate neighbor of Detroit's former Union Trust tower (pp. 144–145), the most spectacular presence on Detroit's nocturnal skyline before World War II. The new building, owned by the same company, was specifically designed to take over this role with a contemporary lighting approach adapted to the different forms and materials of modern architecture. The building was faced with a white quartz aggregate that brightly reflected the sun during the day. The building's lighting design somewhat ironically thematized the fact that electricity at that point had all but taken over gas' former role in urban and domestic lighting. The ceiling of the glass-enclosed lobby was covered by a series of plastic modular domes with incandescent lights and sparkling blue prisms giving the impression of gas flames suspended from the ceiling. The office floors glowed warmly at night, thanks to a system of separate perimeter ceiling modules with fluorescent

lights—an idea that had probably been influenced by Richard Kelly's and Mies van der Rohe's solution at the Seagram Building (pp. 188–190).

The 27th and 28th stories were set back six feet, while a masonry screen continued the line of the building up to the roof. A sixty-foot openwork tower was situated atop these two stories, set back thirty-six feet from the main building's edge. Floodlights were installed on these upper floors and projected onto both the tower and the inner wall, against which the masonry screen was silhouetted. The original installation included red, green and blue filters. Connected to a dimmer switch, these lights could go through alternating washes of color and be preset for a variety of different effects to mark holidays and other special events. The building became known, however, for its tower installation of deep blue lights. Set above a base of white lamps, the color was chosen to give the impression of a gigantic gas pilot light. K. B. / D. N.

Michigan Consolidated Gas, night view with skyline, postcard, c. 1965

Selected Bibliography:

"Detroit Skyscraper: Headquarters Office, Michigan Consolidated Gas Co." *Architectural Record* 128 (August 1960): 142–146.

Andrews, John J. "In Detroit's Newest Office Building … Coordinated Engineering Elements." *Illuminating Engineering* 56 (August 1961): 507–510.

Carlson, David B. "A Different Sort of Skyscraper Puts New Life into Downtown Detroit's Skyline." *Architectural Forum* 118 (May 1963): 98–113.

World's Fair · New York, New York · 1964

The organization of the 1964 World's Fair was overshadowed by heated discussions about New York City's mayor Robert F. Wagner Jr.'s decision to appoint Robert Moses as head of the organizing committee. Moses, the city's planner for decades, had been increasingly criticized for his uncompromising role in slum clearance and urban renewal projects. Moses tried hard, but eventually without success, to make the fair a profitable enterprise. For parts of the 646-acre site, he used the existing plan of the 1939 fair (pp. 176–179), and had most of the 156 pavilions commissioned by commercial enterprises. Only a few foreign countries were represented.

The main complaint from architectural and design critics was the fair's perceived lack of coherence ("If this is architecture, God help us," wrote Vincent Scully). Robert Moses had declared in 1961 that "the fair administration belongs to no architectural clique, subscribes to no esthetic creed, favors no period or school and worships at no artistic shrine" (Robert Moses, quoted in Stern, p. 1028), an approach which had caused the entire design committee to resign. But in handing over the conception and execution of the fair to those who could afford the high ground rents, Moses unwittingly facilitated a more contingent and historical coherence. Space-age technology and the celebratory enlargement of commodities (be it U.S. Rubber's Ferris wheel in the form of a tire, or Chrysler's gigantic motor) constituted strong thematic links both ideologically and visually. In addition, a certain visual coherence simply stemmed from the fact that the fair happened at a time when "the conventions of Modernism were widely accepted and its American interpretation was the virtually unchallenged world standard." (Stern, p. 1027)

A 120-foot-diameter globe symbolized the fair's theme, "Peace through Understanding." Made out of 470 tons of stainless steel, the Unisphere was placed at the center of a pool, surrounded by fountains, and floodlit in changing colors at night. It had been financed by the U.S. Steel Corporation and used a spherical frame with landmasses picked out in solid steel. Inset lights were used to mark national and state capitals. Three steel rings surrounded the globe representing satellite orbits. In many ways space exploration was

one of the key motifs and it connects the fair directly to its historical moment; the success of the Soviet satellite Sputnik in 1957 had released vast resources of U.S. energy and money in a "race" for space. Though critics resolutely scorned the structure, photographs of the dramatically illuminated Unisphere became the most reproduced images of the fair.

Philip Johnson's New York State Pavilion was the fair's most visually dominant building. An open, circular exhibition hall with the world's largest suspension roof was accompanied by a smaller, round theatre and a cluster of three slender towers with circular observation decks. All major vertical and horizontal lines were studded with illuminated white and colored glass spheres.

The "Exposition After Dark Is an Electrical Fantasy of Glowing, Glittering Colors" wrote the *New York Times* (Apple) and the frequent application of colored floodlights convincingly helped to transform the appearance of a number of exhibition pavilions. For example, the massive egg-like bubble or typewriter ball of the IBM pavilion by Eero Saarinen and Charles Eames, propped up thirty-two feet off the ground, only really achieved the condition of a heavily floating solid at night.

The Electric Power and Light Pavilion, sponsored by a national consortium of electrical utility companies, carried the long-

Unisphere, photograph, 1964

Dates: **April 22–October 18, 1964,**
April 21–October 17, 1965

Architects: **Kahn and Jacobs: Eastman Kodak Pavilion**

Sol King and Alberg Kahn Assoc.: General Motors Pavilion

Welton Becket and Associated: General Electric Pavilion

Eero Saarinen and Charles Eames: IBM Pavilion

Philip Johnson, Richard Foster: New York State Pavilion

Javier Carvajal Ferrer and Kelly & Gruzen: Spain Pavilion

Synergetics, Inc. and Robinson-Capsis-Stern Assoc.: Tower of Light (The Electric Power and Light Pavilion)

Gilmore D. Clarke and Peter Müller-Munk Assoc.: Unisphere

Charles Luckman Associates: United States Pavilion

Lighting Designers: **Monte Cutler (General Electric), V-E-K Assoc. Power & Light Exhibit, and others**

Selected Bibliography:

"Lighting Progress in 1964." *Illuminating Engineering* 60 (Jan. 1965): 1–5.

Apple Jr., R. W. "Exhibits Ablaze Under Night Sky." *New York Times* (22 April 1964): 24.

Benjamin, Philip. "General Electric Pavilion Sheds Colored Light on World's Fair." *New York Times* (30 January 1964): 23.

Huxtable, Ada Louise. "Architecture: Chaos of Good, Bad and Joyful." *New York Times* (22 April 1964): 25.

Moses, Robert. *The Fair, The City and The Critics* (pamphlet, New York: New York World's Fair 1964–1965 Corporation, 1964).

Official Guide New York World's Fair 1964/1965 New York: Time Inc., 1964.

Schmertz, Mildred F. "Architecture at the New York World's Fair." *Architectural Record* 136 (July 1964): 143–50.

Smith, Michael L. "Making Time: Representations of Technology at the 1964 World's Fair." In Richard Wightman Fox and T. J. Jackson Lears, eds. *The Power of Culture: Critical Essays in American History.* Chicago and London: University of Chicago Press, 1993: 222–244.

Stern, Robert M., Thomas Mellins and David Fishman. "1964–65 New York World's Fair." *New York 1960: Architecture and Urbanism Between the Second World War and the Bicentennial.* New York: Monacelli Press, 1995: 1027–57.

The Mighty Fair: New York World's Fair 1964–1965: A Retrospective, exh. cat. New York: Flushing Gallery, 1985.

standing tradition of a central exhibition tower to its extreme by producing a "Tower of Light." From a phosphorescent crystalline building, a vertical beam of light from a twelve-billion-candlepower searchlight (the equivalent of 340,000 car headlights) emerged skywards at night, appearing at times as solid as a tower.

The most impressive nocturnal sight was the illuminated 200-foot-wide dome of the General Electric Pavilion by Welton Beckett. Lighting designer Monte Cutler installed a system of 2,112 lights in the triangular elements of the space frame construction. The 150-watt lamps were spotlights with new "dichroic" filters, which produced amber, blue and green lights. A "computer tape" (Benjamin) controlled a continuously running fifteen-minute-long light performance, during which bands of color seemed to be marching around the exterior of the dome. The same technology was used at the ten-story-tall, inclined aluminum facade of the General Motors building, whose thirty-eight vertical strips could be illumined separately in any conceivable color.

In the official guide the diverse attitudes and attractions of the fair were stressed: "It is a circus and a classroom, a voyage around the world, a look back at the past, a peepshow to the future" (*Official Guide* p. 42). Both the fair's didactic qualities and the shortcomings visible during the day vanished at night when the brilliance of the lighting spectacle provided the dominant impression. B. H. / D. N.

New York State Exhibition Building, postcard, 1964

General Electric Attraction Building at night, World's Fair, New York City, 1964 >

Balthazar Korab. General Electric Attraction Building at night, World's Fair, New York City, 1964. Gelatin silver print. American Friends of the CCA/Gift of Elliott and Carolyn Mittler. Collection Centre Canadien d'Architecture / Canadian Center for Architecture, Montréal >

Chrysler Building · New York, New York · 1981

Architect: **William Van Alen**

Location: **405 Lexington Avenue**

Construction Dates: **1929–30. Extant**

Installation Dates: ***c.* 1935, 1981. The building is currently illuminated.**

Installation Type: **Original, unexecuted lighting scheme had included 50-watt incandescent bulbs in the triangular windows of the tower and some floodlighting at lower levels. 1981: 480 40-watt fluorescent tubes mounted on 120 triangular windows in tower. Lights are mounted behind glazing on floors 67–74 and are mounted on exterior channels on floors 75–77. Four 400-watt metal halide floodlights at base of spire. One 1,000-watt metal halide floodlight at each 58th-story corner, three 1,000-watt metal-halide floodlights at each 61st-story corner.**

Lighting Designers: **1981: William Di Giacomo and Steve Negrin, W. A. Di Giacomo Associates. Based on designs of William Van Alen.**

Selected Bibliography

"A Plea for Light." *New York Times* (2 January 1931): 20, col. 7.

"Cooperation as One Architect Sees It: An Interview with William Van Alen." *Electrical World* 95, no. 11 (1930): 539–540.

"Decorative Lighting Restores Grandeur of Skyscraper Tower." *Electrical Construction and Maintenance* 81 (November 1982): 58–60.

Curcio, Vincent. *Chrysler: The Life and Times of an Automotive Genius*. New York: Oxford University Press, 2000.

Kernan, Michael. "The Night Light: Lighting Up the N. Y. Night." *Washington Post* (16 September 1981): C1.

Robinson, Cervin. "Chrysler." *Architecture Plus* 2 (May–June 1974): 50–55.

Often considered the quintessential Art Deco skyscraper, the Chrysler Building, at seventy-seven stories, was the tallest building in the world for the short interval between its completion and the construction of the Empire State Building (pp. 156–157). Architect William Van Alen was deeply involved in the lighting designs for his works and complained that the lighting experts he worked with were "too anxious to please and ... short on both facts and imagination." (Cooperation...) He had at first planned to cap the building with a glass dome lit from within, then contemplated having the top "floodlighted according to a most unusual scheme" (Cooperation ...) before he decided upon the now famous spire. The metallic surface of these upper floors, composed of stainless chromium nickel steel, was not suitable for floodlighting, so Van Alen had metal troughs built into both sides of the glazed triangular windows, into which incandescent bulbs were placed. To the great disappointment of New Yorkers ("A Plea for Light"), these were not employed immediately because of financial constraints caused by the Great Depression, but in later years, the bulbs were used for holiday illumination. Floodlighting was also included on some of the lower stories. For decades after the 1950s, however, the spire remained dark at night.

In 1979, a new owner of the building learned of the existence of the trough lights and decided to restore and expand upon the original illumination. The new scheme followed closely the original plans of Van Alen, but replaced the incandescent bulbs with fluorescent tubes, resulting in a brighter and less subtle appearance. For the unglazed windows on the top three stories, special weatherproof units were used. The fluorescent tubes outline the windows of all four sides in a series of inverted Vs, emphasizing the geometric pattern of ornamentation. The needlelike spire at the very top had been the surprise feature that allowed the Chrysler Building to claim its title as the world's tallest skyscraper over a competing tower at 40 Wall Street. The spire is now separately illuminated with four metal halide floodlights, and the same type of lamp is used to light the structure below the metal top. This lighting installation, although based on the original scheme, presents an appearance closer to our contemporary tastes and technology than to its original design.   K.B./D.N.

Chrysler Building, night view, postcard, *c.* 1932

Chrysler Building, night view. © Nathan Benn/Corbis, *c.* 2000 >

Tower of Winds · Yokohama · 1986

Architect: **Toyo Ito**

Location: **Yokohama Station**

Construction Date: **1986. Extant**

Installation Dates: **1986–c. 1995**

Installation Type: **30 floodlights, 12 neon bands and 1,200 small lamps, backed by mirrored surface and programmed to adjust in response to outside stimuli.**

Lighting Designers: **Toyo Ito with Kaoru Mende, TL Yamigawa Labs and Masami Usuki (programmer)**

Selected Bibliography:

"Creating a Tower of Wind." *Lighting Design & Application* 17 (October 1987): 13.

"Trends in Urban Lighting in Japan." *Philips Lamps & Gear Magazine* 4, no. 1. (2000).

Auer, Gerhard. "The Aesthetics of the Caleidoscope. Artificial Light in Japanese Cities." *Daidalos*, no. 27 (15 March 1988): 42–47.

Berwick, Carly. "An Interview with Toyo Ito." *The Take* (1997 / 1998). Online. Available: http: // www.thetake. com / take / html / 42ndst.html. 24 July 2001.

Ito, Toyo. "The Gate of Okawabata and the Tower of Winds in Yokohama." *Lotus* 75 (1993): 54–59.

Meyhöfer, Dirk. *Contemporary Japanese Architects.* Cologne: Benedikt Taschen Verlag, 1994.

In order to celebrate the thirtieth anniversary of the Yokohama West bus terminal, the architect Toyo Ito was commissioned to renovate and improve the adjacent utilitarian ventilation and water tower. Ito transformed the structure into a magical work of art that manages both to stand out in a crowded city and to actively respond to its surroundings. Ito covered the original, cubic concrete tower with a set of mirrors. Over these he erected a steel framework, on which are installed thirty floodlights and 1,200 small light bulbs. Twelve neon bands also encircle the tower at regular intervals. Perforated steel sheets provide the outer covering to form a seventy-foot-tall oval column. The lighting designer Kaoru Mende wrote after working with Ito on the Tower of Winds: "We are getting fewer opportunities to enjoy the sense of changing time. Part of the reason is that we have become accustomed to lighting environments which always stay the same." ("Trends in Urban Lighting"). He integrated all the lights into a computer program, which made them change in response to the external forces of wind (its direction and speed indicated by the patterns of movement) and of noise from the street.

The tower, which appears to be made of solid metal during the day, becomes seemingly transparent at night, defined only by its moving patterns of light, which Ito himself described as the transformation of architecture into "environmental music" (Berwick). A critic called the tower an "audio-visual seismograph" with a "repertoire of lighting, ranging from glowing sparks of flashing strobe lights, from geometrically regular intervals to amorphous shifts and flows, from retarded slow-motion to stroboscopic excitement, with all kinds of transitions and variants in between." (Auer) Rarely has the early claim that the best nocturnal architecture would dissolve materiality into color and light been realized more convincingly. Yet, in part because the range of color and abstract patterns is wisely limited, the work also provides something of an oasis in the neon-lit pandemonium of a modern Japanese city. Ito notes that "although the winking lights of the tower are less spectacular than other illuminated neon advertisements, it is said to create the impression that the air around the tower is being filtered and purified." (Lotus, p. 55). Toyo Ito continued to make electric light and its transformational qualities a central issue in his architectural designs, be it the Gate of Okawabata (the "Egg of Winds") in Tokyo (1991), or the recent Mediathèque in Sendai (2000). Due to a lack of funds and maintenance, the Tower of Winds has not (or only partially) been illuminated in recent years.

K. B. / D. N.

Tower of Winds, night view, photograph, c. 1986

Tower of Winds, night view, photograph, c. 1990 >

Bank of America Tower (originally CenTrust Tower) · Miami, Florida · 1987

Architects: **Pei Cobb Freed & Partners**
(I. M. Pei & Harold Fredenburgh, lead designers)
with Ferendino / Grafton / Spillis / Candela

Location: **100 Southeast 2nd Street**

Construction Dates: **1980–87. Extant**

Installation Dates: **continuously lit since 1987.**

Installation Type: **387 1,000-watt metal halide floodlights with changeable colored gels.**

Lighting Designer: **Douglas Leigh**

The building was originally erected as the CenTrust Tower, and this company invited lighting and advertising designer Douglas Leigh to develop a lighting scheme for the forty-six-story skyscraper. As a result of Leigh's collaboration with the architect I. M. Pei, the building's curved main facade, which overlooks the waterfront and the causeway to Miami Beach, features shallow setbacks to house batteries of floodlights, much like

The prevailing color is white, but colored floodlights are sometimes used to signify local events or important dates. When, shortly after its opening, Elizabeth Taylor came to Miami, the tower was lit in a deep violet; on the Fourth of July the colors of the American flag are displayed, and in winter the building appears blue, with a few large snowflakes applied to its facade (rather ironic in a sub-tropical climate). No computerized lighting

Bank of America, detail, photograph, *c.* 1987

Bank of America, general view at night with Miami Retro Rail lit by neon lights. © Eyewire Collection / Getty images

Bank of America, general view at night, photograph, *c.* 1987. © Thorney Lieberman. Courtesy of Pei Cobb Freed & Partners >

Selected Bibliography:

"Best Beacon." *Miami New Times*. 1999. Online. Available: http://www.miaminewtimes.com/bom/1999/citylife/024.html. 11 November 2000.

"Best Magic City Icon." *Miami New Times* (17 May 2001) Online. Available: http://www.miaminewtimes.com/issues/2001-05-17/citylife14.html. 11 July 2001.

"CenTrust Tower." Pei Cobb Freed & Partners website. Online. Available: http://www.pcfandp.com/a/p/8002/s.html. 30 July 2001.

De Gale, Annabelle. "Miami, City of Lights." *Miami Herald* (30 December 1999).

Harper, Paula. "Power Skyline." *Art in America* 76 (September 1988): 54–65.

its counterparts of the 1930s. The three remaining sides rise up in straight vertical planes. Ribbon windows alternate with horizontal white enameled aluminum bands. Although the reference to the setback sky-scraper of the 1920s and their typical light-ing schemes is obvious, thanks to much-improved lighting technology the building appears quite different from its predecessors. The enameled aluminum has a high reflec-tivity and the wider reach of new floodlights permits the even lighting of all forty-six stories, isolating the tower as a luminous beacon in the skyline.

effects are used here: the colored lenses are changed by hand, a job that takes two workers four hours to perform. The tower has become "the star of the downtown night skyline" in Miami (Harper, p. 55) and was the catalyst for a citywide illumination plan, with dozens of buildings and bridges now lit at night, many in changing colors.   K. B. / D. N.

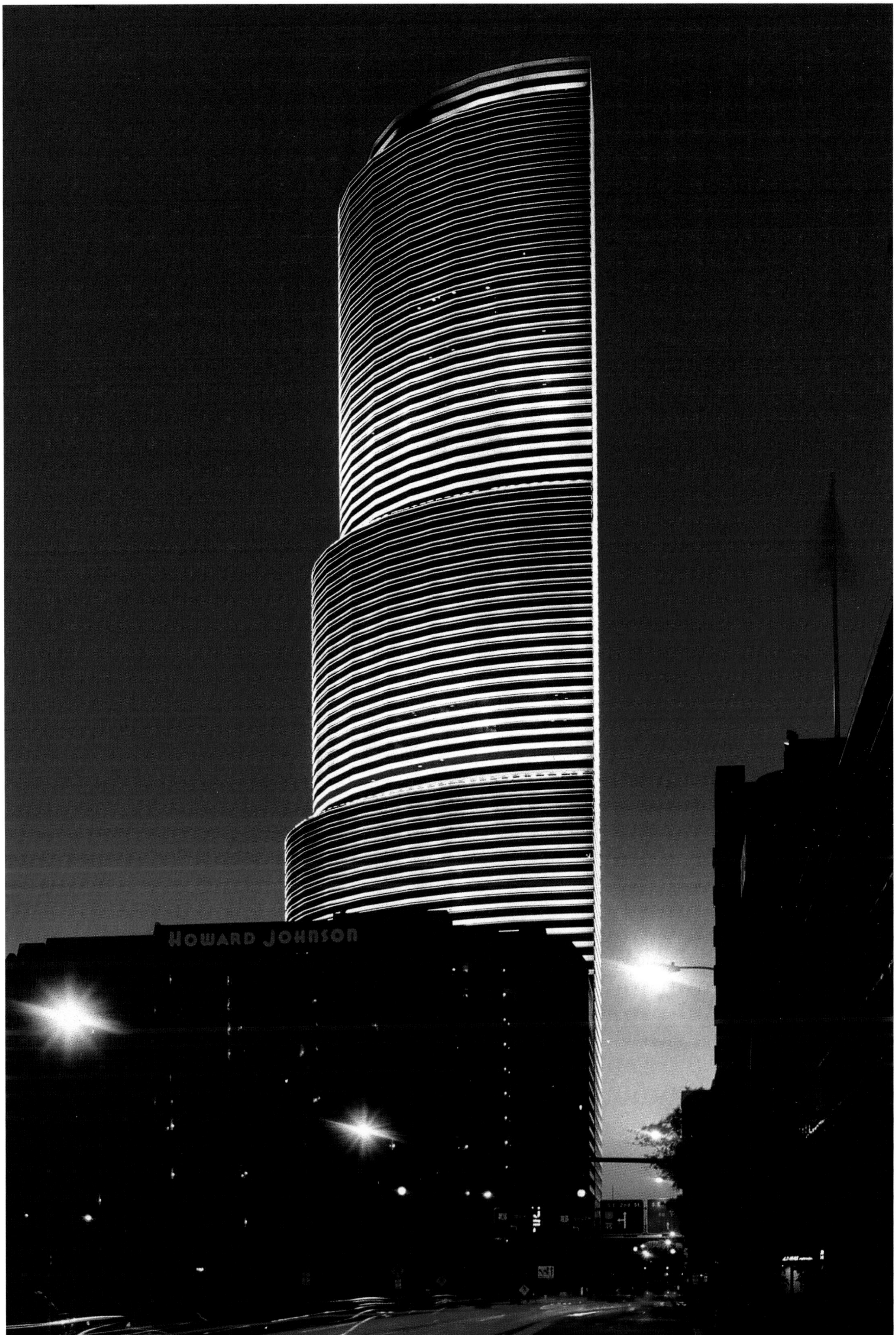
HOWARD JOHNSON

Kirin Plaza · Osaka · 1988

Architect: **Shin Takamatsu, interior design with Kazuko Fujie**

Location: **Shinsaibashi-suji**

Construction Dates: **1987–88**

Installation Date: **since 1988**

Installation Type: **White neon lights behind translucent opal glass. Colored neon lights as part of an occasional computer-generated light show.**

Lighting Design: **Shin Takamatsu**

The building that the hotel and insurance division of the Japanese brewery Kirin placed in a major commercial and entertainment district in Osaka contains in its seven floors bars, restaurants, exhibition and performance spaces. Situated at a prominent intersection of the Shinsaibashi-suji shopping street and the Dotonbori bridge, the building is visible from a considerable distance on two sides. The almost windowless edifice seems to consist of a huge box clad in black granite, whose somewhat forbidding, introverted facades are punctured by gleaming metal elements, sug-

puter-programmed sequence of bright white and colored lights appeared three times a night, as if to prove that the building could, if needed, participate in the visual cacophony around it. Now the white lights are used alone and at very reduced capacity in order to save energy.

Shin Takamatsu was faced with a problem that had already been discussed in Europe in the 1920s—the need to survive in an environment of wildly growing advertisements with an architecture whose form either integrates advertising or converts the entire building into a recognizable icon. As Takamatsu put it, "Kirin Plaza is a new challenger in the battle of advertisements. While the signs surrounding Kirin may be colorful, their haphazard sizes and arrangement render them ineffective in comparison to Kirin's grandeur.... Rather than to the confusing flashes of color, the night stroller is attracted to the stable, white light towers of Kirin Plaza Osaka." (Takamatsu)

D. N.

Kirin Plaza, view from the Dotonbori canal, photograph, c. 1995

Kirin Plaza, photograph, c. 1995 >

Selected Bibliography:

Watanabe, Hiroshi. "Japan: High-rise Beacons Mounted on a Mysterious Black Box." *Architecture: the AIA Journal* 77, no. 9 (September 1988): 6869.

Menard, J.-P., "Entre le Zen et le Kitsch." *Architectes Architecture* 192 (November 1988): 35.

Takamatsu, Shin, "The Canal, the Clock and Kirin Plaza, Osaka." *Japan Architect* 63, no. 5 (May 1988): 39–46.

Vorreiter, Gabriele, "Kirin Articulation: Entertainment Building, Osaka, Japan." *Architectural Review* 184, no. 1098 (August 1988): 58–62.

gesting a gigantic mechanical toy. From the upper half of this box, four luminous slabs of white translucent glass emerge vertically, extending far beyond the roofline of the building (as they don't contain usable space, an exception from the height limits was granted). Their uninterrupted white surfaces and the absence of any advertising on the building provide a striking contrast to the visual density of its neighbors, whose facades are covered beyond recognition with illuminated, colorful signs. Critics were reminded of a grouping of four *andons*, the traditional Japanese floor lamp, and aptly diagnosed a mixture of "Zen and kitsch." (Menard) Initially, a short, com-

NEC Supertower · Tokyo · 1990

Architect: **Nikken Sekkei**

Construction Dates: **1989–90. Extant**

Installation Date: **1990. The building is currently illuminated.**

Installation Type: **11 lighting fixtures installed in plaza on north and south sides of the building. Each fixture contains four 1.8-kilowatt metal halide lamps and seven 1-kilowatt xenon search-lights, two with color filters.**

Lighting Designer: **Motoko Ishii, Motoko Ishii Lighting Design, Inc.**

NEC Supertower, night view, photograph, c. 1994

Selected Bibliography:

"NEC Supertower." *Japan Architect*, no. 2 (February 1991): 110–113.

"Tokyo's Watch Tower." *Lighting Design & Application* 22 (February 1992): 24.

Misu, Kunihiro. "NEC Supertower." *Japan Architect* 65, no. 11–12 (November–December 1990): 86–92.

The forty-three-story headquarters building of the NEC Corporation in Tokyo is one of the more recognizable skyscrapers on the Tokyo skyline and a structural tour de force, designed by one of Japan's largest building and design contractors. The heavy base contains an enormous twelve-story atrium with a removable glass roof. Above this, two pairs of inclined braces support the suspended twenty-story main tower, culminating in a penthouse. The 138-by-49-foot-wide opening at the bottom of the vertical shaft improves the wind performance around the building and allows daylight to enter the atrium and entrance hall.

The lighting design for the building was planned in conjunction with the construction and was intended to insure that the building would remain a highly visible component of the skyline after dark. Lighting designer Motoko Ishii analyzed the differences in the appearance of the building as seen from various points in the city. With these studies and the limits to the use of energy that the company had imposed, she decided to illumine only the upper floors of the tower. In addition she used changing lights to tell time at night. Metal halide and xenon lamps were concealed within the vegetation of the plaza and focused on the upper floors of the narrow, windowless south and north sides of the structure. Connected to separate circuits, the lights were timed to turn off in stages, from the bottom to the top of the tower, as if facing an imaginary second sunset. Every hour between seven and midnight another group shut down, and as the building gradually grew darker, passersby could gauge what time of night it was, earning the building the nickname "watchtower." Different colors were used to signify different seasons, with coral used in the fall and winter, and blue employed during the rest of the year. The ribbon windows on the east and west sides are equipped with perimeter lighting in the ceiling, consisting of white fluorescent lights behind translucent panels, in order to achieve a nocturnal appearance similar to that of the Seagram Building (pp. 188–189). The result was striking enough to earn an international award for exterior lighting.   K. B. / D. N.

Petronas Towers · Kuala Lumpur · 1996

Architects: **Cesar Pelli & Associates: Cesar Pelli (design principal), Fred Clarke (project principal and collaborating designer)**

Location: **Kuala Lumpur City Center, Jalan Ampang**

Construction Dates: **1991–96. Extant**

Installation Date: **1996.**

Installation Type: **More than 250 lighting fixtures on each of two towers. Metal halide floodlighting projectors with 70, 150 and 400-watt lamps, long-range projectors with 1,800-watt lamps. Spheres (made of concentric stainless steel tubes) at the base of each finial lit from within by 8 400-watt floodlights, brushed stainless steel spheres at tips of finials lit by 16 1,800-watt narrow floodlights.**

Lighting Designers: **Howard Brandston, Scott Matthews, Chou Lien, Jung Soo Kim of H. M. Brandston & Partners**

The most prominent element of a master plan for a new commercial center in Kuala Lumpur, the Petronas Towers are currently the tallest buildings in the world, although the Sears Tower in Chicago still contains the highest useable floor space. Commissioned by Malaysia's national oil company, Petronas, and promoted by Prime Minister Mahathir Mohamad, the eighty-eight-story towers soon became a symbol of the country's new international status. Required to reflect the culture of the

Petronas Tower, night view, photograph, c. 2001.
© Mary Shepard

Petronas Towers, night view. © Jeff Goldberg/Esto. >

predominately Muslim country in his design, architect Cesar Pelli employed the traditional Islamic form of two intersecting squares, forming an eight-point star. He then made the walls between each point curve outwards in an arabesque form, furthering the Islamic motif. A bridge at the forty-first and forty-second stories links the two towers and helps to emphasize the intervening space, which Pelli believes is the vital element that bestows upon the buildings their iconic status. It was this space that the lighting designers, in consultation with Pelli, chose to emphasize, elevating the structure far beyond its rather ordinary function as an office building. "What

matters is that the form in the void is balanced and accentuated and reads beautifully at night.... The form helps to create a powerful sense of a huge, well-defined space, like a great door to infinity. Lighting is instrumental in accentuating this characteristic, giving form and presence to that space in the night sky." (Pelli, quoted in Trauthwein, p. 33) The towers are faced with glass and linen-finish stainless steel that reflect the sunlight during the day but can be difficult to illuminate at night. Designers at Brandston Partnership installed metal halide floodlights on the five-story common podium of the two towers as well as on the skybridge. These flood the two interior faces with light from bottom to top, while leaving the outer walls largely unlit. Uplights were then mounted on each of the projecting corners and bays of the five setbacks above the sixtieth floor, encircling the towers with light at each level and providing a convincing reminder of lighting practices in the U.S. during the 1920s and '30s. At the base of the two finials are twelve-foot spheres, composed of stainless steel tubes and lit from within, while the terminating pinnacles feature five-foot spheres illumined by narrow floodlight beams, topping the towers with two brilliant balls of light. The uplighting of the towers extends into the skies, so that the clouds above reflect the illumination. The intricate lighting scheme of the Petronas Towers won an award of merit from the Illuminating Engineering Society in 1999.   K. B.

Selected Bibliography:

Asencio Cerver, Francisco. *The Architecture of Skyscrapers.* New York: Hearst Books, 1997.

Pearson, Clifford A. "Other Than Their Status as the World's Tallest Buildings, What Else do Cesar Pelli's Petronas Towers Have Going for Them?" *Architectural Record* 187 (January 1999): 92–101.

Trauthwein, Christina. "Twin Peaks." *Architectural Lighting* 14 (August / September 1999): 32–34.

Tower of Time · Manchester · 1996

Architect: **Renton Howard Wood Levin Partnership**

Location: **Bridgewater Hall, Mosley Lower Street**

Construction Date: **1996, Extant**

Installation Date: **1996. The building is currently illuminated.**

Installation Type: **AR500 Irideon luminaires with colored lamps mounted on interior and exterior of facade, cold cathode tubes at base of each floor.**

Lighting Designer: **Jonathan Speirs, Jonathan Speirs & Associates**

This eight-story detached tower for Bridgewater Hall in Manchester was designed to hold all of the building's technical equipment, ensuring that no extraneous noise would interfere with the auditorium's concert performances. Lighting designer Jonathan Speirs took this mundane building component and turned it into a "Tower of Time," a nightly display of color that, like Motoko Ishii's NEC Supertower (pp. 210–211) in Tokyo, serves as a huge, abstract clock. Colored lights are mounted on both the interior and exterior of the translucent, curved glass facade, which surrounds the actual concrete core and partially hides the technical equipment within from view. The interior lights change color in coordination with the signs of the Zodiac. Those on the exterior reflect the time of year, starting with green for spring, and running through yellow, red and blue, denoting each subsequent season in a gradual wash of colors. Five lines of tubing delineate the floors. The first line is illuminated on Monday, and on each day an additional line is added, until all are lit on Friday. Every quarter hour there is a sequence of fast-changing colors, acting as the building/clock's "chime." As with Anne Militello's Forty-second Street Studios (pp. 222–223) in New York, the lighting scheme also includes special programs related to the days of the week, with a faster-paced design used for Saturday nights and a quieter one for Sundays. While Bridgewater Hall itself won awards from the Royal Institute of British Architects and the Civic Trust for its contribution to the appearance of a city center, Jonathan Speirs' lighting installation won a special award from the International Association of Lighting Designers in 1999 for the innovative use of light and color.   K. B.

Tower of Time, Manchester, night view.

Selected Bibliography:

"Special Citation for Innovative Use of Light & Color: The Tower of Time." *Architectural Lighting* 14 (July 1999): 40.

"Tower of Time." Irideon Architectural Lighting Company website. Online. Available: http://www.irideon.com/projects/proj2/time.html. 12 July 2001.

"Tower of Time." Lighting Architects Group website. Online. Available: http://www.lightarch.com/lightarch99/pr_ttm.html. 12 July 2001.

Kunsthaus Bregenz · Bregenz · 1996

The municipal art museum in Bregenz, capital of the Austrian state of Vorarlberg, occupies a prominent position on the banks of Lake Constance. The facade of the ninety-foot-tall uniform cube consists of an uninterrupted pattern of large frosted-glass shingles and conveys a minimalist purity characteristic of both its structural and visual concept: this "body of light" (Achleitner) was conceived as a receptacle of daylight for its exhibition spaces and as a luminous box at night. From the translucent walls, light either enters the interior spaces directly or reaches the inside via the translucent ceilings. The building's outer skin rests on a steel structure three feet from the actual building's concrete and glass core, the gap providing spaces for cleaning, air circulation and the installation of floodlights below ground. The diffusing glass creates an ambient glow inside and out.

Before realizing the architect's vision for the building's nocturnal appearance, the museum commissioned lighting and video artists James Turrell, Keith Sonnier, and Tony Oursler to develop nocturnal installations.

The radical simplicity of the design concept is reminiscent of German projects of the 1920s, such as Mies van der Rohe's 1928 designs for department stores in Berlin and Stuttgart (p. 39). The "mystical presence" of the Kunsthaus Bregenz was celebrated as a "triumph of intellect and imagination." (*Architectural Review*)   D.N.

Architect: **Peter Zumthor**

Location: **Karl Tizian Platz**

Construction Dates: **1993–96**

Installation Date: **1998. The building is currently illuminated**

Installation Type: **Lamps between the two layers of glass. Installation, supervision and financing: Vorarlberger Kraftwerke VKW**

Lighting Designers: **Peter Zumthor, James Turrell (1997), Keith Sonnier (1999), Tony Oursler (2001)**

Kunsthaus Bregenz, night view, main entrance, 1997.
© Florian Holzherr

Kunsthaus Bregenz, night view detail, 1997.
© Florian Holzherr

Selected Bibliography:

"Mystical Presence." *Architectural Review* 202, no. 1210 (December 1997): 46–53.

Friedrich Achleitner. "Peter Zumthor: Museo d'Arte, Bregenz, Austria." *Domus* no. 798 (November 1997): 36–43.

Hubertus Adam. "Glashaus aus Beton: Peter Zumthor's Kunsthaus in Bregenz" *Bauwelt* 88, no. 35 (12 September 1997): 1910–17.

Wolfgang Bachmann. "Peter Zumthor: Kunsthaus Bregenz." *Baumeister* 94, no. 9 (September 1997): 50–57.

Website of the museum: http://www.kunsthaus-bregenz.at/

Verbundnetz AG, Administration Building · Leipzig · 1997

Architects: **Becker, Gewers, Kühn & Kühn, Berlin**

Location: **Braunstrasse 7**

Construction Date: **1997. Extant**

Installation Date: **1997. The building is currently illuminated.**

Installation Type: **Digitally-programmed 980-volt cold cathode neon lamps.**

Lighting Designer: **James Turrell**

This office building and computer center for the natural-gas industry in eastern Germany features an advanced energy efficiency system. With its own small gas-fueled power station to create electricity, the building is independent from outside power sources and is even capable of feeding surplus electricity into the local network. Its two-layer glass facade and central atrium allow the building's heating and air circulation systems to adjust to the weather conditions outside.

The building is part of a long tradition in which power companies used their facilities to showcase the potential of current energy technology. One of the architects, Eike Becker, also considered the nocturnal illumination as a potential merging of art and architecture in the historical, Baroque sense of a "Synaesthesia" (Becker). James Turrell won a limited competition for the lighting installation. He placed colored neon tubes in the floors between the two outside layers of glass in the tower at the northeast corner of the building (forty-six feet wide and seventy-two feet high). Three tubes in red, yellow and blue are installed under glass and cast their light towards the ceiling and louvered blinds, which then reflect it outside. Controlled by a computer program, the lights change continuously and cast shifting hazes of color over the glass tower, from blue to red, or orange to green and blue. The color changes reference the varying temperatures that the energy supplier constantly reacts to and provides. "Light should be a material with which we build," declared James Turrell (quoted in Cooley), echoing a suggestion that light designers had formulated again and again throughout the twentieth century. "An illuminated building can be a princess at night and a commoner during the day."

D. N.

Verbundnetz AG, Administrative Building, Leipzig 1997
© Willebrand

Selected Bibliography:

Bachmann, Wolfgang. "Verwaltung der Verbundnetz Gas AG in Leipzig." *Baumeister* 94 (May 1997): 36–39.

Becker, Eike. *Hauptverwaltung der Verbundnetz AG.* Munich: Prestel, 1999.

Cooley, Renee. "Interview with James Turrell: Adventures in Perception." *Architectural Lighting* (March 2001).

Laganier, Vincent. "James Turrell, ou Comment Percevoir l'Architecture Autrement: Trichromie et Virtualisation." *L'Architecture d'Aujourd'hui* 331 (November–December 2000): 106–109.

Victorian Arts Centre · Melbourne · 1997

The Arts Centre of the state of Victoria hosts several cultural institutions, including the Melbourne Symphony Orchestra, Australian Ballet, and the Victorian Opera. The building, which was designed shortly after Frei Otto's design for the Olympic Stadium roof in Munich, applied a similar formal language and structure. Due to structural problems, its latticework spire was replaced in 1996. The rebuilt spire, at 532 feet, was both taller and thinner than the original and featured a striking new lighting installation. Designer Barry Webb replaced the original 106 floodlights with an array of thousands of individual lights and eight separate lighting systems. At the base, or skirt, of the structure, are sprinkled 14,000 incandescent bulbs, creating a type of lighting design that is as old as electric architectural illumination itself. The effect achieved, however, in combination with the rest of the illuminating equipment is completely up-to-date. Distributed throughout the iron framework of the spire are over 22,000 feet of fiber optic cable, some of which is used to create an

overall twinkling effect. At the tip of the spire are neon tubes and strobe lights, while the interior is lit with vertical spotlights, and color changers are located on the edge of the spire's base. The eight separate lighting systems allow for numerous, permutable effects. The newly lighted tower has caused a sensation in Melbourne: "the spire lighting is truly spectacular and occasionally threatens traffic chaos as enthralled drivers catch their first glimpse (Molloy)." K. B. / D. N.

Victorian Arts Centre, night view, photograph, c. 1997

Victorian Arts Centre, night view with skyline, photograph, c. 1997

Architects: **Original building and spire: Roy Grounds. Redesigned spire: Peter McIntyre and Bob Sturrock**

Location: **100 St. Kilda Road**

Construction Dates: **Original building and spire: 1973–84. Redesigned spire: 1996. Extant**

Installation Date: **1997. The building is currently illuminated.**

Installation Type: **Originally lit by 106 floodlights. 1997: 22,310 feet of fiber optic cable, including end-emitting twinkle lamps and side-emitting cable throughout the structure, connected to 174 150-watt metal halide light sources. 1-watt white and 3-watt blue incandescent lights on the skirt, halogen high-intensity spot lamps at specific levels, 460 feet of neon tubing and strobe discharge lamps at tip of spire, high-power narrow-beam vertical spotlights in center of structure. Ten custom-designed color changers on outer edges of base, rigged onto metal halide floodlights.**

Lighting Designer: **Barry Webb, Barry Webb & Associates with Stephen Found, Bytecraft Australia**

Selected Bibliography:

"Aurora Australis." Lighting Design & Application (May 1999). Online. Available: http://www.iesna.org/LDA_5-99/feature_aussie1.htm. 19 July 2001.

"Site History." Victorian Arts Centre homepage. Online. Available: http://www.svc060.bne101v.server-web.com/aboutus/history.html. 26 July 2001.

Molloy, Jacqueline. "An Inspired Vision." *Lighting Dimensions* (December 1997).

Los Angeles International Airport Theme Building and Light Columns · Los Angeles, California · 1997

Architects: **Theme Building: Charles Luckman, William Pereira, Welton Becket & Paul R. Williams. Light Columns: Nadel Architects**

Location: **Los Angeles International Airport. Theme building: 201 Center Way. Pylons on Century and Sepulveda Boulevards**

Construction Dates: **Theme Building: 1960–62. Pylons: 2000.**

Installation Dates: **Theme Building: 1962, 1997. Pylons: 2000. Both are currently illuminated.**

Installation Type: **Theme Building: Exterior: 56 Irideon AR500 wash luminaires (high-output floodlights with internal dichroic color-changing mechanisms) mounted at base and on observation deck. Pylons: Total of more than 700 lighting fixtures. Glass pylons lit from within by architectural color-changing fixtures. Century Boulevard: in each tower 16 to 40 color-changing 150-watt metal halide lamps. Sepulveda Boulevard: in each tower 32 automated color-changing washlights with metal halide lamps.**

Lighting Designers: **Theme Building: Michael Valentino, Walt Disney Imagineering**

Light Columns: **Dawn Hollingsworth, Jeremy Windle, Erin Powell (Moody Ravitz Hollingsworth Lighting Design, Inc.)**

Selected Bibliography:

"LAX Restaurant Changes its Spots." *Architectural Record* (April 1997): 148.

"LAX Themed Building." Irideon Architectural Lighting Company website. Online. Available: http://www.irideon.com/projects/proj2/lax.html. 1 August 2001.

"Los Angeles Airport theme building is designated landmark." *Historic Preservation News* (1993 March–April): 33, no. 3: 4.

Trauthwein, Christina. "Dusk 'til Dawn." *Architectural Lighting* 15 (January/February 2001): 24–27.

Weathersby, William Jr. "Close Encounter." *Lighting Dimensions* (June 1997).

The evocative and futuristic LAX Theme Building opened in 1962 and was illuminated from the very beginning. Initially only lit with amber lights, it was meant to symbolize the optimism of a future Los Angeles in the jet age. The building's characteristic 350-foot-wide intercepting arches (supposedly adding earthquake stability) rise to a height of eighty-five feet and anchor the restaurant, which is supported by a central column. Stylistic influences range from sources as diverse as Oscar Niemeyer's Brazilian architecture to Martian space ships from the film *War of the Worlds* (1954—the set designer was Hal Pereira, brother of the architect.) The building is in turn said to have influenced the design of the popular TV cartoon series, *The Jetsons*, which aired for the first time on 23 September 1962.

Unable to project floodlights onto the exterior without blinding patrons inside the building's windows, the designer for the new lighting scheme chose instead to mount lamps with dichroic color-changing devices at the base of the central core, lighting the structure from below. Additional lights were installed on the observation deck to illumine the arches that soar over the main structure. The lights are programmed to change gradually during a cycle of fifteen minutes. "One of the nice things with the fixtures, because they are dichroic, is that when you fade over a minute to two minutes, the building actually goes through a myriad of colors—everything from dark blue to aqua. Even though I programmed up to five looks within the fifteen-minute segments, you actually see quite a few more" (Valentino, quoted in Weathersby). Every fifteen-minute sequence uses different color effects within one color range per segment: "We didn't want to make this look like a disco. This is a rather elegant building and we wanted to treat it with a lot of respect." (Weathersby) On the quarter hour, the slow fades are augmented by a thirty-second display of rapid changes. The show starts with one leg of the structure lit all in white, and this then washes over the rest of the building, followed by quick fades of one color after another. The interior of the restaurant carries out the futuristic theme of the original structure, with neon-outlined amoeba shapes on the ceiling, dichroic mirrors, and lava lamps with special flying saucer tops.

The illumination of the Theme Building was soon followed by a further attempt to enliven the airport at night. Fifteen 110-foot-tall glass cylinders now stand in a circle at the airport's entrance, while an additional eleven pylons line Century Boulevard, rising in size from twenty-five to sixty feet in imitation of the flight path of a departing plane. The pylons are all made of translucent glass and lit from within by color-changing fixtures, taking on a theme of colored light columns that was popular at many European exhibitions during the 1920s, such as the Barcelona World's Fair (pp. 138–139). Nicknamed the "Psychedelic Stonehenge" (Trauthwein, p. 24), the two sets of pylons produce numerous, changing color effects and all together form the largest installation of automated lighting in the world. This latest addition to the L.A. Airport's decorative lighting scheme won designer Dawn Hollingsworth the title of Architectural Lighting Designer of the Year from Lighting Dimensions International.   K. B. / D. N.

LAX, Light Pylons, night view, photograph, *c.* 1997

LAX Theme Building, night view, photograph, *c.* 1997 >

LAX, Light Pylons, night view, photograph, *c.* 1997 >

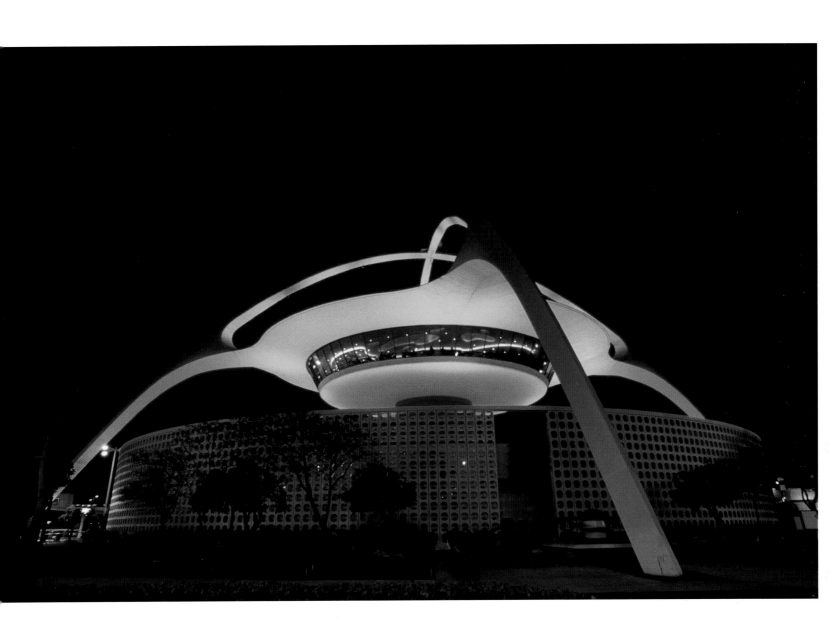

Burj al Arab Hotel · Dubai · 1999

Architect: **W. A. Atkins & Partners: Tom Wright (design director)**

Location: **Jumeirah Beach Resort**

Construction Date: **1999. Extant**

Installation Date: **1999. The building is currently illuminated.**

Installation Type: **Exoskeleton lit by metal halide projectors and by 90 strobe lights. Crown and fabric facade are lit by *c*. 150 color-changing luminaires, installed on poolside bar, cantilevered restaurant, helicopter pad, and island bridge. Adjacent to helicopter pad: Four 4.7-kilowatt Xenon Skytracker searchlights can project beams into the sky. (660 feet from the hotel) projection room on mainland: Four 7-kilowatt PIGI large format scrolling slide projectors focused on the membrane of the eastern facade.**

Lighting Designers: **Jonathan Speirs, Gavin Fraser, Malcolm Innes, Alan Mitchell, James Mason and Iain Ruxton, Jonathan Speirs & Associates. Lighting controls designer: Paul Gregory, Focus Lighting.**

Burj al Arab, night view, photograph, *c.* 1999

Selected Bibliography:

"Burj Al Arab." Lighting Architects Group website. http://www.lightarch.com/Content/lightarch/lightarch2001/pr_burjalarab.html.

Currimbhoy, Nayana. "Color Washes Turn a Dubai Hotel into a Huge, Animated Lighting Spectacular." *Architectural Record* 188 (May 2000): 320–321.

Linn, Charles. "Lighting …" *Architectural Record* 188 (May 2000): 315.

McBride, Edward. "Burj al Arab." *Architecture* 89 (August 2000): 116–127.

Speirs, Jonathan. "Radiating Resort." *Lighting Design & Application* 30 (August 2000): 32–35.

T., W. "Case Study." *Architectural Record* 188 (September 2000): 160.

The Burj al Arab Hotel, at 1,053 feet and sixty stories the tallest hotel in the world, and with seven stars the world's most luxurious, was commissioned by Dubai ruler Sheikh Muhammad bin Rashid al Maktoum to create an attraction for world travelers and to give his city a fitting architectural symbol. Built across from the Jumeirah Beach Resort on a man-made island off the coast of Dubai, about fifteen miles from the city center, the V-shaped structure consists of an external steel frame, or exoskeleton, with a reinforced concrete tower that holds the 202 guest suites. The open, eastern side of the V, which includes a 600-foot-high atrium, is covered with a translucent Teflon-coated fiberglass fabric that helps to filter the desert sun and is meant to evoke the sail of a ship.

It is upon this fabric that the building's light show is projected. Metal halide projectors provide a base by illuminating the inner components of the exoskeleton with white lights. The crown of the building and the tensile fabric of the facade are then lit by color-changing luminaires. These are situated on the roof of a ground level bar, a cantilevered restaurant and helicopter pad, both located near the building's crown, and on the bridge to the island.

Although numberless color patterns and quick sequences would be possible, the creators point out that "the shows are designed so that the effect is not too kinetic, but colorful, hypnotic, fun and expressive.... Changes take place on the hour and half hour, so that much of the time the tower is static in a single 'look,' with enough movement and change in the two small shows per hour to be dynamic and powerful without being overly dominant." (Lighting Architects Group website) The building may appear as all white, all one color, or as a combination of different hues. Strobe lights are mounted within the exoskeleton, allowing for such effects as colored light pulses running along the length of the building. For special events, xenon projectors can project huge images, such as portraits of Arab leaders, onto the fabric facade, while searchlights project beams into the sky. Because of the translucency of the fabric facade, the colors can also be seen from inside the hotel's towering atrium.

This dramatic lighting display transplants a modernized version of the old concept of mobile color floodlighting from the heart of urban America to a developing beach resort in the Middle East. In contrast to the crowds in American cities, here only guests of the hotel, of the Jumeirah Beach Resort (1996, also lit by Speirs and Major) on the mainland, and the local population can witness the nocturnal spectacle. By promising its visitors the splendor of "1,001 Nights" the hotel's public relation planners skillfully exploit the vague associations between colorful lights and the orient, often voiced in conjunction with lighting projects in urban America in the 1930s. The project won an International Illumination Design Award in 2000.   K. B. / D. N.

Forty-Second Street Studios · New York, New York · 2000

Architects: **Platt Byard Dovell**

Location: **229 West 42nd St.**

Construction Date: **2000. Extant**

Installation Date: **2000, the building is currently illuminated.**

Installation Type: **Total of 225 lighting fixtures. Translucent shades inside the windows lit by custom fluorescent fixtures with colored gels. Each bay of the facade structure is lit in each floor by 2 575-watt PAR fixtures with halogen lamps and dichroic glass, plus 1 metal halide lamp, reflected by steel blades set at 30-degree angles from the facade. 5 automated luminaires with HID lamps mounted above the marquee, with dichroic color-changing elements. 175-foot-tall light spire on west side, composed of connected linear sections of acrylic tubes lined with optical film and fed by automated luminaires with dichroic HID lamps.**

Lighting Designers: **Anne Militello, Vortex Lighting. James Carpenter (Light fin and dichroic glass square)**

42nd Street Studios, night view, photograph, 2000

Selected Bibliography:

Dunlap, David W. "Choreographing Times Sq. Into 21st Century." *New York Times* (16 September 1993): sec. B, 1, col. 2.

Gener, Randy. "New 42nd Street Studios Building Lights Up its Facade." Theatre.Com. Online. Available: http://www.theatre.com/news/public/newsprint.asp?newsid=7858. 24 April 2001.

Giovannini, Joseph. "Times of the Signs." *New York Magazine* (26 June 2000).

Goldberger, Paul. "Busy Buildings." *New Yorker* 76 (4 September 2000): 90–93.

Weathersby, William, Jr. "Choreographed Illumination of a Rehearsal Center's Facade Creates its own Street Theater on Broadway." *Architectural Record* 188, no. 11 (November 2000): 196–200.

The ten-story structure of the Forty-second Street Studios, just around the corner from Times Square, provides low-cost rehearsal space for actors, dancers, and musicians in a neighborhood where affordable rents have become increasingly scarce. With its glass curtain-wall facade, the building invites daytime passersby to look in upon the studios and enjoy the impromptu theater created by the artists at work. The current revitalization plans for Times Square that were developed in 1993 by a team led by architect Robert Venturi and graphic designer Tibor Kalman require all new buildings to plan for the accommodation of lighted signs into their facades. The architects Charles Platt and Ray Dovell convinced the client, the non-profit group "New 42nd Street Inc." to take the concept one step further, forego the considerable revenue that a lighted advertisement might have generated and to integrate an abstract illumination scheme into the structure of the building itself. Working closely with lighting designer Anne Militello, they constructed a steel framework of perforated, horizontal blades separated into bays by vertical elements and mounted in front of the facade's top seven stories. During daytime, the blades act as "brises soleils" to protect the interior from direct sun exposure on its southern facade. At night, they reflect the light from lamps hidden on the steel armature, as well as from automated color-changing luminaires mounted on the marquee. Behind the glass wall, translucent shades are pulled down at night and lit by fluorescent lamps with colored gels to create a luminous background for the more animated installation on the surface. On the building's western edge, a 175-foot-tall spire of light goes through yet another series of color fades. Below this, a thirty-by-thirty-foot square of reflective glass with dichroic fins recalls with its outline the brick theater facade that previously stood on the spot and also provides a daytime show of refracted light (both designed by glass artist James Carpenter). A total of 256 colors are available to create more than 500 computer-controlled patterns after dark. The display is programmed to grow in intensity as the week progresses, starting out with relatively slow-changing effects on Monday and reaching its apogee on the weekends, when the facade takes on a different appearance every few seconds. Militello states that the building was "conceived as illumination itself. It is as if, at times, the building is a lighting fixture … an object that gives forth light," rather than a structure that has been illuminated from an outside source. (Militello, quoted in Gener).

These ever-changing color patterns are the logical next step in the evolution of mobile color lighting that had begun in the 1920s and demonstrate once again the potential of nocturnal illumination as a fundamental component of architectural design. Paul Goldberger's critique in the New Yorker similarly echoes sentiments expressed during the most intense phase of architectural lighting in the 1930s: "… the facade of the building literally becomes a performance. It glows, it flashes, it changes from red to blue and then to yellow, orange and green. The lights do not cover up the architecture, like the commercial billboards up and down the rest of the street; they are completely in tune with the structure of which they are a part. They make it dance." (Goldberger)

K. B. / D. N.

Goodman Theatre Center · Chicago, Illinois · 2001

Architects: **Kuwabara Payne McKenna Blumberg Architects and Decker Legge Kemp Architecture**

Location: **170 North Dearborn Parkway**

Construction Dates: **2000–2001. Extant**

Installation Date: **2001. The building is currently illuminated.**

Installation Type: **Facade: 192 color light fixtures utilizing LEDs and digital technology. Fixtures project light onto screens behind 96 glass panels. Rotunda: 240 LED fixtures. All controlled by lighting console with an internal clock for seasonal variations. Audio component for sound and light shows.**

Lighting Designer: **Rich Locklin, Lightswitch in conjunction with Color Kinetics (lighting technology).**

The idea of a lighting design for the new Goodman Theatre Center began with the building's owner, Albert Friedman, who wanted an installation that would announce the move of Chicago's seventy-five-year-old Goodman Theatre into the heart of the city's North Loop theater district. The new building incorporates the facade of two existing 1922 theaters, bringing with it the old marquee and vertical illuminated sign, which now mark the entrance to the center's 840-seat proscenium auditorium. Working closely with a digital lighting company and the architects, lighting designer Rich Locklin turned the facade and entrance for the 400-seat flexible perfor-

rotunda on the corner of the building culminates in an oblique crown of LED fixtures, which change and harmonize with the effects on the facade.

Clearly a descendant of the mobile color lighting effects first seen in the late 1920s and '30s in such installations as the Kansas City Power & Light Company (pp. 154–155) or Chicago's own McJunkin building (p. 112), this design makes use of a technology that is more sophisticated and versatile. In place of colored filters and dimmers, a computer controls all color changes and the illusion of movement, resulting in an installation that is very low-maintenance, energy-efficient, and easy to revise. Locklin plans to set the lights to music, which will be triggered on the hour and will, he notes, turn the facade into the projection screen of a giant color-organ, once again bringing modern technology to an old concept. K. B. / D. N.

Selected Bibliography:

Connor, Thomas. "Another Toronto firm wins prized U. S. commission—Did you hear an echo?" *Architectural Record* 188 (June 2000): 45.

Geary, Dawn. "Block Party." Color Kinetics project description, 2001.

Pattison, Kathy. "Digital Lighting Sets the Stage." *Lighting Design & Application* 31 (July 2001): 32–35.

Shulman, Ken. "The Color of Money." Metropolis Magazine. Online. Available: http: // www.metropolis-mag.com / html. 22 June 2001.

The Goodman Theatre website. Online. Available: http: // www.goodman-theatre.org / index.html. 8 December 2001.

mance space into one of the most animated structures in nighttime Chicago. The forty-by-one-hundred-foot facade is composed of ninety-six individual glass panels and crowned by an elevated, floodlit cornice. Shades behind the panels are each lit by two fixtures that use LED and digital technology for a number of special effects. The system can combine red, blue and green LEDs to produce up to 16.7 million colors as well as such effects as fades, washes, and variations in speed and intensity, all of which play continuously from sunset to sunrise. In addition, the glass

Goodman Theatre, night view, photographs, 2001

Sony Center · Berlin · 2001

Architect: **Helmut Jahn**

Location: **Potsdamer Platz**

Construction Date: **2000**

Installation Date: **2000. The building is currently illuminated.**

Installation type: **Continuous neon lights for peri-meter lighting of the glass-clad Potsdamer Platz Office Tower and adjacent facades. 24 1,200-watt spotlights, 24 1,800-watt 'washlights' with automatic color changers for the suspended roof structure.**

Lighting Designers: **Yann Kersalé and L'Observatoire International, New York**

One of the two key pieces of land emerging from Renzo Piano's masterplan at the heart of the Potsdamer Platz development in Berlin was the roughly triangular plot of 285,000 square feet for the Sony Corporation, designed by Helmut Jahn and containing office spaces, residential sections, an "urban entertainment center" with a cinema and museum complex, and a 43,056-square-foot atrium at its center. Not unlike a half opened umbrella, the transparent and translucent roof construction above this atrium became the focus of a lighting

While critics suggested that such an installation was "without any relevant history" (Meyer), the sequential changing of projected color for a calculated urban impact is a direct repetition of the most popular form of urban lighting in the United States in the 1920s and '30s.

The curvilinear form of the slender, twenty-eight-story office tower in the acute angle of the triangular site can be read as a late homage to Mies van der Rohe's famous 1921–22 designs for a skyscraper at Berlin's

Sony Center, night views, 2001

Selected Bibliography:

Meyer, Uli. "21 Sekunden Sonnenuntergang: Licht-installation am Sony Center, Berlin" *Bauwelt* 92, no. 10 (9 March 2001): 22–23.

Schulz, Bernhard. "Gläsernes Quartier: Sony Center am Potsdamer Platz in Berlin von Helmut Jahn" *Baumeister* 97, no. 4 (April 2000): 4.

Phillips, Duane. "Sony Center: Architecture for the Masses" *World Architecture* no. 84 (March 2000): 62–66.

concept by French light artist Yann Kersalé, one of the pioneers in the 1970s rebirth of this genre. The architecture surrounding the ten-story atrium became the backdrop for a theatrical projection of colored lights onto the folded glass fiber membranes above. In response to the famously gloomy fall and winter days in this northern European city, the installation begins with an "extension of daylight" at four o'clock in the winter and 6 o'clock in the summer: bright white light is projected against and then reflected from the artificial sky above the piazza. When dark-ness falls, a continuous sequence of twenty-one-second-long sunsets is played all evening with colors changing from cyan blue to magenta red. At midnight the projection changes into a continuous dark night blue, to be replaced by a bright white light in the early morning hours, until daylight sets in.

Friedrichstrasse, which was supposed to achieve a similar degree of immaterial trans-parency. The continuous neon lights along the upper edge of each floor of the office tower and adjacent buildings surrounding the atrium respond to the desire to conserve and enhance the building's form at night, when typically the scattered lights of individual offices would distract from the overall form. The solution found here by L'Observatoire International is a modern-day successor to Mies van der Rohe's and Richard Kelly's original perimeter lighting of the Seagram Building (pp. 188–190) in 1956, which was too costly to be continued beyond the energy crisis of 1973.   D.N.

Lighting Designers—Selected Biographies

Karen Bouchard, Dietrich Neumann

De Nyse W. Atwater
(c. 1895–1948)

An important innovator in the use of color, D.W. Atwater, an engineer at Westinghouse, designed the first full-scale colored floodlighting installation for an exposition at the Sesqui-Centennial in Philadelphia in 1926. He worked on large-scale installations from the early 1920s until his death, including street decorations for festivals in New York and Washington, D.C. and the Century of Progress Exposition in Chicago in 1933. Atwater was instrumental in promoting architectural flood-lighting as a tool of urban planning ("Skylines beyond the twilight zone").

Arthur Alanson Brainerd
(1891–1966)

An illuminating engineer at the Philadelphia Electric Company (PECO), A.A. Brainerd designed an early mobile color floodlighting installation for his company's Edison Building in 1928. A proponent of the promotional value of floodlighting, Brainerd also designed early schemes for the Lincoln-Liberty Life Insurance Building in Philadelphia and the Atlantic City Auditorium, as well as a luminous panel installation for one of PECO's district offices in 1935.

Howard Brandston
(b. 1935)

Beginning as a theatrical lighting designer, Howard Brandston soon turned to architectural illumination and went on to design more than 2,500 projects, among them the Petronas Towers in Malaysia (1996), the updated installation on the Niagara-Hudson Building in Syracuse (1999), and, perhaps his favorite commission, the newly restored Statue of Liberty in 1986. A tireless promoter of the lighting profession, Brandston is well known in his field not only as a designer, but also as a teacher, an author, and a designer of light sculptures.

Adolph F. Dickerson
(n.d.)

As Walter D'Arcy Ryan's assistant at General Electric, A.F. Dickerson was a key figure in the design and implementation of illumination schemes for a number of international expositions, including the Panama-Pacific of 1915, the Brazil Centennial of 1922, and the Century of Progress of 1933. After helping to bring floodlighting and the use of color to the forefront with Ryan, Dickerson went on to become the head lighting designer for San Francisco's Golden Gate Exposition of 1939.

Abe (Abraham H.) Feder
(1910–97)

Abe Feder began his career in the theater, working on more than 300 Broadway shows and being the first stage lighting designer to be credited in the playbill. In the 1940s, he branched out into the large-scale public spectacle of the urban night. As the first architectural lighting designer with an independent practice, Feder redefined the professional profile. Together with Richard Kelly and Douglas Leigh, he managed to reinvent architectural lighting for the new forms of modern architecture. Among his most important lighting commissions were the United Nations Headquarters (1949), the Philharmonic Hall at Lincoln Center and Rockefeller Center (1984), all in New York. In addition, he designed installations in such varied places as Montreal, Washington, D.C., and Jerusalem. When he died in 1997, the illuminations of Rockefeller Center and the Empire State Building were turned off for an hour in his honor.

Samuel Galloway Hibben
(1888–1972)

Director of Applied Lighting at Westinghouse, S.G. Hibben was a member of the lighting committee for both the 1939 and the 1964 New York World's Fairs. He also created the 1945 design for the Statue of Liberty's illumination and modernized the lighting of the Washington Monument. Hibben was known in his field for his lectures on lighting practices, which he delivered nationwide to audiences at all levels of expertise.

Motoko Ishii
(b. 1938)

One of the most honored of contemporary lighting designers, Motoko Ishii established her own firm in Tokyo in 1968. Since then, she has enjoyed a remarkably varied career, with designs ranging from city illumination plans and exposition lighting (beginning with Expo '70 in Osaka) to laser shows, architectural lighting, and even the illumination of a coral reef off the coast of Japan. The Illuminating Engineering Society of North America has honored her with over forty awards for such works as the NEC Supertower (1990), the Dae-Han Insurance Company Headquarters in Seoul (1986), and the Electric Power Pavilion at Expo '85 in Tsukuba. In 1994, she received her profession's highest honor, the Paul Waterbury Award of Distinction, for the Rainbow Bridge of Tokyo Bay.

Fernand Jacopozzi
(c. 1878–1932)

Italian lighting expert Fernand Jacopozzi became famous for his installations in Paris during the 1920s and '30s. Beginning with his transformation of the Eiffel Tower into a gigantic billboard for Citroën during the 1925 exposition, Jacopozzi went on to create floodlighting installations for the Place de la Concorde, the Arc de Triomphe, and the Cathedral of Notre-Dame, to name just a few. Working on camouflage architecture during World War I, Jacopozzi had a counterfeit Gare de l'Est built outside Paris, illuminated at night to deceive potential airborne attackers. He was working on plans to erect entire make-believe cities for the night, to save the real City of Light from attack, when the war ended.

Bassett Jones
(1877–1960)

An inventor, technological planner and consulting engineer, Bassett Jones was one of the founding members of the Society of Illuminating Engineering. He was also one of the first to address, in 1908, key questions of architectural lighting and to urge a collaboration between illuminating engineer and architect. Beginning in stage lighting, where he developed revolutionary new techniques, Jones later planned rather theatrical architectural illuminations for the Chicago Tribune Tower and the American Radiator Building. He was a consultant on illumination at the New York World's Fair of 1939. Here, Jones moved from the common use of floodlighting to a more sophisticated employment of fluorescent and diffuse lighting, helping to bring about a new phase in architectural illumination.

Richard Kelly
(1919–77)

Richard Kelly was one of the most influential lighting designers for mid-century modern architecture in the United States. Trained as both an engineer (at Columbia University) and an architect (Yale University), his lighting designs significantly shaped our understanding of buildings such as Louis Kahn's Yale Art Museum as well as his Kimbell Museum, Richard Neutra's Kaufman House, Philip Johnson's Glass House and Mies van der Rohe's Seagram Building. In Rio de Janeiro he designed the lighting for the Sugarloaf Mountain and Copa-cabana's waterfront. Instead of using floodlighting from vantage points outside the building, his lighting solutions usually were evolved from a deep understanding of the architectural structure. With his definition of different types of artificial light in architecture ('focal glow,' 'ambient luminescence' and 'sparkling brilliance') he helped to formulate an emerging language and theory of architectural lighting. Kelly received several awards from the lighting industry for his work and was honored posthumously with the Gold Medal of the Illuminating Engineering Society in 1979.

John Kennedy
(b. 1935)

John Kennedy belongs to the third generation of lighting engineers at General Electric's Nela Park research facility in Cleveland after men such as Alvin L. Powell and Matthew Luckiesh had first set the defining parameters for architectural lighting design. During his long career at General Electric, Kennedy taught industrial and outdoor lighting and was responsible for a large number of architectural lighting projects, among many others the lighting of Cleveland's Terminal Tower, the Golden Gate Bridge and the Boston Museum of Fine Arts. Kennedy continues to provide consulting for lighting designs with his own firm, KLS Inc.

Yann Kersalé
(b. 1955)

Perhaps the most prominent of today's lighting designers in France, Kersalé's work was crucial in the rediscovery of architectural illumination in the 1980s. Trained as an artist at the Ecole des Beaux Arts at Quimper, he has, since 1983, executed numerous temporary and permanent lighting installations around the world, from the lighting of the Eiffel Tower in 1983 to the Opera de la Bastille in 1989, the recent Sony Center in Berlin (2001) and parts of O'Hare Airport in Chicago. His rhythmic lighting concept for Jean Nouvel's renovation and extension of the Opera of Lyon, refers to one of his most impressive installations, the lighting of the Grand Palais in 1987, which used increasing and diminishing blue light to turn the building into the city's pulsating heart of glass.

Heinrich Kramer
(*b.* 1941)

Heinrich Kramer is one of the most prominent architectural lighting planners in Germany. In 1971, he received a Ph. D. from the University of Bochum and he has been teaching at the university of Aachen since 1989. He cofounded the firm Lichtdesign GmbH with H. T. von Malotki in 1980, and became its president in 1990. Kramer has designed the lighting concepts for a number of key buildings in central Europe, such as the Städtisches Museum in Mönchengladbach by Hans Hollein, the Institut du Monde Arabe in Paris by Jean Nouvel, the Commerzbank Skyscraper in Frankfurt by Norman Foster, and the German Historical Museum in Berlin by I. M. Pei. Kramer is a member of the Lichttechnische Gesellschaft Deutschlands as well as the Commission Internationale Eclairage and the European Lighting Designer Association.

Douglas Leigh
(1907–99)

Best remembered for his flamboyant and innovative animated billboard advertisements, including the famous smoke-ring-blowing Camel cigarette man, Douglas Leigh took up the profession of architectural lighting designer fairly late in life. Leigh's influence on the nighttime appearance of New York City is deeply felt to this day. The first person to light the Empire State Building in color (in 1976), Leigh also created schemes for the Citicorp, Helmsley and Crown Buildings, among others. In addition, he designed the lighting for the CenTrust Tower in Miami in 1987, the Nationsbank Tower in Baltimore in 1994 and lighting plans for entire cities, including Cincinnati in 1987 and Atlanta in 1996.

Matthew Luckiesh
(1883–1967)

Although Matthew Luckiesh designed few installations, he was a leading figure in the fledgling illuminating engineering profession of the early twentieth century. Director of Applied Science at General Electric (1920–49), Luckiesh conducted research into the nature of light in order to produce better illumination. His interest in the use of color led to his work on a color organ from 1921 onwards, and to GE's broad support for research into colored light projection and abstract art. Luckiesh was a prolific inventor and writer, introducing the science of lighting to the average person in layman's terms, while also influencing his fellow practitioners with more technical articles and books.

H. Herbert Magdsick
(1888–after 1953)

An employee of General Electric, H. H. Magdsick designed some of the first true floodlighting installations of architecture in the United States, including those of the Woolworth Building in 1915 and the Statue of Liberty in 1917. Magdsick was instrumental in promoting the new technology of gas-filled tungsten-filament incandescent lighting as a substitute for arc lamps in street lighting. He also believed that a partnership of lighting with the new architectural forms of the 1920s could be a means of transforming the appearance of American cities at night, a prophecy that would largely come true.

H. E. Mahan
(n. d.)

A member of General Electric's Illuminating Laboratory for forty-three years, H. E. Mahan worked on many lighting projects, including the Panama-Pacific Expo in 1915, the Century of Progress in 1933, and the Golden Gate in 1939. Mahan promoted the use of mobile color floodlighting in a number of articles that appeared in the electrical, architectural, and real estate journals of the time, helping to spread the idea beyond the world of illuminating engineering professionals.

Kaoru Mende
(*b.* 1950)

After receiving his degrees from Tokyo University in industrial and environmental design, Kaoru Mende founded his own lighting firm in 1990. He has worked with a number of Japanese architects, such as Toyo Ito, with whom he developed the lighting for the Tower of Winds in Yokohama in 1986 and the Mediatheque in Sendai, 2001, as well as Fumihiko Maki, Arata Isozaki and Tadao Ando (Chapel on the Water). He emphasizes a central concern for architecture in his work, as there are too "many examples of architecture wounded by careless lighting." Mende has received numerous awards from international lighting associations, among them an award of excellence from the International Association of Lighting Designers for Rafael Vinoly's "Tokyo International Forum" in 1997.

Anne Militello
(*b.* 1957)

As a successful theatrical lighting designer, Anne Militello won an Obie Award for Sustained Excellence of Lighting Design while still in her twenties. After working for Disney's Imagineering in the early '90s, she started her own firm, Vortex Lighting, in 1995. Branching out into the field of architectural lighting, she quickly won acclaim for her innovative designs. Militello was named Lighting Designer of the Year for 1999 by Lighting Dimensions International, and in 2001 she received the highest honor in architectural lighting, the Paul Waterbury Award of Distinction, for her design for the 42nd Street Studios in New York. Most recently, she has enjoyed success with a gallery exhibition of her lighting art, and she continues to produce works of illumination for architecture, concert tours and the theater.

John David Mooney
(n. d.)

After earning a degree in painting from the University of Illinois in 1965, John Mooney discovered light as one of his principal mediums in the mid-seventies.

Soon he was involved in large-scale lighting projects, such as Light Space 1977, the first public art project commissioned by the city of Chicago, which consisted of sixteen moving searchlights along Lake Michigan, and was reminiscent of some of the searchlight displays of the 1930s. A comparable but much larger display with a more complex score followed in 1990 to celebrate the opening of O'Hare's new American Airlines Terminal. Several of his most memorable pieces involved skyscrapers, such as the installation "Lightscape 89" that celebrated IBM's seventy-fifth birthday with the placing of light sources in more than 7,000 windows of Mies van der Rohe's IBM tower in Chicago, or a comparable color illumination of the windows of the Chicago Tribune for the building's seventy-fifth birthday in 1997.

Alfred Paulus
(n. d.)

An important designer of mobile color floodlighting installations, Alfred Paulus was a member of Westinghouse's commercial engineering department. In this position, he worked on the Atlantic City Auditorium in 1930, the relighting of the Statue of Liberty in 1931, and New York's Cities Service Building in 1932. In addition, Paulus helped to design the innovative color lighting effects used at the Philadelphia Sesqui-Centennial Expo of 1926 and Chicago's Century of Progress in 1933.

Alvin L. Powell
(1889–1940)

Director of the Edison Lighting Institute at General Electric, Alvin Powell supervised illumination designs throughout the United States. Similar to Matthew Luckiesh, Powell saw lighting design in a larger cultural context. He expected electricity's potential to unleash new artistic expressions as new and powerful as those of the Renaissance. He brought back many new lighting techniques from his travels to Europe and explored in detail the parallels between colored light and music, about which he published an illustrated brochure on behalf of General Electric in 1930. Powell's initiatives were of central importance to GE's unique attempts during the 1920s and '30s to move beyond the role of an energy provider towards that of a shaper of new artistic expressions.

Henry Rustin
(1865–1906)

Along with Luther Stieringer, Henry Rustin was responsible for the first great American exposition lighting schemes, including those of the Transmississippi of 1898 in Omaha and the 1901 Pan-American in Buffalo. Replacing powerful arc lamps with incandescent outline lighting, Rustin helped to create a new art form that thoroughly delighted turn-of-the-century fairgoers. In 1904, Rustin was solely responsible for the lighting of St. Louis' Louisiana Purchase Expo, where he experimented with changing colored lights and new ways of turning on the illumination at dusk. This was his last great work before his untimely death in 1906.

Walter D'Arcy Ryan
(1870–1934)

One of the great figures in the history of illumination, Walter D'Arcy Ryan was director of General Electric's laboratory in illuminating engineering, the first of its kind in the world. Moving beyond the contemporary practice of outline lighting, Ryan created memorable new designs employing first arc lamps and then incandescent floodlights. He was responsible for the first full exterior illumination of a skyscraper when he lit New York's Singer Tower in 1907, and in 1909 he orchestrated the Hudson-Fulton Celebration, creating a huge lighting display that utilized colored filters, steam engines, and a battery of moving searchlights known as the Scintillator. His triumph was undoubtedly the Panama-Pacific Expo of 1915, the first to be lit extensively by floodlights. Ryan went on to design the lighting for the 1922 Brazil Centennial Expo and 1933's Century of Progress International Exhibition in Chicago, all the while maintaining his reputation as the dean of American illuminating engineers.

Jonathan Speirs
(b. 1958)

Jonathan Speirs formed his own lighting firm, Jonathan Speirs & Associates, in Edinburgh in 1992. His longtime collaboration with Mark Major led to the founding in 1996 of a London studio called Speirs and Major, and the two offices are united under the larger entity known as The Lighting Architects Group. The firm's reputation as innovative designers quickly spread from Britain to Europe, the Mideast, and North America, and they have garnered numerous awards for such colorful and animated designs as the Burj al Arab in Dubai, the Manchester Tower of Time, and the Millennium Dome in London. Speirs was named International Architectural Lighting Designer of the Year by Lighting Dimensions in 1998.

Luther Stieringer
(c. 1845–1903)

Luther Stieringer, a protégé of Thomas Edison, was largely responsible for the development of architectural lighting as a new art form in the late nineteenth century. In charge of the illumination for the first exhibition in the United States to be lit entirely by electricity, the Southern Exposition of 1883 in Louisville, Stieringer went on to design the lighting for every major American exhibition up to the Pan-American of 1901. With Chicago's Columbian Expo of 1893, Stieringer moved beyond simple arc lighting to create a delicate scheme of incandescent outline that turned the fair's array of buildings into a fairyland at night and moved contemporaries to rhapsodize about the union of art and science. An innovator always looking for ways to improve his art, Stieringer continued to develop new ideas until his premature death in 1903.

Joachim Teichmüller
(1866–1938)

Teichmüller was one of the key figures in the debate about light and architecture in 1920s Germany. He had studied electrical engineering in Hanover, Berlin-Charlottenburg, and Darmstadt, and became a professor at Karlsruhe University in 1899. In 1919, he became the director of the university's Light Technology Research Institute. Besides numerous publications about electrical engineering, his (re-) introduction of the term *Lichtarchitektur* (Light Architecture) at the Gesolei Exhibition in Düsseldorf 1926 as well as his subsequent articles about the topic were an important contribution to the architectural debate. His institute in Karlsruhe was one of the prime experimental sites for the art of architectural lighting.

James Turrell
(b. 1943)

The American installation artist James Turrell has used artificial light in his work since the 1970s, and has in recent years worked on a number of architectural illumination projects. Besides the Verbundnetz AG in Leipzig, Turrell has worked on two skyscrapers for major German banks in Frankfurt and provided a new lighting design for the Pont du Gard near Nimes. Particularly impressive was Turrell's temporary installation at architect Peter Zumthor's Kunsthaus Bregenz.

Joseph Urban
(1872–1933)

Joseph Urban's career illustrates best the numerous crossovers among the disciplines connected with architectural illumination. Born and trained in Vienna, Urban came to the U.S. in 1912 as art director for the Boston Opera. He worked as an illustrator, set designer for the theater and the movies, as architectural designer, and he also played an important role in the history of architectural illumination. His early stage designs in Vienna were influenced by the revolutionary work of Gordon Craig and Alphonse Appia, replacing conventional sets with colored lights. His compelling film sets led to the first architectural commissions, which would later include the Ziegfeld Theatre (1927–29), the Hearst International Magazine Building (1929) and the New School for Social Research (1930). Architectural lighting played an important role in these designs, as well as in other unexecuted projects, such as the Max Reinhardt Theatre of 1929, which included European-style luminous bands in its facade. Shortly before his death he crowned his career with the elaborate color and light design for the Chicago World's Fair of 1933.

Historical Glossary

Karen Bouchard

Ampere

The basic unit of electric current in the International System of measurement. The term was coined in 1881 and named after the French physicist André Marie Ampère (1775–1836), who devised Ampère's law on the magnetic force between two electrical currents.

Arc lamp

The first practical commercial electric light source. Light is produced by briefly bringing together two pieces of carbon (conductors) that are connected to an electrical supply. The usually rod-shaped conductors are then pulled apart, and a spark reaches across the open space, forming an arc, while the tips of the carbon rods are heated to a white-hot intensity. Later developments added flame-producing salts to the carbon, allowing the arc itself to give off light and producing an even more brilliant illumination. The lamp was first developed by Sir Humphrey Davy in 1807 but became practical as a lighting source only around 1878, with improvements in the electric generator. At this time, Paul Jablochkoff developed an arc lamp that was used for streetlights in Paris and was exhibited at the Exposition Universelle of 1878. Jablochkoff "candles" were soon in use in other major cities, including London. At 500-candlepower intensity and up (incandescent lamps would soon be available with intensities as low as 1 candlepower), the arc lamp was too bright for domestic use and was restricted to large interiors such as factories and stores, as well as to exterior lighting. The lamp's brilliant light allowed expositions to stay open after dark, and exhibitors quickly took advantage of this development. Every major exhibition of the late nineteenth century was illuminated at least in part by arc lamps, but by 1904, the promoters of the Louisiana Purchase Exposition in St. Louis were already boasting that they had employed no "old-fashioned" arc lights in the main exhibition area of their fair. Arc lights were also used as searchlights, one of the few areas of lighting where they are still employed today. Although the term is usually reserved for carbon arc lamps, it is sometimes used to describe discharge lamps in general. In the meantime a late successor to the arc lamp has appeared in the form of the "short arc lamp." A mercury or xenon discharge lamp produces a high-power discharge between electrodes that are placed less than a centimeter apart. It produces a very intense light that is utilized in searchlights and movie projectors, among other applications. Short arc mercury lamps were used for the revolving beacon that was installed on the Empire State Building in 1956.

Candela (Candlepower)

International standard unit of luminous intensity. Adopted in 1979. A lamp's candlepower is measured in candelas. Candlepower used to be determined by the light from a spermaceti candle of a specific weight and rate of burning and is today measured by a certain frequency of a light source.

Cathode

In discharge lamps, the electrode that emits electrons and causes the gas contained within the tube to glow. Two types are in use: cold cathode and hot cathode.

Cold cathode tube

A type of discharge lamp in which the current flows without producing heat. Lamps of this type can be bent into special shapes and are often used in signs. Includes most neon lamps and some fluorescent lamps.

See also: Hot cathode tube.

Dichroic filter and reflector

A type of glass filter coated with thin layers of metallic or other interference film. The layers allow only one part of the spectrum, one color from a beam of light, to pass through. The remaining colors are reflected back into the fixture, which results in a deep, saturated color. Developed in the years following World War II, their fragility and high cost meant that they did not come into general use until the 1980s, when they were used in automated fixtures. However, they had been employed for the very first time in the roof of the General Electric Building at the 1964 World's Fair and included in an installation on the Indianapolis Power & Light Co. Building as early as 1968. Currently, they are in use on the Forty-second Street Studios in New York and the LAX Theme Building in Los Angeles. The same principle also allows cold light reflection, when a glass reflector is coated with a dichroic film allowing the heat to escape sideways, whereas the light is reflected towards the main direction of the projector.

Dimmer

A device used to control the intensity of light, producing differences not only in brightness but also in color. In the late nineteenth century, the rheostat was developed, a resistance dimmer connected in series with incandescent lamps. By dividing the incoming voltage between the lamps and the resistance, the rheostat produced a dimming effect (installed, for instance, in the Savoy Theatre in London in 1881). The Festival Hall at the Louisiana Purchase Exposition in St. Louis was lit in three different colors that were each brought up in turn with the use of a rheostat. Rheostats have been used as late as the 1968 installation on the Indianapolis Power & Light Co. Building. However, as lighting grew more complicated, the reactance dimmer became the standard. First patented by Westinghouse in 1887, this type of dimmer was common by the 1920s. A popular reactance dimmer of the 1930s was the thyratron tube dimmer, produced exclusively by GE. This dimmer employed thyratron (hot cathode) tubes as a means of control and was the first remote control, preset system, allowing dimming effects to be set ahead of time. Thyratron dimmers were used for the first time to produce mobile color effects on Decatur's Staley Building in 1930, Los Angeles' Southern California Edison Building and the Kansas City Power & Light Co. Building, both in 1931. It is much more complicated to dim fluorescent tubes than incandescent lamps. One of the reasons for the fact that mobile color illumination was discontinued after the 1920s and 1930s was the fact that incandescent lamps were widely replaced with the more efficient discharge lamps. Resistance and reactance dimmers are now obsolete and most dimming effects are computerized.

Discharge Lamp

After the arc lamp and incandescent lamp, the discharge lamp is the third major type of device for electric illumination. Light is produced by passing electricity between two electrodes in a gas-filled tube, thereby causing the gas to glow. Different colors are obtained by varying the type of gas in the tube. There are high- and low-pressure discharge lamps.

After Humphrey Davey had made some experiments early in the nineteenth century and J. Heinrich Geissler developed a working model, the Geissler tube, in 1855, the first commercial display was at the Diamond Jubilee of Queen Victoria in 1897. In 1898, D. McFarland Moore, an assistant to Thomas Edison, developed a lamp that contained nitrogen, air, or carbon dioxide, the latter giving off a strong white light. Although much more energy-efficient than the incandescent bulb, Moore lamps were cumbersome to install and quickly disappeared after an improved tungsten filament lamp was devised. A few were used for architectural outline lighting, and Moore installed one of his lamps in the foyer of Madison Square Garden in 1899. The next important development was the low-pressure mercury vapor lamp, invented by Peter Cooper Hewitt in 1901 with a research stipend from George Westinghouse. The lamp produced a blue-green color, demonstrating a common disadvantage of early discharge lamps: their limited ability to render accurate color. In about 1910, Georges Claude publicized his neon lamp, which was very quickly adopted for use in electric signs. Later developments included the high-pressure mercury and low-pressure sodium lamps (both in 1932), the fluorescent lamp in 1938, the metal halide lamp in 1960, and the high-pressure sodium lamp in 1962.

DMX control system

DMX (Digital Multiplex) is the standard interface between control systems and dimmers, color scrollers, projectors, strobes, and other lighting equipment. The DMX standard was developed in 1986 by the U.S. Institute for Theatre Technology. Allows up to 512 pieces of lighting equipment to be controlled by one system, using a single cable. Used in conjunction with automated luminaires, it allows for the most sophisticated color changing abilities yet available. DMX systems are used on the Burj al Arab in Dubai, among many other installations.

EPOK

Animation screen consisting of electric bulbs connected to a grid of photoelectric cells. Cartoons and text are projected onto the cells and then transmitted as flashing lights. Invented in Germany, the device was adopted by Douglas Leigh in the 1930s and used to create many memorable, animated advertising signs.

Filter

A device placed in front of a lamp to modify the light beam. Neutral filters are used to reduce the intensity of light without changing the color. Color filters allow selective colors to pass through while absorbing or reflecting others. Color filters have been in use since the beginnings of projected light. Glass was the first material employed. Arc lamp searchlights were covered with glass filters to produce multi-colored beams at international expositions during the nineteenth century. Sheets of colored glass strung on wires were used to produce changing color effects in a fountain at the 1889 Exposition Universelle in Paris. Later filters were made of gelatin or of plastic. Color floodlighting was accomplished as early as 1908 on the Singer Building in New York but came into its own during the late 1920s.

See also: Dichroic filter; Mobile color floodlighting.

Floodlight

While searchlights had been used to occasionally flood buildings with arc or incandescent light (New York's Singer Tower was illuminated in this manner in 1908 and several other New York City buildings during the Hudson Fulton Celebration in 1909), the term "floodlight" appears in lighting journals only after GE's development of an improved incandescent bulb in 1913, which initiated an important rethinking of architectural lighting. Walter D'Arcy Ryan, the chief illuminating engineer at General Electric, probably invented the term, when he, in 1912, suggested replacing the common outline lighting, which he felt was detrimental to the appearance of the architecture, at the 1915 Panama-Pacific Exposition with a system of hidden light sources whose powerful illumination would be cast under a wide angle close to the building's walls. Also in 1915, New York's Woolworth Building was illuminated solely by floodlights. In the following years the term became so successful that it quickly lost its specificity and was indiscriminately used for all forms of external light projection. Initially incandescent, and occasional gas lamps were used, later the mercury vapor lamps as well as high-pressure sodium and metal halide lamps.

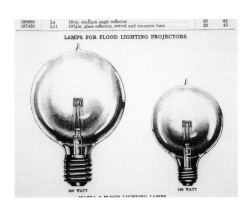

LAMPS FOR FLOOD LIGHTING PROJECTORS

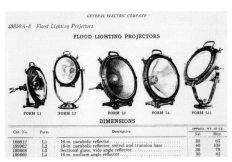

GENERAL ELECTRIC COMPANY

48850A-8 Flood Lighting Projectors

FLOOD LIGHTING PROJECTORS

Fluorescent lamp

A type of discharge lamp consisting of a glass tube filled with mercury and a rare gas, usually argon but sometimes krypton. Electrons flow between the electrodes, or cathodes, located at either end of the tube and ionize the gas, producing ultra-violet radiation. The interior of the tube is coated with powdered phosphors, substances that absorb the radiation and fluoresce, i.e., transform it into visible light. By varying the type and number of phosphors, many different colors can be produced. The first fluorescent tubes, using neon and other rare gases in combination with phosphors, were introduced by Georges Claude's company in 1933, although experimental lamps were produced as early as 1926. The first large-scale exterior installation was at the International Exposition of 1937 in Paris, where colored fluorescent tubes decorated the Eiffel Tower. The lamp as it is known today became commercially available in 1938 and was displayed to the American public at the 1939 World's Fairs in New York and San Francisco. Installations on Seattle's Mutual Life Building in 1939 and New York's GE Building in 1940 followed. Since then, fluorescent tubes have revolutionized mostly interior illumination.

Footcandle

Unit of luminous intensity equal to one lumen per square foot. Equivalent to the illumination produced by one candle at a distance of one foot. Coined *c.* 1905–10.

Gaslight

Light produced by a gas flame, usually from coal gas (a byproduct of coke production). Developed in England in the 1790s and demonstrated publicly in London in 1807. The light produced was much brighter and cleaner than that of oil lamps or candles, and its use quickly spread throughout the western world. Until the invention of the gas mantle in the late 1880s (a hood made of oxides was placed around the flame, improving the access to oxygen and glowing when heated), gaslights were simply open flames. Progress in gas lighting depended on central gas production. In the second half of the nineteenth century, gas flames began to be used for architectural illumination and advertising. The 1889 Exposition in Paris, the first world exposition to use electric lights as architectural illuminants, was also partially lit by gas, with small globes lining the various tiers of the Eiffel Tower, mixed with incandescent bulbs and arc searchlights. Although gaslight was gradually replaced with the advent of improved electrical lamps, it was still being used to illuminate exposition grounds as late as the Panama-Pacific in 1915 and continued in general use into the 1930 and '40s.

High-intensity discharge lamp

Subset of discharge lamps in which the gas-containing tube is pressurized slightly above atmospheric pressure. There are three types: high-pressure mercury vapor, developed in 1932, metal halide, patented in 1960, and high-pressure sodium, announced to the public in 1962 but not released for sale until 1965.

See also: Discharge lamp, high-pressure sodium, metal halide lamp, high-pressure sodium lamp

High-pressure sodium lamp

A type of high-intensity discharge lamp using sodium as its gas medium, with a small amount of mercury and either argon or xenon. A wide-spectrum light source that allows most colors to be seen, although an orange tint is discernible. First practically available in 1965, after ten years of development, the lamp is often used in street lighting. Employed in architectural illumination when a warm, golden tone is desired. Current installations include Chicago's Merchandise Mart and Cleveland's Terminal Tower.

See also: Low-pressure sodium lamp.

Hot cathode tube

A type of discharge lamp in which the cathode, or electrode, must be heated in order to emit electrons. Used with high-pressure lamps. Includes sodium, metal halide, and most fluorescent lamps.

See also: Cold cathode tube.

Illuminating Engineering Society

Founded in 1906, the Illuminating Engineering Society of North America (IES) is the lighting industry's foremost professional organization. Among its founding members was Walter D'Arcy Ryan, possibly the first person to call himself an illuminating engineer. The organization's membership includes lighting designers, engineers, architects and others. IES was instrumental in gaining recognition for illuminating engineering as a distinct profession. Through its sponsorship of scientific research, the IES has become the recognized authority in North America for illumination practices in all areas of lighting. The IES has produced a scholarly professional journal since its inception and is still a vital force in the field of illuminating engineering with 10,000 members around the world. Soon after its foundation, similar societies were established in many countries, such as the Deutsche Beleuchtungstechnische Gesellschaft in 1912 (later called Deutsche Lichttechnische Gesellschaft). Since the early 1980s, the American Lighting Designers have had their own professional organization, the Association of Lighting Designers (IALD), with many international affiliations.

Incandescent lamp

A lamp containing a filament that gives off light when heated to incandescence by an electrical current. The incandescent lamp was not the first electric light. Arc lamps had come into general use in the 1870s but were too bright and inconvenient for domestic use. A number of inventors at the time were working on a lamp that would "sub-divide the light," producing a small amount that would be useful indoors. Sir Joseph Swan, Heinrich Goebel and Thomas Edison developed lamps that consisted of a carbon filament inside a glass bulb from which the air had been removed. Edison, however, is given credit for the first practical incandescent lamp, which was successfully demonstrated in

October of 1879. The incandescent lamp was first displayed on a large scale at the International Electrical Exhibition, held in Paris in 1881. The first electric sign (spelling Edison's name) was displayed at the London Electrical Exhibition in 1882. The decorative possibilities of incandescent lighting were quickly developed. Outline lighting, in which strings of exposed bulbs, sometimes tinted different colors, were used to delineate building features, became the most popular means of architectural illumination. In the early years of the twentieth century, experiments were made with metallic filaments, with tungsten eventually becoming the standard. With the development of the gas-filled tungsten filament lamp of 1913, incandescent floodlights became a practical reality. William Coolidge had developed a bendable tungsten wire for lamps in 1909, and Irving Langmuir soon afterward coiled the wire and added gas to the bulb (instead of the vacuum previously employed), producing a lamp that would last much longer and would be more energy-efficient. This is basically the same lamp in use today. These new bulbs were marketed as Mazda lamps, named after the Persian God of Light and Wisdom, Ahura Mazda. Although many of its exterior lighting duties have since been taken over by discharge lamps, the incandescent lamp remains the most popular type of light for domestic use today.

See also: Tungsten halogen lamp; Floodlight; Outline lighting.

Jablochkoff candle

See: Arc lamp.

Light-emitting diode (LED)

A semiconductor device that emits light when an electrical current is passed through it. The first practical LED device was produced in 1962 and used for indicator lights and flat-panel computer displays. Originally available only in red, followed by amber and green. Available in blue and white since the mid-1990s. In 1996, George Mueller and Ihor Lys combined LEDs by computer to create more than 16 million hues that can be changed inch by inch for mobile color effects, as seen, for example, at the Goodman Theatre in Chicago or the advertising screens in Times Square.

Low-pressure sodium lamp

Type of discharge lamp using sodium vapor as its gas medium. Introduced commercially by Philips Lighting Corporation in 1932. The most efficient of all lamps, but produces a strong yellow light that reduces colors to shades of gray. Popular in Europe for street lighting but largely replaced by the 1950s in the U.S. with high-pressure mercury lamps. Used to produce a golden effect on the Palais de Chaillot at the Paris Exposition of 1937.

See also: High-pressure sodium lamp.

Lumen

Unit of luminous flux (the time rate of light flow) equal to that emitted by a source of one candle intensity.

Lux

International System unit of illumination. Equal to the amount of illumination resulting when one lumen is evenly distributed over one square meter.

Mazda lamp

See: Incandescent lamp.

Mercury capillary lamp

Compact mercury discharge lamp whose arc is enclosed in a narrow tube (i.e. capillary). Because of the high wattage contained in a small volume, the tube must be cooled with water to prevent steam from forming. Developed for use in searchlights. First used extensively for building illumination at the 1939 World's Fair in New York.

Mercury vapor lamp

One of the first practical discharge lamps. The low-pressure mercury vapor lamp was invented by Peter Cooper Hewitt in 1901. The blue-green color of the gas limited its usefulness for general lighting. In 1932, GE introduce the high-pressure mercury vapor lamp. Highly efficient, the first such lamp available was a 400-watt model that produced as much light as a 1000-watt incandescent bulb. This new lamp contained argon as well as mercury and was soon popular for street lighting. A phosphor coating is now often added to the inside of the tube to reduce the bluish tone of the gas. After the 1930s, mercury vapor lamps began to be used as floodlights with such installation as the Tishman Building in New York (1958) and the Calgary (Alberta) Power Building in 1969.

Metal halide lamp

A high-intensity discharge lamp similar in construction to the high-pressure mercury lamp but also containing metal halides (compounds of a metal and a halogen). The added halides produce a whiter light that makes these lamps useful when color rendering is important. The process was first patented by Charles Steinmetz at GE in 1912, but a practical lamp was not available until the 1950s. Gilbert Reiling at GE developed the modern metal halide lamp, which GE publicly announced in 1962. One of the earliest public installations was at the 1964 World's Fair in New York. The lamp's small size contributed to the development of automated luminaires in the early 1980s. Now very common in floodlighting applications, as its white light shows the true color of building materials at night. Early installations included the Exchange National Bank in Tampa and the Calgary Power Building, both in 1969.

Mobile color floodlighting

The term used to describe animated colored floodlighting effects in the late 1920s and 1930s. Lamps with colored filters were connected to one or more dimmers, which continually changed the intensity of the light. Two systems were employed. In the wash system, only white lights were connected to the dimmer, while the colored lights remained stable. The color would gradually be faded out as the white lights were brought up to full intensity. In the cycle system, both the white and colored lights were dimmed for preset time periods. The process quickly became very popular in the U.S. and installations were found on the Philadelphia Electric Company's Edison Building (1927), the Staley Building in Decatur, IL (1930), and the Kansas City Power & Light Co. Building (1931), among many others. Although the term was not generally used after the 1930s, mobile color installations enjoyed a short-lived revival in the 1960s, as seen, for instance, in the Indianapolis Power & Light Co. Building scheme of 1968. They currently are enjoying renewed popularity, largely due to the advent of automated luminaires, with such installations as the Burj al Arab in Dubai, the LAX Theme Building in Los Angeles, and the Entel Tower in Santiago, Chile.

See also: Dimmer.

Neon lamp

One of the earliest discharge lamps. In 1907, Georges Claude continued the experiments of McFarland Moore, and discovered that noble gases such as argon, or the recently discovered neon, would radiate colored light when they were exposed to electricity. While argon shone in blue-gray, the neon light's bright red color made it impractical for general illumination, but ideal for advertising signs. Neon tubes could be bent into shapes and used to spell out words or create decorative designs. Among the first installations were those on the Grand Palais in Paris and the Church of St. Ouen in Rouen, both in 1910. America's first Neon sign was the name "Packard" at a Los Angeles Car Dealership in 1923. The term "neon lamp" eventually became the generic name for the entire genre of colored tubing used for signs and decoration, even though other gases were used. Claude soon realized that a combination of mercury and argon could be used to produce a blue tube. Enclosing the blue tube in an outer layer of yellow glass produced a green lamp. The effect of a white light could be obtained by using two lamps in concert: one of neon and another of mercury. In 1933, phosphors were added, producing fluorescent tubes that made many more colors available. Neon signs quickly changed the look of cities worldwide. Among the many important architectural applications were the blue lines on the facade of Erich Mendelsohn's Herpich Store in Berlin, 1930 and Simpson's Department Store in London in 1936.

Novagems

Glass "jewels" made to resemble diamonds, rubies, sapphires, and emeralds and cut so as to refract light. Made by craftsmen in Austria. Used by Walter D'Arcy Ryan in 1915 at the Panama-Pacific Exposition in San Francisco. Ryan gave the jewels the name "Novagem." When installed on the Tower of Jewels at the fair, the gems refracted sunlight during the day and the beams from floodlighting projectors at night. Hung from wires, they moved easily with the slightest breeze, creating a scintillating effect. Ryan used the gems in many later installations, including at the Brazilian Centennial Exhibition in Rio de Janeiro 1922 or San Francisco's seventy-fifth anniversary in

1925, when he installed them on an arch outside City Hall.

Opal glass

A type of glass used for architectural installations, in which small particles (such as fluorines) are imbedded in the clear glass, giving it a translucent or opaque, milky white appearance. Comes in two varieties: flashed opal, in which a thin opaque layer is carried over a clear glass layer, and Pot opal, in which the particles are scattered throughout the glass. Opal glass is a very efficient light diffuser and became popular in the 1920s in Europe and soon after in the U.S. for luminous panels in advertising and architectural applications.

Outline lighting

A frequent motif in architectural illumination already before the advent of electricity (achieved with oil lamps or gas flames rendering the main lines of a building visible at night), it was easily adapted to incandescent bulbs in the late nineteenth century. Bulbs could be directly attached to the building or hung like festoons on strings or wires. Both clear and colored bulbs were used. Outline lighting was used for every international exposition beginning with the Southern Exposition in Louisville, Kentucky, in 1883, and continuing until the advent of floodlighting at the 1915 Panama-Pacific. By the time of the Pan-American Exposition in Buffalo in 1901, the practice had become an art form that went far beyond mere outlining. Decorative designs and patterns were used to create a nighttime architecture that was very different from the one seen by day. Outline lighting continues to be seen at festivals and in amusement parks worldwide.

Quartz lamp

A mercury vapor lamp made of quartz instead of glass. As quartz resists heat better than glass, higher currents can be used. It also allows the passage of ultra-violet rays that would be absorbed by glass. First developed in the 1920s. The term is also sometimes used for tungsten halogen lamps.

Reflector

A concave metal or glass surface located behind the lamp in a light fixture and used to redirect light beams, improving the lamp's efficiency. Older floodlights usually employed silvered glass, chromium plate or polished aluminum and were often painted white. A dull metal surface was preferred in order to produce a diffuse light. Parabolic reflectors (PAR fixtures) reflect light in parallel rays, which is useful for search and floodlights.

Strobe light

Short for stroboscopic light. A type of discharge lamp that employs high voltage to send regular, short but intense pulses of electric current through either xenon or krypton gas. Produces a very strong white light, but each pulse lasts for less than a second. In architectural illumination, used for special, pulsating effects, as on the Victorian Arts Centre spire in Melbourne or the Burj al Arab in Dubai. Developed in the mid-twentieth century.

Thyratron tube dimmer

See: Dimmer

Tungsten halogen lamp

A type of tungsten filament incandescent lamp filled with a halogen vapor (iodine, chlorine, bromine or fluorine). The halogen combines with the tungsten particles that evaporate while the lamp is running, and re-deposits them on the filament, thereby keeping the lamp from blackening and giving it a much longer life span. Developed during the 1950s, the first lamp was put into production by GE in 1962. They were subsequently used on the Unisphere at the 1964 World's Fair in New York. Because a high temperature must be maintained in the bulb, quartz was generally used in place of glass. Iodine was the original halogen used, so the first of these bulbs were known as quartz-iodine lamps. Later, other halogens were utilized, as well as a harder glass, and the name tungsten halogen was adopted. Early installations of the lamp include New York's GE Building in 1965, the Empire State Building in 1964, and the Indianapolis Power & Light Co. Building in 1968.

Watt

The standard unit of electrical power, measuring the rate of energy consumption by an electrical device. Equal to 1/746 horsepower. Coined in 1882, after James Watt, the Scottish inventor.

Selected Bibliography

"Architecture of the Night." General Electric Company, *Bulletin* GED-375 (February 1930).

"Lighting is Architecture." *Progressive Architecture* (September 1958): 139–145.

Atwater, D.W. "Skylines beyond the Twilight Zone: A discussion of modern principles and practice in floodlighting" (published by the Westinghouse Lamp Company, ca. 1935)

Auer, Gerhard. "The Aesthetics of the Caleidoscope. Artificial Light in Japanese Cities." *Daidalos*, no. 27 (15 March 1988): 42–47.

Baatz, Wilfried (ed.) *Gestaltung mit Licht*. Ravensburg: Otto Maier, 1994.

Bartetzko, Dieter. *Illusionen in Stein. Stimmungsarchitektur im deutschen Faschismus*. Reinbek: Rowohlt, 1985.

Blühm, Andreas and Louise Lippincott. *Light! The Industrial Age 1750–1900. Art & Science, Technology & Society*. London: Thames & Hudson, 2000.

Canesi, Giovanni and Antonio Cassi Ramelli. *Architetture Luminose e Apparecchi per Illuminazione*. Milan: Ulrico Hoepli, 1934.

Castiglione, Piero, Chiara Baldacci and Giuseppe Biondo. *Lux: Italia 1930–1990*. Milan: Berenice, 1991.

Cox, James A. *A Century of Light*. New York: Benjamin/Rutledge, 1978.

Eskilson, Stephen. "America the Spectacle: Discourses of Color and Light 1914–1934" (Ph.D. diss., Brown University, 1995).

Feder, Abe. "Light as an Architectural Material." *Progressive Architecture* (September 1958): 124–131.

Fillaud, Bertrand, *Les Magiciens de la Nuit*. Antony: Sides, 1993.

Fisher, Thomas. "Night Lights." *Progressive Architecture* 68 (September 1987): 150–155.

Flagge, Ingeborg (ed.) *Architektur – Licht – Architektur*. Stuttgart: Krämer, 1991.

Flagge, Ingeborg (ed.) *Jahrbuch für Licht und Architektur/Annual for Light and Architecture*. London: John Wiley & Son, 1993–1998, 2000, 2001/02

Frank, Michael. "City lights." *Metropolis* (April 1993): vol. 12, no. 8: 23–27.

Gardner, Carl and Raphael Molony. *Transformations: Light*. Crans-Près-Céligny: RotoVision SA, 2001.

Granet, André. *Décors Ephemères: Les Expositions Jeux d'Eau et de Lumière*. Paris: Desfossés, 1948.

Haas, O.F. and K.M. Reid. "Floodlighting." General Electric Company, *Bulletin* LD-16 (June 1931).

Hashizume, Shinya. "Exposition and illumination: Electrifying the city life in modern Japan." *Jimbun kenkyu* (Studies in the humanities), Bulletin of the Faculty of Literature and Human Sciences (Osaka City University, 2000): 53, no. 8: 47–60.

Horváth, József. *The Floodlighting of Budapest*. Budapest: Hungexpo, 1989.

Ishii, Motoko. *My World of Lights*. Tokyo: Libro Port, 1985.

Jakle, John A. *City Lights. Illuminating the American Night*. Baltimore: Johns Hopkins University Press, 2001.

Kalff, L.C. *Kunstlicht und Architektur*. Eindhoven: N.V. Philips' Gloeilampenfabrieken, 1943.

Keller, Max. *Light Phantastic. The Art and Design of Stage Lighting*. Munich: Prestel 1999.

Kelly, Richard. "Lighting as an Integral Part of Architecture." *College Art Journal* 12 (Fall 1952): 24–30.

Kersalé, Yann. *Lumière Matière*. Tokyo: Toto Shuppan, 1998.

Köhler, Walter and Wassili Luckhardt. *Lighting in Architecture: Light and Color as Stereoplastic Elements*. New York: Reinhold, 1959.

Kramer, Heinrich and Walter von Lom. *Licht: Bauen mit Licht*. Cologne: Rudolf Müller Verlag, 2002.

Leach, William. *Land of Desire: Merchants, Power, and the Rise of a New American Culture*. New York: Pantheon, 1993.

Lotz, Wilhelm. *Licht und Beleuchtung*. Berlin: H. Reckendof, 1928.

Lozano-Hemmer, Rafael. *Alzado Vectorial, Vectorial Elevation*. Mexico City: Publications Department, National Council for Culture and the Arts and Impresiones y Editiones San Jorge, 2000.

Luckiesh, Matthew. *Artificial Light: Its Influence upon Civilization*. New York: Century Co., 1920.

McKinley, Robert W. (ed.) *I.E.S. Lighting Handbook*, 1st ed. New York: Illuminating Engineering Society, 1947.

Millet, Marietta S. *Light Revealing Architecture*. New York: Van Nostrand Reinhold, 1996.

Nye, David E. *American Technological Sublime*. Cambridge: MIT Press, 1996.

Nye, David E. *Electrifying America. Social Meanings of a New Technology, 1880–1940*. Cambridge, Mass.: MIT Press, 1990.

Philips, Derek. *Lighting in Architectural Design*. New York: McGraw-Hill, 1964.

Phillips, Derek. "The Second Aspect: Buildings after Dark." *Light and Lighting* 61 (May 1968): 130–134.

Potter, Wentworth M., and Phelps Meaker. "Luminous Architectural Elements." GE Company (December 1931): 5–49.

Powell, A.L., *The Coordination of Light and Music, General Electric, Edison Lamp Works* (LP 101): August 1930.

Ranaulo, Gianni. *Light Architecture. New Edge City*. Basel: Birkhäuser 2001

Rub, Timothy. "Lighting up the Town: Architectural Illumination in the Jazz Age." *Architectural Record* 174, no. 9 (1986): 73, 75, 77.

Schivelbusch, Wolfgang. *Disenchanted Night. The Industrialization of Light in the Nineteenth Century*. Berkeley: University of California Press, 1988.

Schlör, Joachim. *Nights in the Big City*. London: Reaction Books, 1991.

Schwarz, Michael (ed.) *Licht und Raum*. Cologne: Wienand, 1998.

Ward, Janet. *Weimar Surfaces. Urban Visual Culture in 1920s Germany*. Berkeley: University of California Press, 2001.

Wright, Henry. "Lighting is Architecture." *Progressive Architecture* (September 1958): 115–123.

Zapatka, Christian. "The Edison Effect: The History of Lighting in the American City." *Lotus International* 75 (1993): 60–77.

Acknowledgements

Since research for this book began, at first tentatively, in 1989, I have had the great fortune to work with a number of people who share my enthusiasm and their ideas, information and time. The field of discovery turned out to be much richer, more complex and fascinating than I had originally expected and laying the groundwork by assembling the countless articles in (often hard to find) journals, magazines and daily papers would have been impossible without plenty of help from others.

I have always been grateful for the superb working conditions at Brown University, and its grants have both provided me with free time during the final phase of the project and supported a number of research assistants, Andrea Diaz, Adelaide Egan, Douglas Klahr, Jonathan Mekinda, Peter Niles, Kaveri Singh and Edward Orloff whose work laid the foundation for this project. I would like to thank in particular the staff at Brown's Slide Library, Assistant Curator Karen Bouchard for her immense work on the project (see below), Curator Norine Duncan, for her patience and encouragement, Erica Boyd for her technical expertise, and Terry Abbott for assistance with the production of images. Stephen L. Thompson, Bill Wood and Mark Shelton provided expert reference advice.

Assembling the rather diverse visual material was only possible because many individuals went out of their way to provide us with images, information, last-minute copyright clearances and the like, and we gratefully acknowledge their help: Jerry Aloi, Robert F. Dischner & Al Wager of Niagara Mohawk Company, Rex. M. Ball and David Halpern, William C. Barrow of the Cleveland State University Library, Kim Batchelor-Davis of the Detroit Regional Chamber, Christine Boldizsar of Unigard Insurance, Patricia Bornhofen at Electronic Theatre Controls, Christian Braig of the PECO Library, Howard Brandston, Ivan K. Charley of Ipalco, Larry Cohn of the Lurie Company, Chicago, Georgia Colao, Roger Dudley and Ed R. Legge of Xcel Energy, Barbara Dey of the Colorado Historical Society, Tom DiFilippo of the Delaware County Historical Society, W. A. Di Giacomo Associates, Melissa Dollman of Horton Lees Brogden, Lighting Design, Jane Ehrenhart of the Illinois State Historical Library, Herr Fischer at Thyssen in Düsseldorf, Seymour Fortin, owner of the Denver Gas & Electric Building, Leigh A. Gavin of the Chicago Historical Society, Dawn Geary of Color Kinetics Inc., Angela Giral of the Avery Library, Yvonne Goulbier and Thomas N. Smith, Ed Gorczyk of Michigan Consolidated Gas Company, Laurie Jane Greene of Martin Professional, Paul Gregory of Focus Lighting Inc., Deborah Gust at the Lake County Museum, Carol M. Herrity of the Lehigh County Historical Society, Allentown, PA., Louis A. Hieb of the University of Washington, Special Collections Library, Rose Mary Hoge of the Cleveland Public Library, Kathleen James-Chakraborty at UC Berkeley, John Johnston of Sussman Prejza, Barbara Jones at the John David Mooney Foundation, Yoko Kanii of

Motoko Ishii Lighting Design, Bob Keller of Forest City Enterprises, John Kennedy , Janet Lill, Beth Wassarman and Meg Guroff, Rich Locklin at Lightswitch, Laura Lee Linder, Helen Welting and and John Anderson at the GE Hall of Fame in Schenectady, Garry Lowe of Barry Webb & Associates, Rafael Lozano-Hemmer, Mary E. Matiya of Tate & Lyle North America, David McBrayer of the Kansas City Power & Light Company, Ed McDowall of AmerenCIPS, Terry McGowan, Mrs. LaVerne Roston, of Lighting by Feder, Maggie McManus of MidAmerican Energy Co., Marjorie G. McNinch of the Hagley Museum and Library, Dennis Northcott of the Missouri Historical Society, David Pulliam of the Kansas City Star, Drew Rolik of Tower City Archives, Timothy J. Ryan and Mike Crone of Cinergy, Melissa Scroggins of the Fresno County Public Library, Robert Shook of Schuler & Shook, Inc., Jonathan Speirs, Tracy Stone, Reference Librarian at Oklahoma City Downtown Library, Greg Tesone of the Atlantic City Convention Center, Eva Thole at the Kunsthaus Bregenz, James W. Tottis of the Detroit Institute of Arts, Jon Tremayne of Pacific Gas & Electric, Gary Welch of the Wilson Company, Tampa, Sarah Wesson, Richardson-Sloane Special Collections Center, Davenport Public Library and Carol Zsulya at the GE Lighting Information Center at Nela Park in Cleveland.

The most enjoyable aspect of this journey into uncharted territory (apart from the actual moments of discovery) have been the many conversations about it with students, colleagues and friends, who provided insights, references and critical questions. In the fall of 2000, conversations with my students at Yale, as well as with Robert A.M. Stern, Alec Purves, Eeva-Liisa Pelkonen, Alan Plattus and Diana Balmori, helped to formulate the structure and arguments in this book. During the last phase of this project I had the good fortune of enjoying the hospitality, rich resources and stimulating intellectual atmosphere of the Centre Canadienne de l'Architecture in Montréal and then at the Institute for Advanced Study in Princeton. At the CCA I would like to thank Phyllis Lambert and Nicholas Olsberg for their time, comments and challenging questions. I fondly remember the countless fruitful lunchtime conversations and post-lecture discussions with the members of my class, among them James Ackmerman, Mark Jarzombek, Panos Matziaras and Brigitte Desrochers. Among the staff of the CCA's superb research collection I have had great help from Louise Désy, Louis Martin, Manon Gosselin, Anne Troise and at the library from its director Gerald Beasley, as well as Paul Chenier, Renata Guttman, Rosemary Haddard, Francoise Roux and Alexis Sornin. During my time at the Institute for Advanced Study in Princeton I profited greatly from the extensive discussions in our seminars with Marilyn and Irving Lavin, Oleg Grabar and Kirk Varnedoe, my 'classmates' John Walsh, Martin Jay, Karl Luedeking, Ludger Derenthal and Mark Hansen

and my colleagues at the architecture school Beatriz Colomina and Mario Gandelsonas.

In addition I would like to acknowledge the help, insights and suggestions of Hansgeorg Bankel, Christiane Collins, Steven Eskilson, Gail Fenske, Hendrik Gerritsen, Walter Leedy, Stephen Litt, Christopher Mead, Margaret Maile, Pat Malone, Daves Rossell, Michelangelo Sabbatini, Sarah K. Stanley, Anne Troise, Fred Scott, Chris Thomas, Bob White and John Zukowsky. My sister Elisabeth conducted research in Germany and both she and my father proofread large parts of the German manuscript in the final phase of the project, for which I am immensely grateful. Deborah's warm support and companionship, her infectious enthusiasm and clear judgement have helped this project in more ways than she might imagine.

I cannot thank the staff of Prestel Verlag enough for supporting this project even when it took longer than expected. Jürgen Tesch convinced me to finally enter the final phase of writing it, Angeli Sachs helped to shape the concept, the incredibly patient and friendly Curt Holtz saw it through, the professional staff at Wigel Design, among them Petra Lüer, Aisha, and Fred Feuerstein, turned it into reality.

Lastly and most importantly I would like to thank Karen Bouchard, Associate Curator at Brown University's Art Slide Library, for the countless hours she spent on this project. Karen wrote or co-wrote most catalogue entries, biographical sketches and the historical glossary. In addition, she conducted an enormous amount of research, did all the proof-reading and managed the entire project by calmly and reliably keeping track of innumerable images, facts, names, copyright details and sources of information. This book simply could not have happened without her.

Providence, R.I., July 2002
Dietrich Neumann

Photographic Credits

Abbreviations: left (l), right (r), center (c) top (t), bottom (b), top left (tl), top right (tr), center left (cl), center right (cr), bottom left (bl), bottom right (br)

Akademie der Künste Berlin, Sammlung Baukunst: 36b; *Architectural Forum* (October 1958): 186; (February 1957): 190br; *Architectural Record* (Dec. 1932): 162t, (Dec. 1959): 196l, 196r; Avery Architectural and Fine Arts Library, Columbia University in the City of New York: 60t, 60b; *Bauwelt* (January 2 1930): 130l; Bier, Justus, "Über Architektur und Schrift." *Der Baumeister* (Nov. 1929): 32t, 32b; Canesi, Giovanni and Antonio Ramelli, *Architetture Luminose e Apparecchi per Illuminazione* (Milan: Ulrico Hoepli 1934): 41b; Chicago Architectural Photographic Co.: 0-8605.: 140t; Cochran, Edwin A. "*The Cathedral of Commerce*" (New York, Munder-Thomsen, 1916): 102; *Control Equipment for Mobile Color Lighting* General Electric (1931) (GEA 1444): 152l; Courtesy of Color Kinetics. Photographs by James Budd, Rosebudd Productions: 224, 225; Courtesy of Jonathan Speirs and Associates.: Photograph by Gavin Fraser: 214, Photos by Iain Ruxton: 221l, 221r; Courtesy of Murphy/Jahn, Inc; Photographs by Engelhardt/Sellin, Aschau i.CH., Germany: 226l, 226r, 227; Courtesy of Pacific Gas & Electric Company: 118l; Courtesy of Vortex Lighting, Photo by Andrew French: 223; Dickerson, A. F. "Color: New Synthesis in the West." Reprint by General Electric from *Architectural Record* (1939): 180, 181; Diderot, Denis, *Encyclopedie*, (Paris Briasson, 1765) "Lumiere:" 28b; *Electrical World* (30 August 1930): 144; *General Electric Review* (March 1914): 101, (Dec. 1930): 149; Granet, André. *Décors Emphèmeres: Les Expositions Jeux d'Eau et de Lumière*. (Paris: Desfossés, 1948): 172b. Haas, O. F. and K. M. Reid, "Floodlighting." General Electric Company, *Bulletin LD-16* (June 1931): 57t, 57c. Häring, Hugo, "Lichtreklame und Architektur," *Architektur und Schaufenster*, 24, no. 8 (1927): 5–8.: 39t. Hartmann, Sadakichi, "Recent Conquests in Night Photography" The Photog. Times 41 (Nov. 1909): 72tr, 72b. *Illuminating Engineering* (August 1965): 182l; (April 1968): 185; *Illumination Design Data* (General Electric 1936): 57b; *Illumination of the Pan-American Exposition*. (Brooklyn, NY: A. Wittemann Publisher, 1901.) 90, 91t, 91b; Johnson, Philip, Mies van der Rohe (New York City: Museum of Modern Art 1947): 138l, 138r; Kalff, L. C.. *Kunstlicht und Architektur* (Eindhoven: Phillips, 1943): 33t, 33c, 171t, 171b; Kansas City Power & Light Co.: 155; Klein, Adrian Bernard. *Coloured Light : An Art Medium : Being the Third Edition Enlarged of "Colour-Music."* (London:

Technical Press, 1937): 22, 23t, 23b, 24; *Scientific American*, 10 April 1915: 25b; Kramer, Heinrich ©Lichtdesign Ingenieurgesellschaft GmbH: 183; *L'Illustration* (29 June 1889): 21; László, Alexander, *Die Farblichtmusik*, (Leipzig: Breitkopf & Härtel, 1925): 42t, 42b; *Le Genie Civil* (5 December 1931): 159; Library of Congress, Prints and Photographs Division, Gottscho-Schleisner Collection: LC-G612-T-05710 DLC: 77, LC-G612-T-05710 DLC: 115, LC-G612-T01-21012 DLC: 163, LC-G613-T01-35154 DLC: 179b, LC-G612-71723 DLC: 189; *Life Magazine* (12 May 1968): 187t, 187b; *Light* (April 1927): 65; Lighting designed by Motoko Ishii, Motoko Ishii Lighting Design Inc.: 211; Lotz, Wilhelm, *Licht und Beleuchtung* (Berlin: Reckendorf, 1928): 117tl, 131l, 134r; Lubschez, Ben Judah *Manhattan the Magical Island*. (Press of the American Institute of Architects, 1927): 74l; Luckhardt/Köhler. *Lighting in Architecture*. (New York: Reinhold 1959): 29t, 29b; Mendelsohn Erich, *Amerika*, Bilderbuch eines Architekten (Berlin: Mosse, 1926): 25; Mittag, Martin. *Thyssenhaus : Phönix-Rheinrohr-AG Düsseldorf*. (Essen: Bauzentrum-Ring, 1962): 192l, 192r; Mujica, Francisco *History of the Skyscraper* (Paris: Archeology & Architecture Publishers, 1929): 119r, 121; 124; Murphy/Jahn Inc., Architects, Chicago IL: 80; Museum of the City of New York, The Byron Collection, 93.1.3.1112.: 182r. Niagara Mohawk Co., Syracuse: 63, 160b, 161; Perry, John and W. E. Ayrton, "On the Music of Colour and Visible Motion." *Proceedings of the Physical Society*, III (1880): 18–19: 19; Photo by James Palma, Courtesy of Pei Cobb Freed & Partners: 206l; Photo courtesy of Allan Toft, Martin Professional: 218, 219bl, 219br; Photo courtesy of ETC Architectural: 219t; Photo: John M. Gerard. Courtesy of Larry Qualls: 178; Photograph Bognar, Botand © 1996: 204, 208, 209; Photograph by Tomio Ohashi. Courtesy of Toyo Ito & Assoc., Architects.: 205; Photographs courtesy of Barry Webb & Associates.: 217l, 217r; Postcards, contemporary illustrations: 9 tr, 9 cr, 9 br, 10 l, 12 t, 13 b, 18, 20, 25, 27, 31t, 33b, 40t, 46t, 46b, 48, 62t, 67, 68b, 75b, 89t, 89bl, 89br, 92l, 92r, 93, 96, 98l, 98r, 99, 100l, 100r, 103, 105t, 105b, 106l, 107r, 108l, 120, 123b, 126l, 126r, 127, 129l, 129r, 130r, 131r, 132, 133, 134l, 138b, 140b, 141, 143, 144, 146l, 146r, 147, 148, 149, 150, 152r, 153r, 162, 165, 166t, 167t, 167b, 168, 172tr, 173l, 173r, 179t, 174, 184l, 184r, 190tl, 193, 194; 197; 198, 199, 200, 201t, 202; Private Collection: 172tl, 177; *Progressive Architecture* (September 1958): 188; 190bl, 191r, 191l; Roux-Spitz, Michel, *Exposition des arts décoratifs*, Paris, 1925 (Paris: A.Lévy, 1928): 117 tc, 117tr, 117b; Schaefer, Philipp. Neue Warenhausbauten der Rudolph Karstadt A.-G. (Berlin: Hübsch, 1929): 136, 137; Semsch, Otto, *A history of the Singer building construction*. (New York, Shumway & Beattie, 1908): 97; *Souvenir Book of the Louisiana*

Purchase Exposition: Day and Night Scenes. (St. Louis: Official Photography Co., 1904): 95t, 95b; Stair, Jacob L., "The Lighting Book," (Chicago: Curtis Lighting, 1930): 113r; Talbot, Frederick, *Electrical Wonders of the World*, vol.2, (London: Cassell, 1921): 109; Teichmüller, Joachim, *Moderne Lichttechnik in Wissenschaft und Praxis*, vol. 1. Union Verlag, 1928: 28ctr.; *The Hudson-Fulton Celebration 1909* (State of New York, 1909): 12 b, 54b, 55l, 55r; *The Illuminating Engineer* (February 1932): 28t; *The Magazine of Light* (Summer 1934): 54t, 61t. (Nov. 1931): 62b; *Transactions of the American Institute of Electrical Engineers* (no. 1, 1916): 107; *Transactions of the Illuminating Engineering Society* (*TIES*) (Oct. 1922): 110; (July 1924): 112l, 112r, (December 1926): 122, (1929): 128l, 138t, (1930): 58b, 123t, 125 (May 1930): 59r, 1931: 58t, (March 1931): 153l, (Feb. 1934): 166b, (Nov. 1938): 61b; Universal Studios, Universal City Walk Orlando Florida, all rights reserved: 81t; Wainwright, David, *The British Tradition – Simpson – A World of Style*. (London: Quiller Press, 1996.): 169.

The author and publisher would like to thank those copyright owners who have kindly given their permission to reproduce their works in this volume. The publisher would be pleased to hear from any copyright holder who could not be traced.

Front cover: "Architecture of the Night." General Electric Company, *Bulletin.*
Photograph courtesy of the Burndy Library at the Massachusetts Institute
of Technology (Fagan Collection), see page 59.
Back cover: LAX Theme Building, night view, photograph, *c.* 1997, see page 219.
Frontispiece: De Volharding Building, photograph, *c.* 1928, see page 133.
Page 228: Martin Lewis, *Manhattan Lights*, etching, 1931, private collection.
© With kind permission from Robert K. Newman, The Old Print Shop, New York, N.Y.

Prestel Verlag
Königinstrasse 9, 80539 Munich
Tel. +49 (89) 381709-0
Fax +49 (89) 381709-35

4 Bloomsbury Place, London WC1A 2QA
Tel. +44 (20) 7323-5004
Fax +44 (20) 7636-8004

175 Fifth Avenue, New York NY 10010
Tel. +1 (212) 995-2720
Fax +1 (212) 995-2733

www.prestel.com

Prestel books are available worldwide.
Please contact your nearest bookseller or write to any of the
above addresses for information concerning your local distributor.

The Library of Congress Control Number: 2002112898

The Deutsche Bibliothek lists this publication in the Deutsche
Nationalbibliografie; detailed bibliographic data is available on the
Internet at http://dnb.ddb.de

The essay by Werner Oechslin was translated by Steve Martin, Pawtucket, R.I.

Editorial direction by Curt Holtz
Editorial assistance by James Young
Copyedited by Danko Szabó, Munich
Designed and Typeset by WIGEL, Munich
Lithography by ReproLine, Munich
Printed and bound by Passavia Druckservice GmbH, Passau

Printed in Germany on acid-free paper

ISBN 3-7913-2587-6